A

PICTORIAL SCHOOL HISTORY

OF THE

UNITED STATES;

TO WHICH ARE ADDED

THE DECLARATION OF INDEPENDENCE,

AND THE

CONSTITUTION OF THE UNITED STATES

WITH

QUESTIONS AND EXPLANATIONS

BY

JOHN J. ANDERSON, A. M.,

LATE PRINCIPAL OF GRAMMAR SCHOOL NO 31, NEW YORK CITY.

NEW YORK:
CLARK & MAYNARD, PUBLISHERS,
5 BARCLAY STREET.
1870.

SCHOOL HISTORIES

BY

JOHN J. ANDERSON, A. M.,

LATE PRINCIPAL OF GRAMMAR SCHOOL No 31, NEW YORK CITY.

---

1. Introductory. School History of the United States. Illustrated with maps. 194 pp. 16mo.

This work, though arranged on the catechetical plan, may be read independently of the questions as a continuous narrative, the text having been fully written before the questions were prepared. IT IS DESIGNED FOR CLASSES OF ADVANCED AS WELL AS LOWER GRADES, IN WHICH ONLY AN OUTLINE OF UNITED STATES HISTORY IS TAUGHT

2. Common School History of the United States. Illustrated with maps 350 pp 16mo

This work is more catechetical than the preceding, since the answers are more independent of each other. IT IS DESIGNED FOR LARGE GRADED SCHOOLS.

3. Grammar School History of the United States. With one series of maps showing the places referred to in the work, and another showing the progress of the country, with its territorial extent at different periods in its History 252 pp 16mo

The narrative plan has been adopted in this book, with one set of questions at the bottom of the pages, and another for topical review at the end of the sections THIS WORK WILL MEET ALL THE WANTS OF GRADED SCHOOLS AND ACADEMIES.

4. Pictorial School History of the United States. Fully illustrated with maps, portraits, vignettes, &c 402 pp 12mo.

This work is also on the narrative plan but more circumstantial in its statements than any of the preceding IT IS DESIGNED FOR HIGH SCHOOLS AND ACADEMIES

*** All of the above-named works contain the Declaration of Independence and the Constitution of the United States, with questions and explanations, and in the Grammar School History will also be found Washington's Farewell Address

5. A Manual of General History. Copiously illustrated with maps, and accompanied with questions, Chronological Tables, Tables of Contemporaneous History, etc. etc 420 pp 12mo

THIS WORK HAS BEEN PREPARED WITH GREAT CARE ON THE NARRATIVE PLAN ITS STATEMENTS ARE BRIEF AND CLEAR. DESIGNED FOR ADVANCED CLASSES

6. Anderson's Bloss's Ancient History. Illustrated with colored maps and a chart. 445 pp 12mo. DESIGNED FOR HIGH SCHOOLS AND ACADEMIES

ONE OF THE LEADING AIMS IN ALL OF ANDERSON'S HISTORIES IS TO CONNECT THE GEOGRAPHY WITH THE CHRONOLOGY.

CLARK & MAYNARD, PUBLISHERS,

5 BARCLAY ST, New York.

PREFACE.

THE work here offered embraces several features which, it is thought, will not fail to recommend it to such teachers as desire that their pupils should acquire a more comprehensive knowledge of the history of our country than can be obtained from either of the author's previous and more elementary works.

(It has been the leading aim, in the present one, to state every important fact in the history in clear and concise language) so that the pupil may be able readily to comprehend it, and, at the same time, to see its connection with the events preceding it.(No important event, it is believed, has been omitted, nor any of the particulars necessary to make it fully understood.)

The questions at the bottom of the pages are more numerous than in any other school history. This has been done as much for the benefit of the teacher as of the pupil; for, though the former may not actually need them, they will facilitate his labor, and secure better recitations from his pupils, by requiring greater precision, on their part, in the selection of their answers. In this way, the important habit of giving exact and explicit answers will be greatly encouraged. Discursiveness in recitation may, indeed, sometimes be allowed, but always with great caution, so as to avoid that rambling and immethodical mode of thought which is so tiresome and injurious.

By the plan of this work, every fact is learned with a due regard to its relative importance, and all are linked together so as to constitute, in the mind of the pupil, a complete and uninterrupted chain. It may be objected, that the plan of requiring only brief answers is not calculated to encourage this logical connection of events on the part of the young student. This objection has been obviated by the insertion, at the end of every few pages, of a list of review questions of an entirely different character, and much more comprehensive than those at the foot of each page.

These review questions are, in the author's estimation, one of the chief recommendations of the book. They directly call into active exercise the pupil's power of continuous thought, the answer to a single question very often requiring the substance of several paragraphs of the text. The pupil is thus made to perceive more clearly the connection between the events, and habits of thoughtful study are necessarily induced.

It will be also observed that the work is copiously illustrated with maps; that dates are inserted with great frequency; and that the chronological tables of battles, the settlement and admission of the States, the inauguration of the Presidents, and the general events in the history of the country from its discovery, are given with fullness and precision.

These maps and tables do not serve merely to enhance the attractive appearance of the work, but will contribute, it is believed, greatly to its usefulness and value. Not only are they constantly referred to in the text, but a series of questions running through the book, and connecting the geography with the chronology, brings them forcibly before the pupil's attention, and thus serves to give additional accuracy as well as permanency to his knowledge of the subject.

The pronunciation of proper names has also been given more copiously than in either of the author's previous works, the authorities used being the gazetteer of Baldwin and the dictionaries of Webster and Worcester.

While returning thanks to his fellow-teachers for the favor with which his former works have been received, the author submits this new one, with the hope that it may not prove less acceptable.

CONTENTS.

CONTENTS.

MAPS.

INTRODUCTION.

1. The geographers of ancient times had no knowledge whatever of America; though it has been asserted that, several years before Christ, navigators had sailed out of the Mediterranean Sea, and, being wafted across the Atlantic Ocean by the trade-winds, had reached the Western Continent.

2. About 'five centuries previous to the discovery of America by Columbus, the Northmen, a people from Norway and adjoining countries, colonized Iceland and Greenland, and made explorations in America as far south as New England. Settlements are also said to have been made in these regions by them, and intercourse kept up for some time with the mother country. These expeditions, however, seem not to have attracted any general attention; nor were their results permanent, or known to the other nations of Europe.

3. It is almost certain that when Columbus set sail on his eventful voyage in 1492, he had not the least knowledge of the existence of a second continent; nor is there any evidence whatever that he even imagined there was such a continent. His great aim was to find a shorter and better route to India than the one then traveled by way of Egypt and the Red Sea. The route around the southern extremity of Africa was not discovered until five years after. To him, nevertheless, is justly ascribed the honor of being the discoverer of the New World, since it was

through his enterprise and sagacity that its existence came to be generally known.

4. At the time of Columbus's discovery the continent of America, from the icy latitudes of the North to the regions far south of the equator, together with most of its islands, was inhabited by various races who differed in many respects from Europeans. As the country at that time, and until Balboa discovered the Pacific Ocean (p. 15), was supposed to be a part of India, these inhabitants were called Indians. In some parts of the country they were found to have attained a considerable degree of civilization; in others they were in the savage state, being divided into tribes, living in rude huts called wigwams, and existing mostly by fishing and hunting. They spoke different languages, and their religion consisted in worshiping an unknown and invisible Deity, whom they called the "Great Spirit."

5. Whence did they come? How did they reach America? How long had they been living there? These questions have been asked a great many times, but have never yet been satisfactorily answered. Many theories have been advanced to solve the difficulty; but the origin of these various races, both civilized and uncivilized, remains as much a mystery as ever.

6. According to one of these theories, America received its first inhabitants from eastern Asia, by way of Behring's Straits; while other and more probable statements are, that vessels were at various times wafted by the trade-winds across the Atlantic Ocean from the Old World, and that thus people of different races being accidentally carried to the other continent, settled there, and founded the different nations which inhabited it at the time of its discovery by Columbus.

7. Of one thing there can be no doubt. When America was discovered by Columbus, it had been inhabited for centuries; and the previous occupants of certain portions of it had attained a degree of civilization not possessed by their inhabitants at the time of this discovery. The evidences of this are still abundant in the ruins of temples and other buildings, and in the articles of copper and silver found buried beneath these ruins. Curious specimens of pottery of great antiquity have also been found; and mounds of remarkable extent are seen in certain parts, the origin of which was unknown to the uncivilized Indians.

8. After Columbus led the way, expeditions were undertaken by Europeans of different nations, in order to explore the New World and make settlements in various parts of it. None were marked by more heroism and self-sacrifice than those conducted by the French Catholics in their efforts to explore the country in the region of the great lakes, and along the Mississippi River and its tributary streams. Marquette (*mar-ket'*), La Salle (*sal*), and others, penetrated the vast wilderness by way of the St. Lawrence; and they were followed by others, who established stations at various places, and labored to convert the Indians to their faith (p. 212).

9. At the close of the Revolutionary War the western boundary of the territorial possessions of the United States extended only to the Mississippi (p. 186). By the "Louisiana Purchase," in 1803, the limits were extended to the Rocky Mountains (pp. 203, 204). The coast strip about fifty miles wide, between Florida and Louisiana, claimed by Spain as a part of Florida, was occupied by the United States at the beginning of the "War of 1812," and, under the claim that it was part of the "Louisiana Purchase," was retained. In 1819, Florida was acquired by cession

from Spain (p. 249), all the "rights, claims, and preten-
sions" of Spain, to territory west of the Mississippi and
north of the 42d parallel, being, at the same time, also
ceded to the United States.

10. The region west of the Rocky Mountains, extending
from latitude 42° to about 548, with the Pacific for its western boundary, was long known as Oregon. It was claimed by the United States, because, among other reasons, its
principal river had been discovered by an American—
Captain Gray, of the ship Columbia, of Boston—in 1792,
and because, during the administration of President Jefferson, it was explored by Captains Lewis and Clark, commanding an overland expedition sent out by the United
States government. Gray gave the name of his vessel to
the river he discovered. By the treaty made with Spain
in 1819, the United States strengthened their claim to the
region.

11. Great Britain also claimed Oregon until 1846, when
by treaty, the boundary line between the possessions of
the two nations was fixed at the 49th parallel; and thus
was settled a controversy which had been continued for a
number of years, and which, at one time, threatened to
produce a war between the two countries. In 1845, Texas
became a member of the Union, by annexation (pp. 269,
270). California, New Mexico, Arizona, Utah, and Nevada
were acquired from Mexico by conquest; and their possession was confirmed by a treaty made at the close of the
war with that country (p. 284), and by a subsequent treaty
made in 1853. Alaska was purchased from Russia in 1867
(p. 343).

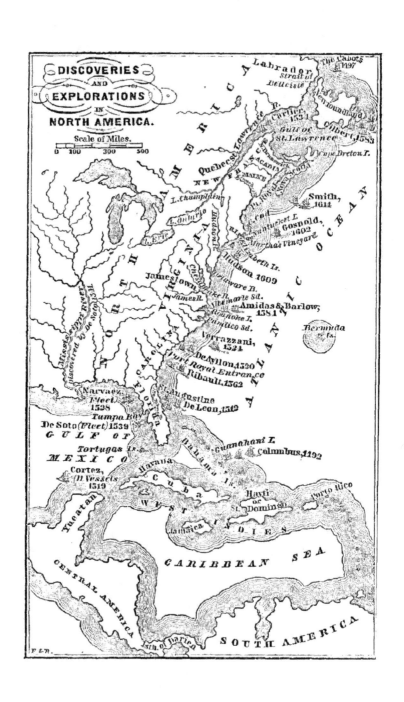

HISTORY OF THE UNITED STATES.

SECTION I.

Discoveries and Explorations.

EXTENDING FROM THE DISCOVERY OF AMERICA, IN 1492, TO
THE SETTLEMENT OF VIRGINIA, IN 1607.

COLUMBUS.

I. CHRISTOPHER COLUMBUS,* the discoverer of America, was born in the city of Genoa (*jen'-o-a*), Italy. At an early age he manifested a predilection for the sea, and the most of his life, previous to its great event, was passed on the waters of the Mediterranean, and the west coast of Africa; and he even made a voyage towards Greenland, passing beyond the island of Iceland.

II. In those days, when navigation was yet in its infancy, the usual route to India—the country in the southeast part of Asia with the adjacent islands being so called—was by way of Egypt and the Red Sea. Columbus, believing the earth to be round, concluded that by sailing westward he would sooner

---

* Columbus was born about the year 1435. He died at Valladolid, Spain, in 1506.

I. QUESTIONS.—1. By whom was America discovered? 2. Where was Columbus born? 3. How is Genoa situated? (See map of Europe.) 4. How did Columbus spend the most of his time previous to his discovery of America?

II. 5. By what route did European travelers reach India at that time? 6. What part of the earth was then known as India? 7. What theory did Columbus have as regards a more direct route to India? 8. By what religious conviction was he also influenced?

reach India than by taking this route. He was also influenced by the conviction that he was commissioned by Heaven
to carry the Gospel to the heathen of unknown lands.

III. His first application for aid was to the government of
Genoa: it was refused. After applying, without success, to
the monarchs of England and Portugal, he was assisted by

Isabella (*iz-ă-bel'-lah*), Queen of
Spain, and he set sail from Palos
(*pah'-los*), at the mouth of the river
Tinto, in that country, with three
vessels, namely: the Pinta (*peen'-
tah*), Santa Maria (*san'-tah ma-re'-
ah*), and Nina (*ne'-nah*). The first
land which he saw was one of the
Bahama Islands, called by the
natives Guanahani (*gwah-nah-
hah'-ne*), by him San Salvador, now sometimes known as Cat
Island; and thus, in 1492,* was America discovered.

ISABELLA.

IV. Columbus made three other voyages to the New
World, in the first of which, as well as in the one just described, his discoveries were confined to the islands between
North and South America; but in his third voyage, in 1498,
he discovered the mainland, at the mouth of the river Ori-

---

* According to a theory, advanced by a German author, there have been three different discoveries of
America; namely:—the first, during the period from one thousand to six hundred years before Christ, by
navigators who sailed from Asia, through the Mediterranean; the second, in the tenth century after
Christ, by the Norwegians; and the third, in 1492, by Columbus.

III. QUESTIONS.—9. To whom did he first appeal to assist him in testing his theory? 10. With what success? 11. To whom did he afterwards appeal? 12. What
was the result? 13. Who finally did help him? 14. Of how many vessels did his
fleet consist? 15. Give their names. 16. From what place did he set sail? 17. In
what part of Spain is Palos situated? (See map, p. 2.) 18. The island which he first
discovered belonged to what group? 19. How are the Bahama Islands situated?
(See map, p. 10.) 20. What did the Indians call the island discovered? 21. What
name did Columbus give to it? 22. What is the meaning of the name San Salvador?
Ans.—Holy Saviour. 23. By what name is the island now known? 24. In what direction is it from Cuba? (See map, p. 10.) 25. From St. Augustine? (See same map.)

IV. 26. How many voyages in all did Columbus make to America? 27. What
can you say of the first two? 28. When did he make his third voyage? 29. What
discovery did he then make? 30. What did he accomplish in his fourth voyage?
31. In what conviction, touching the discovery of America, did Columbus die?

noco, in South America; and in the fourth and last, he examined the coast of Darien. He still, however, believed that the lands which he had discovered were a portion of Eastern Asia ($\bar{a}'$-she-$\dot{a}$), instead of a new continent, and in this conviction he died, being, as intimated, entirely ignorant of the real grandeur of his discovery.

V. In 1499, the year after Columbus discovered the continent, Amerigo Vespucci* (a-$m\bar{a}$-$r\bar{e}'$-$g\bar{o}$ ves-$poot'$-$sh\bar{e}$), an Italian navigator, visited the eastern coast of South America, and, in 1501, made a second voyage to the same regions. He prepared accounts of these two voyages, which were published in Europe, in which he claimed to be the first European that had landed on the western continent. In consequence of the claim set up by him, as well as from the fact that his were the first published accounts of the newly discovered country, it was called America.

SEBASTIAN CABOT.

VI. In 1497, one year before Columbus discovered the continent, and two years previous to Amerigo's visit, John Cabot and his son Sebastian, while sailing under a commission from Henry VII., of England, discovered the coast of Labrador, and thus were the first to discover the continent of America. In a second voyage, made by Sebastian Cabot in 1498, the coast

---

* Amerigo Vespucci was born in Florence, Italy, in 1451. He died in Seville, Spain, in 1512.

V. QUESTIONS.—32. When did Vespucci visit America? 33. What part of America did he visit? 34. How did the country come to be called America?

VI. 35. What discovery was made in 1497? 36. What large island southeast of Labrador? (See map, p. 10.) 37. Did the Cabots or Vespucci first discover the continent? 38. Was the honor of naming this country rightly bestowed? 39. Did that honor belong either to the Cabots or Vespucci, rather than to Columbus? 40. When did Sebastian Cabot make a second voyage. 41. Give an account of it. 42. Of what special importance did the successes of the Cabots prove?

from Labrador to Chesapeake Bay—some say to Florida—
was explored; landings were made in several places, and
natives were seen, clad in the skins of beasts and making use
of copper. These achievements of the Cabots, the discovery
and explorations, proved of momentous importance, especially
to England, as, by reason of them, that country based her
claim to all the region from Labrador to Florida.

VII. Twenty years after Columbus's first and great discovery, Ponce de Leon* (*pōn'-thā dā lā-ōn'*), an aged Spaniard,
sailed from Porto Rico (*re'-co*), in search of a wonderful fountain, which, it was said, existed in one of the Bahama Islands,
and would impart immortal youth to all who might drink of
its waters. After visiting several islands of the Bahamas,
and tasting the waters of every river, lake, and fountain found,
he turned to the northwest, and, in 1512, discovered an unknown land. This was thought to be an island; and, from the
abundance of flowers with which the forests were adorned,
and because the discovery happened on Easter Sunday, which
the Spaniards call *Pascua Florida* (*pah'-scoo-ah flo-re'-dah*), it
received the name of Florida. He continued his search along
the coast of Florida, and among the Tortugas Islands, but, of
course, without finding any such fountain.

VIII. Several years after, he made another voyage to
Florida for the purpose of making a settlement, he having been
appointed governor of the country upon the condition that
he would colonize it. He effected a landing, but was met by
the natives with determined hostility; and, in an attack made
by them, the Spaniards were killed or driven back to their

---

* Juan Ponce de Leon was born in Leon, Spain. He died in 1521.

VII. QUESTIONS.—43. In what year did De Leon make a voyage in search of a
wonderful fountain? 44. From what place did he sail? 45. Was he an old or a young
man at the time? 46. What tradition then existed, in relation to the fountain? 47.
What efforts did De Leon make to find the fountain? 48. When did he discover Florida? 49. Why did he call it Florida? 50. Among what islands did he search besides the Bahamas? 51. In what direction from Florida are the Tortugas Islands?
(See map, p. 10.)

VIII. 52. Why did De Leon go to Florida a second time? 53. What appointment had he received? 54. What further account can you give of him?

ships, and De Leon himself received a mortal wound of which he died in Cuba.

IX. In 1513, Balboa,* the Governor of the Spanish colony at the Isthmus of Darien, the first colony established on the American Continent, while crossing the isthmus gained the summit of a mountain from which he discovered the Pacific Ocean. After falling upon his knees and thanking God for the privilege of being the discoverer of this great ocean, he descended to the sea-shore and took possession of the whole coast in the name of the Spanish crown.

X. About the time of De Leon's defeat in Florida, De Ayllon (*dā ile-yone'*), a Spanish adventurer, was engaged in an enterprise having for its object the procuring of a large number of Indians to work the plantations and mines of St. Domingo (*do-ming'-gō*). At a place in the southern part of South Carolina, a great number of natives were treacherously captured; but the undertaking proved unsuccessful, for of the two vessels employed, one was lost while on the return to St. Domingo, and many of the captives in the other sickened and died.

XI. It was not many months after this unprofitable speculation, that De Ayllon obtained the appointment as governor of Chicora (*che-kō'-rah*), the name given to that part of Carolina which he had visited, and he wasted his fortune in fitting out an expedition to conquer the country. The issue of this second enterprise was likewise disastrous: one of his ships, the largest and best, was stranded and lost; many of his men were killed by the natives, in revenge for the treachery

---

* Vasco Nunez de Balboa was born in Spain, in 1475. Having been superseded in the governorship of the colony at Darien, and afterwards charged by the new governor with the design of making other discoveries without authority, he was tried and found guilty. Although he persisted that he was unjustly condemned, he was beheaded in conformity with the sentence, in 1517.

IX. QUESTIONS.—55. By whom was the Pacific Ocean discovered? 56. When was the discovery made? 57. What civil position did Balboa hold at the time? 58. Where was he when he discovered the Pacific? 59. What ceremony did he observe?

X. 60. Who was De Ayllon? 61. What enterprise did he engage in? 62. What was the result?

XI. 63. What appointment did he afterwards receive? 64. What was the object of his second expedition? 65. What account can you give of it?

which he had previously been guilty of; and he himself barely made good his escape.

XII. In 1517, Cordova, a Spanish navigator, sailed from Cuba and discovered the northern coast of Yucatan. Upon his return he gave such a favorable account of the civilization and riches of the people whom he had seen, as to awaken a keen desire among the Spaniards to undertake their conquest. Accordingly Velasquez (*va-lah'-sketh*), the governor of Cuba, sent an expedition under the direction of Juan de Grijalva (*gre-hahl'-vah*), the result of which was very satisfactory. Grijalva, after an exploration of the southern coast of Mexico, returned with a large amount of treasure, obtained by trafficking with the natives.

CORTEZ.

XIII. Velasquez, then determining to conquer the Mexicans and get possession of their wealth, sent an expedition, consisting of eleven vessels and more than six hundred armed men, under the command of Fernando Cortez. Cortez landed, in 1519, near Vera Cruz (*vā'-rah kroose*), and was at once met by friendly deputations from Montezuma (*mon-ta-thoo'-mah*), the Mexican emperor. By perseverance and a course of falsehood and duplicity, he succeeded in reaching the city of Mexico, the Indian capital; and by stratagem and boldness, and with the aid of Indian tribes opposed to the Mexican rule, finally

XII. QUESTIONS.—66. When was Yucatan discovered? 67. By whom? 68? What can you say of the account which he gave? 69. What expedition was sent in consequence of this account? 70. What did Grijalva accomplish?

XIII. 71. What did Velasquez then determine upon? 72. Who commanded the expedition against Mexico? 73. Of how many vessels did his fleet consist? 74. When did he land in Mexico? 75. At what place? 76. By whom was he met? 77. What account can you give of Cortez's further movements?

completed the conquest of the people, and Mexico became a province of Spain in 1521.

DE SOTO.

XIV. In 1528, Narvaez (*nar-vah'-eth*), having been appointed governor of Florida by the Spanish sovereign, sailed from Cuba to conquer and possess the country. The attempt proved most disastrous; for, of the three hundred men who landed in Florida and penetrated the wild regions, only four, after years of wandering, succeeded in reaching a Spanish settlement in Mexico. These four men asserted that Florida was the richest country in the world, a statement which the people of Spain generally believed; but to no one was credulity more disastrous than to Ferdinand de Soto* (*da so'-to*), a brave cavalier who had gained riches and military honors with Pizarro, in Peru.

XV. De Soto having solicited permission to conquer Florida at his own expense, the Spanish sovereign not only granted his request, but appointed him governor of Cuba, and of the immense territory to which the name of Florida was then vaguely applied. With a fleet of ten vessels and a gay company of six hundred armed men, he sailed for the New World in 1538. Leaving his wife to govern Cuba, he proceeded to Florida, landed on the shores of Tampa Bay, and, in the summer of 1539, commenced his march into the interior, toward the fancied land of gold.

XVI. After wandering for nearly three years in the wilder-

* De Soto was born in Spain, in 1500. He died in 1542.

XIV. QUESTIONS.—78. What expedition was undertaken in 1528? 79. What was the result? 80. What opinion did De Soto entertain with regard to the wealth of Florida? 81. What successes had he previously met with?

XV. 82. What request did he make of the Spanish sovereign? 83. How was the request treated? 84. When did he sail for America? 85. Where did he leave his wife? 86. Where did he land? 87. In what part of Florida is Tampa Bay? (See map, p. 10.) 88. When did he commence his march?

ness, encountering the hostility of the natives and suffering disasters and disappointments, De Soto sickened and died. To conceal his death from the natives, who regarded him with fear, his body was sunk beneath the waters of the Mississippi, a river which he had discovered in 1541. After vainly trying to reach Mexico through the forests, the remnant of his followers built seven frail barks, sailed down the Mississippi, and along the coast of Mexico until they arrived at a Spanish settlement.

XVII. In 1524, Verrazanni (*vä-rat-tsah'-ne*), a Florentine navigator, while sailing in the service of France, explored the coast of North America from the Carolinas to New-foundland (*new'-fund-land*). To the whole region thus explored he gave the name of New France, a name which was afterwards restricted to the territory

VERRAZANNI.

of Canada, and which was so retained while that country remained in the possession of the French.

XVIII. No other explorations were made by the French until 1534. In that year and the following James Cartier* (*car-te-ä'*) made two successful voyages, discovered the river St. Lawrence, explored its banks, and took possession of the whole country in the name of his king. Though Cartier and the Lord of Roberval (*ro-bare-val'*), some years after, undertook to colonize Canada, the French effected no permanent

---

* Cartier was born at St. Malo, France, in 1494. The time of his death is not known, though it is supposed he lived to an advanced age.

XVI. QUESTIONS.—89. What river did he discover? 90. When did he discover the Mississippi? 91. How long did he wander in the wilderness? 92. What finally became of him? 93. What was done by his followers after his death?

XVII. 94. What exploration was made seventeen years before De Soto discovered the Mississippi? 95. What name did Verrazanni give to the region which he explored? 96. To what territory was that name afterward restricted? 97. How long did Canada retain the name of New France?

XVIII. 98. When, after the exploration made by Verrazanni, did the French make other explorations? 99. Who commanded the expeditions? 100. How many voyages did he make in 1534 and 1535? 101. Through what strait did he sail? (See map, p. 19.) 102. In what year did he discover the St. Lawrence? (See map, p. 10.) 103. When was Quebec settled? 104. By whom was it settled? 105. How is Quebec situated? (See map, p. 10.)

settlement until one was made on the site of Quebec, in 1608, by Champlain.

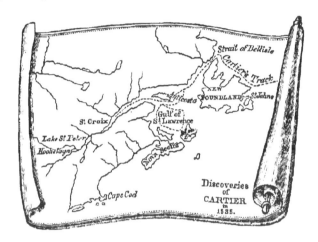

XIX. Quebec is not, however, the oldest French settlement in America, as Port Royal, now Annapolis, in Nova Scotia (*scō'-she-ah*), was settled three years before by De Monts (*dŭ-mong*), a wealthy *Huguenot*. Port Royal was then spoken of as being in Acadia, a name which, at the time, was applied to the whole territory now included in Nova Scotia, New Brunswick, and the adjacent islands.

XX. More than forty years before the settlement of Port Royal, in Nova Scotia, the Huguenots, or French Protestants, undertook to establish a colony—first in South Carolina and afterwards in Florida—as a place of refuge for their people. Their expeditions were undertaken by direction and aid of Jaspar Coligny* (*ko-leen'-ye*), Admiral of France. The first, intrusted to the command of John Ribault (*rē-bō'*), reached the

---

* Coligny, or, as the name is sometimes written, Coligni, was born in France, in 1517. He was murdered at Paris, in 1572.

XIX. QUESTIONS.—106. Which is the oldest French settlement in America 107. In what year was Port Royal settled? 108. How is Port Royal situated? (See map, p. 10.) 109. By what name is Port Royal now known? 110. What territory was then called Acadia ?

coast in 1562. The colonists landed at Port Royal entrance, selected their place of refuge, and built a fort, to which they gave the name of Carolina, in honor of King Charles (Carolus) of France. It was thus that this country received its name, a century before it was occupied by the English. Ribault, leaving twenty-six men to keep possession, returned to France for reinforcements; but the promised aid not arriving, the colonists in despair embarked for their native land. The second expedition was sent out in 1564, when a settlement was made on the banks of the St. John's River, Florida.

XXI. Hardly had the news reached Spain of the Huguenot settlement on the St John's River than Melendez, who had been appointed governor of Florida upon condition that he would conquer the country within three years, departed on his expedition of conquest. After forming a settlement at St. Augustine (*aw-gus-tēne'*) in 1565, which is the oldest in the United States, he proceeded against the Huguenots, whom he surprised; and massacring men, women, and children, broke up the colony. This did not long go unavenged; for, in little more than two years after, De Gourges (*dŭ-goorg*), a brave soldier of France, having fitted out three ships at his own expense, surprised two Spanish forts on the St. John's River, and hung two hundred captives upon the trees.

XXII. The first enterprise on the part of the English for the purpose of planting a colony in America was undertaken in 1579, by Sir Humphrey Gilbert, who sailed from England under a patent which had been granted by Queen Elizabeth; but severe storms and Spanish war vessels compelled him to put back, and the scheme, for a time, was abandoned. In

XX QUESTIONS.—111 Where had the Huguenots previously undertaken to establish a colony? 112. What object had they in view? 113. Who aided and directed them? 114. Who commanded their first expedition? 115. Give an account of it 116. In what direction from St Augustine is Port Royal entrance? (See map, p 10) 117 When was the second expedition sent? 118 Where was a settlement made? 119. Describe the St. John's River. (See map, p 10)

XXI. 120. What was the fate of the Huguenot settlement on the St John's? 121 When and where did Melendez make a settlement? 122. What can you say of that settlement? 123. How was the massacre of the Huguenots avenged?

1583 he sailed a second time for America, and landed at Newfoundland; but accomplished little more than the erection of a pillar bearing the arms of his government. While returning to England, in the same year, his vessel foundered, and he, with all on board, perished.

XXIII. Sir Walter Raleigh* (*raw'-lē*), not disheartened by

RALEIGH.

the sad fate of his step-brother, Gilbert, obtained from Elizabeth an ample patent, and sent two vessels, under the command of Amidas, and Barlow. The voyagers arrived on the coast of Carolina, visited the islands in Pamlico and Albemarle Sounds, took possession of the country in the name of Elizabeth, and, after trafficking with the natives, returned to England. So glowing an account did they give of the country, that Queen Elizabeth declared the event to be the most glorious in her reign; and, in memorial of her unmarried state, named the region Virginia. Upon Raleigh she conferred the honor of knighthood.

XXIV. Two attempts were afterwards made by Raleigh to establish a colony in America; one in 1585, and the other in 1587. In the first, more than a hundred persons were sent.

---

* Raleigh was born at Hayes, in Devonshire, a county of England, in 1552. The death of Queen Elizabeth, in 1603, proved fatal to his fortunes. He was tried on a false charge of high treason, convicted, and, after a period of fifteen years, thirteen of which he passed in confinement, he was beheaded in London, on the 29th of October, 1618.

XXII. QUESTIONS.—124. What account can you give of the first English enterprise to establish a colony in America? 125. When did Gilbert sail a second time? 126. At what place did he land? 127. What body of water is on the west of that island? (See map, p. 10.) 128. What became of Gilbert?

XXIII. 129. How were Gilbert and Raleigh related? 130. What patent did Raleigh obtain? 131. How many vessels did he send to America? 132. Who commanded them? 133. When did Amidas and Barlow reach America? (See map, p. 10.) 134. What exploration did they make? 135. What else did they do? 136. In what direction is Roanoke Island from Jamestown? (See map, p. 29.) 137. What can you say of the account which Amidas and Barlow gave of the country they visited?

These, with Ralph Lane as governor, were conveyed by a fleet of seven vessels, under the command of Sir Richard Grenville. They proceeded to Roanoke, an island on the coast of North Carolina, where a settlement was commenced. After a year of distress, they all embarked for England with Sir Francis Drake, who had stopped at Roanoke on his way from the West Indies.

XXV. The second colony was composed of agriculturists and artisans with their families. Having reached Roanoke, and there, on the site of the former settlement, commenced building "the city of Raleigh," John White, the governor, went to England for supplies. When he returned, after an absence of nearly three years, Roanoke was deserted, and no trace of the colonists could be found

XXVI. The next attempt, after Raleigh's, to plant an English colony in America, was made by Bartholomew Gosnold, in 1602. After discovering the promontory which he called Cape Cod, also Nantucket, Martha's Vineyard, and the group known as the Elizabeth Islands, he landed on one of the last named, where he selected a position for a settlement and built a storehouse and fort. The persons chosen to remain becoming alarmed at the menaces of the Indians and at the want of supplies, the design was abandoned, and the whole party returned to England.

XXVII. Gosnold made such favorable reports of the country, that the merchants of Bristol were induced to fit out two

---

XXIV. QUESTIONS.—138. How many attempts did Raleigh make to establish a colony in America? 139. When were they made? 140. Give an account of the first XXV 141 Of whom did the second colony consist? 142 Who was their governor? 143 Where did they commence to build a city? 144 What name did they give to the city? 145 Why did the governor of the colony leave? 146. How long was he gone? 147 What did he find upon his return to Roanoke?

XXVI 148 When was the next attempt made to plant an English colony in America? 149. Who commanded the undertaking? 150 What discoveries did Gosnold make? 151 In what direction from Martha's Vineyard is Nantucket? (See map, p. 23.) 152 At what place did Gosnold make preparation to make a settlement? 153 What are the Elizabeth Islands now called? (See map, p. 23.) 154 Why did not the settlement on Elizabeth Islands prove permanent?

vessels, under the command of Martin Pring, for exploration and trade. During the first voyage, made in 1603, the shores and several large rivers of Maine, as well as the coast as far south

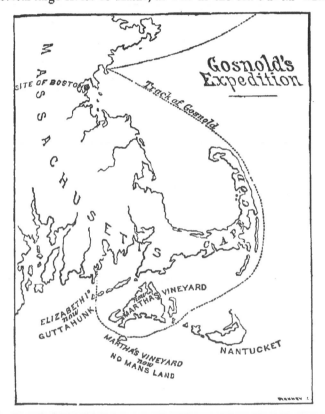

as Martha's Vineyard, were examined, and a profitable traffic was carried on with the natives. Three years later, Pring repeated his previous voyage, and made a more accurate survey of Maine.

XXVIII. The territory which the English claimed, basing

their claim, as has been previously stated, principally upon the discoveries of the Cabots, extended from the 34th to the 45th degrees of north latitude. In 1606, James I. granted the northern portion, from the 41st to the 45th, to an association of "knights, gentlemen, and merchants of the west of England," known as the Plymouth (*plim'-uth*) Company, calling the region North Virginia. The southern portion, from the 34th to the 38th, called South Virginia, he granted to an association of "noblemen, gentlemen, and merchants, in and about London," known as the London Company.

VICINITY OF CHESAPEAKE BAY

XXIX. During the following year, 1607, the Plymouth Company sent a number of planters, who began a settlement at the mouth of the Kennebec River, in Maine; but the intense cold of the winter, the destruction of their storehouse

---

by fire, and the death of their president, George Popham, discouraged them, and they returned to England.

XXX. The London Company were more successful. They sent a fleet of three vessels, commanded by Christopher Newport, and carrying more than a hundred colonists. During the long voyage of four months, dissensions arose among the leading men, and John Smith, whose genius had excited their jealousy, was placed in confinement. The design of the colonists was to form a settlement on Roanoke, but a storm carried the vessels farther north, into Chesapeake Bay. They sailed about fifty miles up a large stream which they named James River, and, selecting a place for a settlement, called it Jamestown.

XXIX. QUESTIONS.—161. When did the Plymouth Company attempt to make a settlement? 162. At what place? 163. Describe the Kennebec River. (See map, p. 10.) 164. What else can you say of the settlement on the Kennebec?

XXX. 165. Were the London Company more or less successful? 166. Of how many vessels did the fleet, sent by them, consist? 167. Who commanded the fleet? 168. How many colonists were there on board of the three vessels? 169. How long a voyage did they have? 170. How was John Smith treated during the voyage? 171. At what place did the colonists intend to make their settlement? 172. Why did they not do so?

REVIEW QUESTIONS

2

SECTION II.

Colonial History.

EXTENDING FROM THE SETTLEMENT OF VIRGINIA, IN 1607, TO THE COMMENCEMENT OF THE FRENCH AND INDIAN WAR, IN 1754.

VIRGINIA.

VIRGINIA.

In 1584 Amidas and Barlow visited the coast of North Carolina. Upon their return to England, Queen Elizabeth, in memorial of her unmarried state, named the region Virginia, a name which was afterward applied to the whole country explored by Sebastian Cabot, but finally restricted to the present State. On the Seal of Virginia (given above) is the motto of the State, *Sic semper, &c.*, meaning, *So be it ever to tyrants.*

I. THE first settlement in Virginia was made in 1607, at Jamestown.* The colony was governed under a charter granted by James I., the supreme government being vested in a council resident in England, and the local government in a colonial council, the members of both deriving their appointment from the king.

II. The first* council consisted of seven persons, among whom were Bartholomew Gosnold, John Smith,† and John Ratcliffe, with Edward Wingfield, an avaricious and unprincipled man, for governor.

---

* With the exception of the ruins of two or three houses, and of a church and fort, nothing remains of the ancient town.

† John Smith was born in Willoughby, county of Lincolnshire, England, in 1579. His life was a most eventful one, and, considering the age in which he lived, he was indeed a remarkable man. The narrative of the part he took in wars against the Turks, of his captivity by them, and his escape, seems more like a romance than a reality. He died in London, in 1631.

VIRGINIA.—I. QUESTIONS.—1. When was Virginia first settled? 2. At what place? 3. How was Jamestown situated? (See map, p. 29.) 4. In what direction from the Bermuda Islands was Jamestown? (See map, p. 10.) 5. How was the colony at first governed? * Colonial.

Smith, at first, was not permitted to take a seat in the council, because of a false charge of sedition made against him by his colleagues ; but they were soon compelled to restore him to his station.

III. For a time the colony did not prosper. The scarcity of provisions, the hostility of the natives, the want of industrial habits among the settlers, and sickness, which carried to the grave fifty men in less than four months, proved nearly fatal to its existence. Bartholomew Gosnold, the projector of the settlement, and a man whose influence had greatly contributed to promote harmony in the council, was among those who died.

IV. Wingfield, the president, having embezzled the public stores, and become concerned in a plot to abandon the settlement, in a vessel belonging to the colony, was expelled from the council. He was succeeded in the presidency by Ratcliffe ; but, in consequence of the inefficiency of the latter, the management of affairs fell into the hands of Captain John Smith. Several months later, upon the actual deposition of Ratcliffe, Smith was formally elected in his place.

V. To the efforts of the new president, almost unaided as they were, the salvation of the infant colony was owing. He made frequent excursions into the neighboring country, and returned with supplies of corn. He also explored Chesapeake Bay, ascended the James and other rivers as far as he could in boats, and made his knowledge, thus acquired, of great use in the government of the colony.

II. QUESTIONS.—6. Of how many persons did the council consist? 7. Name four of the most prominent men belonging to the first council. 8. Who was the first governor? 9. What was his character? 10. How was Smith at first treated by the council?

III. 11. Did the colony, at the beginning, prosper or not? 12. What were the causes? 13. What is said of Gosnold?

IV. 14. Of what two crimes was Wingfield guilty? 15. By whom was he superseded? 16. What is said of Ratcliffe's management? 17. What was the consequence?

V. 18. What is said of the efforts of Smith? 19. What of his excursions for corn? 20. Of his explorations?

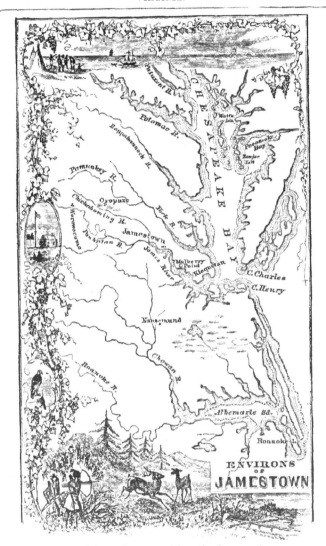

(*Questions to be answered from the above map.*)

Name five rivers that flow into Chesapeake Bay. What two capes are at the entrance of the bay? To what large body of water is Chesapeake Bay tributary? *Ans.—The Atlantic Ocean.* How was Jamestown situated? Into what body of water does the Chowan River flow? What other river flows into Albemarle Sound? How is the Island of Roanoke situated? In what direction is it from Jamestown?

JOHN SMITH.

VI. On one of his expeditions up the Chickahominy, in search of corn, he was surrounded by about three hundred Indians, and, after a desperate struggle, captured. In triumph they conducted him through the country, showing him to the various tribes on the Rappahannock and Potomac Rivers, and then took him to a chief, dwelling near the fork of the York River. After being detained for three days he was sent to Powhatan, the principal chief, or "emperor of the country," whose subjects numbered about eight thousand. His residence was on the York River. The Indian warriors met in council, and, after a long and solemn consultation, determined that Smith should be put to death.

VII. Accordingly he was bound, and his head placed upon a large stone; but, just as the savages were raising their clubs

POCAHONTAS.

to dash out his brains, Pocahontas, the beloved daughter of Powhatan, a child only twelve years old, rushed forward, clasped the captive's head in her arms, and begged that his life might be spared. Her generous and heroic conduct touched her father's heart, and the sentence was revoked. Smith was not only set at liberty, but an escort of twelve men was provided to conduct him to Jamestown.*

---

* This story is disputed. It had its origin in the narrative published by Smith after the death of Pocahontas.

VI. QUESTIONS — 21 How was he captured? 22. To whom did the Indians con-

VIII. On arriving there, after an absence ot seven weeks, he found every thing in disorder. The colony was reduced to forty men, the strongest of whom were preparing to quit the country. The attempt at desertion was prevented by decisive action; order was restored; and a large accession to

THE ATTEMPT AT DESERTION SUPPRESSED.

their number by the arrival of Newport, who had been to England, revived the drooping spirits of the colonists. Smith, by his captivity and frequent expeditions, gained considerable knowledge of the language and manners of the Indians, and of the country and its resources, which enabled him to establish a peaceful intercourse between the settlers and the tribes of Powhatan.

duct him? 23. Where did Powhatan live? 24. Describe the York River. (See map, p. 29.) 25. What sentence was pronounced against Smith?

VII. 26. How did the Indians undertake to carry out the sentence? 27. State how Smith was saved. 28. What else did Powhatan do for Smith?

VIII. QUESTIONS.—29. What condition of things did Smith find at Jamestown upon his arrival there? 30. Of what value did Smith's captivity prove to Jamestown?

IX. The administration of the affairs of Jamestown, however, gave no satisfaction to the company in England. Believing that under a new charter, conferring greater privileges, their dreams of profit would be realized, they sought and obtained one, in 1609, and appointed Lord Delaware, a nobleman distinguished for his virtues as well as his rank, governor for life.

X. Christopher Newport, Sir Thomas Gates, and Sir George Somers, who had been appointed commissioners authorized to administer the affairs of the colony till the arrival of Lord Delaware, were dispatched to America with a fleet of nine vessels and more than five hundred emigrants. While on the passage a severe storm dispersed the fleet. One of the vessels, that bearing the commissioners, was wrecked on one of the Bermuda Islands, and one small one foundered: the other seven reached the James River in safety.

XI. Although no person had yet arrived authorized to supersede the president, Smith at first made no attempt to maintain his power; but the disorder and disaster that ensued so alarmed the better portion of the colonists, that, at their request, he resumed his abandoned functions. While returning from a visit to one of the settlements near Jamestown which he had established, he was so severely injured by an explosion of gunpowder, that, feeling the need of the best surgical skill, he returned to England towards the close of 1609.

XII. No sooner had Smith fairly departed than the colonists gave themselves up to idleness and vice. The Indians be-

IX. QUESTIONS—31 When did the London Company get a second charter? 32 Why did they ask for it? 33. What appointment was conferred upon Lord Delaware? 34 What can you say of Lord Delaware?

X 35. Who had been authorized to precede Lord Delaware in the management of the affairs of the colony? 36. How many vessels and emigrants did they have? 37 What accident happened to the fleet?

XI 38. How was the colony governed after the arrival of the seven vessels? 39. What accident happened to Smith? 40. What did he do in consequence?

XII 41. How did the colonists behave after his departure? 42. What was the consequence? 43 What was that period of time called? 44 What determination did the colonists finally come to? 45 Why was not the determination carried out?

came hostile, the horrors of famine ensued, and, in less than six months after, not more than sixty, of the five hundred persons whom he had left, remained. This period of distress and gloom was long remembered as the "starving-time." In consequence of the destitute condition to which the colonists were reduced, and of the gloomy prospects ahead, it was determined to desert Jamestown entirely, and seek safety among the English fishermen at Newfoundland. In four vessels they embarked; but just as they were drawing near the mouth of the river, Lord Delaware appeared with emigrants and supplies, and persuaded them to return.

XIII. Under the administration of the wise and good Delaware, order and contentment prevailed, and the affairs of the colony began to prosper; but, unfortunately, his health failed, and he was compelled to return to England, leaving the government to be administered by a deputy. New settlements were made in the vicinity of Jamestown, and notwithstanding the laws were harsh and strict, the colony continued to prosper. The company in England, however, with a view to greater advantages, obtained another charter, their third, in 1612. A remarkable feature of the new charter allowed the company to hold meetings for the transaction of business, thus giving to the body a democratic form of government.

XIV. In 1613 occurred the marriage of Pocahontas to a young Englishman named John Rolfe (*rolf*). This event proved to be of great importance, as it had the effect of establishing a confirmed peace with Powhatan, as well as with the powerful Chickahominy Indians. Three years after her marriage, Pocahontas accompanied her husband to England, where she was an object of great interest to all classes

---

XIII. QUESTIONS.—46. What is said of the affairs of the colony under the administration of Lord Delaware? 47. What, unfortunately, was he compelled to do? 48. When did the London Company procure their third charter? 49 What remarkable feature did the new charter contain?

XIV. 50. What interesting event took place in 1613? 51 Of what importance did it prove? 52. What further can you state of Pocahontas?

2*

of citizens, and was presented at court. While preparing to return to her native land she suddenly died, leaving a son, from whom are descended many well-known families in Virginia.

XV. During the year 1613 two expeditions were sent from Virginia, under the command of Samuel Argall, an avaricious man, who afterwards became deputy-governor of the colony. Argall's object was the protection of the fishermen off the coast of Maine; but discovering a French settlement near the Penobscot, he destroyed it, and dispersed the inhabitants. In his second expedition he reduced and plundered Port Royal, in Nova Scotia.

XVI. The commencement of negro slavery in the English colonies dates from its introduction into Virginia, in 1620, when a Dutch vessel entered the James River with negroes, twenty of whom were landed and sold into perpetual slavery. The culture of cotton was begun the next year. A large number of colonists were sent to Virginia during the year 1620, among whom were about a hundred young women of good reputation, who were disposed of to the planters as wives, each purchaser giving one hundred pounds of tobacco, being the cost of the woman's passage to America.

XVII. After the marriage of Pocahontas, until the death of her father, peaceful relations existed between the settlers and the Indians; but, in 1622, Powhatan's successor commenced a bloody war, in one day massacring about three hundred and fifty men, women, and children. The settlers retaliated, slaughtering great numbers of the Indians and driving the rest into the wilderness.

XV. QUESTIONS.—53. Who was Samuel Argall? 54. Give an account of his first expedition from Virginia. 55. Of his second. 56. Describe the Penobscot River. (See map of Maine.) 57. How is Port Royal situated? (See map, p 10.)

XVI. 58. How was negro slavery introduced into the English colonies in America? 59. What can you say of the commencement of cotton culture? 60. How did the planters get their wives?

XVII. 61. How long did peaceful relations continue between the whites and Indians? 62. Give an account of the first massacre.

XVIII. The affairs of the colony caused frequent meetings of the London Company. These were largely attended by the stockholders, and exciting debates. often of a political character, took place. The freedom of speech manifested on such occasions displeased King James, and he determined to accomplish the dissolution of the company. Under the pretext, therefore, that the disasters to the colony were the result of bad government, the dissolution was effected, and, in 1624, Virginia became a royal province.

XIX. The celebrated "Navigation Act," which secured to English ships the monopoly of the carrying trade with England, and seriously abridged the freedom of colonial commerce, was passed by Parliament in 1651. It was not at first enforced against Virginia, but after its re-enactment in 1660, with new provisions, it was rigorously executed, despite the remonstrances of the colonists. In 1673, Charles II., of England, granted to Lord Culpepper and the Earl of Arlington, "all the dominion of land and water called Virginia," for the term of thirty-one years.

XX. The complaints of the people grew louder and louder. In addition to this lavish grant, and the oppressiveness of the " Navigation Act," the colonists were restricted in the elective franchise; were required to conform to the doctrines and rituals of the Church of England ; and the taxes levied were unequal and oppressive. They wanted but an excuse for appearing in arms, and it was soon found in the invasion made by the Susquehanna Indians. The invaders penetrated Virginia from the north, and carried desolation and death to many a lonely plantation.

XVIII. QUESTIONS —63 Why did the London Company have frequent meetings? 64 What can you say of the meetings? 65. What did King James determine upon? 66. Why? 67 When did he accomplish his purpose? 68. What was his pretext for so doing?

XIX 69 When was the celebrated "Navigation Act" passed? 70. What was its most obnoxious feature? 71 How did it affect the colonial commerce? 72 What can you say of its enforcement? 73 What grant of Virginia was afterward made to two persons?

XX. 74 Of what did the people complain? 75. What did they seek? 76 What excuse was soon found? 77. What did the Susquehannas do?

XXI. The people, knowing Governor Berkeley's measures for defense to be very inefficient, demanded permission to arm and protect themselves; but, being refused, they united ostensibly to repel the Indian invaders; and thus a struggle for popular liberty broke out in 1676, known as Bacon's Rebellion. Nathaniel Bacon, from whom the movement took its name, was at once pointed out as the leader. His social position was good; he was eloquent and courageous.

XXII. With a force of five hundred men he marched against the Indians, whom he met and defeated; and though Berkeley issued a proclamation declaring those in arms rebels, no notice was taken of the fulmination. The success against the Indians inspired the insurgents with confidence. They made demands which Berkeley consented to grant; but it soon becoming evident that he was acting treacherously, a desultory civil war broke out, in the course of which Jamestown was burned to the ground.

XXIII. Just as the success of the rebellion seemed to be established, and plans in respect to a new government were about to be adopted, Bacon suddenly died. The governor then pursued vigorous measures, and, regaining his former power, caused twenty-two of the insurgents to be hanged. Fines, imprisonments, and confiscations disgraced his administration until he was recalled by the king, in 1677.

XXIV. Berkeley's successor was Lord Culpepper, to whom and the Earl of Arlington the country had been granted in 1673, as previously stated. Virginia then became a pro-

---

XXI. QUESTIONS.—78 What demand did the people make of the governor? 79. Who was the governor? 80. How did he treat their demand? 81. What was the consequence? 82. Who was the leader of the insurgents?

XXII. 83. Relate the incidents of the rebellion.

XXIII. 84. What misfortune befell the insurgents? 85. What was Berkeley's conduct afterwards towards them?

XXIV. 86 Who succeeded Berkeley as governor of Virginia? 87. What change was then made in the character of the government? 88 How long did Virginia continue as a proprietary government? 89. What can you say of the subsequent government?

prietary government. Culpepper continued to rule until 1684, when, in consequence of his mismanagement, the king revoked the grant made to him and Arlington, and deprived him of his office. Virginia thus became a royal province again, and so remained till the REVOLUTION.

MASSACHUSETTS.

FROM ITS SETTLEMENT, IN 1620, TO THE UNION OF NEW ENGLAND COLONIES, IN 1643.

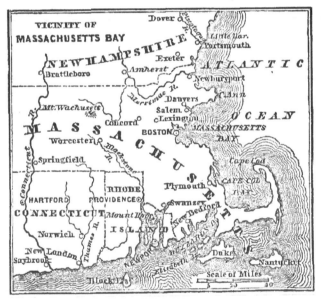

I. CAPTAIN JOHN SMITH, who had performed so creditable a part in the settlement of Virginia, set sail from London in 1614, with two ships, for the purpose of trade and discovery in the region of Cape Cod. He reached the American coast, examined the shores from the Penobscot River to Cape Cod, and prepared a map of the country, to which he gave the name of New England. The luster of the expedition, unfortunately, was very much dimmed by the act of Thomas Hunt, who commanded one of the ships: by him twenty-four of the natives were captured and taken to Spain, where they were sold into slavery.

MASSACHUSETTS.

"The name of this State probably arose from the name of a tribe of Indians formerly at Barnstable, or from two Indian words, *mas*, signifying an *Indian arrow-head*, and *wetuset*, a hill." The State motto, *Ense*, &c., means, By his sword he seeks the calm repose of liberty.

II. The original Plymouth Company having been superseded by another, called the Council of Plymouth, King James granted to the latter, in 1620, absolutely and exclusively, all the territory between the 40th* and 48th parallels of north latitude, extending from the Atlantic to the Pacific. It was not, however, under the direction of this council, or with the aid of the King, that the first permanent settlement in New England was made, but by a small band of Pilgrims, dissenters from the Church of England, who fled from their own country to find an asylum from religious persecution. The sect to which they belonged were known in England as Puritans.

III. They at first went to Amsterdam, in Holland, whence they removed to Leyden (*li'-den.*) At Leyden they lived in great harmony for about eleven years, under the pastoral care of John Robinson; but, from various causes, they became dissatisfied with their residence in Holland, and desired to plant a colony in America, where they might enjoy their civil and religious rights without disturbance. After much solicitation they obtained a grant of land from the London Company, and, being

without means, formed a contract with some London merchants, who furnished the capital for the undertaking.

IV. As many as could be accommodated embarked on
board a vessel called the Speedwell, but the larger portion remained at Leyden with Robinson. The ship sailed to Southampton, England, where she was joined by another ship,
called the Mayflower, with a body of Puritans from London.
The two vessels soon set sail, but had not gone far before
the Speedwell was found to need repairs, and they entered the
port of Dartmouth, England. They started a second time,
but again put back, this time to Plymouth, where the Speedwell was abandoned as unseaworthy.

V. Then, after permitting those who chose to abandon the
enterprise, the Mayflower set sail alone, with one hundred and
one persons,—men, women, and children,—the most distinguished of whom were John Carver, William Brewster,
Miles Standish, William Bradford, and Edward Winslow.
After a boisterous passage of sixty-three days, they reached
the American coast, and in two days after were safely moored
in Cape Cod Bay. In the cabin of the Mayflower, before
they landed, they agreed to and signed a solemn compact, by
the terms of which they were to be ruled, and immediately after
they unanimously elected John Carver governor for one year.

VI. Several days were spent by exploring parties in search-
ing for a favorable locality to commence the settlement. At
length, on the 21st of December, 1620, they all landed at a place
which they called Plymouth, in memory of the hospitalities
which had been bestowed upon them at the last English port

IV. QUESTIONS.—22 Did they all leave Holland? 23. Who remained? 24 On
board of what vessel did they sail? 25 To what place did the Speedwell first go?
26. What accession was made to the company at Southampton? 27 What
then took place? 28. What further can you state of the Speedwell?

V. 29 From what place did the Mayflower set sail alone? 30 With how many
persons? 31. Who were the most distinguished of them? 32 What kind of a
passage did they have? 33 What did they do before leaving the ship?

VI. 34. In what way were several days spent? 35 When did they land?
36. At what place? 37 Why did they call it Plymouth? 38 What can you say
of their sufferings? 39 What befell Carver's family? 40. Who succeeded him as
governor?

from which they had sailed. The winter was severe, and in less than five months nearly half of that Pilgrim band died from the effects of exposure and privations,—Governor Carver and his wife being among the number. William Bradford was thereupon elected to fill the vacancy, and during thirty years he continued to be a prominent man in the colony.

VII. In April, of 1621, a treaty of friendship was made with Massasoit (*mas-sa-soit'*), chief of the Wampanoags (*wom-pa-nō'-ags*), which was sacredly kept for more than thirty years. Canonicus, the great chief of the Narragansetts, who regarded the English as intruders, kept the colonists in fear for awhile; but the decided course of Bradford eventually compelled him to sue for peace.

VIII. In the mean time other influences were at work to extend the range of settlements. A company composed of gentlemen who were interested in the fisheries and trade of New England, having purchased a tract of land, sent out an expedition of a hundred persons, under the charge of John Endicott. These reached Salem in 1628, and made a settlement, thus laying the foundation of the Massachusetts Bay Colony. The proprietors soon after obtained a charter from the king, under the incorporated title of " The Governor and Company of Massachusetts Bay, in New England."

IX. Accessions were rapidly made to the new colony, and settlements at Charlestown and other places were made. An important change took place in 1629, by which the government of the company was transferred from London to New England. This induced men of fortune and intelligence to become interested, among whom was John Winthrop, who

VII. QUESTIONS.—41. What important treaty was made ? 42 For how long a time was the treaty observed ? 43. What can you say of Canonicus ?

VIII. 44. What settlement was made in 1628? 45. In what direction from Plymouth is Salem ? (See map p 37) 46. What led to the settlement of Salem ? 47. When was Salem settled ? 48. What charter was afterward obtained by the proprietors of Salem ?

IX. 49. What can you say of the growth of the Massachusetts Bay Colony ? 50. What induced Winthrop and others to join the colonists? 51. When was Boston settled? 52. By whom was it settled ?

was afterward elected governor, and who set sail for the colony in the beginning of April, 1630. Winthrop* was accompanied by about three hundred families, mostly Puritans, who settled at Boston and adjacent places, in 1630.

X. The banishment of Roger Williams, in 1635, was an event not only important in itself, but also on account of the principle it enunciated. Though a Puritan, Williams denounced the religious intolerance practiced in New England, for which, as well as certain opinions touching civil matters, he was banished. Nor was this the only banishment. A Mrs. Hutchinson,† who persisted in holding meetings of her own sex, and promulgating peculiar views, was also compelled to leave.

XI. An act of the "General Court" at Boston, in 1636, by which about two thousand dollars were appropriated for the purpose of founding a public school or college, led to the establishment of what is now the oldest literary institution in America. In 1638, the Rev. John Harvard bequeathed upwards of three thousand dollars to it, which, in honor of the benefactor, was named Harvard College. Its location is at Cambridge (kāme'-brij), about three miles from Boston.

---

* John Winthrop was born in Groton, county of Suffolk, England, in 1588. He was re-elected governor of Massachusetts every year until 1634. With the exception of two or three years, he was afterwards deputy governor or governor until his death, which occurred in 1648.

† Mrs. Anne Hutchinson, upon being sentenced to banishment, at first went to Rhode Island. After the death of her husband, which occurred in 1642, five years later, she removed with her children to New Netherlands. The Indians and the Dutch were then at war, and, in an attack made by the former, her house was set on fire, and she and all her family, except one child, either perished in the flames or were massacred by the savages.

X. QUESTIONS.—53. What intolerance was shown towards Roger Williams? 54. What towards a woman?

XI. 55. Give an account of the establishment of Harvard College. 56. How is Cambridge situated? (See map, p. 120.)

NEW HAMPSHIRE.

NEW HAMPSHIRE.
In 1629 John Mason obtained a grant of the territory between the Merrimac and Piscataqua Rivers, calling it New Hampshire, in commemoration of the fact that he had once been governor of Portsmouth, in Hampshire county, England. The Seal of the State is shown above. New Hampshire has no motto.

I. The Council of Plymouth, it will be recollected, in 1620 obtained a grant of land including the whole of what is now known as New England. In 1622, a portion of this grant — that extending from the Merrimac to the Kennebec—was ceded by the council to Ferdinand Gorges (*gor'-jez*) and John Mason, two of its most active members. Gorges and Mason called the territory which they thus obtained Laconia, and, in the spring of 1623, sent emigrants who made settlements at Little Harbor, near Portsmouth, and at Dover. These, then, were the first settlements in New Hampshire.

II. In 1629, the Rev. John Wheelwright and others, who evidently did not consider the grant to Gorges and Mason as of much value, purchased of the Indians all the territory be-

NEW HAMPSHIRE.—1. QUESTIONS.—1. How did the Council of Plymouth dispose of a portion of their lands in 1622? 2. Describe the Merrimac River. (See map p. 37.) 3. Describe the Kennebec. (See map, p. 10.) 4. What name did Gorges and Mason give to their country? 5. What rivers bounded Laconia? 6. How is Portsmouth situated? (See map, p. 44.) 7. In what direction from Portsmouth is Dover? (See map, p. 44.)

II. 8. What purchase of territory was made in 1629? 9. How did this purchase conflict with the claims of Gorges and Mason? 10. Into what body of water does the Piscataqua flow? (See map, p. 44.) 11. What grant did Mason obtain in 1629? 12. What name did he give to the country?

tween the Merrimac and Piscataqua. In the same year
Mason obtained from Gorges a grant, in his own name alone
of the country which Wheelwright had purchased, and to
this he gave the name of New Hampshire.

III. The different settlements of New Hampshire in time
came to be governed by different proprietors; but the people
believing their interests would be promoted by a change, in
1641 formed a union, and placed themselves under the pro
tection of Massachusetts. This privilege was enjoyed for
a period of nearly forty years, when, in 1680, the two colo
nies were separated by order of the king, and New Hampshire
became a royal province.

POETSMOUTH AND VICINITY.

IV. In the following year a vex
atious controversy began, as to the
proprietorship of the lands, which
continued for a number of years
This dispute grew out of the claims
which the heirs of Mason had laid to
all the territory between the Merri
mac and Piscataqua, and it was not
terminated until they relinquished
all the unoccupied portions of the
province. During the wars known as King Philip's and King
William's, the settlers of New Hampshire suffered severely
from the incursions of the Indians. In one case, the attack
upon Dover in the latter war, twenty-one persons were killed
and others were captured and taken to Canada.

V. The district of New Hampshire was several times con
nected with Massachusetts,—the first from 1641 to 1680, as
previously stated; but, in 1741, it became a separate prov
ince, and so continued till the Revolution.

III QUESTIONS—13 What change in the government of the New Hampshire
settlements took place in 1641? 14 Give a further account of the political con.
nection between New Hampshire and Massachusetts. (See, also, paragraph V.)
   IV 15. What controversy respecting lands began in 1681? 16. Give some ac
count of it. 17 How did the wars of King Philip and King William affect the set·
tlements of New Hampshire?

CONNECTICUT.

CONNECTICUT.
This State derives its name from its chief river, the Connecticut, a name given to it by the Indians, and signifying in their language *the long river.* In the Seal of Connecticut (given above) is the motto of the State, *Qui transtulit sustinet,* He who brought us hither still preserves.

I. In 1630 the Council of Plymouth ceded to the Earl of Warwick the soil of Connecticut; and this grant, in the following year, was transferred to Lord Say-and-Seal, Lord Brooke, and associates.

II. As the Dutch, at the time, laid claim to all the territory thus ceded, they resolved to prevent any settlements being made within the limits of the new grant. Accordingly, they proceeded from New York, sailed up the Connecticut River to where Hartford now stands, and there erected a fort. The structure was hardly completed when Captain William Holmes and a company from Plymouth sailed up the river, and, though forbidden by the Dutch, who threatened to fire upon them if they attempted to pass the fort, the English kept on unhurt, and commenced the settlement of Connecticut, at Windsor (*win'-zer*), by erecting in that year, 1633, a trading-house there.

III. In the autumn of 1635, a company of sixty men,

CONNECTICUT.—I. QUESTIONS.—1. What grant of land was made in 1630? 2. What, in 1631?

II. 3. What resolution did the Dutch determine upon? 4. What action did they accordingly take? 5. When and where was Connecticut first settled? 6. Describe the Connecticut River. (See map of New England.)

women, and children journeyed from Massachusetts through the wilderness, and settled at Windsor, Hartford, and Wethersfield. At about the same time a colony was commenced at the mouth of the Connecticut, which, in honor of Lord Say-and-Seal and Lord Brooke, was called Saybrook. But the migration conducted by the Rev. Thomas Hooker, in 1636, was one of the most important to Connecticut. With about a hundred persons he departed from the vicinity of Boston, and, after a toilsome journey through swamps and forests, arrived in the valley of the Connecticut. His people settled mostly at Hartford.

IV. It was at this time that difficulties with the Indians began to arise. The Pequods, a warlike tribe inhabiting the southeast part of Connecticut, committed many acts of hostility, and sought an alliance with the Narragansetts in an effort to exterminate the colonists; but, through the exertions of Roger Williams, the league was prevented. The Indians, however, continuing their murderous depredations, a court, summoned at Hartford, in 1637, formally declared war against them.

V. Soon a force of ninety colonists, with about the same number of Mohegan Indians, started against the foe. The expedition, commanded by Captain John Mason, sailed down the Connecticut and along Long Island Sound, and landed at a point in the southwestern part of Rhode Island. Here it was joined by other Indian allies, until the whole force amounted to not less than five hundred men. Mason proceeded by quick marches, and surprised the chief fort of the Pequods, situated

III. QUESTIONS.—7 What account can you give of the settlements made in the autumn of 1635? 8. Of the colony at the mouth of the Connecticut? 9. Of the migration conducted by Hooker?

IV. 10. Who were the Pequods? 11. What alliance did they try to bring about? 12 How was it prevented? 13 When and by whom was war declared against the Pequods?

V. 14 What expedition was sent against them? 15. Give an account of the movements of the expedition 16 At what place was the chief fort of the Pequods situated? 17. How is New London situated? (See map, p. 47) 18. What was the result of the expedition?

on the Mystic River, eight miles northeast of New London. It and the wigwams were burned, and more than six hundred men, women, and children perished by fire or were slain.

VI. The Pequods never recovered from their great loss. The severe blow dealt them was promptly followed by vigorous measures, until finally the survivors, about two hundred in number, surrendered in despair, and were sold into captivity

or incorporated with other tribes. So complete was their overthrow that the very name of Pequods was no longer heard.

VII. A third colony was established in Connecticut, in 1638, called the New Haven colony. The land was bought of the Indians, and under the guidance of the Rev. John Davenport and Theophilus Eaton, a colony, remarkable for the

VI. QUESTIONS.—19. What effect did the blow have upon the Pequods? 20. What further account can you give of the Pequods?

VII. 2. When was a third colony established in Connecticut? 22. By whom? 23. At what place? 24. How is New Haven situated? (See map, p. 47.)

religious spirit that marked its laws, was planted and flourished.

VIII. It will be seen that three colonies were established in Connecticut, namely : the Connecticut colony, embracing Windsor, Hartford, and Wethersfield, the inhabitants of which acknowledged the authority of Massachusetts; the Saybrook colony; and the New Haven colony. The one at the mouth of the Connecticut, Saybrook, maintained its separate existence until 1644, when it was annexed to the Connecticut colony. Then there were only two. These were united in 1665, under a royal charter granted by Charles II, king of England. This charter was exceedingly liberal, and confirmed in every particular the constitution which the people had adopted at Hartford, twenty-six years before.

IX. For a number of years the colonists of Connecticut enjoyed comparative freedom from anxiety and molestation ; but, in 1687, Sir Edmund Andros, who had been appointed royal governor of New England, appeared before the Assembly, then in session at Hartford, and demanded the surrender of their charter. A discussion at once arose which was protracted till evening, when the charter was brought in and laid upon the table ; but just as Andros was stepping forward to take it, the lights were suddenly extinguished. When the candles were relighted, the document could not be found : it had been carried away by Captain Wadsworth, and hid in the hollow of a tree which was afterward known as the Charter Oak.

X. Andros, notwithstanding his inability to procure the charter, assumed the government, and administered it in his own name until he was seized at Boston, in 1689, and sent to England, for trial on a charge of maladministration of public affairs. The people then received the charter from its hiding-

VIII Questions.—How many colonies, in all, were established in Connecticut? 26. Give their names 27 What settlements did the Connecticut colony embrace? 28. What became of the Saybrook colony? 29 What union afterward took place?

IX. 30 What demand was made of the Connecticut people in 1687? 31 Give an account of the proceedings that followed

X 32. What further can you say of Andros? 33 Of the charter?

place, and Connecticut again assumed her position as an independent colony.

RHODE ISLAND.

I. Upon the banishment of Roger Williams* from Massachusetts, he remained several months with the Narragansetts, and then fixed his habitation on the spot where the city of Providence now stands. This was in the year 1636. The place selected by him for settlement was purchased of the Indians, and to it he gave the name which it still bears, to commemorate "God's merciful providence to him in his distress." Williams was prompt to proclaim

RHODE ISLAND.
The Island of Aquetneck was so called by the Indians. When Coddington and his associates settled there, in 1638, fancying it resembled the Island of Rhodes, in the Mediterranean, they called it Rhode Island: hence the name of the State. The State Coat of Arms is given above. The motto is, *In God we hope.*

religious toleration in his new home, and the rules governing the colony were made by a majority of the inhabitants; consequently immigrants came in great numbers, mostly from the oppressed of the neighboring colonies.

II. A year after, William Coddington, who had become dis-

---

* Roger Williams was born in Wales, in 1606. He died in Rhode Island, in 1683.

RHODE ISLAND.—I. QUESTIONS.—1. When was Rhode Island settled? 2. At what place? 3. By whom? 4. How did Williams procure the land? 5. Why was Providence so called? 6. What induced immigrants to flock to Rhode Island?

II. 7. What settlement was made by Coddington? 8. Why did he leave Boston? 9. What was Coddington's settlement afterward called? 10. What was Williams's afterwards called?

3

satisfied with his residence in Boston, in consequence of the church opposition to which he had for a long time been subjected, accepted an invitation from Williams, and, with eighteen others, purchased from the Indians the island of Rhode Island, and settled there. This settlement was afterwards known as the Rhode Island Plantation, and that of Williams as the Providence Plantation.

III. It was claimed on the part of Plymouth, and the assumption was supported by Massachusetts, that the lands whereon Williams and Coddington had settled belonged to Plymouth, and that consequently the two settlements were under the jurisdiction of that colony. Rather than acknowledge this claim, Williams went to England and obtained from Parliament a free charter of incorporation, whereby the two settlements of Rhode Island were united, in 1644, under one government, as the Rhode Island and Providence Plantations.

ROGER WILLIAMS.

IV. After Charles II. ascended the throne of England, Rhode Island, in 1663, obtained a new charter. When Andros assumed the government of New England, operations, under the charter, were for the time necessarily suspended; but immediately after his seizure at Boston, as elsewhere stated, the charter again became the fundamental law of the colony, and was the only constitution of the State till 1842.

III. QUESTIONS.—11. What claim did the colonies of Plymouth and Massachusetts set up? 12. What did Williams do in consequence? 13. When were the two plantations united? 14. Under what name?

IV. 15. By whom was a new charter granted to Rhode Island? 16. When was it granted? 17. What can you say of it? 18. What interruption to its operation was for a time suffered? 19. When was the administration of affairs under the charter resumed? 20. Till what year did the charter then continue in operation? 21. How many years passed from the time it was granted till its final supersedure?

REVIEW QUESTIONS

MASSACHUSETTS.

FROM THE UNION OF THE NEW ENGLAND COLONIES, IN 1643, TO "THE FRENCH AND INDIAN WAR."

I. In 1643 a union was formed by the four colonies of Massachusetts, Plymouth, Connecticut, and New Haven, the object being to secure mutual protection against the encroachments of the Dutch and French, and for better security against the hostility of the Indians. When, five years after, Rhode Island desired to be admitted to the confederacy, the request was not granted, because she refused to be incorporated with Plymouth, as part of that colony, and thus lose her separate existence. The general affairs of the union were managed by a board of commissioners, consisting of two from each colony; and, in this way, the confederacy existed for nearly fifty years. When, at last, it was destroyed, by the loss of their charters, the colonists still cherished a desire for union.

II. In 1656 a lamentable trouble commenced, growing out of the arrival in that year of a number of Quakers from England. A report, which represented them to be a people of peculiar opinions and conduct, had preceded them, and those who first arrived were consequently sent back at once. Shortly after, a law was passed, intended to prohibit their coming into the united colonies at all; but this failing of its object—the Quakers still continuing to come—another law was enacted, decreeing the punishment of death upon all who returned from banishment.

MASSACHUSETTS.—I QUESTIONS.—1. What union was formed in 1643? 2, What request did Rhode Island make? 3. Why was it not granted? 4. How were the general affairs of the union conducted?

II 5, What arrival took place in 1656? 6 What was done with those who first arrived? 7 Why were they sent back? 8 Did this course keep the Quakers from coming? 9 What severe law was thereupon enacted?

III. This also failed of its object. Many of the banished returned, four were executed, some were publicly whipped, and others were cast into prison. The great severity of the law finally caused a general feeling of condemnation; a widespread sympathy for the accused began to be felt, and, after five years of trouble, the atrocious act was repealed.

KING PHILIP'S WAR.

IV. During the life of Massasoit, the treaty of friendship made between him and the people of Plymouth was faithfully kept. After his death, his two sons, Alexander and Philip, were looked upon as being unfriendly to the whites; and when, upon the death of the elder brother, Philip became chief, trouble began to be anticipated.

KING PHILIP.

V. It was evident to the Indians that the spreading settlements were fast reducing their domains and breaking up their hunting-grounds; and they saw plainly, in the growing power of the whites, their own inevitable extinction. Nothing short of a combination of all the New England tribes for the extermination of the colonists, it was thought, could arrest the tide against them; and Philip, so it was alleged, was the leading spirit in plotting the combination. A converted Indian, who had been sent as a missionary among his people, was the principal informer against the chief. This man was afterward found murdered. The execution by the whites of

III. QUESTIONS.—10. What effect did the law have? 11. How were the Quakers then punished? 12. What further can you say of the troubles?

IV. 13. Who was Alexander? 14. Philip? 15. To what position did Philip attain?

V. 16. What became evident to the Indians? 17. How did the Indians suppose they could be saved from extinction? 18. Who was supposed to be the leading spirit in plotting an Indian combination? 19. Who informed against Philip?

three Indians, who had been arrested, tried, and convicted of
the murder, may be considered as the immediate cause of the
war.

INDIAN WARFARE.—THE SURPRISE.

VI. The first attack was made by Philip, in 1675, upon
the people of Swanzey, a village thirty-five miles southwest
from Plymouth. The alarm was given, and he was pursued
by a force consisting of Plymouth troops and volunteers

QUESTIONS.—20. What became of the informer ?   21. What was the immediate
cause of King Philip's war ?
VI. 22. Give an account of the attack upon Swanzey.   23. To what place was
Philip pursued?   24. Where is Mount Hope situated?   (See map, p. 37.)   25. What
can you say of the war that followed ?

from Boston, as far as his home at Mount Hope, which he was forced to abandon. He sought safety in a swamp. Here he was besieged for a number of days, but at length made his escape, with the most of his warriors. The war that followed was of the most desolating character. The savages, grown desperate, burned village after village, and carried death and destruction throughout the country for miles around.

VII. Although a treaty of peace had been made with the Narragansetts, they proved unfaithful to their obligations, and became the allies of Philip. This becoming known, a strong force was sent against them, and, in an immense swamp in the southern part of Rhode Island, they were defeated with great loss. Yet they continued their depredations till the death of Philip, which occurred in 1676. The shot of a faithless Indian terminated the life of the wily chief.

VIII. A controversy, which had been going on for a number of years, between the heirs of Gorges and Mason and the Massachusetts colony, concerning the province of Maine, was, in 1677, decided by judicial authority in favor of the heirs, and Massachusetts then purchased their interest. Three years after, a separation of New Hampshire from Massachusetts was declared, and the former became a royal province —the first in New England ; but the title to Maine was retained by Massachusetts until the year 1820.

IX. The English Parliament, with a view to monopolizing the trade with the colonies, passed the "Navigation Act." The opposition to this, as well as to other obnoxious laws, as shown by Massachusetts, displeased the king, James II., and he therefore deprived that colony of her charter. Sir Edmund Andros, who, by his subsequent career, made himself

---

VII. QUESTIONS —26 How did the Narragansetts behave? 27. What followed? 28. What became of Philip?

VIII 29. What controversy was settled in 1677? 30 How was it settled? 31 What took place three years after? 82 Till what time was Maine a part of Massachusetts?

IX. 83. Why was the "Navigation Act" passed? 34 How was the law treated by Massachusetts? 85. What did the king then do?

infamous, on account of his unjust and oppressive government, was sent to govern New England.

X. These proceedings on the part of the king rendered him exceedingly unpopular,—so much so, that when the news of the English Revolution and James's dethronement reached Boston, it caused great rejoicing. Andros and the most obnoxious of his officers were seized and sent to England, and the former mode of government was again established.

KING WILLIAM'S WAR.

XI. James fled to France, and William, Prince of Orange, and Mary, his wife, the eldest daughter of James, were called to the English throne, as king and queen of that country. The cause of the fugitive king was earnestly espoused by the French monarch, and this, principally, led to a contest between the two powers, known in history as King William's War, in which the respective colonists became involved and suffered terribly.

XII. During the early part of the contest, which lasted from 1689 to the peace of Ryswick (*riz'-wick*), in 1697, the French and their Indian allies made expeditions against Dover, Schenectady (*ske-nek'-ta-de*), and other settlements in the northern colonies, and committed barbarities of the most shocking character. To check these incursions, an expedition, under Sir William Phipps, was dispatched by Massachusetts against Nova Scotia. The capture of Port Royal was easily accomplished, and Phipps returned to Boston with a large amount of booty.

XIII. A second undertaking, of greater magnitude, was

X. Questions.—36. What made James II. unpopular in Massachusetts ? 37. What, consequently, caused great rejoicings there ? 38. What treatment was meted out to Andros?

XI. 39. To what place did James retreat? 40. Who then was made king of England? 41. Who, queen? 42. What was the principal cause of King William's War?

XII. 43. How long did the war last? 44. What places did the French and Indians attack? 45. How is Dover situated? (See map, p. 44.) 46. How is Schenectady situated? (See map, p. 62.) 47. Give an account of Phipps's expedition against Nova Scotia.

planned by the New England colonies and New York, having for its object the conquest of Canada, though the prospect of plunder gave to it all the vitality it possessed. A large naval force, under Sir William Phipps, left Massachusetts, while a land expedition proceeded from New York; but the undertaking proved a signal failure. The land troops reached the head of Lake Champlain, and then, because no means of transportation were provided, turned back. The expedition by water was pushed with no more energy and dispatch, and it too failed.

XIV. Phipps, after his return, was sent to England, for the purpose of procuring aid in the further prosecution of the war, and also to obtain for Massachusetts a restoration of the charter which King James had taken away. His mission, as regards the first purpose, was unsuccessful: as regards the second, King William refused to restore the old charter, but, instead, he granted a new one, which united Massachusetts, Plymouth, Maine, and Nova Scotia in one royal government, and upon Phipps was conferred the office of governor.

XV. One of the very first acts of the new governor was the formation, in 1692, of a court to try certain persons who were accused of witchcraft, the belief in which, at the time, prevailed among the people of Salem and neighboring towns. Twenty persons were put to death, more than fifty were tortured or frightened into a confession, and many suffered imprisonment. The delusion, which lasted more than six months, was finally dispelled, and the most of those who had participated as prosecutors in the unrighteous work confessed their error; still there were some, the most prominent of whom was Cotton Mather, an eccentric but influential minister, who defended their course to the last.

<hr>

XIII. QUESTIONS.—48. What second undertaking was planned? 49. What gave to it its vitality? 50. Give an account of the land expedition 51. Of the expedition by water. 52. How is Lake Champlain situated? (See map, p. 62.)

XIV. 53. Why was Phipps sent to England? 54. How successful was he?

XV. 55. What was one of the first acts of Governor Phipps? 56. How is Salem situated? (See map, p. 37.) 57. How many persons were put to death? 58. How many were tortured or frightened into a confession? 59. What further account can you give of the delusion?

3*

XVI. King William's War continued to afflict the colonies, extending over a period of about eight years, till it was brought to a close, as before stated, by the treaty of 1697.

QUEEN ANNE'S WAR.

XVII. Upon the death of James II., which occurred in France, in 1701, the French monarch acknowledged his son, who was then in exile, to be the lawful heir to the English throne. This tended to produce a spirit of resentment in England, where the crown had been settled upon Anne (*an*), the second daughter of James. While the English were making preparations for war, King William died, and Anne became sovereign of England. The interference of France in the matter of the succession to the English crown, in connection with other causes, led to a war between England on the one side, and France and Spain on the other, which is known in America as Queen Anne's War, but, in Europe, as the *War of the Spanish Succession.*

XVIII. In consequence of a treaty of neutrality which the confederated tribes of Indians, commonly known as the Five Nations, had made with the French in Canada, New York did not suffer from any invasion from the north, the Five Nations occupying lands within that colony. The weight of the war, therefore, fell upon the people of New England. Bodies of French and Indians made incursions from Canada, fell upon the defenceless villages, and murdered or carried into captivity the helpless inhabitants.

XIX. The capture of Port Royal, in 1710, after an unsuccessful attempt made three years before, was the most important event of the war.* The name of the place was thereupon

---

XVII QUESTIONS.—60. What course did the French monarch pursue, upon the death of James II ? 61. How did this affect the English people? 62 While preparations were being made for war, what occurred? 63. What were the causes of Queen Anne's War? 64. By what other name was the contest known?

XVIII 65. How did New York escape invasion during the war? 66. Where was the weight of the war felt?

* In America

changed to Annapolis, in honor of the English queen, and Acadia was permanently annexed to the British realm. The contest continued about eleven years, hostilities having commenced in 1702, and closed by the treaty of Utrecht (*u'-trekt*), in 1713

KING GEORGE'S WAR.

XX. A peace of nearly thirty years followed, which was broken during the reign of George II., by King George's War. This contest had its origin in European disputes, relating, principally, to the kingdom of Austria, and, for that reason, is known in Europe as the *War of the Austrian Succession.*

XXI. War having been declared between England and France in 1744, the colonial possessions were at once involved. The most important event was the capture of Louisburg (*loo'isburg*), by a force, mostly of New England troops, under William Pepperill, aided by an English fleet, commanded by Commodore Warren. The contest between the two nations continued about four years, and was terminated by the treaty of Aix-la-chapelle (*ākes-la-sha-pel'*), in 1748, by which all acquisitions of territory which had been made by England and France during the war were mutually restored.

XIX. QUESTIONS.—67 What was the most important event of the war? 68. When was Port Royal captured? 69. What change took place in the name? 70. Why was the name so changed? 71 What permanent annexation was made to the British realm? 72 How long did the war continue?

XX. 73. How long did peace continue after King William's War? 74. What war then broke out? 75. What was the cause of King George's War? 76. By what other name is it known?

XXI. 77. When was war declared? 78 What was the most important event of the war? 79 How long did the war continue? 80. By what treaty was it terminated? 81. What provision did the treaty make as regards acquisition of territory?

NEW YORK.

NEW YORK.

When, in 1664, Stuyvesant surrendered New Netherlands, in compliment to the Duke of York, to whom it had been granted, New Amsterdam was called New York, a name which was also applied to the whole province. Below the Shield of the State (given above) is the motto, *Excelsior*, meaning more elevated, denoting that the course of the State is onward and higher.

I. UNTIL most of the large bays and rivers on the eastern side of North America had been explored, it was generally supposed that there existed a more direct and less dangerous passage by water, from the Atlantic to the Pacific, than the route around Cape Horn. Among those who entertained this belief was Henry Hudson,* an English navigator, who, actuated by the desire to become the fortunate discoverer of such a passage, if any existed, made four voyages to the coast of America.

II. In his third voyage, made in 1609, while sailing in the service of "The Dutch East India Company," he discovered the river which now bears his name. Having sailed up the stream to the head of ship navigation, and explored it in a small boat for some miles further, probably as far as Albany, he returned to Europe.

---

* Hudson made his fourth voyage in 1610. While in Hudson's Bay, a mutiny occurring among his men, he, with eight who remained faithful to him, was put into an open boat and abandoned. Two ships were afterwards sent from England to make search for him, but no tidings of the bold navigator could ever be gained.

I. NEW YORK.—QUESTIONS.—1. Who was Henry Hudson? 2. How many voyages did he make to the coast of America? 3. What was his object?

II. 4. When did he discover the Hudson? 5. In whose employ was he at the time? 6. How far up the Hudson did he proceed? 7. What was his object? 8. Who first discovered the Hudson River? *Ans.*—Verrazani in 1524.

HENRY HUDSON.

III. The Dutch, claiming that Hudson's discovery gave them a title to the country, in 1614 built a fort on Manhattan or New York Island, and, in the following year, built a second fort, at Albany, which they called Fort Orange. Their claim to territory included the whole region from Cape Cod to the southern shore of Delaware Bay, though that part in their possession was the only portion known as New Netherlands.

IV. The actual colonization of the country did not commence until 1623. In that year, under the auspices of a new organization, called "The Dutch West India Company," two settlements were made; one at Fort Orange, the site of Albany, and the other on Manhattan Island, to which the name of *New Amsterdam* was given. The company offered a large tract of land and certain privileges to every individual who would form a settlement of fifty persons. This led, more than two centuries afterward, to very serious disturbances, known as the "anti-rent difficulties."

V. New Netherlands had, in the course of time, four Dutch governors, the first of whom was Peter Minuits : he was succeeded by Wouter Van Twiller, during whose administration a controversy was begun, occasioned by the alleged encroachments of the English on the eastern end of Long Island and on the Connecticut River. Sir William Kieft (*kreft*), the third

---

III. QUESTIONS.—9. What claim to territory did the Dutch make? 10. When and where did they build two forts? 11. How is Albany situated? (See map, p. 62.) 12. What territory was known as New Netherlands?

IV. 13. When was New York first colonized by the Dutch? 14. What settlements were then made? 15. What inducements were offered to settlers? 16. What difficulties followed, a long time after?

V. 17. Give in order the names of the four successive Dutch governors of New Netherlands. 18. What occurred during Van Twiller's administration? 19. What, during Kieft's? 20. What was Kieft's fate?

governor, involved the colony in a strife with the Swedes of Delaware, whose settlements he considered as encroachments upon New Netherlands. He also, by his unwise and inhuman conduct, brought on a disastrous war with the Indians. After an administration of about nine years, the West India Company deprived him of his office. On his return to Europe, the ship in which he sailed was wrecked, and the guilty man perished.

VI. Peter Stuyvesant, the fourth and last of the Dutch governors, arrived in 1647, when he commenced a vigorous though often arbitrary rule. He conciliated the Indians, made a treaty settling boundary disputes with the English,

VI. Questions.—21. What did Stuyvesant accomplish? 22. What was the consequence? 23. What did the people desire? 24. What did they demand? 25. How was their demand treated?

gained by conquest the Swedish settlements on the Delaware,

PETER STUYVESANT.

and by judicious regulations did much to encourage commerce. The consequence was, that many immigrants came from the oppressed, the discontented, and the enterprising of other colonies and European nations; and soon a body of people were gathered together who, notwithstanding all their privileges, desired other and greater ones. They even demanded a share in the government; but Stuyvesant resisted, and his conduct was afterwards approved by the home government.

VII. In 1664 Charles II., in entire disregard of the claims of the Dutch, granted to his brother, the Duke of York, the whole region from the Connecticut River to Delaware Bay, and a fleet, under Colonel Nicolls, was sent to take possession of the territory. In the mean time, all that portion now known as New Jersey was sold by the duke to Lord Berkeley and Sir George Carteret.

VIII. The appearance of the English fleet before New Amsterdam convinced Stuyvesant, when too late, of the imprudence of his conduct in refusing the demand of the colonists. They, hoping to enjoy more freedom under English rule, determined to comply with Nicolls's summons to surrender; but Stuyvesant, faithful to his employers, the Dutch West India Company, declined to sign the articles of capitulation

VII. QUESTIONS.—26. Who was the Duke of York? 27. From whom did he receive an extensive grant? 28. When did he receive it? 29. What region was granted? 30. What was done to procure possession of the territory? 31. What disposition did the duke make of a portion of his grant?

VIII. 32. What mistake had Stuyvesant made? 33. How did it prove to be a mistake? 34. What can you say of Stuyvesant's subsequent conduct? 35. What changes in names took place? 36. Who was the first English governor of New York?

until the town was actually in the possession of the English. The new occupants changed the name of New Amsterdam to New York, a name which was afterward applied to the whole territory under the control of the duke; and Fort Orange was called Albany. Nicolls was the first English governor.

IX. In 1673, during a war between England and Holland, the Dutch regained possession not only of New York, but of New Jersey and the settlements on the Delaware. Their hold, however, proved of brief duration; for, by the treaty of peace, made a few months after, the whole territory was restored to the British crown. To remove all doubts concerning the Duke of York's title to the lands, a new charter, confirming the former grant, was given by the king, and under it Sir Edmund Andros was appointed governor. When Charles II. died, his brother, the Duke of York, ascended the throne as James II. But, in consequence of the arbitrary conduct of James, a revolution took place, the king fled to France, and William and Mary were proclaimed joint monarchs of England.

X. The intelligence of these proceedings in England was received in New York with demonstrations evincing the satisfaction of the people. Jacob Leisler (*lice'-ler*), aided by several hundred armed men, and with the approbation of the citizens generally, took possession of the fort in the name of the new sovereigns. Although never officially recognized as governor, Leisler continued at the head of affairs, managing with prudence and energy, for more than two years, his son-in-law, Milborne, acting as his deputy. Upon the arrival of Governor Sloughter (*slaw'-ter*), bearing a commission direct

IX. QUESTIONS.—37. What occurred in 1673? 38. How long did the Dutch keep possession? 39. What grant was then given a second time? 40. Who succeeded Charles II. as king of England? 41. What can you say of James's rule? 42. What was the consequence?

X. 43. How was the news of the English revolution received in New York? 44. What did Leisler do? 45. How long was he the acting governor? 46. Who was his deputy? 47. When did Leisler surrender his authority? 48. Did this satisfy the enemies of Leisler or not? 49. What was the fate of Leisler and Milborne?

from the English sovereigns, Leisler surrendered all authority into his hands. This would not satisfy the enemies of Leisler: they were bent upon his destruction. So he and Milborne were arrested, tried on a charge of treason, and condemned to death. Sloughter, while drunk at a feast, signed the death-warrant, and both were executed.

XI. In 1741 the Dutch church and other buildings in the city of New York were burned, and a house was robbed by slaves. Witnesses testified that the negroes had conspired to burn the city, murder the inhabitants, and set up a government of their own. An intense excitement among all classes followed, and before it was allayed more than thirty persons, condemned as having been engaged in the plot, were executed, and others were transported to foreign parts. Doubtless a plot of some kind had existed, though the accounts of it were evidently greatly exaggerated, and many innocent persons were made to suffer.

XII. The history of New York during the next few years, and till the commencement of the French and Indian War, contains no events of much importance. During King George's War, which commenced in 1744 and continued nearly four years, the Indians, in alliance with the French, made frequent incursions into the territory between Albany and Crown Point, and a number of skirmishes took place; but in the great final struggle for territory between England and France, which had its beginning in 1754, New York took no inconsiderable part.

XI. QUESTIONS.—50. What took place in 1741? 51. What testimony was produced? 52. What followed? 53. What punishments were inflicted?

XII. 54. When did King George's War commence? 55. By what name is that war known in Europe? *Ans.—As the "War of the Austrian Succession."* 56. How did New York suffer during King George's War? 57. How is Albany situated? (See map, p. 62.) 58. How, Crown Point? (See same map.) 59. What war broke out in 1754? *Ans.—The French and Indian War.*

NEW JERSEY.

NEW JERSEY.

In 1664 the Duke of York sold a tract of land to Lord Berkeley and Sir George Carteret. In honor of Sir George, who had been governor of the Island of Jersey, in the English Channel, and had held it for King Charles in his contest with the Parliament, the tract was named New Jersey. The State motto is, *Liberty and Independence*.

I. THE territory of New Jersey was included in the Dutch province of New Netherlands. The precise date of the first settlement within its limits is not ascertained: it is known, however, that the Dutch had a trading settlement at Bergen as early as 1622; and, in 1623, they built Fort Nassau, on the east side of the Delaware River, a few miles below Philadelphia; but the settlement made at Elizabeth, in 1664, by emigrants from Long Island, is considered as the beginning of colonization in New Jersey.

II. As stated in the colonial history of New York, the Duke of York, to whom the English king had granted, in 1664, the whole province of New Netherlands, in the same year sold New Jersey to Lord Berkeley and Sir George Carteret. Philip Carteret, brother of Sir George, was the first governor; and, by settling at Elizabethtown, now called Elizabeth, made it the first capital.

NEW JERSEY.—I. QUESTIONS.—L. In what province was the territory of New Jersey included? 2. Where, at an early period, did the Dutch have a trading settlement 3. When did they build Fort Nassau? 4. How was the fort situated? 5. When was New Jersey first colonized? 6. At what place? 7. By whom?

II. 8. How did Berkeley and Carteret acquire New Jersey?

III. The liberal constitution published by the proprietors, by which it was provided that no rents for the use of lands would be required for the space of five years, induced many persons to settle. The attempt to collect the rents, after the five years, produced a great deal of ill feeling, especially among those who had purchased lands of the Indians, they asserting that a deed from the aborigines was superior to any other title. After disputing about two years, the settlers revolted and elected James Carteret, a dissolute son of Sir George, governor.

IV. After the Dutch had resigned possession of New Netherlands by treaty stipulations, in 1674, New Jersey, a portion of the territory so given up, was again granted to the Duke of York. In disregard of the rights of Berkeley and Carteret, the duke appointed Andros governor over the entire reunited province, but afterward agreed to restore New Jersey to the rightful proprietors. This promise he only partially performed.

V. Berkeley having sold his interest in the proprietorship of New Jersey to Edward Byllinge (*bil'-linge*), an English Quaker, the purchaser, in consequence of pecuniary embarrassment, made an assignment to William Penn and two other Quakers. The proprietors then divided the whole territory into two portions, Carteret taking the eastern, which thereafter was known as East Jersey, and the Quakers taking the western, known as West Jersey. In 1682 New Jersey became the exclusive property of Quakers, William Penn and eleven of his brethren having, in that year, purchased the eastern division.

III. QUESTIONS.—9. What induced persons to settle in New Jersey? 10 What was the consequence when an attempt was made to collect the rents? 11. After disputing two years, what did the people do?

IV. 12. When did the Duke of York get possession of New Jersey a second time? 13 What wrong did the duke then perpetrate? 14. Did he persist in the wrong?

V. 15. What did Berkeley do with his interest in New Jersey? 16 What did Byllinge do with his? 17. What division was then made of the territory? 18. What was the condition of things, as regards ownership, in 1682?

VI. When the Duke of York, as James II., ascended the throne of England, in seeking to annul the colonial charters, he placed New Jersey under the jurisdiction of Andros ; but the revolution in England, and the expulsion of the tyrannical governor from America, put an end to the obnoxious rule. The Jerseys were in an unsettled condition until the proprietors, in 1702, surrendered their powers of government to the crown.. The two provinces were then united, and for thirty-six years New Jersey was a gubernatorial dependency of New York, with a distinct legislative assembly of its own.   In 1738 the connection was severed forever, and from that time to the Revolution New Jersey was a separate royal province.

REVIEW QUESTIONS.

MARYLAND.

MARYLAND.
The province granted to Cecil Calvert, second Lord Baltimore, in 1632,
was named in the charter *Terra Ma-
riæ*, Mary's Land, in honor of Queen
Henrietta Maria, wife of Charles I.,
the English monarch, and daughter
of Henry IV., King of France. The
motto of the State, translated, is, *Increase and Multiply*.

I. By the charter granted to the London Company in 1609, the limits of Virginia were extended, and embraced all the territory now forming the States of Maryland, Virginia, and North Carolina. The dissolution of the company having been effected in 1624, the whole region became the property of the crown.

II. In 1631, William Clayborne obtained from Charles I. a license to traffic with the Indians. Under this authority, which was afterward confirmed by the Governor of Virginia, he established two trading-posts: one on Kent Island, in Chesapeake Bay, and the other at the mouth of the Susquehanna; but the permanent settlement of Maryland was accomplished by other agencies.

III. Influenced by a desire to provide an asylum for Catholics, then persecuted in England, Sir George Calvert, a Roman

MARYLAND.—I. QUESTIONS.—1. Was Maryland once a part of Virginia? 2. What other State was also a part? 3. When and how did they become such? 4. When and by whom was the right to make divisions of the whole region afterward acquired?

II. 5. What license did Clayborne obtain? 6. What did he do under its authority? 7. How is Kent Island situated? (See map, p. 24.) 8. Describe the Susquehanna River. (See map, p. 85.) 9. What large city is situated southwest from the mouth of the Susquehanna? (See same map.)

III. 10. Who was Sir George Carteret? 11. For what did he apply to the king? 12. What desire influenced him? 13. Why was the charter issued to his son?

Catholic nobleman, whose title was Lord Baltimore, applied for a charter to establish a colony in America. King Charles readily agreed to make the grant, but before the document received the royal seal, Calvert died. It was then issued to Cecil (*se'-sil*) Calvert, son of Sir George, who, by the death of his father, inherited the title of Lord Baltimore.

LORD BALTIMORE (SECOND).

IV. This charter was the most liberal one, in every respect, that had thus far been granted by the English crown. It secured to emigrants equality in religious rights and civil freedom, and made the government of the colony independent of that of England. It also provided that no tax should be levied upon the colonists by the crown, and that no law should be established without the sanction of the freemen or their deputies. The province was called Maryland, in honor of Henrietta Maria, wife of Charles I.

V. The first body of emigrants sent by Lord Baltimore consisted of about two hundred persons, mostly Roman Catholics. Leonard Calvert, brother of the lord proprietary, who conducted them from England, became the first governor. They arrived in 1634, and at once commenced a settlement, which they anticipated would become a great city, calling it St. Mary's.*

VI. Clayborne, from the first, claimed Kent Island, and refused to submit to the authority of the governor. Having determined to defend his claim by force of arms, a severe skirmish took place, in which his party suffered defeat. Clay-

---

* Scarce a trace of the settlement now remains.

IV. QUESTIONS.—14. What is said of the charter? 15. Name four of its provisions. 16. What is said of the colony's name?

V. 17. When, where, and by whom was Maryland settled?

VI. 18. What claim did Clayborne insist upon? 19. Give an account of the skirmish that followed. 20. What further account can you give of Clayborne?

borne himself had fled to Virginia just previous to the battle, but the Maryland Assembly having declared him guilty of treason, the Governor of Virginia sent the fugitive to England for trial.

VII. His claim was refused; but, being acquitted of the charge of treason, he returned to Maryland, and, in 1645, incited a rebellion, in the course of which he made himself complete master of the province, and compelled the governor, in his turn, to fly into Virginia. In the following year, however, Calvert appeared at the head of a military force and recovered possession.

VIII. After the governor's resumption of office, the assembly enacted a law known as the "Toleration Act," which secured the free exercise of religious opinions to all persons professing belief in Jesus Christ. Although, by the terms of the charter, religious freedom was guaranteed to every individual, yet, by the passage of this act, the guarantee received the sanction of law.

IX. During the supremacy of Cromwell and the Puritans in England, Parliament appointed commissioners, of whom Clayborne was one, to administer the government of the colony. An act of the assembly declared that Catholics were not entitled to the protection of the laws of Maryland: this led to a civil war between the Catholics, who adhered to the proprietor, and the Protestants, who sided with Parliament. After Cromwell's death the rights of Lord Baltimore were restored, and, for nearly thirty years, the colony enjoyed repose.

X. Upon the death of the second Lord Baltimore, his son, Charles Calvert, inherited his title and became the proprietor of the province. He retained possession until 1691, when

VII Questions.—21. Give an account of "Clayborne's Rebellion."

VIII 22 Of the Toleration Act.

IX 23. How did Clayborne get to be a commissioner to administer the affairs of Maryland? 24. Give an account of the civil war 25. What change took place after the death of Cromwell?

X. 26 What further can you state of the colonial history of Maryland?

King William constituted Maryland a royal province, in which condition it continued for a space of more than twenty years. Finally, in 1715, the proprietor's rights were restored to his infant heir, the fourth Lord Baltimore, and Maryland remained a proprietary government from that time till the Revolution.

PENNSYLVANIA.

I. In the early part of 1681, William Penn,* whom we have already spoken of in the history of New Jersey, actuated by a desire to found a colony where civil and religious liberty would be enjoyed, and where the people might dwell together in the bonds of peace, obtained from Charles II., in payment of a debt due to his father, a grant of all the territory within the present limits of Pennsylvania. The permanent settlement of the colony dates from the founding of Philadel-phia,† in 1682, by Penn,

PENNSYLVANIA.

The word *sylva* means a wood or forest. Wm. Penn, thinking that *Sylvania* would be a name applicable to a land covered with forests, suggested it for his territory. The secretary who made out the patent prefixed *Penn* to *Sylvania*, in honor, as the king afterward said, of Penn's father. The motto of the State is, *Virtue, Liberty, and Independence.*

---

* William Penn was born in London, in 1644. He died at Ruscombe, Berkshire County, England, in 1718.
† Philadelphia, signifying *brotherly love*, though the name of a city in Asia Minor, was so called by Penn because of its intrinsic significance.

PENNSYLVANIA.—I. QUESTIONS.—1. What grant of land was made in 1681? 2. What was Penn's ruling desire? 3. When was Pennsylvania settled? 4. At what place? 5. Where and by whom had previous settlements been made?

though small settlements of Swedes had been previously made on the Island of Tinicum and on the western bank of the Delaware.

II. In addition to the grant from King Charles, Penn became, by purchase and grant from the Duke of York, the proprietor of all that section now constituting the State of Delaware: this, he called the "Territories" or the "Three Lower Counties on the Delaware." As the natural consequence of these two grants being made to the same party, all the territory embraced in both was united under one government.

III. Penn's arrival in America was greeted by the settlers of Delaware, and those whom he had sent to Pennsylvania in the previous year, 1681, with great enthusiasm; and, after several meetings for conference with the Indians, he made his famous treaty with the "red men" beneath a wide-spreading elm, at a place now called Kensington, a suburb of Philadelphia, and paid them for their lands. This treaty was "never sworn to and never broken."

WILLIAM PENN.

IV. His treatment of the Swedes on the Delaware was also marked by a spirit of liberality. To them he gave assurances that they should not be molested in their religion or laws. The wisdom of his course toward the Indians, as well as of his government generally, was soon apparent, for the colony had a more rapid and peaceful growth than any other in America.

II. Questions.—6. What territory was added to Penn's jurisdiction? 7. How was it so added? 8. What name did Penn give to the territory acquired from the Duke of York?

III. 9. How was Penn received in America? 10. What took place at Kensington? 11. Where is Kensington? 12. What statement is made respecting the treaty?

IV. 13. How did Penn treat the Swedes? 14. What assurances did he give them? 15. What was soon apparent? 16. How was it made apparent?

V. After devoting himself zealously for two years to his duties, he intrusted his government to a council, and, terminating his first visit to America by sailing for England, left a prosperous colony behind of seven thousand persons. After a lapse of fifteen years he made a second visit to Pennsylvania; but during his absence the "Three Lower Counties on the Delaware" had become dissatisfied and withdrawn from the union. In England he had been imprisoned on account of his supposed adherence to the cause of James II., the deposed king, and the government of his province had been conferred upon Colonel Fletcher, the Governor of New York, who reunited Delaware to Pennsylvania.

VI Penn found his colonists discontented and clamorous for greater political privileges. He thereupon offered them a new frame of government, more liberal than the former one, which the people of Pennsylvania gladly accepted; but the Delaware colonists declined it, declaring that they preferred to exist as an independent colony. Their preference was so far acquiesced in, as to allow them an assembly of their own.

VII. Penn directed his attention to various reforms, having reference, especially, to the condition of the Indians and negroes; but his plans were arrested by tidings from England of a ministerial project for abolishing all the proprietary governments in America. Deeming his presence in England necessary to the defeat of the project, he sailed from the colony in 1701, and never visited it again.

VIII. Upon his death, which occurred in 1718, he left his American possessions to his three sons, who continued to administer the government, most of the time by deputies, until the Revolution, when their claims were purchased by the commonwealth of Pennsylvania

V QUESTIONS —17 What was the length of Penn's first visit to America? 18 How many colonists were there then in Pennsylvania? 19 When did he again visit Pennsylvania? 20 What had occurred during his absence?

VI 21. How did Penn find his colonists? 22 What did he offer them? 23 Did they accept his offer? 24 What was done as regards Delaware?

VII. 25. To what did Penn direct his attention? 26. What arrested his plans? 27. What followed? VIII. 28. Give the subsequent colonial history of Pennsylvania

DELAWARE.

DELAWARE.
Delaware Bay and River were so named in honor of Lord Delaware, who was governor of Virginia in 1611. When the present State of Delaware came into the possession of Wm. Penn, he called it the "territories or three lower counties on the Delaware;" hence the name of the State. The motto of the State is, *Liberty and Independence.*

I. THE settlement of Delaware may be said to have its origin in the desire of Gustavus Adolphus, the renowned king of Sweden, to found a free colony in the New World for all persecuted Christians. His death occurring before the project was undertaken, a delay of several years followed: but finally a charter was granted by the government of that country to the Swedish West India Company.

II. In 1638 a body of about fifty emigrants, sent out by the company, arrived at Cape Henlopen. After purchasing of the Indians all the lands from the Cape to the Falls of the Delaware, at Trenton, they erected a fort and commenced a settlement on Christiana Creek, near Wilmington. The territory thus purchased they called New Sweden, and, under the direction of Peter Minuits, a former governor of New Netherlands, settlements were multiplied and contentment prevailed.

III. The Dutch of New Netherlands were far from looking

DELAWARE.—I. QUESTIONS.—1. What was the origin of the settlement of Delaware ? 2. What charter was granted ?

II. 3. When was Delaware settled ? 4. What purchase of lands did the Swedes make ? 5. How is Cape Henlopen situated ? (See map, p. 24.) 6. In what part of Delaware is Wilmington situated ? (See map, p. 24.) 7. What did the Swedes call their territory ? 8. Who was the first governor of New Sweden ?

upon these proceedings with favor. They protested against, what they considered, the intrusion upon their territory, and menaced the settlements with destruction ; but the Swedes, anxious to retain their possessions, heeded neither protest nor menace. On Tinicum Island, situated a few miles below Philadelphia, they built a fort, and there established the capital of the province. A fort which the Dutch afterward constructed, near their settlement on Christiana Creek, they destroyed.

IV. In revenge for these defiant measures, Stuyvesant, then governor of New Netherlands, with a force of more than six hundred men, proceeded, in 1655, against the Swedes, subjected them to the authority of Holland, and thus put an end to Swedish power in America.

V. The Dutch retained possession of Delaware till they, in turn, were overpowered by the English, in 1664. From that time till 1682 it was connected with the province of New York. By the grant made to William Penn, in 1682, Delaware was joined to the government of Pennsylvania, and the connection existed, with more or less closeness, until the Revolution.

III. QUESTIONS.—9 How did the Dutch look upon the Swedish settlements ? 10 What can you say of their protests and menaces ? 11. What did the Swedes do at Tinicum Island ? 12. How is Tinicum Island situated ? (See map, p. 68.)

IV. 13. What did Stuyvesant do ? 14. When was the colony of New Sweden broken up ?

V. 15 How long did the Dutch retain possession of Delaware ? 16. What further account of the colony can you give ?

NORTH AND SOUTH CAROLINA.

NORTH CAROLINA.

A body of Huguenots, under command of Ribault, landed at Port Royal entrance, in 1562, and built a fort to which they gave the name of Carolina, in honor of King Charles (Carolus) of France. It was thus that Carolina received its name. The Seal of North Carolina is given above. The State has no motto.

I. THE earliest attempts to settle North Carolina, as before described, were made by parties of English emigrants, sent out by Sir Walter Raleigh, in 1585 and 1587. The whole region extending from Albemarle Sound to the St. John's River in Florida, and designated as Carolina, was granted, in 1630, to Sir Robert Heath; but as he made no attempts at colonization, or at least none that were successful, the grant was subsequently declared forfeited.

II. In 1663 this same territory was granted by Charles II. to Lord Clarendon and seven other noblemen of England. Previous to this, in or about 1650, a number of emigrants from Virginia had made a settlement upon the Chowan River, near the present village of Edenton, which was afterward called "The Albemarle County Colony." After the grant to Clarendon and his associates had been made, it was discover-

NORTH AND SOUTH CAROLINA.—1. QUESTIONS.—1. When and by whom were the first attempts made to settle North Carolina? 2. What grant was made in 1630? 3. Why was it afterward declared forfeited?

II. 4. What grant was made in 1663? 5. When, where, and by whom was North Carolina settled? 6. Describe the Chowan River? (See map, p. 79.) 7. How is Edenton situated? (See same map.) 8. Which colony was called the "Albemarle County Colony?"

ed that the settlement upon the Chowan was outside of the northern boundary of the province: a new grant was therefore given, by which the limits of Carolina were extended from Virginia to the middle of Florida.

III. A second settlement was made in North Carolina, previous to the grant to Clarendon and others, by a band of New England adventurers. This was near Wilmington; but as it did not prosper it was soon abandoned. In 1665 a company of planters, from Barbadoes, founded a permanent settlement not far from the site of the former one near Wilmington, which was afterwards called "The Clarendon County Colony."

IV. As it was anticipated by Clarendon and the other proprietors that Carolina would become a powerful empire,

III. QUESTIONS.—9. What is said of a second settlement in North Carolina? 10. Of the " Clarendon County Colony?"

IV. 11. What anticipation did Clarendon and his associates entertain? 12. What, therefore, did they decide upon? 13. What accordingly was done? 14. How did the constitution work?

they decided to have a form of government adequate to the grandeur of their anticipation. Accordingly, a constitution was prepared by the Earl of Shaftesbury, a statesman of ability, and John Locke, the eminent philosopher ; but, as might have been expected, it proved unsatisfactory to the colonists, not being suited to their circumstances ; and, after a strife of more than twenty years, it was repealed.

SOUTH CAROLINA.

In 1729 Carolina was sold to the King of England, and then separated into North and South Carolina. The Seal of South Carolina is given above. The motto of the State is, *Animis opibusque parati*, Ever ready with our lives and property.

V. The earliest attempt to plant a colony in South Carolina was made by the Huguenots at Port Royal entrance, as before stated, in 1562. In 1670, more than a century after, a colony was founded on the western bank of the Ashley River, near its mouth, which, in honor of one of the grantees of Carolina, was called "The Carteret County Colony." In the course of time most of "The Clarendon County" settlers removed to the southern colony, and thus, as only two colonies remained in Carolina, the northern one was designated as North Carolina, while the other was known as South Carolina.

VI. The people of the southern colony, in a few years, came to the conclusion that the site of their settlement had not been well chosen, and that a location at the junction of the Cooper and Ashley Rivers would give them better facilities for commerce. Acting upon this conviction, they abandoned their first settlements, after an occupancy there of ten years, and, in 1680, laid the foundation of their new town, calling it Charleston, in honor of Charles II., King of England.

VII. In 1729 Carolina was sold to the King of England, and then separated into North and South Carolina. From that time till the Revolution they were royal provinces.

GEORGIA.

I. THE territory of Georgia, it will be recollected, was included in the grant of Carolina, made in 1663, to Clarendon and others. After a period of sixty-six years it again became the property of the crown, at which time it was still a wilderness, unoccupied except by savage tribes.

II. Though claimed by Spain as a part of Florida, the English king, George II., disregarded the claim, and, in 1732, granted to a corporation of twenty-one trustees, for twenty-one years, all that tract between the Savannah and Altamaha (al-ta-ma-haw') Rivers, which, in honor of the king, was called Georgia. The object of the corporation was to provide an asylum in America for the destitute of England, the grant being "in trust for the poor."

VI. QUESTIONS.—20. What did the people of the southern colony conclude upon, in the course of time? 21. How long did they stop at the first place settled? 22. When was Charleston settled? 23. How is Charleston situated? (See map, p. 79.)

VII. 24. What took place in 1729? 25. What is said of the subsequent colonial history of the two Carolinas?

GEORGIA.—I. 1. In what grant was the territory of Georgia at first included? 2. How long did it remain as a part of that grant? 3. What did it then become?

II. 4. What claim was set up by Spain? 5. Notwithstanding the claim, what was done by the English king? 6. Describe the Savannah River. (See map, p. 79.) 7. The Altamaha. (See map of Georgia) 8. Why was Georgia so called? 9. What was the object of the corporation?

4*

GEORGIA.

Georgia was so called in honor of George II., king of England, by whom the territory was granted, in 1732, to a corporation entitled the "Trustees for settling the Colony of Georgia." The seal of the State is given above. The State motto is *Wisdom, Justice, and Moderation.*

III. The first settlement was made in 1733, the year after the grant, by one hundred and twenty persons, under the guidance of James Oglethorpe * (ŏ′-gl-thorp), a member of the British Parliament, one of the trustees, and governor of the colony. On a high bluff overlooking a river, the foundation of a town was laid, which received the name of Savannah.

IV. The colony made rapid increase in numbers, but, owing to the poverty of the settlers, and to their being unaccustomed to habits of industry, as also to the impolitic regulations established by the trustees, it did not grow much in wealth. Oglethorpe made two visits to England: in the first, returning with about three hundred emigrants; and in the second, with a regiment of six hundred men for the defense of the southern frontier, which was threatened by the Spaniards.

V. In consequence of the conflicting claims to territory,

---

* General James Oglethorpe was born in England, in 1688. He died there in 1785.

III. QUESTIONS.—10. When and where was Georgia settled? 11. Who was Oglethorpe? 12. How is Savannah situated? (See map, p. 79.)

IV. 13. What is said of the colony's growth in population? 14. Of its growth in wealth? 15. How many visits did Oglethorpe make to England? 16. Whom did he bring with him on his first return to the colony? 17. Whom, on his second? 18. Why did he bring the regiment?

and during a war between England and France, the colonists became involved in hostilities with
their Spanish neighbors. An expedition, under Oglethorpe, invaded Florida to go against St.
Augustine, but returned unsuccessful. In 1742, two years after,
this invasion was retaliated, and a
Spanish fleet, with a large number
of men, appeared at the mouth of
the Altamaha River. The troops

JAMES OGLETHORPE.

landed captured one fort, and were proceeding against another,
situated on St. Simon's Island, when, by a stratagem conceived
by Oglethorpe. they became alarmed, retreated to their shipping, and sailed for Florida.

VI. Peace was soon after restored; but, though the colonists
were free from one source of trouble, they were not satisfied
with the rule of the corporation. This state of things, nevertheless, existed until 1752, when, wearied with their trouble-
some charge, the trustees surrendered their charter to the
crown, and Georgia became a royal province.

V. QUESTIONS.—19. What was the cause of the hostility between the people of
Georgia and Florida? 20. Give an account of the expedition against St. Augustine. 21. How is St. Augustine situated? (See map, p. 320.) 22. Give an account of
the retaliative expedition. 23. How is St. Simon's Island situated?

VI. 24. How did the colonists feel after the war? 25. How long did the trustees
continue to rule? 26. What took place then?

REVIEW QUESTIONS.

(Questions to be answered from the above map.)

How is Williamsburg situated? Where was Fort Le Bœuf? In what direction did Washington travel, in going from Williamsburg to Fort Le Bœuf? What two rivers, uniting, form the Ohio? Where did Fort Duquesne stand? What two forts were on Lake Champlain? Where was Fort William Henry? Fort Oswego? Fort Niagara? Fort Schuyler? Fort Edward? Fort Venango? Fort Necessity?

SECTION III.

THE FRENCH AND INDIAN WAR.

I. Although the boundaries between the British and French possessions in America had been, for more than a quarter of a century, a subject of dispute, the treaty of Aix-la-Chapelle, made in 1748, left them still undefined.

II. The English, basing their title upon the discoveries made by the Cabots, laid claim to all the territory from New-foundland to Florida, extending from the Atlantic to the Pacific. The French claimed all the interior portion adjacent to the rivers St. Lawrence and Mississippi and their tributaries, upon the ground that they had been the first to explore and occupy it; and, the better to secure their claim, they erected forts at various places through this region, so as to make a complete chain of defenses from Nova Scotia to the mouth of the Mississippi.

III. In consequence of these conflicting claims, a war broke out between England and her colonies on the one side, and France and her colonies, largely aided by the Indians, on the other, which is generally known as "The French and Indian War," or "The Old French War." It was a contest for territory and dominion in America.

EVENTS OF 1753.

I. The first hostile act, it was alleged, was perpetrated by the French. They seized three British traders, whom they

regarded as intruders upon their territory, and im- 1753.
prisoned them at Presque Isle (*pres keel*), now Erie,
situated in the northwestern extremity of Pennsylvania.

II. At the time of this event, there was in existence an
organization which had been chartered in 1749, four years
before, by the name of " *The Ohio Company.*" This association consisted of gentlemen, principally Virginians, who had
obtained from the King of England a grant of six hundred
thousand acres of land, on and near the Ohio River, for the
purpose of carrying on the fur trade with the Indians and of
settling the country.

III. The French saw, in the formation of the Ohio Company, a systematic scheme, the first, perhaps, in a series of
similar ones, to deprive them of their possessions, and, as a
consequence, of their traffic and influence among the Indians:
hence their seizure and imprisonment of the three traders;
hence, too, the vast preparations for hostile contingencies
which they began to make, not the least of which was the
erection of forts between the Alleghany River and Lake Erie.

IV. The Ohio Company, on learning of these hostile measures, laid their complaints before the lieutenant-governor of
Virginia, Robert Dinwiddie. As the grant to the company
was within the original charter limits of Virginia, and as, perhaps for no less a reason, the lieutenant-governor was a stock-
holder in the concern, the complaints were listened to with a
willing ear.

V. It was at once determined to send a letter to the French
commander, remonstrating against the aggressive acts of his

II. QUESTIONS —4 Give an account of the origin, composition, and purposes
of the Ohio Company

III 5. How did the French regard the Ohio Company ? 6. How then did the
French justify their seizure of the three traders ? 7 Where did they erect forts to
oppose the Ohio Company ? 8. What three forts were erected between the Alleghany River and Lake Erie ? *Ans.*—One at Presque Isle, and (for the other two see
map, p 85.)

IV. 9. To whom did the Ohio Company complain ? 10 Why did the governor
listen to their complaints?

men, and demanding their withdrawal from the territory. This message was intrusted to George Washington, then a young man not twenty-two years of age, who had, by the manner in which he had discharged the duties of adjutant-general of one of the districts of Virginia, acquired a reputation for prudence and ability.

VI. Washington set out on his mission on the last day of October, 1753, from Williamsburg, then the capital of Virginia. After a difficult and dangerous journey of four hundred miles, more than half of which was through a wilderness inhabited by hostile Indians, he reached Fort Venango (*ve-nang'-gō*), whence he was conducted to Fort Le Bœuf (*buf*). Here he found St. Pierre (*pe-āre'*), the French commander.

VII. St. Pierre's reply was also by letter. He stated, in substance, that he could not leave the territory, as he was acting by the orders of his superior officer, the Marquis du Quesne (*kane*), Governor-general of Canada, whose head-quarters were at Montreal (*mont-re-aul'*).

EVENTS OF 1754.

I. After an absence of eleven weeks, during which he encountered on his journey severe hardships, amid snow, icy floods, and hostile Indians, Washington reached Williamsburg and delivered St. Pierre's letter to Dinwiddie. This document, and the report which Washington made of the ex-

V. QUESTIONS.—11 What did Dinwiddie at once determine upon? 12 To whom was the message intrusted? 13 How old was Washington at the time? 14. What military position had he held? 15. How had he discharged its duties?

VI 16. When and from what place did Washington set out? 17 Give an account of the journey to Fort Le Bœuf. 18 How was. Fort Venango situated? (See map, p 85.) 19. What village now occupies the site of Fort Venango? *Ans.—Franklin.* 20 How is Fort Le Bœuf situated? (See map, p 85.) 21 What village now occupies the site of Fort Le Bœuf? *Ans.—Waterford.* 22. Where did he find the French commander? 23 What was the commander's name?

VII 24 Did St. Pierre return a verbal or written reply? 25. What did he state in the letter? 26. How is Montreal situated? (See map, p. 85.)

EVENTS OF 1754.—I 1 How long was Washington absent on his mission? 2 Give an account of his homeward journey 3 What report did he make? 4. Of what were Dinwiddie and his council convinced?

tensive warlike preparations he had discovered on
his journey, convinced the lieutenant-governor and
1754.
his council that the French were intending to penetrate the
territory of Virginia and take military possession. No time
was therefore to be lost.

II. At the confluence of the Alleghany and Monongahela
Rivers the Ohio Company commenced the construction of a
fort; and an expedition, of which Washington, at first second
in command, soon became chief, was sent to protect the work-
men, assist in the building, and afterwards to garrison the
place.

III. But the French were too quick for the English : before
the fort was half completed, a strong force, augmented greatly
by Indians, had come from Venango and summoned the men
there to surrender. What could the English do? Less than
forty in number, they capitulated and withdrew. The French
completed the works, and called the place Fort Duquesne.

IV. Washington, it will be seen, did not reach the fort.
Learning that it had fallen into the hands of the enemy, and
that a strong force was marching to intercept him, he fell back
and took a position in a place called the Great Meadows.
Here word came to him that a detachment of the French had
advanced to within a few miles of his position, where they were
skulking, evidently with hostile intent. With the determination
of forestalling their .design, he sallied forth, came upon the
foe by surprise, and, in the contest that followed, killed or
captured all but one,—their commander, Jumonville (*zhoo-
mong-veel'*), being among the slain.

II. QUESTIONS —5. Where did the Ohio Company commence to build a fort? 6.
Describe the Alleghany River. (See map, p. 85.) 7. Describe the Monongahela River.
(See same map.) 8. What expedition did Washington have the command of?

III. 9. How much of the "new fort" did the English succeed in building? 10.
What then took place? 11. What name did the French give it?

IV. 12 Did Washington reach the fort or not? 13 Why not? 14. Where were
the Great Meadows? (See map, p. 85) 15. What word came to him at the Great
Meadows? 16. Describe the battle that followed 17. By what name is the battle
known? *Ans.—The battle of the Great Meadows.*

1754.   V. This battle, fought on the 28th of May, 1754, was Washington's first, as it was also the first of the war. Though the numbers engaged in it were small, its effects in the grand contest, of which it was the precursor, were by no means unimportant.

VI. Washington's first care was in relation to the prisoners. These he sent, without delay, to Dinwiddie, and at once began to make preparations to resist the strong force coming against him. At his position in the Great Meadows, a fort which he had previously commenced was completed: and, owing to the pinching famine that prevailed during its construction, he named it Fort Necessity.

VII. Here he was attacked by a force of fifteen hundred French and Indians, commanded by De Villiers (*vil-le-āre'*). After a brave defense of ten hours, continued till near midnight, while a violent rain-storm prevailed, he capitulated on the following morning, July 4th, 1754; and, before noon, marched out of the fort with the honors of war.

VIII. Although war as yet had not been formally declared between the two nations, England and France, the British ministry, in anticipation of that event, recommended the colonies to unite in some plan for their common defense. In conformity therewith, a congress, held at Albany, made a treaty with the Indians of the Six Nations; and adopted a plan of union, which had been prepared by Dr. Franklin, a delegate from Philadelphia.

IX. The plan, however, was never carried into effect: the colonial assemblies rejected it because it gave too much power

---

V. QUESTIONS.—18. When was the battle of the Great Meadows fought? 19 What further can you say of it?

VI. 20. What was Washington's first care? 21. What did he do with them? 22. What preparations did he then begin to make? 23. What fort was built? 24. What name was given to it, and why?

VII. 25. Give an account of the battle that took place there?

VIII. 26. What recommendation did the British ministry make? 27. What was accordingly done?

IX 28. What further can you say of the plan? 29 What was then determined upon?

to the crown, while, singularly enough, the crown 1754. also rejected it because it gave too much power to the people. It was then determined that the war should be carried on with British troops, and such auxiliary forces as the colonial assemblies might voluntarily furnish.

EVENTS OF 1755.

I. The disaster at Fort Necessity, together with the hostile attitude of the French government, aroused the attention of the British ministry, and preparations, on an extensive scale, were speedily made for aggressive operations in America.

II. Four expeditions were accordingly planned for 1755: one to expel the French from Nova Scotia; another against Crown Point, to be led by Sir William Johnson; the third against Niaagara, to be commanded by Governor Shirley (*shur'-le*), of Massachusetts; and the fourth against Fort Duquesne. General Braddock,* an officer of distinction,

GENERAL BRADDOCK.

who had been sent to America as commander-in-chief of all the royal forces in the colonies, took the immediate charge of the expedition against Duquesne.

III. Colonel Monckton (*monk'-tun*), commanding the first expedition, landed at the head of the Bay of Fundy, where he was joined by General Winslow, a New Englander, with

---

* General Edward Braddock was born in Perthshire County, Scotland, about the year 1690. Before he came to America he had been forty years in the British army, and had served with credit in the wars against Spain, Portugal, and Germany.

EVENTS OF 1755.—I. QUESTIONS.—1. What aroused the attention of the British ministry? 2. What preparations followed?

II. 3. How many expeditions were planned for the year? 4. What were they? 5. What part was assigned to Braddock?

III. 6. Who commanded the expedition against Port Royal? 7. Give an account of it.

1755. about three thousand troops from Massachusetts.
The two forts of the French situated there were
captured in June, 1755 ; the settlements of the Nova Scotians
were wantonly destroyed ; a beautiful and fertile country was
reduced to a solitude, and the inhabitants, by thousands, were
driven on board the English ships, and scattered among the
colonists of New England and other places.

IV. Of the four expeditions planned for the year's campaign, Washington became enlisted in the one against Fort
Duquesne, and, during the memorable and disastrous battle
that occurred, distinguished himself by his courage and presence of mind. Braddock, who was arrogant and conceited,
marched his troops through the wilderness with great formality,
as if against a foe of European tactics, in disregard of the
suggestions of Washington, who was acting as his aide-de-
camp, and who was well acquainted with the mode of warfare
practiced by the Indians. The result was, that when within
ten miles of the fort he fell into an ambush, and was defeated
with great loss.

V. The British troops retreated in great disorder until they
reached the Great Meadows, a distance of forty miles, where
Braddock, who had been mortally wounded in the engagement, died. This battle, sometimes called the battle of the
Monongahela, occurred on the 9th of July, 1755, a little more
than a year after Washington's capitulation at Fort Necessity.

VI. By the death of Braddock, Shirley became the commander-in-chief of the royal forces in America. His expedition, though less disastrous than the one against Duquesne,
was also a failure. His troops, assembled at Oswego, were delayed for months; the disaster of the Monongahela para-

---

IV. QUESTIONS.—8. In which expedition did Washington take part? 9 What
is said of his conduct in the battle that occurred? 10 What was Braddock's character? 11 What illustration of his character is given? 12. What was the result?

V 13 What was Braddock's fate? 14. When did the battle occur? 15. By
what name is it sometimes known?

VI 16 Who succeeded Braddock as commander-in-chief? 17. What account
can you give of his expedition?

lyzed his efforts; the Indian allies deserted; and, finally, the expedition was abandoned.　1755.

VII. The expedition under Johnson, though not resulting in the capture or destruction of Crown Point, was a successful one. The troops employed were mostly from Massachusetts, Connecticut, and New Hampshire. At the "carrying-place," between the Hudson River and Lake George, a force of about six thousand men assembled under General Lyman, and constructed a fort, which was at first called Fort Lyman, but, owing to the jealousy of Johnson, was subsequently named by him Fort Edward. Upon the arrival of the commander of the expedition, he moved forward with the main body of his men to the head of Lake George, fifteen miles from Fort Edward.

VIII. While encamped here, the Indian scouts brought word that the enemy, French and Indians, two thousand strong, were on their march to attack Fort Edward. They were commanded by the Baron Dieskau (*de-es-ko'*), who had proceeded from Montreal (*mont-re-aul'*) to Crown Point, and thence to the head of Lake Champlain. Losing no time, Johnson sent Colonel Williams with a thousand New England troops, and the renowned chief Hendrick, with two hundred Indian warriors, to intercept the enemy.

HENDRICK

IX. But Dieskau changed his plan. As he approached the fort, his Indian allies, fearful of its cannon, refused to

VII. QUESTIONS.—18. From what places did the men of Johnson's army come? 19. Where did a large force assemble? 20. Who, at first, commanded them there? 21. What building did they construct? 22. Where was Fort Edward situated? (See map, p. 85.) 23. Upon Johnson's arrival what did he do? 24. In what direction from Fort Edward is Lake George? (See map, p. 85.)

VIII. 25. What word was brought to Johnson? 26. By whom was the invading force commanded? 27. What route had Dieskau taken? 28. What did Johnson at once do?

1755.

proceed to the attack; he therefore took another direction to go against the army at the lake, and, in so doing, took the road by which the forces sent out by Johnson were marching. Through his Indian scouts he soon heard of the approaching enemy. The result was, that the English and their allies were drawn into an ambush, on the 8th of September, and, after being defeated with signal slaughter, losing among their killed both Williams and Hendrick, they fled back to Johnson's camp, pursued by Dieskau.

X. From behind a hastily formed breastwork of trees Johnson fired upon the assailants, but, being slightly wounded early in the action, retired to his tent. The defense, which was most gallantly kept up by the New England troops, was turned into an attack by General Lyman, the next in command, and the French and their Indian allies were routed with great slaughter.

XI. Dieskau was found by the pursuers, wounded and alone, leaning against the stump of a tree. As they approached, he felt for his watch, to insure kind treatment by delivering it up : a soldier, thinking he was feeling for his pistol, shot him, inflicting an incurable wound. He was conveyed a prisoner

to the English camp, and subsequently sent to Europe. After suffering for ten years, he died of the injuries which he had received.

XII. Johnson, instead of following up the victory, as he was urged to by his officers, loitered away the autumn, doing nothing except building a useless fort of wood near his encampment, which received the name of Fort

SIR WILLIAM JOHNSON.

IX. QUESTIONS.—29. What change took place in Dieskau's movements? 30. Describe what followed.

X. 31. Give an account of the battle at Johnson's camp.

XI. 32. Give the subsequent history of Dieskau.

William Henry. This he garrisoned, as also Fort
Edward, and then, as winter approached, he retired
to Albany. Though General Lyman was the real hero of
the campaign, Johnson* received the thanks of Parliament
for the victory, was voted £5,000, and created a baronet of
Great Britain.

1755.

EVENTS OF 1756.

I. Shirley's career as commander-in-chief of the royal forces
in America drew to a close in the spring of 1756, when he
was superseded by General Abercrombie, who was appointed
to act until the arrival of Lord Loudon. Dieskau's successor
as commander-in-chief in Canada was the Marquis de Montcalm (*mont-kam'*).

II. Although for a long time hostilities had been carried on
in America between England and France, yet no formal declaration of war was made until May of 1756, when England
proclaimed hostilities against France, and, soon after, the
latter power issued a declaration against England.

III. The plan of the campaign for 1756, adopted by a convention of colonial governors held at Albany, did not differ
much from that of the preceding year—Crown Point, Niagara, and Fort Duquesne being the places aimed against. No
part of it, however, was carried out, nor, beyond some tardy
preparations, even attempted. Abercrombie, deeming the
forces under his command inadequate, waited for the arrival
of Loudon, and the earl, when he came, effected nothing.

---

* Sir William Johnson was born in Ireland, in 1715. He died at his residence near Johnstown, Fulton
County, New York, in 1774.

XII. QUESTIONS.—83. What should Johnson at once have done? 34. What did
he do instead? 35. How was he rewarded? 36. State why the reward was not
justly bestowed. 87. How is Fort William Henry situated? (See map, p. 85.)

EVENTS OF 1756.—I. 1. What changes took place in the commanders of the respective forces?

II. 2. What is said of the declaration of war?

III. 8. What is said of the plan of operations for 1756? 4. Was the plan carried
out or not? 5. State the cause.

1756.   IV. Not so the French. In an expedition against Oswego, which was then defended by two forts, Montcalm laid siege to the place, drove the garrison out of one

OSWEGO.

of the forts into the other, killed the commander, Colonel Mercer, and compelled the English to surrender. Fourteen hundred prisoners and a large amount of stores and money fell into the hands of the victors. After demolishing the forts, to allay the jealousy of the Indians, Montcalm left Oswego a solitude, and returned to Canada.

V. The defeat of Braddock, in 1755, left the western frontier in a defenseless condition. Incited by French emissaries, the tribes of the Ohio commenced the work of desolation, and killed or carried into captivity about a thousand of the inhabitants. It was therefore evident that the inroads of the savages must be checked, or, in a short time, not a single white man, friendly to the English, would remain in that region.

VI. A party of less than three hundred men, commanded by Colonel Armstrong, undertook to destroy Kittanning, the chief town of the perfidious tribes. The march through the forest was long and perilous, but the stronghold was reached, thirty or forty warriors were killed, and Kittanning was left a smoking ruin.

EVENTS OF 1757.

I. Loudon's plan of operations for 1757 was limited to an expedition against Louisburg (*loo'-is-burg*). He sailed from

IV. QUESTIONS.—6. Give an account of Montcalm's success against Oswego. 7. What did he do there after the victory ? 8. How is Oswego situated ? (See map, p. 96.)

V. 9. What induced the tribes of the Ohio to become hostile to the English settlers ? 10. What deeds of wrong were they guilty of ? 11. What became evident ?

VI. 12. Give an account of the expedition against Kittanning. 13. How is Kittanning situated ? (See map, p. 85.)

EVENTS OF 1757.—I. 1. Give an account of Loudon's operations during 1757. 2. How is Halifax situated ? (See map, p. 108.) 3. How is Louisburg situated ? (See same map.)

New York with about six thousand men, and, at Halifax, was joined by a powerful naval armament **1757.** and land force from England; but, learning that the French were prepared for defense, he abandoned the enterprise and returned to New York.

II. This, like the previous year, through the energy and ability of Montcalm, showed a marked superiority to the French arms. In the beginning of August that commander, with nine thousand men, two thousand of whom were Indians, laid siege to Fort William Henry. For six days, its commander, Colonel Monroe, kept up a vigorous defense, trusting to receive aid from General Webb, who, at the time, was in command of a large force at Fort Edward.

III. At length, learning that no assistance would be sent, and being entirely without ammunition, he was compelled to surrender on the 9th, capitulating that his men should have a safe escort to Webb's quarters. Notwithstanding this stipulation, the English had hardly left the fort before the Indian allies of Montcalm, incited by the hope of plunder, attacked them and massacred a large number. Fort William Henry was demolished by order of Montcalm; and thus the year 1757 passed, like its predecessor, without a single advantage to the English.

WILLIAM PITT.

IV. In consequence of the

II. QUESTIONS.—4. How did the operations of 1757 compare with those of the previous year? 5. When and by whom was Fort William Henry besieged? 6. Who commanded the fort? 7. What is said of his defense?

III. 8. What unwelcome information reached Colonel Monroe? 9. How was he not in a condition to make a further defense? 10. Give an account of the massacre. 11. What became of the fort? 12. Where did it stand? (See map, p. 85.)

IV. 13. What change took place in the British Government? 14. What as regards the command of the royal forces in America?

5

1757.   disgraces of the American campaigns a new administration of the British government was formed, with William Pitt,* afterward Lord Chatham, as prime minister. Loudon, who by his inactivity had disappointed the anticipations of the people, was recalled, and preparations were made to carry on the war with greater vigor.

* William Pitt, first Earl of Chatham, was born at Westminster, England, in 1708. At the beginning of the American Revolution he was opposed to the measures of the British ministry in the American colonies, but, at the close of a speech, made in 1778 in Parliament, in which he spoke against a motion to acknowledge the independence of America, he fell in an apoplectic fit, and was borne home, where he died in a few weeks afterward.

REVIEW QUESTIONS.

EVENTS OF 1758.

I. The campaign of 1758 opened, on the part of the English, with fifty thousand men in the field. These forces were divided into three distinct bodies: one, under General Amherst, for the subjugation of Louisburg, and the Island of Cape Breton (*brit'-on*); another, under Abercrombie, who had succeeded Loudon as commander-in-chief, was to proceed against Ticonderoga and Crown Point; and the third, under General Forbes, was to undertake the reduction of Fort Duquesne.

II. Amherst made Halifax, in Nova Scotia, his rendezvous, from which place he embarked in the fleet of Admiral Boscawen. A landing was effected near Louisburg, then defended by the strongest fortress in America, and a siege, memorable for its length and desperate resistance, commenced. At length, on the 26th of July, the French surrendered by capitulation, and, with the town, the whole Island of Cape Breton, as well as that of St. John's, fell into the hands of the British.

JAMES WOLFE.

III. During the siege two persons particularly distinguished themselves by their courageous conduct. These were James Wolfe and Richard Montgomery (*mont-gum'-er-e*); the first, the real hero of the enterprise, was slain at Quebec in the following year, while fighting for his king; and the other, Montgomery, was also slain at

---

Events of 1758.—I. Questions.—1. What was the plan of the campaign for 1758?

II. 2. Where did Amherst rendezvous? 3. On whose fleet did he embark his troops? 4. Where did he land his troops? 5. How is Louisburg situated? (See map, p. 103.) 6. How was Louisburg defended? 7. What was the result of the expedition? 8. In what direction from Cape Breton Island is the Island of St. John's? (See map, p. 103.)

III. 9. Give the names of the persons who distinguished themselves during the siege of Louisburg. 10. What is said of the further history of Wolfe and Montgomery?

Quebec, but several years later, while contending for the cause of liberty. 1758.

IV. While success was crowning the arms of the British at the east, Abercrombie was slowly making his way northward. At the head of about sixteen thousand men, he descended Lake George, and, debarking at its northern extremity, commenced a march through the dense forests towards Ticonderoga,* then commanded by Montcalm.

V. An advance force suddenly coming upon a detachment of the French, on the 6th of July, a severe conflict ensued, in which, though the enemy were routed, Lord Howe, an officer greatly beloved by the army and the American people, was killed.

VI. The death of Howe, who was the leading spirit in the expedition, was keenly felt. For awhile it put a complete check upon operations, and the most of the army fell back to the landing-place at the foot of the lake; but, on the 8th of July, an advance was made in full force, and the fort was assaulted. The British fought gallantly, though fruitlessly. After losing nearly two thousand of their number in killed and wounded, they withdrew once more to the landing-place; whence, fearing an attack from the enemy, on the following morning, they re-embarked for the head of the lake.

VII. The failure of this expedition was somewhat relieved

---

* Fort Ticonderoga was built by the French in 1755. It was then called Carillon (chime of bells), in allusion to the music of the waterfalls in the outlet of Lake George, near it

IV. 11. What was Abercrombie doing while Loudon was operating in Nova Scotia? 12 In what direction from Albany is Lake George? (see map, p 85) 13 On what lake is Ticonderoga situated? (See map, p 85)

V 14. Describe the action of the 6th of July

VI 15 What effect did the death of Howe have upon the expedition? 16 Describe the action of the 8th of July 17 What movement did the British make after their defeat?

VII 18. How was the failure of the expedition against Ticonderoga relieved? 19 What was Bradstreet's object in his enterprise? 20 In what direction from Lake George was Fort Frontenac? (See map, p. 85.) 21. What city is situated where Fort Frontenac then stood? (See page 102) 22 What route did Bradstreet take? 23 Why was the blow a severe one to the French? 24. How did Bradstreet dispose of his captures?

1758   by the success of an enterprise conducted by Colonel Bradstreet, an officer under Abercrombie. While the main army was wasting away the season at the head of Lake George, Bradstreet obtained permission to go against Fort Frontenac, situated where Kingston now stands, on the north side of the entrance of Lake Ontario. Proceeding by way of the Mohawk and Oswego, he crossed the lake, and, on the 27th of August, captured the fort, the garrison having either fled or surrendered at discretion. This was a severe blow to the French, as the place, besides being in a commanding position, contained a vast amount of military stores intended for Fort Duquesne, and in the harbor were several armed vessels. Bradstreet, after sending two of the vessels, laden with the spoils, to Oswego, destroying the others, and dismantling the fort, returned to Lake George.

VIII. In the third expedition planned for the year, that against Fort Duquesne, Washington held an important command under Forbes. Instead of advancing by the old road which Braddock had taken in 1755, it was decided, against the judgment of Washington, that a new one further east should be opened for the expedition. As was to have been expected, the progress made was exceedingly tedious. Winter was fast approaching, and yet Forbes was many miles from Duquesne. A feeling of discouragement pervaded the troops, which was augmented by a defeat, and loss of three hundred men, sustained by Major Grant while leading an advance detachment.

IX. In this strait Forbes called a council of war, the result of which was a determination to abandon the expedition. Before, however, the order to return was given, intelligence of an encouraging character was received. The march was

---

VIII. QUESTIONS.—25. In which expedition did Washington hold a command? 26. By what road was the advance against Duquesne made? 27. What was the result? 28. What check was experienced by Grant?

IX. 29. What was determined upon in a council of war? 30. Why was not the determination carried out? 31. What success finally rewarded the efforts of the expedition? 32. Why had the French abandoned the fort? 33. What did the English do with the fort?

therefore resumed, and when, towards the latter part
of November, Duquesne was reached, it was found in 1758.
ruins. The French had set fire to it and retreated down the
Ohio. The destruction of Frontenac had cut off all hope
of reinforcements and supplies; their savage allies, when des-
titution and danger threatened, had deserted—hence the ruin
and abandonment of the fort. The English at once repaired
and garrisoned the place, and, in honor of their illustrious
statesman, changed the name to Fort Pitt.

EVENTS OF 1759.

I. The great object of the campaign of 1759 was the re-

duction of Canada; and General Amherst, who had gained
great favor by his success at Louisburg, was appointed com-

EVENTS OF 1759.—QUESTIONS.—I. 1. What was the object of the campaign of
1759? 2. What change took place in the commanders? 3. What was the plan of
operations?

1759. mander-in-chief, to succeed Abercrombie. By the plan of operations, General Wolfe was to lay siege to Quebec ; Amherst was to reduce Ticonderoga and Crown Point, and then co-operate with Wolfe; while a third division, under General Prideaux (*prid'-o*), after capturing Niagara, was to proceed against Montreal.

II. Early in July, Prideaux reached Niagara, and at once commenced a siege, during which he was unfortunately killed by the bursting of a shell. Sir William Johnson, having succeeded to the command, defeated a force of twelve hundred French and Indians who were advancing to the relief of the place, and compelled the besieged to capitulate. Instead, however, of proceeding against Montreal, according to the plan of operations, he garrisoned the fort which he had taken, and then made his way to Albany.

III. In the mean time Amherst had reached the vicinity of Ticonderoga. As he advanced, the French fled from both Ticonderoga and Crown Point without striking a blow, and retired to an island in the Sorel River. Neglecting to follow up his successes as he should have done, he allowed the summer to pass before he made any attempt at pursuit. Then a succession of storms damaged his fleet; and the cold weather approaching, he went into winter quarters at Crown Point, and thus failed to co-operate against Quebec.

IV. Of the three expeditions, that under Wolfe can be said to have been the only one completely successful. With an

---

II QUESTIONS.—4. What is said of Prideaux's operations and fate? 5. Who succeeded him? 6. What success did Johnson meet with? 7. In what respect did he deviate from the original plan of operations? 8. How is Niagara situated? (See map, p. 85.)

III. 9. How far had Amherst proceeded, in the mean time? 10. How are Ticonderoga and Crown Point situated? (See map, p. 85.) 11 Of what lake is the Sorel River the outlet? (See same map.) 12. By what other name is the Sorel sometimes known? (See map, p. 124.)

IV. 13. With how many men did Wolfe advance against Quebec? 14. What route did he take? 15. On what small island did he land his men? 16. In what direction from Quebec is that island? (See map, p. 103.) 17 Where is Point Levi? 18. What did Wolfe do at Point Levi? 19. With what success?

army of eight thousand men, he ascended the St. Lawrence River as far as the Isle of Orleans, where, in 1759. the latter part of June, he landed his whole force in safety. Taking possession of Point Levi, opposite Quebec, he established a battery there, which, though it destroyed the buildings near the river's edge, did but little damage to that part of the city situated on the promontory.

THE ST. LAWRENCE, IN 1759.

V. Becoming convinced that the battery was not near enough to accomplish the reduction of the place, he determined upon a bold attack. Accordingly, on the 31st of July, an attempt was made upon the enemy's intrenchments, but it resulted in defeat and the loss of nearly five hundred men. This contest is known as the battle of the Montmorenci.

V. QUESTION.—20. Give an account of the battle of the Montmorenci.
5*

1759.   VI. Not discouraged by the disaster, Wolfe resolved upon another plan. During the night of the 12th of September his troops effected a landing, at a place about two miles above the city, and, climbing by a narrow path the steep bank of the St. Lawrence, at daylight, on the following morning, they stood on the Plains of Abraham in battle array.

VII. Montcalm, who was in command of the French, refused at first to believe that the force on the Plains was any thing more than a small foraging or marauding party, such confidence did he feel in the unapproachableness of the place in that direction. But, becoming convinced of his error, he abandoned his intrenchments, and led his troops against the enemy. A fierce and bloody battle followed, which resulted in the defeat of the French. Wolfe fell in the moment of victory, and Montcalm,* mortally wounded in the action, expired soon after. The French, fearing a famine, and dreading the horrors of an assault, surrendered the city five days after the battle.

EVENTS OF 1760, AND CLOSE OF THE WAR.

I. Although the British had captured Quebec, the reduction of Canada, which was the object of the campaign of 1759, was not yet accomplished. This failure undoubtedly was owing to the want of activity on the part of Amherst. His long stay, too, at Crown Point, gave De Levi, Montcalm's successor, an opportunity to make preparation for the recovery of Quebec.

---

* Montcalm was born in France, in 1712. At the close of the battle in which he was mortally wounded, on being told that he could not live long, "So much the better," he said, "I shall not live to see the surrender of Quebec." He died on the morning of the 14th of September.

VI QUESTIONS.—21. What plan did Wolfe then determine upon?

VII 22. How was Montcalm surprised? 23. Give an account of the battle that followed. 24. By what name is that battle known? *Ans.*—The battle of the Plains of Abraham. 25. On what day did it occur? 26. When did Quebec surrender?

EVENTS OF 1760.—I. 1. Why had not the British completed the reduction of Canada before the close of 1759? 2. What, beside, was the result of Amherst's inactivity? 3. Who succeeded Montcalm in the command of the French?

II. As soon as the St. Lawrence was free of ice, De Levi proceeded to besiege the city. The British, instead of await-ing the approach of the enemy, and defending themselves from the strong position which they occupied, marched about three miles above the city, and there, on the 28th of April, 1760, was fought one of the most desperate battles of the war. After losing a thousand men or more, the British were compelled to fall back to the defenses which they had unwisely abandoned. The opportune arrival of a British fleet, some days after, changed the scene completely ; and the French lost no time in raising the siege and retreating to Montreal.

III. It was not till September that Amherst, taking the indirect route by way of Oswego, made his way into Canada and invested Montreal. The French governor, unable to re-sist, signed a capitulation, by which not only Montreal, but the whole of Canada, was surrendered into the hands of the English.

IV. On the 10th of February, 1763, a treaty of peace be-tween Great Britain and France was signed at Paris. France, by the terms of the treaty, ceded to Great Britain all her American possessions east of the Mississippi, north of the Iber-ville River, in Louisiana (*lou-e'-z-ah'-na*). At the same time a treaty was made by which Spain ceded her possessions of East and West Florida to Great Britain. Thus, it will be seen, the French and Indian War lasted more than eight years. The first gun was fired in Washington's engagement with Jumonville, in 1754, and the contest was brought to a close by the treaty of Paris, in 1763.

V. Among the dependencies which were surrendered to

II QUESTIONS.—4. Give an account of De Levi's operations. 5. How was Que-bec saved to the English?

III. 6. By what route did Amherst proceed against Montreal? 7. How is Quebec situated? (See map, p. 103.) 8. How, Montreal? (See map, p. 85.)

IV. 9. By what treaty was the war brought to a close? 10. What territory did Great Britain acquire? 11 What other treaty was made at the same time?

V. 12. What stations or posts were included in the surrender of territory to the English? 13. What is said of this transfer? 14. Of what did the Indians soon make themselves masters?

Great Britain by the treaty, were several stations or posts between the lakes and the Ohio, and in the valley of that river. The transfer of these places from the French, with whom the Indians had been on friendly terms, to the English, whom they disliked, greatly exasperated the savages in that region, and they, in a short time, made themselves masters of all the posts, except those of Niagara, Fort Pitt, and Detroit; and hundreds of families were butchered or driven from their homes.

VI. Detroit was besieged for six months, but was finally relieved. The Indians at last were compelled to sue for peace, though Pontiac (*pon'-te-ak*), their principal chief, from whom the war takes its name, refused to submit. He wandered towards the Mississippi, endeavoring to stir up the western tribes against the English, till his career was terminated by the hand of one of his own people.

PRINCIPAL BATTLES OF THE FRENCH AND INDIAN WAR.

DATES.	BATTLES.	COMMANDERS.		VICTORS.
		English	French.	
1754.				
May 28,	Great Meadows......	Washington	Jumonville.	English.
July 4,	Fort Necessity	Washington	De Villiers	French
1755.				
June 16,	Fort Beausejour.. ...	Monckton..	De Vergor.	English.
June 17,	Fort Gasperau........	Monckton..	De Villerai.	English
July 9,	Monongahela........	Braddock ..	Beaujeu....	French.
Sept. 8 {	Near Lake George...	Williams ..	Dieskau....	French.
	Head of Lake George..	Johnson...	Dieskau....	English.
1756.				
Aug. 14,	Oswego	Mercer	Montcalm..	French.
1757.				
Aug. 9,	Fort William Henry.	Monroe. ...	Montcalm..	French.
1758.				
July 6,	Near Ticonderoga....	Howe	De Trepesee	English.
July 8,	Ticonderoga.	Ab'rcrombie	Montcalm ..	French.
July 26,	Louisburg........ ..	Amherst...	Drucourt..	English
Sept. 21,	Near Fort Duquesne..	Grant	Aubry.....	French.
1759.				
July 25,	Fort Niagara	Johnson...	Aubry	English
July 31,	Montmorenci........	Wolfe	Montcalm..	French.
Sept. 13,	Plains of Abraham..	Wolfe	Montcalm..	English.
1760.				
Apr. 28,	3 miles above Quebec.	Murray	De Levi....	French

VI. 15. What is said of the siege of Detroit? 16. By what name is the war known? 17. What is said of the closing career of Pontiac?

REVIEW QUESTIONS.

SECTION IV.

THE AMERICAN REVOLUTION.—CAUSES OF THE WAR.

I. THE expenses which Great Britain had incurred in the French and Indian War had increased her national debt more than three hundred millions of dollars. The English ministry, asserting that this had been done in defending the colonies, declared that the Americans ought of right to share in the burden; and, accordingly, it was proposed by the ministry, George Grenville being at its head, that a direct revenue should be drawn from the colonies by a system of taxation. It was also affirmed that, regardless of the manner in which the national debt had been contracted or augmented, or even in the absence of any debt whatever, Parliament possessed the inherent right to tax America.

II. On the other hand, it was maintained that the colonies had been founded at their own expense; and that they had already contributed more than their fair proportion in defending themselves, while the advantages accruing from their preservation were shared by England in common with themselves. The colonists also maintained that they could only be justly taxed by a legislature in which they were represented. Inasmuch, therefore, as they were not allowed to send representatives to the British Parliament, that body had no right to impose upon them any taxes whatever.

III. Beside, the policy of Great Britain towards her American colonies, from the very beginning of their existence, as

CAUSES OF THE REVOLUTION.—I. QUESTIONS.—1 How much did the French and Indian War add to Great Britain's debt? 2. What assertion did the British ministry make? 3. What declaration did they deduce therefrom? 4. What proposition was accordingly made? 5. What strong affirmation was made?

II. 6. What was maintained by the Americans, as regards the founding of their colonies? 7. What, as regards their contribution for defense in connection with the advantages? 8. What, as regards the principle of taxation?

III. 9. What is said of the policy of Great Britain? 10. What were the "Writs of Assistance?"

shown in the "Navigation Act," with the oppressive measures that preceded and those that succeeded, even down to the authorization of the "Writs of Assistance," in 1761, had been unjust and illiberal, and calculated to incite a rebellious spirit. These "Writs of Assistance" were general search-warrants, which empowered custom-house officers to break open ships, stores, and private dwellings, in search of merchandise which, it was suspected, had paid no duty; and the writs also empowered the officers to compel sheriffs and others to assist in the odious task.

IV. When, therefore, the news of the Stamp Act, passed by Parliament in 1765, reached America, intense indignation was produced throughout the country. By the provisions of the act, all instruments in writing, such as deeds, bonds, and notes, as well as printed pamphlets, newspapers, almanacs, etc., were to be executed on stamped paper, to be purchased from the agents of the British government.

V. The first burst of opposition appeared in the legislature of Virginia, where Patrick Henry* distinguished himself by his bold and manly eloquence. In Massachusetts too the opposition was fearless, and, upon the recommendation of her Assembly, a Colonial Congress, composed

PATRICK HENRY.

* Patrick Henry was born in Virginia, in 1736. He died in 1799, the year of Washington's death.

of delegates from nine colonies, with Timothy Ruggles,* of Massachusetts, for president, was held in New York, to consult with reference to the general safety. The result of their deliberations was the adoption of a Declaration of Rights, a Petition to the King, and a Memorial to both Houses of Parliament.

VI. So intense was the popular indignation against the Stamp Act, as also against the officers appointed to distribute the stamps, that when the day came on which the obnoxious law was to go into effect, there were no officials courageous enough to carry it into execution. All the stamped paper was either destroyed or concealed; and, for a time, all transactions requiring stamps were entirely suspended.

VII. At length business resumed its previous course, being conducted without stamps. In addition to this general opposition, the merchants of New York, Philadelphia, Boston, and other places, agreed to import no more British goods while the Stamp Act remained a law. A change in the British ministry occurring, William Pitt and others exerted themselves in opposition to the obnoxious measure, and it was repealed in 1766, the year after its enactment.

VIII. The news of the repeal caused great rejoicing throughout America, but, as the sequel proved, without adequate cause; for, notwithstanding the repeal of the Stamp Act, Parliament, still claiming the right to tax the colonies, passed, at the same time, another law, called the Declaratory Act, which affirmed the right claimed, in all its length and breadth. It

---

* Notwithstanding the patriotic stand taken by Ruggles before the hostilities of the Revolution actually commenced, he soon headed a body of loyalists and fought against the Americans. At the close of the war he went to Nova Scotia, and there resided till his death

VI. QUESTIONS.—21 What was the effect of the feeling against the Stamp Act? 22. What was done with the stamped paper? 23. What was the consequence, for a time, as regards transactions?

VII. 24. How did business afterward shape itself? 25. In what way did the merchants show their opposition to the Stamp Act? 26. Give the closing history of the act.

VIII. 27. How was the news of the repeal received in America? 28. How did it appear that the cause for rejoicing was illusory? 29. How was the asserted right to tax the colonies shown in 1767?

was attempted to exercise the right so claimed by the passage of a bill, in the following year, 1767, for levying duties on glass, paper, painters' colors, and tea, imported into the colonies. Two other obnoxious acts were also passed during the same year.

IX. The intelligence of these enactments produced a revival of the feelings which had been caused by the passage of the

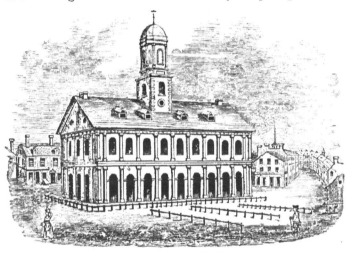

FANEUIL HALL, IN 1776.*

Stamp Act. Non-importation associations were formed, the members of which were pledged not to import or use any articles of British production, subject to duty. The Massachusetts Assembly issued a circular to the other Colonial Assemblies, asking their co-operation in efforts to obtain redress: in response, the most of them adopted resolutions protesting against the odious enactments.

* Faneuil Hall, in Boston, was used by the patriots during the Revolution, and, for that reason, is often called the "Cradle of American Liberty." The original building, comprising a market-place on the ground floor, a town-hall, and other rooms, was erected by Peter Faneuil, permission having been previously granted by the authorities of Boston. In 1761 it was destroyed by fire, but in 1763 it was rebuilt at the expense of the town, and when the British occupied Boston, in 1775, they used the hall for a theatre. In 1805 the building underwent considerable alteration, when it was also enlarged.

IX. QUESTIONS.—30. How did the news of these enactments affect the colonists? 31. What organizations were formed? 32. What was done by the Massachusetts Assembly? 33.8. How did the other colonies respond?

X. The people of Boston were particularly decided in their opposition to one of the enactments known as the "New Revenue Law;" and, in consequence, repeated collisions took place between them and the custom-house officers. For the purpose of overawing the Bostonians, the Governor of Massachusetts requested General Gage, the commander-in-chief of the British forces in America, to station troops in the city. In compliance therewith, two regiments arrived from Halifax, in September, 1768; but their presence still more exasperated the people, and affrays ensued, in one of which, called the "Boston Massacre," the soldiers fired upon the populace, killing three men and wounding others.

XI. Before the news of the "massacre" reached England, an act was passed by Parliament, revoking all the duties laid in 1767, excepting that of threepence per pound on tea. As, however, the people of America were contending, not against the *amount* of taxes imposed, but against the *principle* of taxation without representation, the concession was by no means satisfactory. The Non-importation associations continued, but, of course, only as against the importation and use of the article upon which a duty was still laid. The tea for New York and Philadelphia was sent back to London, without being landed; in Charleston it was stored in cellars, where it perished.

XII. At Boston, on a cold moonlight night in December, 1773, a party of men, disguised as Indians, boarded the ships, broke open the chests of tea, emptied their contents into the water, and then quietly retired. In retaliation for

X. Questions.—34. Wherein did the people of Boston evince particular opposition? 35. What was the consequence? 36. What request did the governor of Massachusetts make? 37. Why did he make the request? 38. How was the request complied with? 39. Give an account of the Boston massacre.

XI. 40. What concessions were made by Parliament in 1770? 41. Why was not this concession satisfactory to the colonists? 42. To what extent did the agreement of the Non-importation associations continue? 43. How was the tea which arrived disposed of?

XII. 44. Give an account of the doings of the "Boston Tea Party." 45. How was the act retaliated? 46. How did the Salem people behave upon the occasion? 47. How, the people of Marblehead? 48. What other obnoxious act was also passed?

his defiant destruction, the British government determined to punish Boston ; and the Boston Port Bill, intended to close that port to all commerce, and transfer the seat of the colonial government to Salem, was accordingly passed. But the people of Salem refused to thrive at the expense of their neighbors, and Marblehead, fifteen miles distant from the despoiled town, offered her port, free of charge, to the Boston merchants. Other acts, which were considered gross violations of the charters and rightful privileges of the colonies, were also passed. Among these was one for quartering the king's troops on the colonies, at the people's expense.

XIII. Meanwhile, delegates were chosen to represent the colonies at Philadelphia. Here, in September, 1774, a general congress, known as "The First Continental Congress," or the "Old Continental Congress," convened, to deliberate on such measures as the united interests of the colonies might require. Fifty-one delegates, representing all the colonies except Georgia, were present, and Peyton Randolph,* of Virginia, was chosen President.

XIV. Their first act was the passage of a resolution commending the conduct of the people of Boston in their opposition to the obnoxious laws of Parliament. They also agreed upon a declaration of rights, recommended the suspension of all commercial intercourse with Great Britain, and voted an address to the king, another to the people of Great Britain, and a memorial to the Canadians.

XV. General Gage, who, in addition to his position as commander-in-chief of the king's forces, had been recently ap-

---

* Peyton Randolph was born in Virginia, in 1723. As stated above, he was the President of " The First Continental Congress." He was also elected President of the second Congress, held at Philadelphia in the following year, but political duties calling him to Virginia before the close of its session, he was succeeded in the position by John Hancock, of Massachusetts. His death was sudden, occurring at Philadelphia, towards the close of October, 1775.

XIII QUESTIONS.—49 What convention took place in 1774 ? • 50 How many delegates were present? 51 Name the twelve colonies that were represented. 52. Who was chosen president of the Congress ?

XIV 53 What measures did they pass ?

XV 54. What appointment had Gage received ? 55. What did he determine upon ? 56. What did he do in conformity with the determination ?

pointed governor of Massachusetts, determined, in this crisis, upon more active measures. He fortified Boston Neck, and seizing the military stores which the Americans had collected at Cambridge and Charlestown, conveyed them to his head-quarters.

XVI. The people everywhere were excited, but their feelings were controlled by a prudence befitting the solemnity of the occasion. A conflict with the "mother country" seemed to be inevitable. The Massachusetts Assembly, though dissolved by the governor, had again convened as a Provincial Congress, and adopted a plan for organizing the militia. The men in Massachusetts capable of bearing arms were daily trained in military exercises, and pledged to take the field at a minute's notice; hence their name of "minute men." Military measures were also adopted in other colonies, and a general determination was manifested to resist, even with arms, the new oppressions attempted to be imposed by Great Britain.

EVENTS OF 1775.

I. The British government was not idle. Gage's forces at Boston had been so augmented by arrivals from England that in the beginning of April, 1775, he found himself in command of three thousand troops.

II. For the purpose of destroying the stores which the Americans had collected at Concord, a town about sixteen miles from Boston, he dispatched, at night, a detachment of eight hundred men, under Colonel Smith and Major Pitcairn;

but notwithstanding the intended secrecy of the expedition, the alarm was given, and the "minute men" were aroused in every direction by messages and signals from Boston. When the British reached Lexington, half the distance to Concord, before sunrise, on the morning of the 19th of April, between sixty and seventy of the citizens were drawn up under arms.

CONCORD, MASS., IN 1774.

III. Pitcairn rode forward and shouted, "Disperse, you rebels; throw down your arms and disperse;" but, not being obeyed, he ordered his men to fire. Then was shed the first blood of the Revolution. Eight of the men of Lexington were killed, nine were wounded—a quarter of that heroic band had thus fallen—and the others dispersed. The British proceeded to Concord, and destroyed all the stores they could find. In the mean time the "minute men" from all directions had begun to assemble, and a skirmish ensued, in which several per-

III. QUESTIONS.—9. Describe what took place at Lexington. 10. At Concord.

1775.   sons were killed on both sides. Towards noon the invaders began their retrograde march for Boston.

IV. The Americans pursued the retreating troops, keeping up a constant fire upon them from behind trees and stone fences. Colonel Smith was severely wounded, and his men, fainting and exhausted, were in danger of being entirely cut off, when they were joined at Lexington* by a re-enforcement of nine hundred men, under Lord Percy. A short interval for rest and refreshment was allowed, and then the united detachments of the British continued the retreat, taking the road to Charlestown. The minute men followed as before, keeping up the pursuit until after sunset. The loss of the British during the memorable affair of this day was about two hundred and eight, in killed, wounded, and missing; that of the Americans was about ninety.

V. The tidings of the day's contest spread with wonderful rapidity, and the militia from New Hampshire, Connecticut, and other parts of New England, hastened to join their brethren of Massachusetts in forming a camp in the neighborhood of Boston. Here General Artemas Ward, of Massachusetts, was exercising a limited command, by virtue of an appointment from the Provincial Congress of that colony; but the men from the different colonies appeared mostly as independent corps, under leaders of their own choosing. This was not all. The effect of the day's strife took a direction which nobody could have anticipated,—people began to talk of a separation from England, and of an independent government of their own.

VI. It being deemed important to secure Ticonderoga and Crown Point, in May, 1775, a number of volunteers from Ver-

---

* Lexington, the scene of the first encounter between the British and Americans in the Revolutionary contest, is situated about ten miles northwest from Boston, and seven miles east from Concord. At the time of the encounter the town contained about seven hundred inhabitants.

IV. QUESTIONS.—11. Give an account of the retreat and pursuit as far as Lexington. 12. How were the British aided at Lexington? 13. Give an account of what afterwards took place.

V. 14. What effect did the battle of Lexington have? 15. Under what organization were the American forces which were collected near Boston? 16. What other effect did the day's strife have?

mont and Connecticut, under Ethan Allen and Bene- 1775.
dict Arnold, captured both places without loss; and, by
this fortunate achievement, a large supply of military and naval
stores fell into the hands of the Americans.

VII. So closely were the British troops at Boston hemmed
in by the provincials, that the place began to experience the
privations of a besieged city. The timely arrival of re-enforcements from England, under Generals Howe, Burgoyne, and Sir
Henry Clinton, enabled Gage to act with more decision; and
that commander issued a proclamation, in which he declared
all Americans in arms to be rebels and traitors, but offered
pardon to those who should return to their allegiance. To
this offer two exceptions were
made — John Hancock* and
Samuel Adams†—their offences
being pronounced too great to
admit of pardon.

VIII. The Americans, antici-
pating that the British had designs against the country beyond Charlestown, determined
to seize and fortify the heights
commanding the neck of the
peninsula. Accordingly, on the evening of the 16th of June,
Colonel Prescott was sent with a detachment of one thousand men to execute this perilous enterprise.

JOHN HANCOCK.

---

* John Hancock was born in Quincy, Massachusetts, in 1737. In 1775 he was elected President of the
Continental Congress, and in 1776 he signed the Declaration of Independence. He died in Quincy, in 1793.
† Samuel Adams was born in Boston, in 1722. He and John Adams were related, having the same
great-grandfather, making them second cousins. He was one of the signers of the Declaration of Independence. His death occurred in Boston, in 1803.

VI. QUESTIONS.—17. Give an account of the capture of Ticonderoga and Crown
Point. 18. How are these two places situated? (See map, p. 85.)

VII. 19. What is said of the condition of the British troops in Boston? 20. By
whom was Gage joined from England? 21. What is said of a proclamation? 22.
Who were excluded from the offer in the proclamation? 23. Why were they excluded?

VIII. 24. On what business was Prescott sent? 25. Why did the Americans
wish to occupy the heights?

1775.   IX. On attaining the ascent of Bunker Hill* he concluded, after consulting his officers, to deviate from the
letter of his orders and fortify Breed's Hill, because the latter
was nearer to Boston, and had a better command of the town
and shipping. The consultation and change delayed matters
until midnight. Then the work commenced.* Every man of
the thousand seized, in his turn, the pick-axe and spade; and
by the dawn of day a strong redoubt was completed.

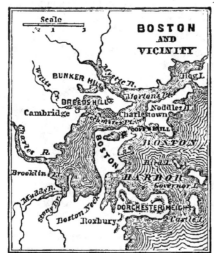

X. The British, on
discovering the works
on Breed's Hill, began
a cannonade from ves-
sels in the harbor, and
also from a battery on
Copp's Hill, in Boston;
but with little or no
effect. They then made
preparations for an as-
sault. About three
thousand troops, under
Generals Howe and
Pigot, crossed over to
Charlestown, while,
mainly through the ex-
ertions of General Putnam, about five hundred men were added
to Prescott's force in the course of the day.

XI. Meanwhile the British had set fire to the village of
Charlestown, by means of shells thrown from Copp's Hill; and,

---

* Bunker Hill monument, an obelisk two hundred and twenty-one feet high, erected in commemoration
of the battle, now stands on the spot where the redoubt was built on Breed's Hill. Its corner-stone was laid
by General Lafayette, on the 17th of June, 1825, the fiftieth anniversary of the battle. An immense con-
course of persons was present on the occasion, including nearly two hundred revolutionary soldiers and
forty surviving patriots of the battle, and President John Quincy Adams, with his entire cabinet. Daniel
Webster delivered the oration.

IX. QUESTIONS.—26. What conclusion did Prescott afterward come to? 27. Why
did he so conclude? 28. How was the work then carried on?
   X. 29. What did the British do on discovering the works? 30. How next did they
proceed?
   XI. 31. When was the battle of Bunker Hill fought? 32. Give an account of it.

amid the glare of its flame, Howe and Pigot advanced
to the attack. Twice did they get to within a few
rods of the redoubt, when the Americans, each time, opened
upon them so deadly a fire that they were repulsed with heavy
loss. General Clinton arriving, the third charge was more
successful; and the Americans, their ammunition being entirely exhausted, were forced to retreat.

XII. The loss to the British,
in killed and wounded, according to their own account, was
more than a thousand men: the
Americans lost less than half
that number, though among their
slain was Joseph Warren,* one
of the ablest and most popular
of the patriot leaders, and an
estimable man. His loss was
deplored as a severe calamity
to the cause of freedom.

JOSEPH WARREN.

XIII. Though the British had
gained the hill—the ground contended for—the victory to
them was more disastrous and humiliating than an ordinary
defeat; while, to the Americans, the defeat had the effect of
a triumph : it gave them confidence in themselves, and consequence in the eyes of their enemies. The day's doings, too,
convinced the people that the military training and experience
which the Putnams, the Starks, and the Washingtons had
acquired, in the "school" of the French and Indian War, had
been gained to some purpose.

---

* Joseph Warren was born in Roxbury, Mass., in 1741. After having been graduated at Harvard College, he studied medicine, and became a physician of extensive practice in the city of Boston. He was
one of the leading men in resisting the unjust and oppressive measures sought to be fastened upon the
colonies by Great Britain, holding as he did, at the time of his death, two of the most responsible civil
positions under the commonwealth of Massachusetts, and a commission as major-general.

XII. QUESTIONS.—33. What loss did the British sustain in the battle? 34. What,
the Americans? 35. What is said of Warren?

XIII. 36. How did the victory affect the British? 37. How, the Americans?
38. Of what did the people become convinced?

1775.   XIV. On the very day of the capture of Ticonderoga, May 10, the second Continental Congress convened at Philadelphia. That body voted to raise an army of twenty thousand men, and, on the 15th of June, by a unanimous vote, elected George Washington commander-in-chief. Washington, who, at the time, was a delegate in the Congress from Virginia, rose in his place, and, with dignity and modesty, accepted the appointment, but declined all compensation for his services: he only asked for the payment of his expenses. He thereupon resigned his position in the Congress, and repaired to Cambridge, three miles from Boston, where, on the 3d of July, he took command of the army, then numbering about fourteen thousand men.

XV. While the revolution was gaining strength at the east, in the south it was also making progress. Lord Dunmore, the governor of Virginia, having seized some powder and removed it to a vessel in the York River, Patrick Henry, at the head of a corps of volunteers, demanded and received compensation therefor. Some months later, in December, a force, consisting of British regulars, tory volunteers, and negroes, which had been collected by Dunmore, attacked a body of Virginia patriots near Norfolk; but the assailants were repulsed with great loss. In revenge, Dunmore, at a later period, reduced the town of Norfolk to ashes.

XVI. It having been ascertained that the British intended to invade the colonies from Canada, Congress determined to anticipate the movement, by carrying the war into that pro-

---

XIV. QUESTIONS.—39. When did Allen and Arnold capture Ticonderoga? 40. What also occurred on that day? 41. What two acts of Congress are mentioned? 42. How did Washington receive the appointment? 43. What did Washington thereupon do?

XV. 44. Describe the York River (See map, p. 85.) 45. What event is mentioned in connection with the York River? 46. What was done by Patrick Henry? 47. Give an account of the battle near Norfolk 48. How did Dunmore gratify his revenge? 49. How is Norfolk situated? (See map, p. 24.)

XVI. 50 What scheme of invasion did the British intend? 51 How was it determined to anticipate the movement? 52. What advantage did the possession of Canada promise? 53. What forces were sent?

vince. Beside, if Canada were gained, its use to the British as a place of rendezvous and supply would be prevented. Two forces were accordingly sent; one by the way of Lake Champlain, under General Schuyler* (*ski'-ler*), and the other by the Kennebec River, commanded by Arnold.

XVII. Schuyler proceeded down Lake Champlain, and encamped on an island at the head of the Sorel (*so-rell'*) River, but sickness compelling his return to Albany, the com-

GENERAL SCHUYLER.

mand devolved upon Montgomery. Ethan Allen,† who, at the setting out of the expedition, had been engaged in reconnoitering the country between the Sorel and the St. Lawrence, was again dispatched in the same direction, this time for recruits. Instead, however, of prosecuting the business on which he was sent, he crossed the St. Lawrence to make an attack upon Montreal. The result of this reckless enterprise was defeat; and he was sent a prisoner to England, in irons. This mishap did not in the least interfere with the operations of the main force; and before the middle of November, Montgomery, by a series of well-directed movements, had acquired

---

* Philip Schuyler was born at Albany, New York, in 1733. He was engaged in the French and Indian war, and accompanied Sir William Johnson in 1755. His death occurred at Albany, in 1804.

† Ethan Allen was born in Connecticut, in 1742, or thereabouts. His parents, soon after his birth, took him to Vermont, and there, when he grew to manhood, he was one of the most determined of the settlers in resisting the claims of New York to the Vermont territory. As colonel of an armed force he protected those who had received grants of land from the Governor of New Hampshire, and drove out of the district the New York settlers. The troubles continued about ten years, when the more important events of the Revolution put an end to the hostile acts, though the controversy was afterward renewed. Allen as stated above, was sent to England in irons. After suffering a captivity of more than two years in England, Halifax, and one of the prison-ships of New York, he was exchanged. He never afterward actively engaged in military service; but died at Burlington, Vt., in 1789.

XVII. QUESTIONS.—54. Near what boundary-line is the head of the Sorel River? (See map, p. 124.) 55. In what direction from the head of the Sorel is Montreal? (See same map.) 56. How long did Schuyler's connection with the expedition continue? 57. Give an account of Allen's doings. 58. Give an account of Montgomery's successes.

1775.   possession of Fort Chambly (*sham'-ble*), St. John's, and Montreal, and was thereby master of a large part of Canada. He then proceeded against Quebec.

PART OF THE SOREL RIVER.

XVIII. In the mean time Arnold, having performed a tedious march through the wilderness, enduring almost incredible toils and hardships, appeared before Quebec ; but not being sufficiently strong to attack the city alone, he retired twenty miles up the St. Lawrence, and there awaited the arrival of Montgomery. A junction of the two forces was effected in the beginning of December, and, with Montgomery in the chief command, the entire army, numbering but nine hundred effective men, proceeded to take a position before Quebec.

XIX. After a siege of three weeks without gaining any advantage, it was resolved to attempt the capture of the place by an assault. Accordingly, at dawn on the last day of the year, and while a violent snow-storm was prevailing, the American army, in four columns, advanced to the attack. Montgomery,* who led one of the columns, had gained some advantage, when a discharge of grape-shot, from a single cannon of the enemy, made deadly havoc, killing him and one of his aides instantly, and mortally wounding others. His column at once retreated. Arnold, who led another of the columns, was severely wounded and borne from the field, and Captain Morgan assumed the command. Morgan took refuge in a stone house, from which he defended himself awhile, but,

---

* Richard Montgomery was born in Ireland, in 1736. In 1775 he was a representative from New York in the Continental Congress.

XVIII. QUESTIONS.—59. What had Arnold been doing in the mean time? 60. When did Montgomery's and Arnold's forces unite? 61. What movement did they then make?

XIX. 62. Give an account of the battle of Quebec.

seeing no prospect of relief, he and his few followers were compelled to surrender.

XX. Arnold, though wounded and disabled, took command of the troops that had effected a retreat, and, in an encampment a short distance from Quebec, passed a rigorous winter. In the spring, General Wooster arrived from Montreal and took the command; and he, in turn, was succeeded by General Thomas. The

GENERAL MONTGOMERY.

British, having received large re-enforcements from England, assumed the offensive, and before June, 1776, the Americans had abandoned one place after another, and entirely evacuated Canada.

XX. QUESTIONS.—63. What did Arnold do after the battle? 64. By whom was he succeeded in the command? 65. What further is stated of military operations in Canada?

REVIEW QUESTIONS.

EVENTS OF 1776.

I. Owing to various causes, Washington's army in the vicinity of Boston had dwindled to less than ten thousand men, but by great exertions it was augmented to fourteen thousand before the close of February, 1776. Congress, believing that this force would be required in other directions, urged Washington to attack the British, and, if possible, drive them from the city. This accorded with his own desire, which had been previously made known; yet, in a council of his officers, the recommendation was rejected as involving too much risk. A plan of action was, however, adopted, by which a line of fortifications was in one night erected on Dorchester Heights, which completely commanded the city and harbor of Boston.

II. Howe, who had succeeded Gage* in the command, seeing that he must either dislodge the Americans at once or evacuate the city, resolved on an attack; but a violent storm preventing it till the Americans were strongly fortified, his only alternative was evacuation. An understanding was thereupon informally entered into, by which the British should be allowed to embark without molestation from the batteries, upon condition that they would not set fire to the city. In accordance therewith, on the 17th of March, 1776, they evacuated Boston, accompanied by fifteen hundred families of loyalists, and sailed for Halifax.

* Thomas Gage was the last royal governor of Massachusetts. He was an active officer during the French and Indian war, and, during Braddock's campaign, he and Washington met.

EVENTS OF 1776.—QUESTIONS.—I. 1. What fluctuations took place in the number of Washington's army? 2 What was Washington urged to do? 3 To whom did he submit the recommendation? 4. What was its fate? 5. What works were erected instead?

II. 6. By whom was Gage succeeded in command of the royal forces? 7. What two alternatives were presented to Howe? 8. Upon what did he resolve? 9. Why did he not carry it out? 10. What is said of a certain understanding? 11 When did the British leave Boston? 12 By whom were they accompanied? 13. In what direction from Boston is Halifax?

1776.   III. A little more than two months before their ae-
parture, a secret expedition, conducted by Clinton, had
been dispatched by water in a southerly direction. Surmising its
destination to be New York, Washington gave General Charles
Lee authority to raise volunteers in Connecticut and march to
the protection of that city. It happened that on the very day
of Lee's arrival in New York, Clinton appeared off Sandy
Hook, just outside the harbor.

IV. Foiled in his design against the city, Clinton sailed
southward; and Lee, who had been appointed to the command
of the southern forces, pushed rapidly on, watching, as best he
could, his movements. At Cape Fear Clinton was joined
by Sir Peter Parker and Lord Cornwallis (corn-wol'-lis), with
a fleet and troops from England, and the whole force proceeded against Charleston, in South Carolina.

V. The people of Carolina had received intelligence of the
intended attack, and were making great exertions in the erection of defenses at various places in the harbor. A fort of
palmetto wood, on Sullivan's Island, garrisoned by about five
hundred men under Colonel Moultrie (mōle'-tre), commanded
the channel leading to the town, and was considered, in connection with Fort Johnson, on James Island, the key to the
harbor. A combined attack by land and water upon Sullivan's Island was commenced on the morning of the 28th of
June, 1776. After a conflict of nine hours, during which
Clinton was foiled in his attempt to reach the island, and the
fleet was much shattered, the vessels drew off, and the British
abandoned the enterprise.

III QUESTIONS—14. What expedition was sent under Clinton? 15. In what
way did Washington undertake to anticipate Clinton's designs? 16. What coincidence occurred?

IV. 17 In what direction did Clinton then sail? 18 What took place at Cape
Fear? 19. Where is Cape Fear? (See map, p. 79) 20 Against what place did the
British then proceed?

V. 21 How were the people of Charleston prepared? 22. What fort is between
Forts Moultrie and Johnson? (See map, p. 129.) 23. Give an account of the battle
of Fort Moultrie.

VI. While success was thus attending the American arms at the South, Congress was preparing to declare a separation of the political relations existing between Great Britain and the colonies. On the 7th of June, Richard Henry Lee, of Virginia, offered the following resolution: "*Resolved*, That these united

VICINITY OF CHARLESTON

colonies are, and of right ought to be, free and independent States; that they are absolved from all allegiance to the British crown, and that all political connection between them and the State of Great Britain is, and ought to be, totally dissolved."

VII. Thereupon a discussion took place which continued for three days, when the further consideration of the subject was postponed to the 1st of July. In the mean time, Thomas Jefferson, John Adams, Benjamin Franklin,* Roger Sherman, and Robert R. Livingston, were appointed a committee to draft a Declaration of Independence. Lee's resolution was passed by a large majority on the 2d of July; and the DECLARATION OF INDEPENDENCE, which had been prepared by

---

* Benjamin Franklin was born in Boston, in 1706. He died in Philadelphia, in 1790.

VI. QUESTIONS.—24. What was Congress doing in the mean time? 25. Recite the resolution which was offered by Lee. 26. When did he offer it?

VII. 27. What is said of the discussion that followed? 28. What committee was appointed? 29. What became of Lee's resolution? 30. Give the further history of the Declaration.

6*

DR. FRANKLIN.

Thomas Jefferson, the chairman of the committee, was unanimously adopted on the 4th of July, 1776.* Everywhere the action of Congress was heartily approved by the people, and the Declaration was received in assemblies, cities, and among the troops, with demonstrations of joy.

VIII. In the beginning of July, General Howe arrived from Halifax, and took possession of Staten (*stat'-in*) Island, at the entrance of New York Bay. This he made the rendezvous for a powerful army intended to act against New York. He was soon joined by his brother, Admiral Lord Howe, from England, and by Clinton from the South : these, with other arrivals, including a body of Germans, or Hessians (*hesh'-ans*), as they were generally called, gave him an army of thirty-five thousand men.

IX. The design of the British was to seize the city of New York and the country along the Hudson River, establish a communication with Canada, separate the New England from the other States, and overrun the populous portions of the revolted districts. Washington's army, in the vicinity of New York city, amounted to twenty-seven thousand men ; but, as many of these were sick, and many others were with-

---

* The old State House, in Philadelphia, where Congress met, is still standing. It is generally known by the name of Independence Hall, though the room in which the Declaration of Independence was adopted and signed, received at first that appellation. The building was erected in 1735, but its bell-tower was not put up until 1750. A bell which was imported from England, expressly for the tower, was found cracked upon its arrival, and thereupon it was recast in the city of Philadelphia, and raised to its place in 1753. Upon fillets around its crown are the words : *Proclaim liberty throughout all the land unto all the inhabitants thereof.* It has a world-wide reputation as the "Liberty Bell."

VIII. QUESTIONS.—31. Of what island did Howe take possession? 32. In what direction from New York city is Staten Island? (See map, p. 131.) 33. By what additions did he acquire an army?

IX. 34. What was the design of the British? 35. What is said of Washington's army?

out arms, his effective force did not exceed seventeen thousand men.

X. Lord Howe and his brother, having been commissioned to grant pardons to all who would lay down their arms and return to their allegiance, undertook to make known their powers by a proclamation addressed to the people, and by letters to Washington. The letters were not received, because they were addressed to George Washington, Esquire, instead of being addressed to him as commander-in-chief of the American army. This rejection of the letters was owing, not to any official pride on the part of Washington, but to a conviction that to receive them would compromise American rights and dignities.

XI. Baffled in the attempt, Howe determined to strike an effective blow without further delay. His troops were accordingly landed on the western end of Long Island, and, in three divisions, by three different roads, they advanced towards the American camp at Brooklyn, which was then in command of General Putnam.*

XII. While two of the divisions were engaging the Americans, the third, under Clinton, having taken a circuitous route, fell upon their rear. Some of the patriots, by a desperate effort, cut their way through the host of foes, but a great many were either killed or taken prisoners. The loss of the

NEW YORK BAY.

---

* Israel Putnam was born in Danvers, Massachusetts, in 1718. He took an active part in the French and Indian war. His death occurred in 1790, at Brooklyn, Connecticut.

X. QUESTIONS.—36. What special commission had Lord Howe and his brother received? 37. How did they undertake to make known their powers? 38. How were the letters addressed? 39. What was their fate? 40. Why were they rejected?

XI. 41. What did Howe then determine upon? 42. Where were his troops landed? 43. What passage of water did he cross in going from Staten Island to Long Island? (See map, p. 131.) 44. What plan of advance did the British adopt?

XII. 45. Give an account of the battle of Long Island.

1776.

Americans, in killed, wounded, and prisoners, was nearly two thousand; that of the British was less than four hundred. This conflict, generally known as the battle of Long Island, was fought on the 27th of August, 1776.

XIII. On the night of the 29th, while a heavy fog was hanging over Brooklyn, and concealing the movements of the Americans, the troops were embarked, under Washington's supervision, and in safety they all crossed to New York city. This retreat was undoubtedly one of the most signal achievements of the war, and redounded greatly to the military reputation of Washington.

XIV. As the evident design of the British was to encompass the American army on the Island of New York, Washington called a council of his officers, and, influenced by their opinion, abandoned the city and retreated to the northern part of the island. A part of the British army, thereupon, crossed the East River and took possession of the city.

XV. Desiring to gain a knowledge of the condition and plans of the enemy remaining on Long Island, Washington applied for a discreet officer to enter their lines and procure this intelligence. Captain Nathan Hale,* of Connecticut, volunteered for the service. Hale reached the British camp, and obtained the information desired, but on his return was arrested. He was taken before Howe, by whom, without even the form of a regular trial, he was ordered for execution the next morning. He died a patriot and a hero, saying with his last breath: "I only regret that I have but one life to lose for my country."

---

* Nathan Hale was born in Connecticut, in 1755. After being graduated at Yale College, he became a teacher. Immediately after the battle of Lexington, he entered the army as lieutenant, and before the close of the year was promoted to be a captain. His death occurred on the morning of the 22d of Sept., 1776. The tree on which he was hung, was one of an orchard owned by Colonel Rutgers, and stood "near the present intersection of East Broadway and Market street," New York city.

XIII. QUESTIONS.—46. Give an account of Washington's masterly retreat to New York.

XIV. 47. Why did Washington abandon the city of New York? 48. To what place did he retreat?

XV. 49. Relate the circumstances connected with the death of Nathan Hale.

XVI. About the middle of September, a large detachment of the British crossed the East River, at a point toward the upper part of New York Island, and formed a line almost across the island. On the morning of the 16th, they advanced, in strong force, towards the American lines, two miles off, when a

GENERAL PUTNAM.

spirited skirmish took place, resulting in the defeat and pursuit of the British. Though the Americans lost Colonel Knowlton and Major Leitch (*leech*), their principal officers engaged, the affair was of advantage, inasmuch as it was the first gleam of success in the campaign, and consequently tended to revive the spirits of the army.

XVII. It was evident, from Howe's movements, that he intended to get above Washington's army and destroy his communications with the Eastern States. While three English frigates were sent up the Hudson to cut off the communication with New Jersey, Howe passed through the strait at the east of New York Island, and landed the greater part of his army in Westchester county, beyond the Harlem River. To render these movements fruitless, Washington withdrew his troops further north, to White Plains, and here, the British following, a partial though severe engagement took place, on the 28th of October, in which the Americans suffered defeat, losing between three and four hundred men, a loss about equal to that of the enemy.

XVIII. During the following night the Americans had so improved and strengthened their position, that Howe con-

XVI. Questions.—50. Give an account of the battle that took place on the 16th of September.

XVII. 51. What did Howe's movements indicate? 52. Describe the movements. 53. Give an account of the battle of White Plains. 54. In what direction from Tarrytown is White Plains? (See map, p. 47.)

1776. cluded not to renew the contest until the arrival of reenforcements; but before these came Washington withdrew his troops still further north, to the hills of North Castle. Instead of following, the British general turned his attention to the American posts on the Hudson, with the apparent design of invading New Jersey, and marching against Philadelphia.

XIX. Leaving one detachment, under Lee, at North Castle, and another, under Colonel Magaw, at Fort Washington, the American commander crossed the Hudson with the main body of his army, and entered New Jersey. On the 16th of November, 1776, the British made an attack upon Fort Washington, situated on New York Island, about eleven miles above the city, and, although they were successful, the victory cost them a thousand men.

XX. They then, in large force, commanded by Cornwallis, crossed the Hudson and took possession of Fort Lee, nearly opposite Fort Washington, which had been abandoned on their approach. Closely pursued by Cornwallis, Washington retreated through New Jersey, and, early in December, crossed the Delaware with his diminished and disheartened army. Congress, then in session at Philadelphia, soon after adjourned to Baltimore.

XXI. Lee,* who had been urged by his commander-in-chief to hurry to the support of the main army, instead of obeying, at first delayed, and then advanced leisurely. Hav-

---

* Charles Lee was born in England, in 1731. He was with Braddock in the battle of the Monongahela, and with Abercrombie in the assault on Ticonderoga. He afterward served in the Russian army. His death occurred at Philadelphia, in 1782.

XVIII. QUESTIONS.—55. Why did not Howe afterward renew the contest? 56. By what movement was Howe foiled? 57. In what direction from Verplanck's Point is North Castle? (See map, p. 47.) 58. What was Howe's next movement?

XIX. 59. On what stream of water was Fort Washington situated? (See map, p. 47.) 60. Give an account of the battle there.

XX. 61. Give an account of the retreat and pursuit. 62. What movement did Congress make? 63. On what river is Philadelphia situated? (See map, p 142.) 64. Baltimore? (See map, p 237.)

XXI. 65. How did Lee obey Washington's order to hurry to his support? 66. What misfortune befell him? 67. What was then done with Lee's detachment?

ing incautiously taken quarters
at a distance from his detachment, he was surprised and
taken prisoner by a scouting
party of the enemy. Sullivan,
who had been made a prisoner
at the battle of Long Island,
and recently exchanged, then
took command of the detachment, and promptly conducted
it to Washington's camp across
the Delaware.

GENERAL LEE.

XXII. Owing to the reverses which the army had sustained, a feeling of gloom and despondency prevailed among
the patriots. This was soon dispelled by a bold enterprise
accomplished by Washington. On the night of the 25th of
December, 1776, a division of the army crossed the Delaware
under his command—two other divisions, in consequence of
the ice, not having succeeded in getting over—and at eight
o'clock on the morning of the 26th, attacked a body of Hessians stationed at Trenton. Rahl,* their commander, was
mortally wounded, between thirty and forty of his men were
slain, and nearly a thousand taken prisoners. Washington's
loss was only four men, two of whom fell in the battle, and
two were frozen to death.

XXIII. Conscious that he could not hold Trenton against
the superior force which the British could concentrate there
in a few hours, he recrossed the Delaware with his prisoners
and spoils. The victory restored confidence to the Americans,

---

* The name of this officer was also spelled Rall, and in other ways. After the battle he was conveyed
to the house of a Quaker family, where Washington and Greene visited the dying man.

XXII. QUESTIONS.—68. In what direction from Philadelphia is Trenton ? (See map,
p. 68.) 69. When did a battle take place there ? 70. Give an account of the battle.
XXIII. 71. Why did Washington abandon Trenton ? 72. What effect did the
result of the battle have? 73. What induced Washington to again proceed to Trenton ?

1776.   while it startled and mortified the British. Encouraged by his success, and finding his army strengthened very much by recent recruits, Washington resolved to act on the offensive. With that view he again crossed the Delaware and took post at Trenton, though the enemy were assembled in great force at Princeton, only ten miles distant.

EVENTS OF 1777.

CENTRAL PART OF NEW JERSEY.

I. After being joined by troops under Generals Mifflin and Cadwallader, Washington's whole force at Trenton, on the 1st of January, 1777, did not exceed five thousand men. Fortunately, Congress had invested him with almost dictatorial powers in all things relative to the operations of war, and, thus empowered, he was making efforts to augment his army by the addition of artillery battalions.

II. Towards the evening of the 2d of January, Cornwallis, at the head of a large body of troops, reached Trenton, and after making several attempts to cross the stream which runs through the town, and being as often repulsed with loss, he concluded to give his wearied troops a night's repose, and defer hostilities until morning, feeling sure of then capturing Washington and his entire army.

III. Washington's situation was indeed critical. To retreat

EVENTS OF 1777.—I. QUESTIONS.—1. How large was Washington's army at Trenton in the beginning of 1777 ? 2. With what extraordinary power had Congress invested Washington?

II. 3. Give an account of what took place on the 2d of January.

III. 4. Describe the situation in which Washington was placed. 5. What bold expedient suggested itself to his mind in this critical position ? 6. In what direction from Trenton is Princeton? (See map, p. 136.) 7. When did the battle of Princeton take place ? 8. Describe it. 9. What officer did the Americans lose?

across the Delaware, which was then very much obstructed by floating ice, or to remain and risk a battle with a superior force, appeared full of danger. In this hour of darkness, a bold expedient suggested itself, and he adopted it. Leaving his camp-fires burning, he marched by a circuitous route toward Princeton, intending to surprise and attack the British troops left there. At sunrise, January 3d, the van of his forces encountered, near Princeton, a part of the British troops, already on their march to join Cornwallis. At first the American militia gave way, but Washington coming up with a select corps, turned the tide of battle and routed the enemy. The loss of the British, in killed, wounded, and prisoners, was about four hundred men; that of the Americans did not exceed thirty, but among them was General Mercer, who was mortally wounded.

IV. Washington's army was encamped at Morristown during the first months of 1777. The place had not been selected for winter quarters, but, being well protected by forests and rugged hills, no change was made until the latter part of May, when the encampment was removed to Middlebrook.

V. Early in 1776, Congress sent Silas Deane to France, to solicit aid for the United States. He was afterward joined by Dr. Franklin and Arthur Lee. France hesitated to extend any open assistance, but secretly aided the Americans by loans and gifts of money, and by supplies of arms, provisions, and clothing. And what aid France did not extend as a nation, was, to

FLAG OF THE UNITED STATES, ADOPTED IN JULY, 1777.

IV. QUESTIONS.—10. Where did Washington's army spend the first months of 1777? 11. Why did the army remain there so long? 12. When and to what place did the army remove? 13. In what direction from Morristown is Middlebrook? (See map, p. 68.)

V. 14. What persons were sent to France for aid? 15. In what way did France respond? 16. What is said of Lafayette?

1777.

some extent, at least, accorded by her citizens. The Marquis de Lafayette was a notable example. At his own expense he fitted out a vessel, and, in the spring of 1777, arrived in America. He at once joined the army of Washington as a volunteer without pay, but was soon after appointed by Congress a major-general.

VI. Toward the close of April, 1777, General Tryon, late royal governor of New York, made an expedition eastward. With a force of two thousand men he marched against Danbury, Connecticut, and, after destroying the stores which had been collected there by the Americans, burned the town. Fearing an attack from the militia, who were assembling in great force, he retreated to his shipping in Long Island Sound, being repeatedly harassed on his retrograde march by detachments of the Americans, commanded by Generals Wooster, Arnold, and Silliman. Tryon's loss, during the expedition, amounted to nearly three hundred men: that of the Americans was not so large, but Wooster was among the slain.

VII. The destructive expedition against Danbury was fully retaliated in less than a month after. Colonel Meigs (*megz*), with a party of Connecticut militia, crossed Long Island Sound, destroyed the British stores and shipping at Sag Harbor, and, carrying off ninety prisoners, returned to Connecticut without the loss of a man.

VIII. This gallant exploit was followed, in July, by another of equal, if not greater daring. Colonel Barton, with a small party of resolute men, at night crossed Narragansett Bay to the Island of Rhode Island, surprised and captured General Prescott, the British commander there, and returned

VI. QUESTIONS.—17. When and by whom was the town of Danbury burned? 18. In what direction from New Haven is Danbury? 19. Give an account of Tryon's expedition 20. What officer did the Americans lose?

VII. 21. How is Sag Harbor situated? (See map, p. 47.) 22. Give an account of the expedition conducted by Colonel Meigs.

VIII. 23. Give an account of the expedition conducted by Colonel Barton 24. What was afterward done with Prescott?

safe to the mainland with his prisoner. This achievement put it into the power of the Americans to recover Lee, an officer of equal rank with Prescott, and the exchange was accordingly effected in May, 1778.

THE JERSEY PRISON-SHIP.*

IX. As spring approached, it became evident that Howe's scheme in New Jersey was to draw the Americans from their camp at Middlebrook, and bring on a general engagement. In furtherance of the plan, he concentrated the main body of his army at New Brunswick, within ten miles of the camp; and, in one attempt, a skirmish took place between a corps under Cornwallis and Stirling's brigade, in which the British had the advantage. The scheme, however, failed: Washington continued to pursue his "Fabian policy," and, at length, the whole force of the enemy in New Jersey was withdrawn to Staten Island, leaving the American commander in complete possession of the State.

---

* During the Revolution, the British used the hulks of their decaying ships for the imprisonment of Americans captured by them. One of these, the *Jersey Prison Ship*, is proverbial in our revolutionary history on account of the great numbers who were confined there, and of the cruel and inhuman treatment they received. She was anchored in the Wallabout, a small bay on the Long Island shore, opposite New York, and used as a prison-ship until the close of the war.

IX. QUESTIONS.—25. What became evident as spring approached? 26. Did the British succeed? 27. To what place did the British withdraw?

1777.

X. The troops thus withdrawn, amounting to eigh teen thousand men, were embarked on board the fleet commanded by Admiral Lord Howe, and the vessels put to sea, leaving a large force under Clinton still at New York, to retain possession there, and make the city a base of other operations then in progress. The destination of the fleet being unknown to Washington, he remained for many days in painful uncertainty about it.

XI. At last the mystery was explained. The object of the British was to get possession of Philadelphia, but, on reaching Delaware Bay, they were deterred from entering by reports that measures had been taken to obstruct the navigation of the Delaware River. The Admiral, it afterward appeared, then determined to make for Chesapeake Bay, and, in that way, approach as near as possible to the city. Accordingly a landing was effected at a point on the Elk River, a stream flowing into the bay from the north. ·

XII. Washington hastened to dispute the march of the British, and, with the main part of his army, took a position at Chad's Ford, on Brandywine Creek. On the 11th of September, the enemy advanced in two divisions, and while one, under Knyphausen (*nip-how'-zen*), made a direct attack upon the left wing of the Americans, the other, under Howe and Cornwallis, crossed the stream above, and unexpectedly fell upon their right. The patriots defended themselves with great valor, but were at length forced to give way. The loss of the Americans, in killed, wounded, and prisoners, was full twelve hundred men; that of the British was about five

X. QUESTIONS.—28. What disposition did Howe make of his troops? 29. On what subject did Washington feel a painful uncertainty?

XI 30. How was the mystery of Howe's movements explained? 31. By what route did the British finally proceed? 32. What town is situated at the mouth of the Elk River? (See map, p 142)

XII. 33. Where did Washington take a position to dispute the march of the British? 34. Is Chad's Ford nearer the mouth of Brandywine Creek than Wilmington? (See map p. 142) 35. Give an account of the battle of Brandywine. 36. What distinguished officer, on the American side, was wounded? 37. What other distinguished officer was in the battle?

hundred. Lafayette, who was wounded, and Pulaski (*pu-las'-ke*), a Polish nobleman, were both in the battle, doing brave service for the cause of liberty.

WASHINGTON'S HEAD-QUARTERS AT BRANDYWINE.

XIII. During the following night, the Americans retreated to Chester, where they rendezvoused, and next day marched toward Philadelphia. Washington, desiring to save the city

1777.   if possible, recrossed the Schuylkill (*skool'-kil*), with the determination of seeking the enemy and giving battle.   The two armies met, and were on the point of engaging, when a violent rain-storm prevented.   To add to the disaster of Brandywine, General Wayne, who had been detached with about fifteen hundred men to get in the rear of Howe's advancing army, and cut off his baggage train, when near Paoli (*pă-o'-le*), on the 20th of September, was surprised by a midnight attack, and defeated with great loss.

XIV. A movement on the part of the British, which threatened the magazine and military stores at Reading (*red'-ding*), induced Washington to make a counter-movement and take a position at Pottsgrove.   Philadelphia, thus abandoned, was entered by the British on the 26th of September, 1777. Howe prepared to make the city his winter-quarters, while the main body of his army was encamped at Germantown, four miles distant.

XV. Some days after, Washington, on learning that a strong detachment of the British had left for the reduction of Forts Mifflin and Mercer, determined to attack the force re-

PHILADELPHIA AND VICINITY.

maining at Germantown. Accordingly, early on the morning of the 4th of October, the Americans advanced upon the encampment of the enemy, and, for a time, had the advantage ; but a fog which prevailed, and a stone house into which several companies of British troops had thrown themselves, favored the party attacked, and, after one of the bloodiest and most obstinate conflicts of the war, the patriots were repulsed. The loss, on the part of the Americans, in killed, wounded, and prisoners, was about a thousand men; on the part of the British, about half that number.

XVI. Seven or eight miles below Philadelphia, the Americans had erected two forts on opposite sides of the Delaware River. One of these, called Fort Mifflin, was at Mud Island, near the Pennsylvania shore, and the other, Fort Mercer, was at Red Bank, on the New Jersey side. It was evident that while these two forts were in the hands of the Americans, and the obstructions remained which had been placed in the river, the British shipping could not ascend to Philadelphia, and consequently the army there would not readily obtain supplies.

XVII. Howe was aware of this, and, in concert with his brother, a plan of operations was agreed upon for the reduction of the forts and the removal of the obstructions. Accordingly, on the 22d of October, both forts were attacked: Mercer, by a land force of two thousand Hessians, under Count Donop; and Mifflin, by a powerful naval force of frigates and other vessels. But, in both cases, the British were most signally repulsed, with heavy loss. Donop was mortally wounded; about five hundred of the Hessians and marines were either killed or wounded, and two of the largest ships were destroyed. Colonel Green, who commanded at Fort Mercer, Colonel Smith, who commanded at Fort Mifflin, and Commodore Hazelwood, who did good service in command of a small fleet of galleys, were thanked by Congress for their courageous conduct, and to each was afterwards voted a sword.

XV. QUESTIONS.—48. In what direction from Pottsgrove is Germantown? (See map, p 142) 49 While at Pottsgrove, what information did Washington receive? 50 When did the battle of Germantown occur? 51 Give an account of it.

XVI 52 How are Forts Mifflin and Mercer situated? 53. What was evident in connection with the two forts?

XVII 54 What plan of operations was agreed upon? 55. When were the two forts attacked? 56 Give an account of the two battles? 57. How was the gallant conduct of the American commanders afterwards noticed?

1777.   XVIII. On the tenth of November a second attempt to reduce Fort Mifflin was commenced. After a heroic defense of five days, during which the British kept up a destructive fire from a battery which they had erected, and also

from their ships-of-war, the garrison set fire to and evacuated the fort, and crossed over to Red Bank at night by the light of the flames. Washington endeavored to keep possession of Fort Mercer, but before he could send a sufficient force, Lord Cornwallis, with two thousand men, appeared before it. As a defense against such odds was hopeless, the place was abandoned.

COLONEL MOULTRIE.

XIX. During the winter of 1777–'78, Washington's troops were quartered in huts at Valley Forge, on the west side of the Schuylkill River, about twenty miles from Howe's head-quarters at Philadelphia. Here they suffered greatly for want of food, clothing, and comfortable quarters, and many of the officers resigned in consequence of not receiving their pay. In a letter which Washington addressed to the President of Congress, on the 23d of December, he says: "We have no less than two thousand eight hundred and ninety-eight men now in camp unfit for duty, because they are barefoot and otherwise naked."

XVIII. QUESTIONS.—58. When did the British a second time undertake to reduce Fort Mifflin? 59. Give an account of what followed. 60. What is said of Fort Mercer?

XIX. 61. Where did Washington's army make their head-quarters during the winters of 1778–79? 62. In what direction from Fort Mifflin is Valley Forge? (See map, p. 142.) 63. What is said of the sufferings of the Americans at Valley Forge? 64. What statement did Washington make in a letter?

BURGOYNE'S INVASION.

I. The failure of the campaign of 1776 against Canada, left the British at liberty to make hostile demonstrations from that quarter, and they were not slow in availing themselves of it. An army of ten thousand men, consisting of British and German troops, and a large body of Canadians and Indians, was concentrated at St. John's, on the Sorel River.

II. The immediate design of General Burgoyne, who commanded this large army, was to invade the United States by the way of Lake Champlain, and force his way to Albany. He further designed to effect a junction of his own army with that of one from New York city, and thus cut off Washington's communications with the Eastern States. Before making any advance, however, he sent a detachment, under St. Leger, to proceed by way of Oswego, capture Fort Schuyler (*ski'-ler*), situated on the Mohawk River, and then rejoin him at Albany.

GENERAL ST. CLAIR.

III. Burgoyne, at the head of his invading host, moved slowly up the lake, and, after taking possession of Crown Point, proceeded to invest Ticonderoga, which was then garrisoned by a force of three thousand men, under General St. Clair.* This commander had determined

---

* Arthur St. Clair was born in Edinburgh, Scotland, in 1735. He was with Wolfe in the battle of the Plains of Abraham, and with Washington in the battles of Trenton and Princeton. He died near Greensburg, Pennsylvania, in 1818.

BURGOYNE'S INVASION.—I. QUESTIONS.—1. What was the consequence of the failure of the Canada campaign in 1776? 2. Where did the British army of invasion concentrate? 3. How is St. John's situated? 4. Is St. John's north or south of Rouse's Point? (See map, p. 124.)

II. 5. Who commanded the army at St. John's? 6. What was Burgoyne's immediate design? 7. What further design did he have? 8. What detachment did he send out?

7

1777. to hold out to the last extremity, but, to his dismay discovering that the enemy had erected batteries on Mount Defiance, a rocky height commanding the fort, he determined upon a speedy retreat.

IV. On the night of the 5th of July, while dispatching his ammunition and stores for Skenesborough (*skeenz'-bur-rŏ*), now Whitehall, the army crossed over to Mount Independence, and took a road through the woods, on the east side of the lake, towards Fort Edward, the head-quarters of General Schuyler, who then commanded the American forces at the north. Early on the morning of the 7th, the rear division of the retreating army was overtaken at Hubbardton, Vermont, and, after a severe battle, routed with considerable loss. The ammunition and stores were also overtaken at Skenesborough, and destroyed.

V. Schuyler, deeming his force, which then numbered only about four thousand men, inadequate to make a successful stand against that of the invaders, gradually fell back to the islands at the mouth of the Mohawk. Burgoyne reached Skenesborough, and thence his march was slow and difficult, owing to the impediments which Schuyler had placed in his way, by destroying the bridges and felling immense trees across the roads.

III. QUESTIONS.—9 In what part of the State of New York is Lake Champlain situated? (See map, p 62) 10. What State is on the east of the lake? (See map, p. 62) 11. How is Crown Point situated? (See map, p 149) 12. Ticonderoga? (Ditto) 13. Mount Defiance? (Ditto) 14 Up what lake did Burgoyne sail? 15. What place did he take possession of? 16. What place did he then proceed to invest? 17. By whom was Ticonderoga defended? 18. What had St. Clair determined upon? 19 Why did he not carry out his determination?

IV. 20. What did St. Clair do with his ammunition and supplies? 21. In what direction from Fort Edward is Whitehall? (See map, p 149.) 22. To what place did the American army cross? 23 Where is Mount Independence? (See map, p. 149) 24 What road did the army then take? 25. When was the battle of Hubbardton fought? 26 How is Hubbardton situated? (See p 149) 27. Give an account of the battle fought there. 28. What became of the ammunition and stores?

V. 29. To what place did Schuyler retire? 30. Into what river does the Mohawk flow? (See map, p 149) 31 Why did Schuyler retire to the islands at the mouth of the Mohawk? 32. What is said of Burgoyne's march after leaving Skenesborough?

VI. While approaching Fort Edward, an act of barbarity was perpetrated which excited wide-spread abhorrence. This was the murder of Miss McCrea. The lady, it appears, was on a visit to a friend residing near the fort. Several Indians, part of one of Burgoyne's marauding parties, burst into the house where Miss McCrea was, and carried her off. On the way, a quarrel arose among the savages as to whose prize the captive was. The dispute becoming furious, one of the Indians, in a paroxysm of rage, killed her, and bore off her scalp as a trophy. According to some authorities Miss McCrea was killed by a shot, intended for one of her captors, which was fired from an American gun at the fort.

VII. St. Leger, who, it will be recollected, had been sent against Fort Schuyler, on reaching the place, and finding it resolutely defended by Colonel Gansevoort, determined upon a siege. The besiegers were a motley force, composed mostly of British and Indians, the latter led by the famous Brant, with some Royalists, Hessians, and Canadians. On the 6th of August,

KOSCIUSKO.*

two days after the commencement of St. Leger's operations, General Herkimer, with a body of militia, while advancing to the relief of Gansevoort, fell into an ambuscade at Oriskany, (*o-ris'-kan-e*), within a few miles of the fort, and was mortally wounded.

---

* Thaddeus Kosciusko, a Polish patriot, was born about 1755. He was with Gates in the two battles of Stillwater, and subsequently distinguished himself as an adjutant of Washington. His death, which occurred in Switzerland, in 1817, was caused by a fall from his horse over a precipice.

VI. Questions.—33. Give an account of the murder of Miss McCrea. 34. How is Fort Edward situated? (See map, p. 149.)

VII. 35. Against what place had St. Leger been sent? 36. Where was Fort Schuyler? (See map, p. 148.) 37. By whom was Fort Schuyler defended? 38. Upon what did St. Leger determine? 39. Why did he not make an attack at once? 40. Of whom did the besiegers consist? 41. Give an account of the battle of Oriskany.

1777.

VICINITY OF FORT SCHUYLER.

VIII. At the same time, and for the purpose of making a diversion in favor of Herkimer, of whose approach Gansevoort had been informed, a spirited sortie from the fort was made upon the camp of the besiegers, who were driven away or fled, and a large quantity of baggage and stores was seized. The Americans retreated in good order to the fort just as St. Leger came up with re-enforcements.

IX. Schuyler, upon hearing that Gansevoort was so closely pressed, sent a detachment of eight hundred men to his relief. Arnold, who commanded it, by contriving to send a report ahead, exaggerating the number of his force, so worked upon the fears of St. Leger's Indian allies that they fled, and the siege was abandoned.

X. While these events were taking place on the Mohawk, others, of no less importance, were being enacted nearer to Burgoyne. That commander, in consequence of the delays to which he had been subjected, found himself in want of supplies for his army. Learning that large quantities were stored at Bennington, he sent a detachment of five hundred men, mostly Hessians, commanded by Colonel Baum, to seize them. The detachment was met a short distance from the town, on the 16th of August, 1777, by a body of New Hampshire militia, under General Stark, and entirely defeated, Baum being killed. The victors then dispersed in various directions about the field.

VIII QUESTIONS.—42. Give an account of the sortie from the fort.
IX. 43. Give an account of Arnold's stratagem.
X 44 What did Burgoyne find himself in need of? 45. How came it that his supplies were gone? 46. By what method did he undertake to procure supplies? 47. How is Bennington situated? (See map, p 149.) 48. When did the battle of Bennington take place? 49. Give an account of it. 50. What error did the Americans commit after the battle?

XI. At this juncture, five hundred Hessians, whom Burgoyne had sent to the aid of Baum, came up. These were joined by many of their countrymen who had fled. Stark was endeavoring to gather together his scattered men, when, fortunately, Colonel Warner,* with a fresh body of militia, arrived from Bennington, and the enemy were again defeated.

XII. The reverses experienced by the British at Fort Schuyler and Bennington, seriously embarrassed the movements of Burgoyne, and weakened and dispirited his whole army. Just then, when the Americans were in good force to confront the British, a change was made in the command of the patriot army of the north—General Gates, by act of Congress, was appointed to succeed Schuyler.

SARATOGA AND VICINITY.

XIII. Gates advanced to Bemis Heights, a little above

---

* Seth Warner was born in Connecticut, about 1744. He took part in the capture of Ticonderoga and Crown Point, in 1775; was at the battles of Bunker Hill, Bennington, and Bemis Heights, and was with Montgomery in Canada. He died in Connecticut, in 1785.

XI. QUESTIONS.—51. What occurred at this juncture? 52. How did fortune favor the Americans?

XII. 53. How did the defeat of the British at Bennington affect them? 54. Who was appointed to succeed Schuyler? 55. What injustice was done to Schuyler by the change?

XIII. 56. To what place did Gates advance? 57. In what direction is that from Bennington? (See map, p. 149.) 58. What movement did Burgoyne make? 59. When was the first battle of Stillwater fought? 60. Give an account of it. 61. By what other name is that battle also known?

1777. Stillwater, and Burgoyne crossed the Hudson, arriving within two miles of the American camp. On the following day, September the 19th, was fought the first battle of Stillwater, sometimes called the battle of Bemis Heights, in which Arnold was the leading spirit, and the bravest among the brave. Both parties claimed the victory; but, though the British remained on the field of battle, their progress toward Albany was effectually checked.

XIV. The two armies remained in sight of each other for more than two weeks, Burgoyne, in the mean time, strengthening his position, to await the co-operation of Clinton from New York. Despairing of aid from that quarter, the British commander determined, if possible, to cut his way through the American lines. Then, October the 7th, occurred the second battle of Stillwater, or, as it is often called, the battle of Saratoga.

GENERAL BURGOYNE.

XV. After a fierce conflict of several hours, in which the British lost General Fraser and other valuable officers, beside over four hundred men, they were compelled to give way. Though having no command assigned him, Arnold was the most active in the battle, and was severely wounded just as victory was deciding for the Americans.

XVI. Burgoyne* retired to Saratoga shortly after, where, finding

* John Burgoyne was born in England, about 1730. After his surrender to Gates he returned to England, being then a prisoner on parole, where he was coldly received in Parliament, of which body he was a member. He died in London, in 1792.

XIV. QUESTIONS.—62. How long did the two armies remain in sight of each other? 63. What did Burgoyne do in the mean time? 64. What did he at last determine to do? 65. When did the second battle of Stillwater occur? 66. By what other name is that battle also known?

XV. 67. Give an account of the second battle of Stillwater.

XVI. 68. To what place did Burgoyne then retire? 69. What was his condition at Saratoga? 70. When did he surrender? 71. What did the Americans acquire by the surrender?

himself so surrounded that all chance of retreat was cut off, and being without provisions, on the 17th of October he surrendered his whole army, numbering more than five thousand men, prisoners of war. By the surrender, the Americans acquired a fine train of artillery, five thousand muskets, and a large quantity of clothing, tents, and military stores.

XVII. In the mean time Sir Henry Clinton had ascended the Hudson as far as Forts Clinton and Montgomery, and captured the two forts; but, instead of hastening to the co-operation of Burgoyne, he sent an expedition to devastate the country, intending thereby to make a diversion in favor of the northern British army. The troops garrisoning Ticonderoga and other forts on the northern frontier, upon hearing of Burgoyne's surrender, abandoned their posts and fled to Canada, and Clinton's expedition returned to New York.

GENERAL GATES.

XVIII. The all-important successes of Gates* at Bemis Heights and Saratoga formed an unsatisfactory contrast with Brandywine and Germantown, and served the purpose of a faction, subsequently known as "Conway's Cabal," who were laboring in secret to undermine the popularity of Washington. The leading conspirator, the one from whom the cabal derived its name, was Thomas Conway, who had come from Europe with a military reputation, and been appointed a major-general in the American army.

---

* Horatio Gates was born in England, in 1728. He was an officer in Braddock's expedition, in 1755, and was severely wounded in the battle of the Monongahela. After the Revolutionary War, he resided on an estate which he owned in Virginia, until 1790. He then removed to New York, where he died in 1806.

XVII. QUESTIONS.—72. What had Sir Henry Clinton done in the mean time? 73. How were the two forts, Clinton and Montgomery, situated? (See map, p. 47.) 74. What expedition did he send? 75. What effect did Burgoyne's surrender have upon the expedition, and the British troops on Lake Champlain?

XVIII. 76. What invidious contrast was made? 77. What is said of the cabal and the leading conspirators?

1777.   XIX. A knowledge of this intrigue coming to Washington, his despondency, occasioned by the distresses at Valley Forge, was very much augmented, but during the trying season he comported himself with dignity; and time fully vindicated the wisdom of Congress in electing him to be the commander-in-chief of the army.

XX. In November, 1777, ARTICLES OF CONFEDERATION for the government of the United States were adopted by Congress. These, however, in consequence of not being ratified by all the States previous to 1781, did not go into effect before that year.

RUINS OF FORT TICONDEROGA.

XIX. QUESTIONS.—78. Did Washington hear of the intrigue against him? 79. How did the knowledge affect him? 80. What was his conduct under the circumstances? 81. What is said of the wisdom of Congress in connection with the subject?

XX. 82. When did Congress adopt the Articles of Confederation? 83. When did the Articles go into effect? 84. Why did they not go into effect sooner?

REVIEW QUESTIONS.

EVENTS OF 1778

I. The success of the Americans at Saratoga decided the negotiations which had been set on foot in 1776. France acknowledged the independence of the United States, and a treaty of alliance and commerce was concluded between the two countries. The commissioners by whom the treaty was made met at Paris,—those on the part of the United States being Benjamin Franklin, Silas Deane, and Arthur Lee,—and on the 6th of February, 1778, signed the important document.

II. In England the tidings of Burgoyne's surrender produced alarm, which was aggravated by apprehensions that France was about to espouse the cause of the Americans; and instead of the determination formerly manifested by the British ministry, to conquer the rebellious colonies at any cost, a more conciliatory spirit began to prevail, and two bills, in keeping with this feeling, were passed by Parliament.

III. Commissioners were sent to America, with all dispatch, to negotiate a restoration of peace; but Congress refused to treat with them until Great Britain should withdraw her fleets and armies, or acknowledge the independence of the United States.

IV. One of the commissioners, in his eagerness to forward the end of his mission, attempted to bribe General Joseph Reed and Robert Morris, members of Congress. Said Reed, in reply, " I am not worth purchasing; but, such as I am, the king of Great Britain is not rich enough to do it."

EVENTS OF 1778 —I QUESTIONS —1 How did the American success at Saratoga affect matters in France? 2 Who were the American commissioners by whom the treaty was negotiated? 3 When was it signed?

II 4 How did the success at Saratoga affect the cause in England? 5 What was done by Parliament?

III 6 Who were sent to America? 7 How did Congress act toward them?

IV. 8 What is said of the attempt at bribery?

V. France, immediately upon the conclusion of the treaty with the United States, fitted out a squadron, commanded by D'Estaing* (*des-taing'*), the first object of which was to blockade the British fleet, then in the Delaware.

VI. In the mean time, General Howe had resigned his command, and General Clinton been appointed his successor. The

D'ESTAING.

British government, fearing for the safety of their fleet in the Delaware, and apprehending a result to their main army similar to that of Burgoyne's, ordered the ships to leave the river, and the troops to abandon Philadelphia, and both forces to proceed to New York. Consequently, D'Estaing, in his first intention, was foiled, for, before his arrival, Admiral Howe had sailed.

VII. On the 18th of June, Clinton completed the evacuation of Philadelphia, crossed the Delaware, and commenced his march through New Jersey toward New York. Washington gave pursuit, and at Monmouth, on the 28th of June, a severely contested battle was fought. In the early part of it, Lee's division fell back, and was in full retreat just as Washington came up. Lee was sharply rebuked by the commander-in-chief, and directed to assist in further operations;

---

* Charles Hector Count d'Estaing was a native of France, born in 1729. He was a member of the Assembly of Notables in the French Revolution, but, falling under the suspicion of the Terrorists, was guillotined in 1794.

V. QUESTIONS.—9. How did France commence to assist the Americans?

VI. 10. What change took place in the British command? 11. In what intention was D'Estaing foiled? 12. What was the cause? 13. Why did Clinton leave Philadelphia?

VII. 14. When did he leave? 15. In what direction did he go? 16. What movement did Washington make? 17. When did the battle of Monmouth take place? 18. In what direction is Monmouth from Philadelphia? (See map, p. 68.) 19. What is Monmouth now called? *Ans.*—Freehold. 20. Give an account of the battle.

1778. he complied, and during the remainder of the battle displayed both faithfulness and courage.

VIII. Though, at the close of the day, the result of the engagement was indecisive, the advantage was clearly with the Americans, and they slept on their arms, intending to renew the contest on the following morning; but Clinton silently departed before dawn, and proceeded on his march. The loss of the British in the battle reached five hundred, and this was increased by more than a thousand desertions, principally among the Hessians, before the march was ended. The Americans lost more than two hundred, many of whom fell from the excessive heat and fatigue of the day.

IX. Lee's pride having been wounded by the rebuke he had received on the battle-field, he addressed two disrespectful letters to Washington on the subject, and, at his own request, was tried by a court-martial. Three charges were made out against him, namely: disobedience of orders, misbehavior before the enemy, and disrespect to the commander-in-chief. A tedious investigation of more than a month was had, when he was found guilty and sentenced to be suspended from all command for a year.

X. Lee never rejoined the army, but, just before the close of the war, died in Philadelphia. It is certain that his conduct, on more than one occasion during the war, gave rise to painful suspicions; and the evidence is now strong that, once at least, he was ready to act a treacherous part.

XI. During the summer of 1778, an enterprise was decided upon by Washington and D'Estaing, having for its object the

---

VIII. QUESTIONS.—21 What is said of the result? 22. What prevented a renewal of the contest? 23 What losses were sustained by each party?

IX. 24. To whom did Lee address two disrespectful letters? 25. Why did he do so? 26. What action was taken at his request? 27 What charges were brought against him? 28 What was the result of the trial?

X. 29 When and where did Lee die? 30. What is said of his conduct during the war?

XI 31 What enterprise did Washington and D'Estaing decide upon? 32 What force did the enemy have there at the time? 33. How did the French and Americans commence operations? 34. In what direction from Providence is Newport? (See map, p 37.)

expulsion of the British from the Island of Rhode Island, which place had been made a military dépôt and stronghold by them. The enemy's force there, at the time, consisted of about six thousand men, commanded by General Pigot, whose head-quarters were at Newport. In accordance with the plan of attack, the French fleet entered the harbor of Newport and anchored near the town, while Sullivan,* commanding the American troops, crossed from Tiverton and landed on the northern part of the island.

XII. Just as arrangements were matured for a combined attack, Lord Howe, who had heard of Pigot's danger, and hastened to his relief, made his appearance with his large fleet. The new-comer entirely diverted the French commander from his object, who, tempted by the hope of a naval victory,

GENERAL SULLIVAN.

sailed out to meet Howe. The two fleets were about to engage when a furious storm came on, which parted and disabled them.

XIII. D'Estaing returned to Newport, but, instead of co-operating with the Americans, as agreed, he announced his intention of sailing for Boston, to refit his ships. Against this contemplated desertion, not only Sullivan, but Lafayette and Greene, who were then with the army at Rhode Island, remonstrated, but without effect. In the mean time, Sullivan had advanced almost to Newport, but, finding himself deserted

---

* John Sullivan was born in Berwick, Maine, in 1740. In consequence of ill health, he resigned his position in the army before the close of the war. His death occurred at Durham, New Hampshire, in 1795.

XII. QUESTIONS.—35. Describe what took place in connection with D'Estaing's fleet.

XIII. 36. Upon D'Estaing's return to Newport, what announcement did he make? 37. How was the announcement received by the Americans? 38. What had Sullivan done in the mean time?

1778. by the French, he withdrew to the northern part of the island, followed up by the British.

XIV. Here, on the 29th of August, occurred an engagement known as the battle of Quaker Hill, or, taking its name from another eminence, on which the Americans had thrown up a redoubt, the battle of Batt's Hill. After a loss, in killed, of over two hundred on each side, the British retired. Learning that a fleet with troops was coming to the aid of Pigot, Sullivan gained the mainland, by a night movement, just in time to avoid being intercepted by Sir Henry Clinton.

XV. A little later in the season, a marauding expedition, commanded by General Grey, committed great devastation, burning vessels in Buzzard's Bay, sacking New Bedford and Fair Haven, and, at Martha's Vineyard, levying an immense contribution in sheep and cattle. But no acts of the enemy during the entire war were considered of greater atrocity than those committed by the Tories and Indians at Wyoming, in Pennsylvania, and at Cherry Valley, in New York.

XVI. Early in July, 1778, a large force of Tories and Indians, under Colonel John Butler, entered the Valley of Wyoming, spread desolation in every direction, and defeated, with great slaughter, a body of the inhabitants, who had marched out to check their ravages. In November, of the same year, a force of the same mixed character fell upon the settlement of Cherry Valley, and killed, or carried into captivity, many of the settlers.

XVII. Towards the close of the year, Sir Henry Clinton sent an expedition of two thousand men to invade Georgia.

XIV. QUESTIONS.—39. When did the battle of Quaker Hill take place? 40. Give an account of it 41. What is said of Sullivan's escape?

XV. 42 Give an account of Grey's expedition. 43. Where is Buzzard's Bay? (See map, p. 37) 44. In what direction from Newport is New Bedford? (See same map) 45. Where is Fair Haven? *Ans.*—On the Acushnet River, opposite New Bedford, with which it is connected by a bridge. 46 Where is Martha's Vineyard? (See map, p. 37.) 47. What acts of the enemy were looked upon as of peculiar atrocity? 48. Where is Cherry Valley? (See map, p. 62) 49. Where, Wyoming? (See map, p. 62.)

XVI. 50. Give an account of the "Massacre at Wyoming." 51. Of the "Massacre at Cherry Valley."

Colonel Campbell (*kam'-el*), who commanded it, proceeded against Savannah, then defended by a force of only six hundred regulars and two or three hundred militia, under General Robert Howe, and, on the 29th of December, made an attack. The Americans were defeated with much loss, and, in consequence, Savannah fell into the hands of the British, and was retained by them until July, 1783.

EVENTS OF 1779.

I. Savannah having fallen into the hands of the British, no other post in Georgia remained to the Americans except Sunbury (*sun'-ber-e*). On the 9th of January, 1779, General Prevost, who had arrived from Florida with a body of troops, captured this post, and, assuming the command of the British forces in the South, ordered Campbell to occupy Augusta, for the purpose of giving encouragement and support to the loyalists in that region.

II The Tories along the western frontiers of Carolina, having organized themselves into a body, and placed Colonel Boyd in command, marched to join the royal army under Prevost. Throughout their entire route, they committed depredations and cruelties upon the property and persons of the patriots; but at Kettle Creek, Georgia, they were attacked, on the 14th of February, by a force of Carolina militia, under Colonel Pickens, and utterly defeated, Boyd being among the killed.

III. Encouraged by this success, General Lincoln (*link'-on*), who had arrived to take command of the American troops at

---

XVII. QUESTIONS.—52. What expedition was sent against Georgia? 53. How is Savannah situated? (See map, p. 164.) 54. When did a battle occur? 55. Give an account of it. 56. What was the consequence?

EVENTS OF 1779.—I. 1. What post in Georgia remained to the Americans after the fall of Savannah? 2. State how and when this, too, was lost. 3. What command did Prevost assume? 4. What order did he give? 5. In what direction from Savannah is Sunbury? (See map, p. 164.)

II 6. What organization of Tories was effected? 7. What is said of their acts? depredations, etc.? 8. When did the battle of Kettle Creek take place? 9. Where did it take place? *Ans.*—At Kettle Creek, Georgia, near its junction with the Savannah River. 10. Give an account of the battle.

1779. the South, sent General Ashe to drive the British from Augusta, and confine them to the country near the sea. Campbell fled at his approach ; but at Brier Creek, Georgia, Ashe was surprised by Prevost, on the 3d of March, and defeated, losing nearly his whole army by death, captivity, and dispersion. Elated with victory, Prevost advanced against Charleston, but the timely arrival of Lincoln forced him to retire.

IV. Learning that a body of British troops was stationed at Stono Ferry, ten miles southwest from Charleston, Lincoln determined, if possible, to drive the enemy from a position so menacing to the city. Accordingly, on the 20th of June, the attempt was made, but, after a severe engagement, the Americans were repulsed.

V. While these operations were being carried on at the South, General Tryon made two more expeditions against Connecticut, and Clinton captured Stony and Verplanck's Points, on the Hudson. In Tryon's second expedition, he destroyed some salt-works at Horseneck, and dispersed a body of troops under Putnam ; in his third, he plundered New Haven, and laid East Haven, Fairfield, and Norwalk, in ashes.

VI. Washington, desiring to recapture Stony Point, planned a midnight attack under General Wayne.* On the 15th of July, Wayne set out, and, dividing his force into two col-

---

* Anthony Wayne was born at Waynesborough, Chester County, Pennsylvania, in 1745. He died at Presque Isle, now Erie, in 1796, while on his way from the West, where he had been on public business.

· III. QUESTIONS.—11 Who succeeded General Robert Howe in the command of the American troops at the South? 12. On what expedition did Lincoln send Ashe? 13. How is Augusta situated? (See map, p. 164.) 14. When did the battle of Brier Creek take place? 15 Into what body of water does Brier Creek flow? (See map, p. 164.) 16. Give an account of the battle.

IV. 17. When did the battle of Stono Ferry take place? 18. Where was the battle fought? 19. Give an account of it.

V. 20. In the mean time, what had the British done at the East and North? 21. How is Stony Point situated? (See map, p. 169.) 22. Which is the nearer to Peekskill, Stony Point or Verplanck's Point? (See map, p. 169.) 23. How are New Haven, Fairfield, and Norwalk situated? (See map, p. 47.) 24. Where is East Haven? Ans.—Four miles east from New Haven. 25. What did Tryon accomplish in his second expedition? 26. In his third?

umns, for simultaneous attacks
on opposite sides of the fort
reached the outworks before
the alarm was given : the two
columns then forced their way
with the bayonet, in the face
of a tremendous fire of grape-
shot and musketry, and, meeting in the centre of the
works, the garrison surrendered at discretion. The entire

GENERAL WAYNE.

loss of the Americans was fifteen killed, and eighty-three
wounded : the British lost upward of six hundred, in killed
and prisoners. This achievement, considered one of the most
brilliant of the war, was effected without the firing of a single
gun on the part of the victors.

VII. Only four days after, July 19, another gallant exploit
crowned the efforts of the Americans. The British post at
Paulus (*paw'-lus*) Hook,* in New Jersey, opposite the city of
New York, was surprised at night by Major Henry Lee, and
one hundred and fifty men of the garrison were made prisoners.

VIII. These two successes were counterbalanced by a complete reverse, experienced about a month later, in Maine. A
squadron of armed vessels, fitted out by Massachusetts, proceeded against a military post which the British had established on the Penobscot River. Just as the Americans were
about to make an assault, after an ill-judged siege of fifteen
days, a British fleet arrived and defeated them with great loss.

---

* Paulus Hook was so called for a number of years. Its name was afterwards changed to " the city of
Jersey," and in 1838, by act of incorporation, it was called Jersey City.

VI. QUESTIONS.—27. What place did Washington desire to recapture ? 28. How is
Stony Point situated? (See map, p. 169.) 29. When was the battle of Stony Point
fought? 30. Give an account of it. 31. How is Wayne's achievement considered ?
VII. 32. Give an account of the exploit at Paulus Hook.
VIII. 33. Describe the Penobscot River. (See map, p. 103.) 34. Give an account
of the reverse on the Penobscot.

1779.   IX. As many of the Indian tribes, especially those in the western part of New York, were constantly warring upon the border settlements, General Sullivan was sent to check their depredations, as also to avenge the " Massacre of Wyoming." On his march, he was joined by General James Clinton, from the vicinity of Albany, when the united forces amounted to about five thousand men. After defeating a body of Indians and Tories at Newtown, now Elmira, in a conflict known as the " Battle of Chemung" (*she-mung'*), he penetrated as far as the Genesee (*jen-e-see'*) River, destroying forty Indian villages and a vast amount of corn. This chastisement greatly intimidated the Indians, and their murderous excursions became less frequent.

X. The winter of 1779–'80 set in early, and was very severe. Washington made his winter quarters at Morristown; and, though he made great exertions for the comfort of his troops, they still were at times on half allowance, and suffered greatly for want of sufficient clothing and shelter.

XI. D'Estaing, it will be remembered, sailed from Rhode Island for Boston, to refit his ships, after they had been disabled in a storm. From Boston he went to the West Indies. In September, 1779, he returned, and prepared to co-operate with Lincoln in an attempt to recover Savannah. On the 9th of October, after a siege of about three weeks, the two commanders made a combined assault, but were repulsed with the loss of nearly a thousand men, in killed and wounded. Among those who fell was the gallant Count Pulaski, a Polish patriot, who had distinguished himself at the battle of Brandywine, and had otherwise rendered good service to the American cause.

IX QUESTIONS —35. Upon what expedition was Sullivan sent? 36. By whom was he joined? 37 Where is Elmira? (See map, p 62) 38. What took place there? 39. What did Sullivan accomplish? 40 Describe the Genesee River (See map, p. 62)

X. 41. What is said of the condition of Washington's army during the winter of 1779–'80?

XI. 42. What is said of D'Estaing's movements? 43 Give an account of the attempt to recover Savannah. 44. What officer of note did the Americans lose?

XII. In September of this year, one of the most obstinate naval engagements ever fought took place off Flamborough Head, England. It was between a small squadron of French and American vessels, commanded by Paul Jones,* and two British frigates that were convoying a merchant fleet. At about seven, on the evening of the 23d, the battle commenced. The Bon-Homme Richard, Jones's flagship, coming in contact with

PAUL JONES.

the Serapis, one of the frigates, commanded by Captain Pearson, Jones lashed the two vessels together. The contest continued with great fury till ten at night, when the Serapis struck. The other frigate in the mean time had surrendered to the Pallas, one of the vessels of the squadron. Jones, finding that his own ship was sinking, was compelled to transfer his crew to the Serapis.

XIII. Great Britain found an additional antagonist this year, in Spain; that power with a view to regaining Gibraltar Jamaica, and Florida, joined France and declared war against her.

EVENTS OF 1780.

I. The principal military operations of 1780 were carried on in South Carolina. Sir Henry Clinton, with a fleet commanded by Arbuthnot, having sailed from New York to pro-

---

* John Paul Jones was born in Scotland, in 1747. At the age of twelve, he was apprenticed to a shipmaster who was engaged in the American trade. When the American Revolution broke out, he was in Virginia. His name was John Paul, to which, for some unknown reason, he added Jones. After the Revolution, he entered the Russian naval service, and died at Paris, in poverty and neglect, in 1792.

XII. Questions.—45. Where did a naval battle take place on the 23d of September, 1779? 46. What was the character of the battle? 47. Give an account of it.

XIII. 48. What additional antagonist appeared against Great Britain?

Events of 1780.—I. 1. Where were the principal military operations of 1780 carried on? 2. When did Sir Henry Clinton appear before Charleston? 3. How is Charleston situated? (See map, p. 164.) 4. What took place at Monk's Corner? 5. Where is Monk's Corner? (See map, p. 164.) 6. Give an account of the surrender of Charleston.

1780.   ceed against Charleston, appeared before that city in February, and, on the 1st of April, commenced a regular siege. While it was in progress, an American force, sta-

tioned at Monk's Corner, to keep open a communication between the city and the interior, was surprised by Colonel Tarleton, and put to flight. On the 12th of May, Lincoln, the American commander, unable to hold out any longer, surrendered, and every man in Charleston became a prisoner of war.

II. To complete the subjugation of South Carolina, as Clinton contemplated, three expeditions were sent into the interior. The first was to scour the country along the Savannah; the second, to go against the post of Ninety-Six; while the third was to pursue a body of troops which had been sent

II. QUESTIONS.—7. Why did Clinton send three expeditions? 8. What special objects had each?

to the relief of Charleston, but, on learning of the surrender of that city to the British, had turned back, and were marching towards North Carolina.

III. The first and second expeditions met with no opposition. As Buford, the commander of the retrograding Americans, was moving very rapidly, and had a long start of the third expedition, Cornwallis, its commander, detached Tarleton with a force of dragoons and mounted infantry, to lead the pursuers. At Waxhaw Creek, on the 29th of May, Tarleton overtook the retreating Americans, and, impetuously falling upon them, gave no quarters, but massacred or maimed nearly every man.

IV. Sir Henry Clinton, believing South Carolina to be completely subdued, sailed for New York, leaving Cornwallis to carry the war into North Carolina and Virginia. In this opinion, however, Clinton was mistaken : for Generals Sumter and Marion, by their partisan warfare, kept alive the spirit of freedom. Although the former was repulsed at Rocky Mount, yet at Hanging Rock, only a week after, he attacked a large body of British and Tories and gained a decided victory.

V. Previous to the surrender of Charleston, Washington had sent the Baron De Kalb with re-enforcements, for the purpose of aiding Lincoln ; but, owing to various difficulties, De Kalb advanced no further than Deep River, in North Carolina, where, hearing of the fate of Charleston, he determined to await further orders. While thus waiting, Gates, who had been appointed by Congress to succeed Lincoln in

---

III QUESTIONS.--9 How did the first and second expeditions succeed? 10 When did the battle of Waxhaw Creek take place ? 11 Give an account of it 12 Into what river does Waxhaw Creek flow? (See map, p 164)

IV 13 Why did Clinton return to New York? 14. Whom did he leave in command? 15 What is said of Sumter and Marion ? 16 What is said of the battles at Rocky Mount and Hanging Rock ? 17 Where are these two places situated? (See map, p 164.)

V. 18. How did Washington endeavor to prevent the loss of Charleston ? 19 Give an account of De Kalb's movements 20 Into what body of water does the Deep River flow ? (See map, p 164) 21 Who was Lincoln's successor in command at the South ? 22. To what place did Gates march his army ?

1780. the command at the South, arrived and took charge.
The army then marched to Clermout, in South Carolina.

VI. At this time there were two large forces of the British in South Carolina: one at Charleston, under Cornwallis, and the other on the Santee River, under Lord Rawdon. On hearing of the approach of Gates, Rawdon concentrated his troops at Camden, twelve miles from Clermont, at which place Cornwallis soon arrived with a small number of troops and took the command. On the 15th of August, Gates sent re-enforcements to aid Sumter in capturing a train of supplies intended for the enemy; and, on the night of the 15th, he advanced towards Camden, for the purpose of attacking the British should they march out in force to repel Sumter.

VII. On the same night, by a singular coincidence, Cornwallis sallied from Camden to attack the camp at Clermont. Just after midnight the two vanguards met at Sanders Creek, and a slight skirmish took place, and early in the morning a

GENERAL DE KALB.

general battle commenced. After a desperate contest, the American regulars, being deserted by the militia, and overwhelmed by superior numbers, were forced to retreat, with a loss in killed, wounded, and prisoners, of about a thousand men. De Kalb* was among the mortally wounded, and died three days after. The loss of the British was between three and four hundred. This contest, fought on the 16th of August,

* The Baron De Kalb was a native of Alsace, a German province in possession of France. He came to America with Lafayette, in 1777.

VI. QUESTIONS.—23. Where, at the time, were the British in force in South Carolina? 24. Describe the Santee River. (See map, p. 164.) 25. How is Camden situated? (See same map.) 26. What movements did Rawdon and Cornwallis make before the 16th of August? 27. What did Gates do on the 15th and 16th?

VII. 28. Give an account of the battle of Sanders Creek. 29. When did it take place? 30. By what other names is it also known? 31. What officer of note did the Americans lose?

1780, is known as the battle of Sanders Creek. It is also known as the first battle of Camden, or, it is quite as often simply designated as the battle of Camden.

VIII. Sumter was successful in capturing the train of supplies; but the defeat of Gates not only left him without any co-operation from that quarter, but let loose the enemy against him. He was pursued by Tarleton, and at Fishing Creek, a tributary of the Wateree, was surprised and routed with great slaughter.

IX. Believing South Carolina to be at last subdued, Cornwallis proceeded to overrun North Carolina. His first measure was to detach Major Ferguson to overawe the inhabitants favoring the patriot cause, and embody the loyalists under the royal banner. A large number of Tories and disreputable persons flocked to Ferguson's standard, and, as a consequence, his progress was attended by many disgraceful excesses.

X. These acts of violence so exasperated the inhabitants, that, on the 7th of October, a hastily-formed force, consisting of bodies of mountaineers and backwoodsmen, under the general command of Colonel William Campbell, of Virginia, attacked the enemy at King's Mountain,* in South Carolina. Ferguson and one hundred and fifty of his men were killed, and the remainder, to the number of more than eight hundred,

---

* King's Mountain is the name of a village in North Carolina. Near it, but in South Carolina, is the eminence of the same name, which was the scene of the battle. The conflict took place about a mile and a half south of the boundary-line between the two States.

VIII QUESTIONS.—32. What is said of Sumter's success and subsequent defeat? 33. By what name is the Wateree River known in North Carolina? *Ans.*—The Catawba. 34. At what place was Sumter surprised and routed by Tarleton? 35. Into what stream does Fishing Creek flow? 36. Into what stream does the Wateree flow? (See map, p. 164.)

IX. 37. Under what delusion did Cornwallis proceed to overrun North Carolina? 38. What was his first measure? 39. What is said of the persons who flocked to Ferguson's standard? 40. What was the consequence?

X. 41. When was the battle of King's Mountain fought? 42. Was the battle fought in North or South Carolina? 43. In what direction is King's Mountain from the Cowpens? (See map, p 164.) 44. Of whom did the American force at King's Mountain consist? 45. Give an account of the battle. 46. What officer did the Americans lose? 47. How did the result of the battle affect Cornwallis?

1780. surrendered. Though the Americans had only twenty men killed, the loss of Colonel Williams, a brave and efficient officer, who was among the slain, was very much felt. The blow was a severe one to Cornwallis, and compelled him to make a retrograde march into South Carolina.

GENERAL MARION.

XI. Marion* ($mā'$-re-un), by his stratagems and expedients, continued to frustrate the purposes of British detachments, and Sumter, appearing again in the field after his rout at Fishing Creek, was victorious in two engagements— one at Fishdam Ford, with Major Wemyss ($wĕmz$), and the other at Blackstocks, with Tarleton.

XII. At the north, in the mean time, events of great importance were taking place. Sir Henry Clinton, having heard that a mutinous spirit was breaking out in Washington's army, deemed the occasion propitious for an expedition. Accordingly, a force of five thousand men, under Knyphausen, advanced into New Jersey, took possession of Elizabeth, and burned "Connecticut Farms," a village now called Union. In a second advance, also led by Knyphausen, the British were met at Springfield, on the 23d of June, and repulsed.

---

* Francis Marion was born in South Carolina, in 1732. The amount of service which he rendered the patriot cause during the Revolution can hardly be estimated. He was sometimes at the head of an independent force, surprising relief and supply parties of the British, and often rescuing captive Americans; and then he and Sumter would be engaged in some daring enterprise, or he would aid Greene. All attempts of the enemy to overreach or baffle him were entirely futile. He was an honest man and a pure patriot. His death occurred in 1795.

XI. QUESTIONS.—48. What is said of Marion's successes? 49. Of Sumter's? 50. Where is Fishdam Ford? (See map, p. 164.) 51. Where is Blackstocks? (See map, p. 164.)

XII. 52. What prompted Clinton to send an expedition into New Jersey? 53. What expedition did he send? 54. What did Knyphausen accomplish in his first advance? 55. How is the village of Union situated? (See map, p. 68.) 56. How is the city of Elizabeth situated? (See map, p. 136.) 57. What was the city of Elizabeth formerly called? Ans.—Elizabethtown. 58. When did a battle take place at Springfield? 59. What was the result? 60. How is Springfield situated? (See map, p. 136.)

TREASON OF ARNOLD.

XIII. The year 1780 is particularly memorable for the treason of
Arnold. In 1778, directly after
the British had evacuated Philadelphia, Washington appointed
Arnold to the command of that
city, as the state of his wound, received at Stillwater, would not per-
mit him to resume active duty.
At Philadelphia he lived at an expense far beyond his income, and,
to meet the demands of his credi-
tors, appropriated public funds to
his own use. Charges were preferred against him, and, though

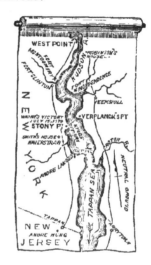

acquitted by a court-martial of actual criminal intent, he was
adjudged to be reprimanded by Washington.

XIV. The decision of the court was received by Arnold
with an ill grace, and with evident emotions of resentment;
and though Washington administered the sentence with great
delicacy and consideration, Arnold felt the disgrace, and determined to effect a plan by which he might wreak his ven-
geance, and, at the same time, repair his fortune.

XV. He had already made secret advances to the enemy,

XIII. Questions.—61. For what is the year 1780 particularly memorable? 62.
When was Arnold appointed to a command at Philadelphia? 63. Why was he not
given a command requiring greater activity? 64. What is said of Arnold's style of
living at Philadelphia? 65. What misappropriation of funds did he make? 66.
What followed?

XIV. 67. How did Arnold receive the decision of the court? 68. How did Washington perform his unpleasant task? 69. Upon what did Arnold determine?

XV. 70. Of what had Arnold already been guilty? 71. What command did he
solicit? 72. What correspondence was he at that time engaged in? 73. What is
said of the importance of West Point? 74. Where is it situated? (See map, p. 169.)
75. How did Arnold's request strike Washington? 76. Why then did he grant the
request?

8

under a feigned name; and while actually engaged in a treasonable correspondence with Sir Henry Clinton, he solicited the command of West Point, then the strongest and most important fortress in the United States. Washington expressed surprise that an officer so remarkable for energy and activity should seek a post where there was comparatively so little to be done; but, having confidence in Arnold's patriotism, he granted the request.

ARNOLD'S HEAD-QUARTERS, OPPOSITE WEST POINT.

XVI. The treasonable correspondence had now been carried on eighteen months. The plot was ripe. Arnold was in the command of an important fortress which he proposed to betray into the hands of the British; and Major André, aide-de-camp to Clinton, was sent to complete the plan of treason and adjust the traitor's recompense. André left New York,

XVI. QUESTIONS.—77. How long had Arnold carried on his correspondence with Clinton before the treasonable plot was ripe? 78. On what mission was André sent? 79. Who was André? 80. How did André reach Arnold?

proceeded up the Hudson, and, at a place about six miles below West Point, met Arnold and completed the bargain.

XVII. Instead of returning by water, as had been previously arranged, circumstances compelled André to cross to the east side of the Hudson, and proceed towards New York by land. When near Tarrytown, he was stopped by three militiamen—John Paulding, David Williams, and Isaac Van Wart—and searched. In his boots were found a number of papers in Arnold's own hand-writing; and he was therefore pronounced a spy. In vain he remonstrated, and attempted to bribe his captors; they conducted him to North Castle, the nearest military station of the Americans.

XVIII. Colonel Jameson, the commander at North Castle, in stead of initiating measures for the capture of Arnold, stupidly dispatched a letter to that officer, informing him of the circumstances of the arrest. The traitor, startled and alarmed upon reading the letter, immediately escaped on board the British sloop-of-war Vulture, the vessel which had been intended for André's return, and took refuge in New York.

BENEDICT ARNOLD.

XIX. André was conveyed to Tappan, a village on the west side of the Hudson, opposite Tarrytown, and there tried by a court-martial, found guilty, and, agreeably to the law

XVII. QUESTIONS.—81. What change was made in André's traveling arrangements? 82. What was the consequence? 83. Where is Tarrytown? (See map, p. 169.) 84. Give the names of the three persons who arrested him. 85. What was the result of the search? 86. Did André endeavor to effect his release, or not? 87. By what means? 88. What did his captors do with him? 89. Where is North Castle? (See map, p. 47.)

XVIII. 90. Who commanded the Americans at North Castle? 91. What folly did he perpetrate? 92. What was the consequence?

XIX. 93. Whither was André taken? 94. How is Tappan situated? 95. Where was he executed? (See map, p. 169.) 96. How was Arnold rewarded for his treachery?

1780. and usages of nations, executed as a spy. Arnold*
was made a brigadier-general in the British service,
and received six thousand three hundred pounds sterling as
an additional reward for his treachery.

---

* Benedict Arnold was born at Norwich, Connecticut, in 1740. After the Revolution he was engaged in business for a time at St John's, New Brunswick. He went to England, and at London, where he died in 1801, he lived in obscurity, everybody avoiding him with disgust.

REVIEW QUESTIONS.

EVENTS OF 1781.

I. The Pennsylvania line of troops, to the number of thirteen hundred, having experienced much suffering through want of pay, clothing, and provisions, left their camp at Morristown, with the intention of marching to Philadelphia and demanding redress from Congress. At Princeton they were overtaken by two emissaries whom Clinton had sent, for the purpose of inducing them by bribes to enter the service of the king.

II. Though smarting under the neglect to which they had been subjected, the troops were not to be bribed. Regarding Clinton's attempt as a reflection upon their fidelity to the cause of freedom, they seized the emissaries and conducted them to General Wayne, to be treated as spies. While at Princeton a committee of Congress met the disaffected soldiers, and, after making concessions and granting relief, settled the difficulty. The two emissaries were tried by court martial, found guilty, and executed as spies.

III. The plan of concession by which the troubles with the Pennsylvania troops were settled, had a pernicious effect; for the example of the Pennsylvanians was soon followed by a part of the Jersey troops, who claimed like treatment; but Washington, by vigorous measures, not only quelled this second mutiny, but repressed all similar manifestations among other portions of the army.

IV. However much these two demonstrations were regretted at the time, they produced a quickening and salutary effect upon Congress. Direct taxes were resorted to, an agent was sent to Europe for aid, the Bank of North America was chartered, and other efficient measures were adopted for the support

Events of 1781.—I. Questions.—1. What is said of the mutiny of the Pennsylvania troops? 2 Where and by whom were they overtaken?

II. 3. What did the troops do with the emissaries? 4 What was finally done with them? 5. How was the difficulty with the troops settled?

III. 6. What is said of the method by which the difficulty with the Pennsylvania troops was settled? 7. How was that soon shown? 8 How were the Jersey troops dealt with? 9 What was the effect?

of the army and the maintenance of the government. Through the exertions of Robert Morris,* as superintendent of the national treasury, and by the help of the bank, was Congress mainly enabled to prosecute the war.

ROBERT MORRIS.

V. Early in 1781, two months after he had joined the British, Arnold was appointed to the command of an expedition against Virginia. With about twelve hundred men, he sailed up the James River to Richmond, plundered and destroyed public and private property there, and all his movements, in every direction, were marked by ravages and distress.

VI. Descending the river, he took post at Portsmouth. An opportunity for his defeat and capture seeming full of promise, Washington arranged a plan by which troops under Lafayette,† co-operating with a French fleet from Rhode Island, were to make the attempt. But the effort failed in consequence of the British fleet, under Arbuthnot, overtaking that of the French off the capes of Virginia, and, after an engagement of about an hour, compelling it to return.

VII. Gates's defeat at Sanders Creek caused his removal from the command of the Southern troops, and the appointment of Greene in his place. Establishing a camp on the

---

* Robert Morris was born in Lancashire, England, in 1734. He came to America when thirteen years old, and was educated at Philadelphia. He was one of the signers of the Declaration of Independence. After the Revolution, he lost, by land speculations, an immense fortune which he had gained in the China trade, and he died at Philadelphia, in 1806, in comparative poverty.

† The Marquis de Lafayette was born in France, of an ancient and distinguished family, in 1757. He was in the battles of Brandywine, Monmouth, and Yorktown, and was a member of the court that tried André as a spy. He died in Paris, in 1834.

IV. QUESTIONS.—10. What is said of the effect which the two uprisings of the troops had upon the Congress? 11. What measures did Congress adopt? 12. What is said of Robert Morris's exertions?

V. 13. When did Arnold commence operations in behalf of those to whom he had deserted? 14. What is said of his expedition? 15. Describe the James River. (See map, p. 85.)

VI. 16. How is Portsmouth situated? (See map, p. 44.) 17. What plan of capture did Washington arrange? 18. Why did it fail?

1781. Great Pedee, the first care of the new commander was to reorganize the army, after which, separating it into

LAFAYETTE.

two divisions, he sent one, under Morgan, to check the devastations of the British in the western part of South Carolina; the other, he retained under his own immediate command.

VIII. Cornwallis no sooner heard of the movement of Morgan, than he dispatched Tarleton to disperse his force or drive it out of the State. Morgan, on receiving intelligence of the approach of the British, was at first inclined to make a stand where he was encamped, but, being informed of the superiority of their numbers, he retreated and took a position near the Cowpens. Here Tarleton found him, on the morning of the 17th of January.

IX. Upon the signal being given, the British rushed forward with a shout, and a conflict ensued, in which, though Tarleton was confident of success, up to almost the very close of the battle, the Americans were completely victorious, inflicting a loss, in killed, wounded, and prisoners, of more than eight hundred men, while their own did not exceed seventy. The battle of the Cowpens was one of the most decisive of the Revolution. The patriots fought, actuated by a desire to revenge the wrongs and outrages which the Tories and English had committed upon them, their neighbors, and their homes,

---

VII. Questions.—19. What change in commanders did Gates's defeat at the South cause? 20. Where did Greene establish a camp? 21. Into what river does that flow? (See map, p. 164.) 22. How did he divide his army, and what did he do with one of the divisions?

VIII. 23. What expedition was dispatched by Cornwallis? 24. What movement did Morgan make? 25. Where is the Cowpens? (See map, p. 164.) 26. When did the battle of the Cowpens take place?

IX. 27. Give an account of the battle. 28. What is said of the decisiveness of the battle? 29. What is said of the desire which actuated the patriots?

and the result was a blow which perceptibly paralyzed the power of the royalists in the South.

X. Morgan* did not linger on the battle-field. Believing that Cornwallis would advance upon him with an overwhelming force as soon as he should hear of Tarleton's defeat, the victor set out in a northeasterly direction, his object being to get across the Catawba before the enemy, then only twenty-five miles distant, could intercept him. Nor was he mistaken with regard to the movement of Cornwallis. That commander soon received the inglorious tidings from the Cowpens, and, starting off in pursuit of Morgan, reached the Catawba at evening, on the 29th, just two hours after the Americans had forded the river. He halted, intending to cross in the morning, but during the night a heavy rain set in, and by daybreak the stream was so swollen as to be impassable.

GENERAL MORGAN.

XI. Greene, who had received intelligence of the victory and pursuit, hurried forward with only a guard of dragoons, and, reaching the east side of the Catawba, took command of Morgan's division, and continued the retreat. After some delay and opposition, Cornwallis effected a crossing, and reached the Yadkin only in time to capture a few wagons which had lingered in the rear of the retreating army. Another fall of rain, which had occurred during the day, overflowed the ford

* Daniel Morgan was born in New Jersey, in 1736. He was with Braddock in the expedition of 1755, performing the humble duties of teamster. At the breaking out of the Revolution, he joined Washington at Cambridge, with a rifle corps. He accompanied Arnold across the wilderness to Quebec, and participated in the attempt to capture that city. In the battle of Bemis Heights he took a distinguished part. His death occurred in 1802, at Winchester, Virginia.

X. QUESTIONS.—30. Why did Morgan hurry away after his victory? 31. What movement did Cornwallis make? 32. How were the Americans aided, as if providentially?

XI. 33. Who now assumed command of the American army? 34. Give an account of the pursuit as far as the Yadkin. 35. Describe the Yadkin. (See map, p. 164.) 36. How were the Americans aided the second time?

1781.

Cornwallis had expected to use, and he was therefore compelled to find a crossing higher up.

XII. By stratagems and manœuvers, Greene succeeded in reaching the Dan River, and effected a crossing just as the astonished enemy appeared on the opposite bank. Grieved and vexed, Cornwallis abandoned the pursuit, and marched southward to Hillsboro (*hilz'-bur-reh*).

GENERAL GREENE.

XIII. Greene * recrossed the Dan, and, with his force increased to over four thousand men, felt himself to be in sufficient strength to confront Cornwallis with boldness. But at Guilford (*ghil'-furd*) Court House, in North Carolina, he was attacked on the 15th of March, and, after one of the severest actions of the war, was forced to retreat.

His loss, in killed and wounded, amounted to four hundred men, in addition to which, many of the militia deserted.

The result, though a victory to the British, cost them, in killed, wounded, and missing, more than five hundred men, and so disabled Cornwallis as to compel him to retreat from the field of victory.

XIV. Undismayed by his reverse, Greene determined to follow the victor, and again give battle. The pursuit was

---

* Nathaniel Greene was born of Quaker parents, at Warwick, Rhode Island, in 1742. He aided, at the beginning of the Revolution, in driving the British from Boston, and he took a distinguished part in the battles of Trenton, Princeton, Brandywine, Germantown, and Quaker Hill; and commanded in the battles of Guilford Court House, Hobkirk's Hill, and Eutaw Springs. He died of "sun-stroke," in Georgia, near Savannah, in 1786.

XII. QUESTIONS.—37. Give an account of the retreat and pursuit after leaving the Yadkin. 38. Describe the Dan River. (See map, p. 164.) 39. To what place did Cornwallis then march? 40. Where is Hillsboro? (See map, p. 164.)

XIII. 41. What bold movement did Greene make? 42. At what place did Cornwallis attack Greene? 43. When was the attack made? 44. How is Guilford Court House situated? (See map, p. 164.) 45. Give an account of the battle.

XIV. 46. What singular pursuit followed? 47. At what place did Greene almost succeed in overtaking Cornwallis? 48. Describe the Deep River. (See map, p. 164.) 49. Where is Wilmington? (See map, p. 164.)

eagerly kept up for several days, and the retreating enemy was almost overtaken at the Deep River; but there, in consequence of the bridge being broken down, and also because of the fatigue of his men, Greene had to give up the chase. Cornwallis did not halt until he reached Wilmington.

XV. Discharging a large number of the militia whose term of service had expired, Greene, with his reduced army, formed the bold resolve of entering South Carolina, and attacking the enemy at Camden. Lord Rawdon, who commanded the post at that place, wrote to Cornwallis, informing him of the threatening danger; but, believing that he would not be able to reach Camden in time to aid in its defense, Cornwallis took advantage of Greene's absence from North Carolina, and marched through that State into Virginia, where his army was strengthened by large additions.

XVI. Greene appeared before Camden, but, finding the enemy there stronger, in position and numbers, than he had anticipated, withdrew to Hobkirk's Hill, about two miles distant. Here he was partly surprised by Rawdon, on the 25th of April, but succeeded in forming his troops and repelling the first advance against him. Victory, for a time, hung in the balance: more than once, the British drove the Americans before them, but were compelled to recede before the impetuous charges of the patriots. At length, a regiment of the Americans was charged so furiously that it broke and fell into disorder. The enemy followed up this success vigorously, until the disheartened Americans retreated in one mass.

XVII. Each party lost about two hundred and fifty men,

XV. QUESTIONS.—50. What movement into South Carolina did Greene then make? 51. Why was his resolve a bold one? 52. Of what did Rawdon inform Cornwallis? 53. Why did not Cornwallis go to the rescue of Rawdon? 54. What did Cornwallis do instead?

XVI. 55. Why did not Greene attack Rawdon at Camden? 56. To what place did Greene withdraw? 57. What occurred there? 58. When did it occur? 59. Give an account of the battle.

XVII. 60. What loss did each party sustain in the battle? 61. Why did not the British follow up their advantage? 62. Whither did Rawdon go, directly after the battle? 63. In what situation did he find himself there? 64. What was he then compelled to do?

1781.   but, as at the battle of Guilford Court House, the British, though victorious, were too much cut up to allow them to pursue the advantage which they had gained. They re-entered Camden, but finding their supplies cut off by the Americans, and realizing that by the northward march of Cornwallis no aid could be expected, they adopted the only alternative, that of evacuation, and Camden was left in flames.

XVIII. A number of successes, in rapid succession, now attended the American arms at the South. In pursuance of Greene's plan of operations, Colonel Henry Lee was detached with a small body of troops, known as "Lee's Legion," and, in consort with Marion, Sumter,* Pickens, and other partisan chiefs, carried on a harassing warfare against the enemy's scattered posts. Forts Watson, Motte, and Granby, fell into the hands of the Americans, and Augusta, Georgia, also surrendered after a siege of about two weeks.

XIX. Only three posts in South Carolina—Ninety-Six, Eutaw Springs, and Charleston—remained in the hands of the British. Greene proceeded against Ninety-Six,† but after besieging it for almost a month, and making an unsuccessful assault, the approach of Rawdon compelled him to raise the siege, and he retreated before the arrival of the enemy. A foray which he subsequently planned, against the British troops in the vicinity of Charleston, was partially successful.

XX. As the fortunes of the British were beginning to de-

---

* Thomas Sumter was born in South Carolina, about 1734. During the Revolution he took an active and able part as one of the partisan leaders at the South. The qualities of bravery, determination, and cheerfulness, which he exhibited, endeared him to his followers, who bestowed upon him the sobriquet of the "Carolina Game-Cock." Fort Sumter, in Charleston Harbor, was so named in honor of him. His death occurred in South Carolina, in 1832.

† The post of Ninety-Six was so called because it was ninety-six miles from Prince George, a frontier fort in the northwestern part of South Carolina.

XVIII. QUESTIONS.—65. How did the American arms then fare? 66. What is said of Colonel Lee and others? 67. Name four of the places that fell into the hands of the Americans. 68. Give the situation of the four places. (See map, p. 164.)

XIX. 69. How many posts were then left to the British? 70. Give the situation of the three places. (See map, p. 164.) 71. Give an account of Greene's attempt against Ninety-Six. 72. What is said of a foray?

XX. 73. What call did Rawdon make upon the people? 74. How came he to make such a call? 75. Who was Colonel Isaac Hayne?

cline, even Charleston itself being threatened, Rawdon called upon all persons who had given in their adhesion to the royal cause, to repair at once to his standard. Among the persons so called was Colonel Isaac Hayne, a distinguished patriot of South Carolina, who had been assured, when he took the oath of adherence, that he would never be required to take up arms against his countrymen.

XXI. Believing this call to be in violation of the agreement, and being thus compelled to assume the sword either for or against the patriots, he did not hesitate to choose the former. At the head of a troop of horse he gained some advantages, but, being surprised and captured, was taken to Charleston. After a brief examination, without any trial whatever, he was sentenced to be hung; and, although the citizens united in petitioning for his pardon, the sentence was duly executed on the 4th of August.

XXII. Towards the latter part of August, Greene, who had been for several weeks on the "high hills of Santee," broke up his encampment to march against Stuart, who was then not twenty miles off. As he advanced, Stuart retreated to Eutaw Springs. Here, on the 8th of September, Greene, with a force not exceeding two thousand men, attacked the enemy, twenty-three hundred strong.

XXIII. The contest was desperate, and, at one time, victory seemed certain for the Americans; but the British rallying, Greene drew off his troops, taking with him about five hundred prisoners. The enemy decamped during the night. In this battle, which may be said to have ended the contest in South Carolina, both parties claimed the victory. Washing

XXI. QUESTIONS.—76. What belief did Hayne hold respecting Rawdon's call? 77 What course did he consequently adopt? 78. What further account can you give of him?

XXII. 79. What movement did Greene make in August? 80. Where was a battle fought in the next month? 81 Near what river did the battle take place? (See map, p. 164.) 82. How did the battle commence?

XXIII 83. Give a further account of the battle 84. What may be said of the battle as regards the contest South? 85. How did Washington consider the result?

1781   ton considered it a victory for the Americans, as the advantage certainly was with them.

XXIV. Cornwallis's operations in Virginia, during the summer of 1781, were very distressing to the patriots, property to the value of several millions having been destroyed thereby. Lafayette had endeavored to check these operations, but owing to the inferiority of his force, was not able to make a stand against Cornwallis.

XXV. Clinton, believing New York to be menaced by a combined force of French and Americans, directed Cornwallis to take a position near the sea, from which he might readily send re-enforcements to the city, when called upon. The order was obeyed. Cornwallis took post at Yorktown, on the south side of York River, Virginia, opposite a promontory called Gloucester (*glos'-ter*).

XXVI. The expected arrival of a French fleet, under Count de Grasse (*dŭ grass*), in Chesapeake Bay, induced Washington to abandon the design which he had meditated against New York and proceed against Cornwallis, but, while doing so, to continue preparations as if against New York. The consequence was, that before Clinton became aware of the real intentions of the American commander, a body of French troops from Rhode Island and Washington's army were well on their way to Virginia.

XXVII. Clinton, finding it too late to adopt any direct measures against the great southward movement wherein the

XXIV QUESTIONS.—86. What is said of Cornwallis's operations during the summer of 1781? 87. What had Lafayette endeavored to do?

XXV 88. What direction was sent to Cornwallis? 89. Why was he so directed? 90. How did Cornwallis obey? 91. How is Yorktown situated? 92. In what direction is Yorktown from Hampton? (See map, p. 237.)

XXVI. 93. Why did Washington abandon his design against New York? 94. What new project did he then determine upon? 95. In what way did he undertake to deceive the enemy? 96. Before Clinton became aware of his intentions, how far had his project progressed?

XXVII. 97. What expedition did Clinton hurry off? 98. What was his object in sending the expedition? 99. When did Arnold reach the harbor of New London? 100. How is New London situated? 101. How was it defended? 102. Into what body of water does the Thames flow? (See map, p. 183.)

French and Americans were combined, undertook to recall Washington by hurrying off an expedition of devastation to the eastward, under the command of Arnold. At daybreak, on the morning of the 6th of September, Arnold appeared off the harbor of New London, with a large fleet, carrying a strong land and marine force. New London is situated on the west bank of the Thames River, three miles from its mouth; and the approach to it was defended by Fort Trumbull, on the west side of the river, and Fort Griswold on the east.

NEW LONDON AND VICINITY.

XXVIII. The invaders were landed in two divisions; one, under Colonel Eyre (*ire*), on the east side, and the other, commanded by Arnold himself, on the west or New London side. Arnold advanced, meeting with but little resistance in taking Fort Trumbull, or in making himself master of the town. The militia which manned the fort, finding it untenable, abandoned their post and went to the aid of Fort Griswold, on the opposite side of the river

XXIX. Meanwhile, Eyre proceeded against Fort Griswold, which had been hastily garrisoned by about a hundred and fifty militia, under the brave Colonel Ledyard. After a desperate contest, in which the assailants were repeatedly repulsed, losing their commander and many men, the fort was at last carried. Irritated by the opposition which they had met, the victors set upon the garrison without mercy, killing and maiming more in the massacre that followed than in the previous contest. Colonel Ledyard was among the first slaughtered. Major Bromfield, a malevolent Tory, who

XXVIII. Questions.—103. In what way did the invaders proceed? 104. What success did Arnold meet with? 105. Whither did the garrison of Fort Trumbull go?

XXIX. 106. By whom was Fort Griswold garrisoned? 107. By whom commanded? 108. What is said of the contest and loss of men before the fort was carried? 109. What is said of the massacre that took place afterward? 110. Relate the case of Colonel Ledyard.

1781. had succeeded to the command, seized the sword which Ledyard was in the act of yielding up, and plunged it through the body of the brave man, killing him upon the spot.

XXX. Arnold, in the mean time, had not been idle. He burnt a number of vessels—all that had not effected their escape up the river—applied the torch to New London, and, while the town was in flames, retreated to his boats.

VIEW OF NEW LONDON.

XXXI. Arnold's expedition against Connecticut, though successful in itself, failed of its main object—the recall of Washington from the South; and consequently Cornwallis's position there was becoming every day more critical. Yorktown was besieged. The troops investing it were from the fleet of De Grasse, in addition to other French troops from Rhode Island, under Count de Rochambeau (*rō-sham-bo'*), and Washington was there as commander-in-chief of the combined

XXX. QUESTIONS.—111. What had Arnold accomplished in the mean time? 112. In what direction from New Haven is New London? (See map, p. 47.)

XXXI. 113. What is said of the success of Arnold's expedition? 114. What was the consequence to Cornwallis? 115. Of what troops were the besiegers composed? 116. What service did De Grasse render?

army, with a large American force. De Grasse blockaded the York and James Rivers and guarded the entrance to Chesapeake Bay.

XXXII. A British fleet, under Admiral Graves, which had been sent from New York for the relief of the besieged, appeared off the capes of Virginia, when De Grasse sallied forth, and a partial action took place. After remaining in sight of the French fleet during five days, Graves, despairing of success, bore away for New York.

LORD CORNWALLIS.

XXXIII. On the 9th of October, the allied armies besieging Yorktown commenced a cannonade so heavy that, in a day or two, most of the British works were demolished, and several vessels in the harbor were burned. In this desperate extremity Cornwallis determined to escape, if possible, by crossing to Gloucester, cutting his way through a French detachment stationed there, and, by rapid marches, to reach New York. But his plan was frustrated. A violent storm dispersed his boats after one division of his army had crossed the river, and the attempt was necessarily abandoned.

XXXIV. His position becoming untenable, and seeing no prospect of relief from Clinton, on the 19th of October, 1781, Cornwallis* surrendered Yorktown and Gloucester, with more than seven thousand British soldiers, to Washington ; his shipping and seamen he surrendered to De Grasse.

---

* Lord Cornwallis was born in 1738. After the Revolution he was appointed to an important command in India, where he inaugurated a series of victories by which the British authority there was finally established. He died in India, in 1805.

XXXII. Questions.—117. What naval movement took place? 118. What did Graves afterwards do?

XXXIII. 119. What is said of the besiegers' cannonade? 120. What attempt at escape did Cornwallis make? 121. What prevented the success of the attempt?

XXXIV. 122. State the circumstances of Cornwallis's surrender.

CLOSE OF THE REVOLUTION, AND EVENTS TO THE BEGINNING OF WASHINGTON'S ADMINISTRATION.

I. The surrender of Cornwallis caused great rejoicings throughout the United States, being considered a death-blow to the war. The effect in England was as might have been anticipated. Public opinion became so decidedly opposed to the further prosecution of hostilities, that, upon the formation of a new ministry, negotiations were entered into for the establishment of peace.

II. A convention of commissioners from the two countries met at Paris, four of whom, John Adams, Benjamin Franklin, John Jay, and Henry Laurens, represented the United States, and, on the 30th of November, 1782, they signed a preliminary treaty. A cessation of hostilities was proclaimed in the American army on the 19th of April, 1783, the eighth anniversary of the battle of Lexington; and, on the 3d of September following, a definitive treaty of peace was signed at Paris.

III. By the terms of the treaty, Great Britain acknowledged the independence of the United States, allowed boundaries extending to the great lakes on the north and the Mississippi on the west, and conceded an unlimited right to fish on the banks of Newfoundland. Florida was, at the same time, returned to Spain.

IV. The close of the war found the national treasury empty : the States were unable to respond to the call of Congress for money, and the resource of foreign loans was about exhausted.

CLOSE OF THE REVOLUTION.—I Questions—1 What effect did Cornwallis's surrender have in America and England?

II 2 Where did peace commissioners from the two countries meet? 3. Who were the American commissioners? 4 When was a preliminary treaty signed? 5 What took place on the eighth anniversary of the battle of Lexington? 6. When was a definitive treaty signed?

III. 7 What did the United States secure by the terms of the treaty?

IV. 8. What was the condition of things at the close of the war? 9 What was the consequence? 10 Where was the influence of Washington felt? 11 What arrangements were soon made?

The government was unable to meet the just claims made upon it, and the consequence was general discontent, particularly among the officers and privates of the army. Through the influence of Washington the discontents in the army were soothed, and arrangements were soon after made by which Congress granted five years' whole pay to the officers, instead of, as by resolution passed in 1780, half-pay for life. Four months' whole pay was granted to the soldiers, in part payment of their claims.

V. In conformity with general orders of Congress, the army was disbanded on the 3d of November, 1783; and on the 25th of the same month, Sir Guy Carleton, who had succeeded Sir Henry Clinton, evacuated New York. After the retirement of the British from the city, Washington met his officers there, and, " with a heart full of love and gratitude," took leave of them.

VI. Washington then repaired to Annapolis, where Congress was in session at the time, and, on the 23d of December, 1783, resigned to that body his commission as commander-in-chief of the American army. His simple and impressive address upon the occasion, and the touching response of General Mifflin,* the president of Congress,

GENERAL MIFFLIN.

* Thomas Mifflin was born in Philadelphia, in 1744. By birth and education he was a Quaker, but, notwithstanding the peace principles of that sect, he was one of the first to enlist in the military service at the breaking out of the Revolution. He was with Washington at Cambridge: in the battle of Long Island he fought with credit, and he was also in the battle of Trenton. His death occurred at Lancaster, Penn., in 1800.

V. QUESTIONS.—12. When was the American army disbanded? 13. When was New York evacuated by the British? 14. After the British left, what affecting scene occurred?

VI. 15. To what place did Washington then repair? 16. Where is Annapolis? (See map, p. 24.) 17. State what took place at Annapolis. 18. To what place did Washington then hasten? 19. How is Mount Vernon situated? (See map, p. 24.)

affected the assemblage to tears. He then hastened to his home at Mount Vernon, where, in the retirement of private life, he hoped to spend the remainder of his days.

MOUNT VERNON.*

VII. Peace was no sooner established than it was found that, by the ARTICLES OF CONFEDERATION, Congress had no power to discharge the debts incurred by the war; and this

---

* Mount Vernon, the home of Washington and the place of his burial, is situated on the western bank of the Potomac, fifteen miles from Washington city. The place, comprising the mansion, the tomb, and two hundred acres of the original estate, was sold, in 1858, by John A. Washington, a nephew of George Washington, to the "Ladies' Mount Vernon Association," for $200,000. "It is the design of the association hold it in perpetuity as a place of public resort and pilgrimage."

VII. QUESTIONS.—20. What difficulty was found in regard to the debts of the Revolution? 21. What was the consequence? 22. How did Congress undertake to raise funds?

condition of things was productive of embarrassments which for a while threatened to deprive the people of the fruits of their seven years' contest for independence. As there was no other alternative, the individual States were called upon for funds, and they, in response, resorted to direct taxation.

VIII. The efforts thus made by the States were productive of great excitement, especially in Massachusetts, where the opposition grew to an open insurrection, known as SHAYS'S REBELLION. Daniel Shays, its leader, made some bold moves against the courts of the State, as well as against the military power; but the outbreak was suppressed, in 1787, with but little bloodshed, by a strong force sent against the insurgents.

IX. This daring attempt to destroy the government, though unsuccessful, filled its friends with gloomy apprehensions. Other causes increased the distrust, until at last it began to be generally felt that the Articles of Confederation were not at all adequate to the exigencies of the Union, and that measures should be taken either to revise them, or substitute others in their place.

X. Accordingly, a convention of delegates from all the States, except Rhode Island, met at Philadelphia, and their first act, by a unanimous vote, was to make George Washington their presiding officer. Instead of revising the Articles of Confederation, as was at first intended, they formed a constitution, after months of deliberation, and adopted it on the 17th of September, 1787. This, with some amendments made in after years, still exists as the Constitution of the United States.

XI. The Constitution was then submitted to the people for ratification, and after a thorough discussion, lasting in some

VIII. QUESTIONS.—23. Give an account of Shays's rebellion.

IX. 24. How did Shays's attempt affect the public mind? 25. What, at last, began to be generally felt?

X. 26 What, accordingly, took place? 27. What was the first act of the convention? 28. What did the convention accomplish?

of the States for two or more years, it was accepted by every one of the thirteen States. When it had been adopted by eleven (the requisite number was nine), it became valid, and went into operation on the 4th of March, 1789.

XI. Questions—29. To whom was the Constitution then submitted? 30 For what purpose? 31. Was the Constitution thoroughly discussed or not? 32. How long did the discussion last in some of the States? 33. How many States finally accepted it? 34. When did it go into operation? 35. How many States had adopted it up to that time? 36. Which of the States had not adopted it when it went into effect? *Ans.*—North Carolina and Rhode Island.

NAMES OF OFFICERS, MENTIONED IN THIS WORK, WHO PARTICIPATED, ON THE SIDE OF THE AMERICANS, IN THE REVOLUTIONARY WAR.

NAME.	DIED.	NAME.	DIED.
Gen. William Alexander (Lord Stirling)	1788	Major Leitch	1776
Col. Ethan Allen	1789	Gen. Solomon Lovell	—
Gen. Benedict Arnold	1801	Gen. Benjamin Lincoln	1810
Gen John Ashe	1781	Gen. Alex. McDougall	1786
Col. William Barton	1831	Gen Francis Marion	1795
Col. Zebulon Butler	1795	Gen. Hugh Mercer	1777
Gen. John Cadwallader	1786	Gen. Thomas Mifflin	1799
Col. William Campbell	1781	Gen. Richard Montgomery	1775
Gen. George Clinton	1812	Gen. Daniel Morgan	1802
Gen. James Clinton	1812	Col. William Moultrie	1805
Gen. Thomas Conway		Capt. Jonas Parker	1775
Baron De Kalb	1780	Col. Andrew Pickens	1817
Count D'Estaing	1794	Col. William Prescott	1795
Gen. Peter Gansevoort	1812	Gen. Casimir Pulaski	1779
Gen Horatio Gates	1806	Gen. Israel Putnam	1790
Count de Grasse	1788	Gen Joseph Reed	1785
Col. Christopher Greene	1781	Count de Rochambeau	1807
Gen. Nathaniel Greene	1786	Gen Arthur St. Clair	1818
Capt. Nathan Hale	1776	Gen. Philip Schuyler	1804
Col. Alexander Hamilton	1804	Gen G. G. Silliman	—
Col. Isaac Hayne	1781	Col. Samuel Smith	1889
Gen. William Herkimer	1777	Gen. John Stark	1822
Gen. Robert Howe	1785	Gen. John Sullivan	1785
Gen. Isaac Huger	1855	Gen. Thomas Sumter	1832
Capt. John Paul Jones	1792	Gen. John Thomas	1776
Col Thomas Knowlton	1776	Col. Seth Warner	1785
Gen. Henry Knox	1806	Gen. Artemas Ward	1800
Col Thaddeus Kosciusko	1817	Gen. Joseph Warren	1775
Gen. Lafayette	1834	Gen. George Washington	1799
Col. William Ledyard	1781	Gen. Anthony Wayne	1796
Gen. Charles Lee	1782	Col Marinus Willett	1830
Col. Henry Lee	1818	Col James Williams	1780
		Gen. David Wooster	1777

PRINCIPAL BATTLES OF THE REVOLUTION.

The asterisk indicates the successful party. † Doubtful.

DATES.	BATTLES.	COMMANDERS.		MEN ENGAGED.	
		American.	British.	Am'rican	British.
1775.					
April 19,	Lexington	Parker	Smith*	unknwn	1,700
June 17,	Bunker Hill. ...	Prescott ...	Gen. Howe*.	1,500	8,000
Dec. 31,	Quebec.	Montgomery	Carleton*	900	1,200
1776.					
June 28,	Fort Moultrie ...	Moultrie* ...	Parker	400	4,000
Aug 27,	Long Island ...	Putnam ...	Gen. Howe*..	10,000	20,000
Oct. 28,	White Plains ...	McDougall	Leslie*......	1,600	2,000
Nov. 16,	Fort Washington ..	Magaw ...	Gen. Howe* .	3,000	5,000
Dec. 26,	Trenton	Washington*.	Rahl	2,400	1,000
1777.					
Jan. 3,	Princeton	Washington*..	Mawhood ...	3,000	1,800
July 7,	Hubbardton.. ..	Warner .	Fraser*	700	1,200
Aug. 6, {	Oriskany†	Herkimer	St. Leger... }	1,000	1,500
	F. Schuyler, sortie	Willett*. .	J. Johnson. }		
Aug 16, {	Bennington (1st).	Stark* ...	Baum. }	2,000	1,200
	(Second battle)	Warner*	Breyman }		
Sept. 11,	Brandywine	Washington	Gen. Howe*	11,000	18,000
Sep. 19,	Bemis Heights....	Gates*	Burgoyne ..	2,500	3,000
Sept. 20,	Paoli...	Wayne	Grey*	1,500	3,000
Oct. 4,	Germantown ...	Washington ..	Gen. Howe*	11,000	15,000
Oct. 6, {	Fort Clinton.	Jas. Clinton }	Sir H. Clinton*	600	3,000
	Fort Montgomery.	Gov. Clinton }			
Oct. 7,	Saratoga, ...	Gates* .	Burgoyne.	8,000	4,500
Oct. 22, {	Fort Mercer...	Col. Greene*..	Donop	450	2,000
	Fort Mifflin	Col Smith* ..	Gen. Howe	400	Mixed.
Nov. 16,	Fort Mifflin	Major Thayer	Gen. Howe* ..	400	Mixed.
1778.					
June 28,	Monmouth	Washington*	Clinton......	12,000	11,000
July 3,	Wyoming .. .	Col Z Butler.	John Butler*	400	1,100
Aug 29,	Rhode Island.. ...	Sullivan* ...	Pigot ..	5,000	5,000
Dec 29,	Savannah	Robert Howe	Campbell*	900	2,000
1779.					
Jan. 9,	Sunbury	Lane	Prevost* ...	200	2,000
Feb. 14,	Kettle Creek ...	Pickens* ...	Boyd. ...	300	700
March 8,	Brier Creek	Ashe	Prevost*	1,200	1,800
June 20,	Stono Ferry ..	Lincoln ...	Maitland*	800	1,200
July 15,	Stony Point	Wayne* .	Johnson	1,200	600
Aug 18,	Penobscot	Lovell..	McLean*	900	8,000
July 19,	Paulus Hook	Major Lee* ...	Sutherland ..	350	250
Aug 29,	Chemung	Sullivan* .	Brant	4,000	1,500
Sept. 23,	Flamboro' Head ...	Paul Jones*	Pearson	squad'n	2 vessels
Oct. 9,	Savannah ...	Lincoln	Prevost*	4,500	2,900
1780.					
April 14,	Monk's Corner....	Huger	Tarleton*	300	600
May 12,	Charleston	Lincoln	Clinton*	3,700	9,000
May 29,	Waxhaw .	Buford ...	Tarleton* .. .	400	700
June 23,	Springfield	Greene*	Knyphausen	6,000	6,000
July 30,	Rocky Mount	Sumter	Turnbull*	600	500
Aug. 6,	Hanging Rock	Sumter*	Brown ...	600	500
Aug. 16,	Sanders Creek	Gates	Cornwallis*	3,000	2,200
Aug. 18,	Fishing Creek .	Sumter	Tarleton*	700	350
Oct. 7,	King's Mountain.	Campbell* ..	Ferguson.....	900	1,100
Nov. 12,	Fishdam Ford	Sumter*....	Weinyss	500	450
Nov 20,	Blackstocks	Sumter* .	Tarleton	500	400
1781.					
Jan. 17,	Cowpens	Morgan*	Tarleton	900	1,100
March 15,	Guilford C. H.	Greene	Cornwallis*	4,400	2,400
April 25,	Hobkirk's Hill ...	Greene	Rawdon*.	1,200	900
June 18,	Ninety-Six	Greene	Cruger*	1,000	550
Sept. 6,	Fort Griswold	Ledyard......	Eyre*	150	800
Sept. 8,	Eutaw Springs†	Greene	Stuart ...	2,000	2,800
Oct. 19,	Yorktown	Washington* .	Cornwallis...	16,000	7,500

(Questions to be answered from the above map.)

Where did the battle of Tippecanoe occur? Harmar's defeat? St. Clair's defeat?
Wayne's victory? How is Fort Mackinaw situated? In what direction is it from
Detroit? From Fort Wayne? From Greenville? How is Sandusky situated?
In what direction is it from Cairo? From Nashville?

REVIEW QUESTIONS

FROM THE BEGINNING OF WASHINGTON'S ADMINISTRATION, IN
1789, TO THE CLOSE OF JEFFERSON'S, IN 1809.

WASHINGTON'S ADMINISTRATION.

I. THE first election
for President of the
United States resulted
in the choice of George
Washington, he receiv-
ing the whole number of
electoral votes. At the
same time John Adams
of Massachusetts was
elected Vice-president.
New York was then
the capital of the Uni-
ted States, and in that
city Washington ap-
peared before the first
constitutional   Con-
gress, and was inaugu-
rated on the 30th of
April, 1789.

GEORGE WASHINGTON
Was born in Westmoreland Co., Va.
on the 22d of Feb., 1732. He was married to Mrs. Martha Custis, in Jan., 1759
He died at Mount Vernon, Va., on the
14th of Dec., 1799, leaving no children.

II. Congress having
created three executive
departments,—of state, treasury, and war,—the heads of which

WASHINGTON'S ADMINISTRATION.—I. QUESTIONS.—1. Who was the first President
of the United States? 2. Who was the first Vice-president? 3. When was Washington inaugurated? 4. Where did his inauguration take place? 5. What political relation did New York hold to the Union at that time?

were to constitute the President's cabinet, Washington appointed Thomas Jefferson, of Virginia, Secretary of State, Alexander Hamilton, of New York, Secretary of the Treasury,

and Henry Knox,* of Massachusetts, Secretary of War. The condition of the treasury was the first thing to be considered, and Hamilton, the secretary of that department, was directed to report a system of revenue. The task imposed upon him was difficult, but it was performed with ability; and, upon his recommendation, the public debts incurred during the war were assumed by the general government.

GENERAL KNOX.

III. In 1790, a law was passed, establishing the seat of government at Philadelphia for ten years, and afterward locating it somewhere on the Potomac; and, in the following year, the Bank of the United States was incorporated. For many years, both New York and New Hampshire† had laid claim to the territory of Vermont, called, originally, the *New Hampshire Grants.* New York having finally yielded her

---

* Henry Knox was born in Boston, in 1750. During the Revolution he commanded the artillery, and was in the battles of Trenton, Princeton, Brandywine, Germantown, Monmouth, and Yorktown. He was a member of the court-martial for the trial of André. His death occurred at Thomaston, Maine, in 1806.

† New Hampshire had laid claim to the territory, and between the years 1760 and 1768, her governor made grants of more than a hundred townships in it, whence it acquired the name of New Hampshire Grants. The claim of New York was based upon the grants made to the Duke of York by Charles II.

---

claim for $30,000, Vermont became the fourteenth State of the Union, in 1791. Kentucky, which had been previously claimed by Virginia, was admitted in the following year; and Tennessee, originally a part of North Carolina, was admitted in 1796.

IV. For a number of years after the Revolution, the British continued to hold certain forts on the northwestern frontier, contrary to the requirements of the treaty of 1783, by which they were called upon

VERMONT.

The principal range of mountains in this State, are the Green Mountains. Vermont was so called from this range, *verd* or *vert*, in French, signifying green, and *mont*, mountain. The State Seal is given above. The motto of Vermont is, *Liberty and Independence.*

to relinquish them to the Americans. This fact, as well as the imprudent language used by the officers of the forts, and by British traders in that region, led the Indians to believe that the people of America would be deprived of their national existence, and be again subjected to Great Britain.

V. This belief made them overbearing and hostile; and, in 1790, they commenced war upon the settlements. Washington at first used pacific means; but, these failing, an expedition, under General Harmar, was sent against the hostile tribes. Harmar destroyed several of their villages, and large crops of corn; and then dividing his army into two bodies, the better, as he thought, for pursuit, reckoned upon a speedy conquest. In this he was doomed to sad disappointment. He encountered

IV. QUESTIONS.—21. What treaty violations were the British guilty of? 22. What belief did the Indians contract regarding the American Government? 23. How was this belief caused? 24. When had a treaty been made by the English?

the savages at two dif-
ferent times, once, on
the 17th of October,
and again, on the 22d,
in the northeastern part
of Indiana, and was
both times defeated,
with severe loss.

VI. A second expedi-
tion was then sent, com-
manded by General St.
Clair; but he was not
more successful than
Harmar. While en-
camped in the western
part of Ohio, in 1791,
he was completely sur-
prised, and defeated
with the loss of about
six hundred men.

VII. A third expedi-

KENTUCKY.

"Conflicts between the white and red races (in Kentucky) were fre-quent: from this fact, it is said, and of its having been the scene of savage warfare for ages, the name Kentucky, meaning, in the aboriginal language, *the dark and bloody ground*, had its origin." The State Seal, with motto, is given above.

tion was then planned, and the command given to General Wayne, the "Mad Anthony" of the Revolution.
Wayne marched against the Indians, defeated them at the
battle of the Maumee, in 1794, and laid waste their coun-

V. QUESTIONS.—25. What did the belief of the Indians lead to? 26. How did Washington at first act towards the Indians? 27. What expedition did he then send? 28. What did Harmar accomplish? 29. Give the further account of the ex-pedition. 30. What town is situated near where Harmar's two battles were fought? *Ans.*—Fort Wayne. 31. How is Fort Wayne situated? *Ans.*—At the confluence of the St. Joseph's and St. Mary's Rivers. 32. What river do the St. Joseph's and St. Mary's form? (See map, p. 192.)

VI. 33. Give an account of the second expedition sent against the Indians. 34. Where did St. Clair's defeat take place? 35. What town is situated near the place? (See map, p. 192.)

VII. 36. What was then planned against the Indians? 37. Give an account of the expedition. 38. Into what body of water does the Maumee flow? (See map, p. 193.) 39. What was the consequence of Wayne's victory and vigorous measures? 40. What elections took place at the expiration of the first presidential term?

TENNESSEE.
"The name of Tennessee is derived
from Tannassee (said to signify a
curved spoon), the Indian name applied to the little Tennessee River." In
the upper part of the Seal of the State
(given above) are the numerical letters
XVI., indicating that Tennessee was the
sixteenth State admitted into the Union.

try. His success, and subsequent vigorous measures, so humbled the savages that, in 1795, they consented to a treaty, by which a large tract of country was ceded to the United States. This treaty was made at Fort Greenville, in the western part of Ohio, where the town of Greenville now stands. Washington, whose first term of office expired on the 4th of March, 1793, was unanimously re-elected: Adams was also rechosen to the vice-presidency.

VIII. The great revolution in France, which broke out during Washington's administration, was powerfully felt, in its principles and effects, in this country. When France declared war against England (the revolution there still being in pro-gress), and looked to us for aid, a large part of the people here, remembering the assistance which she had given us in our struggle for independence, would gladly have seen the United States engaged in the trans-atlantic struggle, siding with their former ally.

IX. M. Genet (*zhe-nā'*), minister to the United States from the French republic, presuming upon the favor with which his country was regarded here, began to fit out privateers in our ports, to cruise against the vessels of nations at war

VIII. QUESTIONS.—41. What is said of the effect of the French Revolution in this country? 42. How did a large part of the people here feel towards France?

with France. Persisting in this course, in opposition to the remonstrance of the President, he was recalled by request of Washington. M. Fouchet (*foo-shā'*), his successor, was instructed to assure the President that France disapproved the conduct of his predecessor.

X. The first measure adopted by the United States government for raising a revenue by internal taxation, was the law of 1791, imposing a duty on domestic liquors. This law, from the first, was very unpopular in certain sections of the country, especially in the western part of Pennsylvania, where the opposition to it grew to an open rebellion in 1794, known as the *Whisky Insurrection*. The approach of a large body of militia, sent by Washington to enforce obedience, had the desired effect, and the rebellion was suppressed without bloodshed.

XI. Although the treaty of 1783 established peaceful relations between the American and British governments, yet it was not long before each party accused the other of having violated its stipulations; and so bitter did the spirit of the complaints and recriminations become, that a war seemed inevitable.

XII. To avoid this calamity, the President sent John Jay* as a special envoy to England, where,

JOHN JAY.

---

* John Jay was born in the city of New York, in 1745. In 1789, when Washington became President of the United States, so exalted was his opinion of Jay's honesty and fitness, that he conferred upon him a choice of the offices in his gift. Jay preferred the bench, and, consequently, was the first Chief-Justice of the United States. His death occurred in 1829, at Bedford, Westchester Co., New York.

IX. QUESTIONS.—43. What did Genet, the French minister, undertake to do? 44. Why did he presume upon such an undertaking? 45. What was the consequence to Genet? 46. Who was his successor? 47. What instructions did Fouchet receive from his government?

X. 48. What was the first government measure for raising a revenue by internal taxation? 49. How was the law regarded by the people? 50. Give an account of the Whisky Insurrection.

XI. 51. What accusations were made by the governments of the United States and Great Britain, each against the other?

in 1794, a treaty was concluded. This was published in the United States, and its provisions at once caused a prodigious storm of excitement and opposition, because they were regarded as being too favorable to the English. In the following year, however, the treaty was ratified, and the threatened conflict happily avoided. At the close of the second term, Washington, having declined a re-election, retired to the quietude of his home at Mount Vernon.

JOHN ADAMS'S ADMINISTRATION.

I. The second President of the United States was John Adams. His inauguration took place at Philadelphia, on the 4th of March, 1797.*

II. The neutral position taken by the United States in the war between France and England, gave offence to the former government; and "Jay's Treaty," which had been ratified in 1795, by the American Senate, considerably augmented the unfriendly feeling. This was boldly made manifest by the act of the French government, in authorizing depredations to be committed upon the commerce of the United States, and in ordering our minister, Mr. Pinckney, to leave France.

III. One of the first acts of President Adams was to convene Congress in extra session, to consider these outrages.

---

* The cabinet selected by Adams consisted of Timothy Pickering, Secretary of State, Oliver Wolcott, Secretary of the Treasury, James McHenry, Secretary of War, and Charles Lee, Attorney General. The navy department was not created until 1798, when Benjamin Stoddard was appointed its head.

XII. QUESTIONS.—52 What did Washington do to avoid a war? 53. What was the result of Jay's mission? 54. By what name is the treaty known? Ans.—"Jay's Treaty" 55. How was the treaty received in the United States? 56. Why was it so received? 57. What course did Washington pursue at the end of his second presidential term? 58. How is Mount Vernon situated? (See map, p 24.)

JOHN ADAMS'S ADMINISTRATION —I. 1. Who was the second President of the United States? 2. When and where was he inaugurated?

II. 3 What offended the French government? 4. How was the offense augmented? 5. How was the feeling of the French government manifested?

III 6. What was one of the first acts of President Adams? 7 How did the American government undertake to adjust the difficulties? 8. With what result?

Three envoys were sent to France, with authority to adjust all difficulties, but the French government refused to receive them, and even ordered two of them, whom they looked upon as less friendly than the third, to quit the country.

IV. The insult to the envoys excited great indignation in the United States; and Congress at once adopted measures for putting the country in a state of defense, authorized a standing army and naval armament, and appointed Washington commander-in-chief of the entire land forces.

V. Hostilities at sea soon commenced. In

JOHN ADAMS
Was born in Quincy, near Boston, Mass., Oct. 19, 1735. In 1764 he married Abigail Smith, daughter of a clergyman. His death occurred at Quincy, on the 4th of July, 1826.

one case, an American schooner was taken, and, in another, a French frigate was captured by the United States frigate Constellation. The decided stand taken by the Americans had its effect upon the French government; and overtures of peace were made, which resulted in a treaty, concluded in 1800, with Napoleon Bonaparte, who had become First Consul of France.

VI. But Washington did not live to see the troubles termi-

IV. QUESTIONS.—9. What was the consequence of the insult to the envoys?

V. 10. What hostile acts actually took place? 11. What was the effect?

VI. 12. What mournful event took place before the troubles with France were terminated? 13. When and where did Washington die? 14. How was his death regarded?

9*

nated: he died at Mount Vernon, on the 14th of December, 1799. His death was regarded as a national bereavement. Congress paid honors to his memory, and the whole people mourned the loss which each person felt that he had individually sustained.

VII. In conformity with the provisions of the law passed in 1790, in relation to the future seat of government, the capital of the United States was removed from Philadelphia to Washington, during the summer of 1800.

THE CAPITOL AT WASHINGTON.

VIII. Adams was President for only one term, or four years. Towards the close of it a fierce strife took place between the two great political parties of the day, the Federalists and the Republicans, in relation to the presidential succession. Thomas Jefferson was the successful candidate, defeating Adams, his opponent; and, at the same time, Aaron Burr, of New York, was elected Vice-President.

VII. QUESTIONS.—15. When was the capital of the United States removed to Washington? 16. How is Washington situated? (See map, p. 24.)
VIII. 17. For how long was Adams president? 18. What took place towards the close of it? 19. Who were the successful candidates?

JEFFERSON'S ADMINISTRATION.

I. The third President of the United States was Thomas Jefferson. His inauguration took place in the new capitol, at Washington, on the 4th of March, 1801.* During his administration, the Ohio Territory,† which had previously formed the eastern part of the Northwest Territory, adopted a State government, and, in 1802, was admitted into the Union as the State of Ohio.

II. In 1803, a most important addition was made to the territory of the United States, by the purchase of an immense tract of land, for which fifteen millions of dollars were paid to France. The territory thus acquired included not only the

THOMAS JEFFERSON Was born at Shadwell, Albemarle Co. Va., April 2, 1743. On the 1st of Jan., 1772, he was married to Mrs. Martha Skelton. His death occurred at Monticello, Va., on the 4th of July, 1826.

H.ORR-CO.

---

* Jefferson's cabinet consisted of James Madison, Secretary of State; Henry Dearborn, Secretary of War; Albert Gallatin, Secretary of the Treasury; Robert Smith, Secretary of the Navy; and Levi Lincoln, Attorney-General.

† After the Revolutionary War, a dispute arose between several of the States respecting the ownership of the Ohio Territory, which was put an end to by the whole being ceded to the United States.

JEFFERSON'S ADMINISTRATION.—I. QUESTIONS.—1. Who was the third President of the United States? 2. When and where did his inauguration take place? 3. When was Ohio admitted into the Union? 4. What is said of Ohio's previous history?

OHIO.

This State was named from the river forming its southern boundary. "The French called the river *La Belle Riviere*, the beautiful river, which signification corresponds, it is said, to that of the Indian appellation, Ohio." The State Seal is given above. Ohio has no motto.

present State of Louisiana, but a vast region extending to the Rocky Mountains. One of the first advantages secured by this purchase was the free navigation of the Mississippi River to the Gulf of Mexico.

III. In the same year, 1803, Commodore Preble (*preb'-el*) was sent to humble the pirates of the Barbary States, who, notwithstanding the tribute which the United States had paid, in imitation of European nations, to secure their commerce in the Mediterranean from molestation, were becoming more insolent and exacting.

IV. Preble first appeared against Morocco, and, after exacting terms of the emperor, proceeded eastward. Before he had time to reach Tripoli, the frigate Philadelphia, one of the vessels of his fleet, which had preceded him, while reconnoitering in the harbor of Tripoli, struck on a rock, and was captured by the Tripolitans, who consigned her crew to slavery.

V. As the captured frigate added to the defenses of the place, and would undoubtedly be sent out to cruise, it was deemed important to recapture or destroy her. The latter

II. QUESTIONS.—5. How was the State of Louisiana acquired by the United States? 6. What advantage accrued from the purchase?

III. 7. What expedition was sent across the Atlantic in that year? 8. What had the Barbary pirates done?

IV. 9. What was the first thing accomplished by Preble? 10. Give an account of the loss of the Philadelphia.

being considered the more prac-
ticable, Lieutenant Decatur,* with
a few brave companions, entered
the harbor on the night of the
15th of February, 1804, boarded
the Philadelphia, killed or drove
into the sea every one of the Tripolitan crew, and, after setting the
vessel on fire, escaped without
losing a man.

COMMODORE DECATUR.

VI. About a year later, Mr.
Eaton, an agent of the United
States, concerted an expedition with Hamet, the exiled though
rightful heir to the throne of Tripoli, against the reigning
sovereign. He left Egypt, accompanied by Hamet, with a
force of about five hundred men, four-fifths of whom were
Arabs: the other fifth was composed of adventurers, principally Greeks, and only nine Americans.

VII. He accomplished a remarkable march of several hundred miles across a desert country, and captured Derne, a Tripolitan city, after a fierce struggle. He held the place for
several weeks, despite the exertions of an opposing army, and
finally routed the enemy in a general engagement, in which
more than three thousand men took part. In the midst of
his successes, a treaty of peace was concluded between the
reigning bashaw and Mr. Lear, the American Consul-General
at Algiers.

---

* Stephen Decatur, Jr., was born in Maryland, in 1779. The affair between the Chesapeake and Leopard, in 1807, in the opinion of Decatur was disgraceful to the Americans, and he did not hesitate to animad-
vert freely upon the conduct of Commodore Barron, who commanded the Chesapeake on that occasion.
The consequence was a duel with Barron at Bladensburg, Md., as late as 1820, in which Decatur was killed,
and Barron was so severely wounded that he was not expected to live, and he only recovered after months
of great suffering.

V. QUESTIONS.—11. What was deemed important with regard to the captured
frigate? 12. Why? 13. What, consequently, was determined upon? 14. Give an
account of the exploit.

VI. 15. What expedition was concerted against the reigning sovereign of Tripoli?
16. From what place did the expedition start? 17. Of whom was it composed?

VII. 18. What is said of the march? 19. What city did Eaton capture? 20.
Give an account of his subsequent successes.

ALEXANDER HAMILTON.

VIII. In July, 1804, the unfortunate duel between Alexander Hamilton* and Aaron Burr† occurred: the latter, at the time, was Vice-President of the United States. This sad affair, which resulted in the death of Hamilton, grew out of a political quarrel between the two men. By it Burr's political influence was completely destroyed; and when Jefferson was re-elected President for a second term, George Clinton, of New York, was chosen Burr's successor as Vice-President.

IX. After his retirement from the vice-presidency, Burr made a journey to the Southwest, and there his conduct subjected him to strange suspicion. He made considerable progress in the organization of an expedition which, it was alleged, was designed for the invasion of Mexico. His ultimate purpose, it was further alleged, was to establish an empire which should embrace one or more of the Southwestern States of the Union.

X. By order of the President of the United States he was arrested, taken to Richmond, Virginia, and there tried on a

---

* Hamilton was born in the Island of Nevis, West Indies, in 1757. At the age of thirteen he was sent to New York to be educated. He was one of the first to take up arms at the beginning of the Revolution, and as captain of an artillery company, performed a creditable part in the battle of Long Island. By his activity and intelligence he attracted the attention of Washington, and, after the battles of Trenton and Princeton, in which he took part, he accepted an invitation from the commander-in-chief to take a place in his staff as aide-de-camp. He afterwards participated in the battles of Brandywine, Germantown, and Monmouth.

† Burr was born at Newark, New Jersey, in 1756. In 1775 he was engaged in the expedition against Canada, and accompanied Arnold upon his toilsome march through the wilderness. He was in the battles of Quebec and Monmouth. His death occurred at Staten Island, N. Y., in 1836.

VIII. QUESTIONS.—21. What sad affair, in which two public men were the principal actors, took place during Jefferson's administration? 22. When did it take place? 23. At what place? Ans.—At Hoboken, New Jersey, opposite the city of New York. 24. What position was Burr holding at the time? 25. What was the cause of the duel? 26. What was the result of it? 27. What was the consequence to Burr?

IX. 28. In what project was Burr subsequently engaged?

X. 29. What order did President Jefferson issue with regard to Burr? 30. What is said of the trial and its result?

charge of treason. The trial was a protracted one; but, under a ruling of the court, which did not involve the merits of the charge, he was acquitted.

XI. The wars in Europe, growing out of the French revolution, continued during Jefferson's administration. That between England and France, though it at first proved profitable to the American shipping interests engaged in the carrying trade between the ports of the two hostile nations, re-

AARON BURR.

sulted in the adoption of measures injurious to our commerce.

XII. To annoy and cripple her adversary, England declared the whole northern coast of France in a state of blockade. Napoleon retaliated by the "Berlin Decree," in which he pronounced the British islands in a state of blockade. But the crowning grievance was the "right of search," asserted by Great Britain, under which claim American vessels were boarded, and all sailors of English birth found on board, were impressed as subjects of the king.

XIII. An event occurred in June, 1807, which brought things towards an issue. The American frigate Chesapeake, when off the capes of Virginia, was attacked by the British frigate Leopard. The Chesapeake, being unprepared for action, struck her colors, after having three men killed and eighteen wounded. Four of her crew, who were claimed by the commander of the Leopard as British deserters, were then

---

XI. QUESTIONS.—31. How did the war between England and France affect American interests?

XII. 32. What did England do to annoy and cripple her adversary? 33. How did Napoleon retaliate? 34. What was the crowning grievance of which Americans complained?

XIII. 35. What event brought the relations of growing hostility between England and America towards an issue? 36. When did it occur? 37. What did the outrage provoke President Jefferson to do?

transferred to the Leopard. This outrage provoked the President to issue a proclamation interdicting the entrance of British armed vessels into the ports or waters of the United States.

XIV. Although the act of the Leopard was disavowed by the English government, no reparation was made; and towards the close of the year the British "Orders in Council," forbidding all trade with France and her allies, were issued. Bonaparte again retaliated by issuing the "Milan Decree," interdicting all trade with England and her colonies.

XV. In consequence of this policy of the two European nations, so destructive to our commerce, Congress laid an embargo upon all American vessels, forbidding them to leave the ports of the United States. As the act of Congress not only failed to obtain an acknowledgment of American rights, but, on account of its ruinous effects upon the shipping interests, was very unpopular among the commercial classes, it was repealed, and the non-intercourse law, prohibiting all commerce with France and Great Britain, was substituted.

XVI. At this point in the history of the country, Jefferson, following the example of Washington, declined a second re-election to the presidency, and terminated his political career. He was succeeded by James Madison, of Virginia.

XIV. QUESTIONS—38. How was the outrage committed by the Leopard treated by the British government? 39. What is said of reparation? 40. When were the British "Orders in Council" issued? 41. What were the "Orders in Council?" 42. How did Bonaparte again retaliate?

XV. 43. What action did Congress take in consequence of the trade-interdicting policy of France and England? 44. Why was the embargo act afterward repealed? 45. What law was substituted for it?

XVI. 46. Why was not Jefferson continued in the presidency for more than eight years? 47. By whom was he succeeded?

REVIEW QUESTIONS.

14

SECTION VI.

MADISON'S ADMINISTRATION.

JAMES MADISON
Was born in King George Co., Va., March 16, 1751. In 1794 he married Mrs. Todd, a Virginia lady. His death occurred at Montpelier, near Orange Court House, Va., June 21, 1836.

I. THE fourth President of the United States was James Madison. His inauguration took place at Washington, on the 4th of March, 1809, at a crisis in the affairs of the nation which required of his administration the utmost caution, prudence, and resolution.* The United States were on the verge of war with Great Britain. Napoleon revoked his hostile "Decrees" in 1810, but the British "Orders in Council" continued in active force.

---

* Madison's cabinet consisted of Robert Smith, Secretary of State; William Eustis, Secretary of War; Paul Hamilton, Secretary of the Navy Albert Gallatin, Secretary of the Treasury; and Cæsar A. Rodney, Attorney-General.

MADISON'S ADMINISTRATION.—I. QUESTIONS.—1. Who was the fourth President of the United States? 2. When did his inauguration take place? 3. What was peculiarly required of Madison's administration? 4. Why? 5. What concession did Napoleon make? 6. What is said of the British "Orders in Council?"

II. In May, 1811, an affair occurred which tended to widen the breach which already existed between Great Britain and the United States, though, in this case, the British were the greater sufferers. The British sloop-of-war Little Belt, Captain Bingham, when off the coast of Virginia, fired into the American frigate President, Commodore Rodgers, but found her fire returned with such heavy broadsides, that, in a few minutes, thirty-two of her crew were killed-or wounded

III. About the year 1804, the Indians on the western frontiers, incited by British emissaries and influenced by the appeals of Tecumseh,* one of their boldest and most active warriors, began to form a confederacy against the people of the United States. A brother of Tecumseh, known as the "Prophet," who by his predictions and promises had acquired great influence over the tribes along the Wabash, was a leading agent in the business of bringing about an alliance.

IV. General Harrison, then governor of the Indian territory, marched towards the western frontier and approached Tippecanoe, the town of the Prophet, situated at the junction of the Tippecanoe and Wabash Rivers, in the present State of Indiana. The Prophet, in the absence of Tecumseh, at once proposed a conference, to take place the next day, and requested the Americans to encamp for the night at a place which he designated. Harrison, suspecting treachery, ordered his troops to sleep on their arms. This proved a fortunate precaution, for, early on the following morning, November 7th, 1811, the Indians made a furious attack upon the American camp; but, after a desperate and bloody contest of

---

* Tecumseh, or, as the name is sometimes written, Tecumtha, was a chief of the Shawnee Indians. He was born on the banks of the Scioto River, in Ohio, about 1770. "The Prophet's" name was Elkswatawa.

II. QUESTIONS.—7. Give an account of the naval affair which took place in May, 1811. 8. What did the affair tend to?

III. 9 What took place among the Indians about the year 1804? 10. Who was Tecumseh's principal co-operator in bringing about the alliance?

IV 11 Where was the battle of Tippecanoe fought? 12 What town is situated not far from the battle-ground? (See map, p. 132.) 13. When was the battle fought? 14. Give an account of it.

two hours, they were repulsed. This battle ruined the plans which Tecumseh had formed, and his next attempt against the Americans was in the alliance which he formed with the English, in 1812.

EVENTS OF 1812.

LOUISIANA.
"In 1682, La Salle* descended the Mississippi to the sea, and, formally taking possession for France of the whole new country watered by the Mississippi from its mouth to its source, he named it Louisiana, in honor of Louis XIV., King of France." The Seal of the State is given above. The motto of Louisiana is, *Union and Confidence.*

V. The United States government had endeavored to induce the British government to abrogate its "Orders in Council," and negotiate terms for suspending the impressment of American seamen, but in vain. That government absolutely refused, and nothing remained but war.

VI. Accordingly, in June, 1812, the President of the United States, in conformity with an act of Congress, issued a proclamation declaring war against Great Britain; and preparations were at once made for raising a large army. General Dearborn, of Massachusetts, an officer who had served with credit in the Revolu-

---

* La Salle, a celebrated French navigator, was born in Rouen, about 1635. His death occurred in 1687. He made four visits to America. In his first, while endeavoring to find a passage by water to China, he explored Lake Ontario. In his third, he descended the Mississippi. The fourth was made for the purpose of settling Louisiana. A fleet, containing more than two hundred colonists, sailed from France, but instead of landing near the mouth of the Mississippi, by mistake they proceeded to Texas. After La Salle had passed two years in Texas, some portion of the time in the vain attempt to reach the Mississippi, his nephew was murdered by one of his few remaining followers, and he was shot by another.

V. QUESTIONS.—15. How had the United States endeavored to avert the war?
VI. 16. When was war declared? 17. Who was placed at the head of the army?
18. Before the commencement of hostilities, what revocation on the part of England took place? 19. But what was still insisted upon?

tion, being appointed commander-in-chief. Before hostilities actually commenced, the British government had revoked its "Orders in Council," but the "right of impressment" was still insisted upon.

VII. At the time of the declaration of war, General Hull, the governor of Michigan (*mish'-e-gun*) Territory, was marching with two thousand men from Ohio to Detroit, his purpose being to accomplish the reduction of the hostile Indians of the Northwest. In anticipation of the war with England, he had been invested with discretionary power to invade Canada.

VIII. Learning, while on the march, that war had been declared, he crossed the Detroit River, with the avowed intention of going against Fort Malden (*maul'-den*); but, instead of at once marching upon the place, he encamped at Sandwich, eighteen miles distant, and thus gave the enemy an opportunity to prepare for defense.

IX. In the mean time Fort Mackinaw, an American post situated on an island at the outlet of Lake Michigan, was surprised by a force of British and Indians, and captured before the garrison had even heard of the declaration of war. This loss was a severe one, as the fort was the key to that section of the country, and the grand dépôt of the fur companies there.

X. Hull, while at Sandwich, sent a detachment to convoy a party who were approaching his camp with supplies. Van Horn, the commander, neglecting to exercise sufficient caution, was led into an ambush near Brownstown, August 5, by six

---

VII QUESTIONS.—20. On what expedition was General Hull engaged? 21 With what discretionary power was he invested?

VIII. 22 What information did Hull receive while on this march? 23. What river did he cross? 24. What was his avowed intention? 25. Where is Fort Malden? (See map, p 214.) 26. Is Sandwich north or south of Fort Malden? (See same map.) 27 What advantage did Hull's halt at Sandwich give to the British?

IX. 28. Give an account of the loss of Fort Mackinaw. 29 Where is Fort Mackinaw situated? 30 In what direction from Detroit is Fort Mackinaw? (See map, p 192.)

X. 31. Give an account of the defeat of Van Horn.

hundred British and Indians, and utterly defeated.

XI. After waiting nearly a month at Sandwich, Hull recrossed the river and took post at Detroit, to the great vexation and disappointment of his troops. Three days after the defeat of Van Horn, a second detachment, under Colonel Miller, was sent to convoy the supply party. As Miller approached Brownstown, on the evening of the 9th, he came upon the British and Indians, who were protected by a breastwork of logs and branches of trees, and, after a sharp contest, completely routed them.

XII. The withdrawal of Hull across the Detroit emboldened General Brock, the British commander, who began to erect a battery opposite the American post. Not being molested, he became still bolder, and, on the 16th of August, crossed the river with seven hundred regulars and six hundred Indians, and demanded an immediate surrender of Detroit.

XIII. The Americans were strongly posted, and confident of victory in the conflict which seemed to be before them; and yet, to the great indignation of his troops, Hull ordered them to withdraw to the fort, and a white flag, in token of submission, to be lifted above the works. By this act of sur-

---

XI. QUESTIONS.—32. What retrograde movement did Hull make? 33. Give an account of the victory gained by Miller.

XII. 34. Give an account of Brock's operations against Detroit.

XIII. 35. What is said of the ability and disposition of the Americans to defend themselves at Detroit? 36. What made them indignant? 37. What did the British acquire by the surrender?

render, not only Detroit, but the whole Territory of Michigan, passed into the hands of the enemy.

XIV. Hull's conduct, two years after, underwent examination by a court-martial, and though he was acquitted of treason, the court pronounced him guilty of cowardice, and he was sentenced to be shot; but, in consideration of his age and revolutionary services, the sentence was remitted by President Madison. Hull's* conduct was severely criticised at the time, as well as in after years; but a series of letters which he published in 1824, and a volume which appeared at a still later period, together form a complete vindication of his surrender, as regards either the charge of treason or cowardice.

XV. During the year 1812 a second invasion of Canada was made in another quarter. On the morning of the 13th of October, Colonel Solomon Van Rensselaer (*van-ren'-se-ler*), with a detachment of only two hundred and twenty-five men, crossed the Niagara River to storm the heights of Queenstown. The commander having been severely wounded at the landing,

* William Hull was born in Connecticut, in 1753. He was in the battles of White Plains, Trenton, Princeton, Bemis Heights, Saratoga, Monmouth, and Stony Point; and in all of them fought with courage. His death occurred in Massachusetts, in 1825.

XIV. QUESTIONS.—38. To what was Hull's conduct afterward subjected? 39. What sentence was pronounced upon him? 40. Why was not the sentence executed? 41. How was Hull's conduct subsequently regarded?

XV. 42. At what place did the second invasion of Canada occur? 43. Describe the event that took place on the morning of the 13th of October. 44. What town, in New York, is opposite Queenstown? (See map, p. 215.)

his troops, led by Captains Ogilvie and Wool, gallantly moved forward, carried a British battery, and
gained the heights.

1812.

XVI. The enemy, re-enforced by several hundred men under
Brock, attempted to regain the battery, but were repulsed,
and Brock was killed. While this struggle was going on at
the west side of the Niagara, a large body of militia was collected at Lewiston, on the east side. General Stephen Van
Rensselaer, a cousin of Solomon, and the superior in command of the troops in that quarter, endeavored to send re-
enforcements across the river, but only about a thousand men
could be induced to go: the rest professed to consider it wrong
to invade the enemy's country.

XVII. On the afternoon of the same day, 13th, the Americans on the heights were attacked by fresh troops, under
General Sheaffe (*shefe*), from Fort George, and nearly all were
killed or taken prisoners. General Van Rensselaer, disgusted
with the conduct of the militia, soon retired from the service,
when the command on the Niagara frontier devolved on General Smyth. Smyth accomplished nothing: after projecting
two invasions of Canada, neither of which was carried out, he
also resigned.

XVIII. The triumphs of the Americans on the ocean, during 1812, were as decided as their reverses on the land. The
first of importance was the capture of the sloop Alert by the
frigate Essex, Captain Porter. The second, of greater importance, was achieved by Captain Isaac Hull,* nephew of
General Hull, on the 19th of August, off the coast of Massa-

---

* Captain Isaac Hull, afterward Commodore, was born in Derby, Conn., in 1775. During the war with
the Barbary States, from 1803 to 1805, he served with distinction in the squadrons of Commodores Preble
and Barron, and co-operated with Eaton in the capture of Derne. He died in Philadelphia, in 1843.

XVI. Questions.—45. Give an account of the repulse and loss sustained by the
British. 46. Where was the main body of the American militia at the time stationed? 47. Why did they not cross over to Queenstown?
XVII. 48. Give a further account of the battle of Queenstown. 49. Who succeeded General Van Rensselaer in the command of the forces on the Niagara frontier? 50. Why had Van Rensselaer resigned? 51. What can you state of Smyth
and his operations?

chusetts. Hull commanded the American frigate Constitution, and Dacres the British frigate Guerriere (*găre-e-āre'*). The action between the two frigates lasted about forty minutes, and resulted in the capture of the Guerriere. The captured vessel had been so much injured it was found impossible to bring her into port, and she was consequently burned by the victors.

XIX. In October, the American sloop-of-war Wasp, Captain Jones, while cruising off the coast of North Carolina, fell in with the British brig Frolic, Captain Whinyates, and after a conflict of three-quarters of an hour, boarded her. A melancholy scene of destruction was presented. The decks were covered with the dead and the wounded. Not twenty of the Frolic's crew escaped unhurt. Scarcely had the enemy's vessel been taken possession of, when an English ship of seventy-four guns hove in sight, and captured both vessels.

XX. A second naval victory by the Americans occurred in this same month, October. The frigate United States, Commodore Decatur, encountered the British frigate Macedonia (*mas-se-do'-ne-a*) west of the Ca-

nary (*ka-nā'-re*) Islands, and, after an action of nearly two hours, compelled her to surrender. She was taken to New York.

COMMODORE BAINBRIDGE.

XXI. A little more than two months later, the Constitution, then commanded by Commodore Bainbridge, gained her second victory, in the capture of the frigate Java (*jah'-va*). The ac-

XVIII. QUESTIONS.—52. What comparison is made between the land reverses and the ocean triumphs? 53. Which was the first important naval victory? 54. The second? 55. When did the action between the Constitution and the Guerriere take place? 56. Give an account of it.

XIX. 57. Give an account of the action between the Wasp and the Frolic. 58. What ~~and deprived Captain Jones of the fruits of his victory~~?

XX. 59. Give an account of the action between the United States and Macedonian.
10

1812. tion took place off.the coast of Brazil, on the 29th of December, and lasted nearly two hours. Bainbridge,* finding the captured frigate so much riddled that it was impossible to get her into an American port, destroyed her by fire, and the Constitution then put into San Salvador, where the prisoners were landed on parole.

XXII. In the belief that the navy of the United States would be entirely destroyed or captured by that of England, it had been decided, at the beginning of the war, to lay up our ships to save them. But, happily, that policy was soon departed from. American privateers, too, scoured the ocean, and British commerce suffered in every direction. During the year 1812, more than three hundred vessels, with not less than three thousand prisoners, beside valuable cargoes, were taken by the Americans.

EVENTS OF 1813.

I. For the campaign of 1813 three armies were raised. That of the West, near the head of Lake Erie, was commanded by General Harrison; that of the Centre, between Lakes Erie and Ontario, by General Dearborn; and that of the North, near Lake Champlain, by General Hampton.

II. The leading object of the army of the West was to recover Michigan and avenge the disgrace of Hull. A division of the army, composed mostly of Kentuckians, commanded by

---

* William Bainbridge was born in Princeton, N. J, in 1774. In 1803 he was in command of the frigate Philadelphia when that vessel struck on a rock and was captured in the harbor of Tripoli. He and his crew, of more than three hundred persons, were taken prisoners by the Tripolitans and held in captivity nineteen months. He died in Philadelphia, in 1833.

XXI. QUESTIONS.—60. Give an account of the action between the Constitution and the Java. 61. What did Bainbridge do with his prize and prisoners?

XXII 62. What policy had been decided upon at the beginning of the war, with reference to American ships? 63. Why was that decision made? 64. What is stated of the successes of the Americans on the ocean, during the year 1812?

EVENTS OF 1813.—I. 1. What armies were raised for the campaign of 1813?

II 2 What was the object of the army of the West? 3. What command did Winchester have? 4. What place did he reach in January? 5. How did his men at first employ themselves there? 6. What did he learn while there? 7. What request did he receive?

General Winchester, reached the rapids of the Maumee on the 10th of January. Here, while constructing huts for the reception of supplies, Winchester learned that Frenchtown, then a small settlement, nearly forty miles distant, was threatened with an attack from a body of British and Indians. He, at the same time, received an urgent request from the inhabitants to come to their assistance.

III. Accordingly, he sent a detachment of five hundred men, under Colonel Lewis, in advance, while he prepared to follow. Lewis, ascertaining that the British and Indians were already in possession of the town, hurried forward, and, on the 18th of January, made a charge upon the enemy, driving them into the woods. On the following day, Winchester arrived. The Americans were, on the 22d, attacked by a force of fifteen hundred British and Indians, commanded by General Proctor. They made a brave defense, but Winchester, who had been made prisoner during the engagement, agreed upon a capitulation, and the Americans surrendered on condition that they should be protected. But Proctor failed to observe the condition: his Indian allies murdered the wounded prisoners who were unable to travel, and then set fire to the houses.

IV. Upon hearing of Winchester's defeat, Harrison took a position on the Maumee River, where he constructed a fortified camp, which, in honor of the governor of Ohio, he called Fort Meigs (*megz*). On the 1st of May, Proctor advanced against this fort, and, with a force of not less than a thousand British and Indians, commenced a siege. Four days after,

---

III. QUESTIONS.—8. How did he act in response to the request? 9. What did Lewis accomplish? 10. What battle took place on the following day? *Ans*—The battle of Frenchtown. 11. Give an account of it. 12. Give an account of the massacre that followed. 13. How is Frenchtown situated? (See map, p. 214.)

IV. 14. Where did Harrison make a stand, upon hearing of Winchester's misfortune? 15. Describe the Maumee. (See map, p. 192.) 16. Is Fort Meigs above or below Toledo? (See map, p. 214.) 17. How was Fort Meigs threatened? 18. Give an account of the event that took place on the 5th of May. 19. When and why did Proctor abandon the siege?

1813. General Clay* arrived, with twelve hundred Kentuckians, and successfully attacked the besiegers, compelling them to disperse; but, unfortunately, a large body of his troops, while pursuing the enemy, was surrounded and captured. On the ninth day of the month, Proctor, deserted by his allies, and despairing of success, withdrew, and returned to Fort Malden.

V. In a little more than two months after, Proctor and Tecumseh again threatened Fort Meigs; but, finding it well garrisoned, terminated a brief siege by a sullen withdrawal. Proctor's next movement was against Fort Stephenson, at Lower Sandusky, now Fremont, situated on the Sandusky River. The place was garrisoned by only one hundred and fifty men, under the command of Major Croghan,† a young man not yet twenty-two years old, and they had but one gun, a six-pounder. Proctor's force consisted of more than twelve hundred men, half regulars and half Indians.

VI. A cannonade was directed against the fort until a breach was effected, when the enemy, on the 2d of August, attempted to carry the place by assault; but they were met by a volley of musketry and a discharge from the six-pounder with such terrible effect, that, panic-struck, they fled in confusion, leaving one hundred and fifty of their number killed or wounded.

VII. The naval supremacy on Lake Erie (*ē'-re*) and Lake Ontario (*on-tā'-re-o*), became an object of much importance to the belligerent governments, and, as early as the beginning of October, 1812, preparations were in progress, on both sides, to

---

* Green Clay was born in Virginia, in 1757. After his success in driving the British and Indians from the siege of Fort Meigs, he was left in command there, and defended the fort when it was a second time threatened. He died in 1826.

† George Croghan was born in Kentucky, in 1791. He was in the battles of Tippecanoe and Fort Meigs (May 5), and served with Taylor in Mexico. His death occurred at New Orleans, in 1849.

V. QUESTIONS.—20. What can you state of the second demonstration against Fort Meigs? 21. To what object did Proctor next direct his attention? 22. In what direction from Fort Meigs was Fort Stephenson? (See map, p. 214.) 23. How was Fort Stephenson prepared to resist Proctor?

VI. 24. Give an account of Proctor's efforts against the fort.

secure it. To Commodore Chauncey* was given the general command of the American naval forces on the two lakes, while to Commodore Perry† was assigned the immediate command on Lake Erie. On the part of the enemy, Sir James Yeo held the general command, and Commodore Barclay the special one on Lake Erie.

VIII. By the first of August, 1813, two squadrons had been fitted out on Lake Erie. One of these, the American, consisted of nine vessels, carrying fifty-four guns; and the other, the British, consisted of six vessels, carrying sixty-three guns. They met, on the 10th of September, near the western extremity of the lake, when a hard-fought battle of four hours' duration took place, resulting in a complete and brilliant victory to the Americans, every vessel of the enemy

having surrendered. In dispatching information of his victory to General Harrison, Perry wrote: "We have met the enemy, and they are ours."

IX. The consequences of the victory were highly important. The Americans completely established their naval supremacy on the lake, Detroit was evacuated by the British, the Indians of Michigan were

COMMODORE PERRY

* Isaac Chauncey was born in Connecticut, in 1772. When a young man, he was engaged in the merchant service, and during a voyage, a mortal sickness prevailed, leaving him on board as the only survivor. He navigated the vessel into port, for which he was rewarded by being appointed to the command of her. He served in the war against Tripoli, and during the war of 1812 he rendered important service on Lake Ontario, by his active coöperation with the land forces. He afterwards served at Washington, in 1840.

† Oliver Hazard Perry was born at Newport, R. I., in 1785. He died at Port Spain, Island of Trinidad, of yellow fever, contracted while he was engaged on government service, up the Orinoco River, in South America.

VII. QUESTIONS.—25. What is said of the naval supremacy on Lakes Erie and Ontario? 26. What command was given to Chauncey? 27. To Perry? 28. To Yeo? 29. To Barclay?

VIII. 30. How large a fleet did Perry command? 31. Barclay? 32. When did the battle of Lake Erie take place? 33. What produced enthusiasm among the Americans? Ans.—A flag floating from the mainmast of Perry's ship, upon which were the dying words of Lawrence: "Don't give up the ship!" 34. Give an account of the battle. 35. How did Perry inform Harrison of his victory?

1813. intimidated, and the way to success for the army at Fort Meigs was clearly opened. Harrison saw his opportunity, and was not slow to profit by it.

X. Having been re-enforced by a large body of Kentuckians, under Governor Shelby, Harrison resolved to seek Proctor and give him battle. While, in conformity with his orders, a regiment of horse, one thousand strong, proceeded by land, crossing the river at Detroit, the rest of the army crossed Lake Erie in Perry's fleet, and landed near Fort Malden. But Proctor, on hearing of Barclay's defeat and Harrison's approach, was seized with alarm; and when the fort was reached, it was found deserted, and Proctor and Tecumseh were in full retreat towards the Thames (*temz*) River. The Americans followed in eager pursuit, and, on the 5th of October, overtook them near the Moravian village on the Thames, about eighty miles from Detroit.

XI. The enemy, seeing that a battle could not be avoided, took a favorable position on a narrow strip of land between the river and an extensive swamp. The Americans charged, breaking the line of the British, and soon compelling them to surrender; but the contest with the Indians was more obstinate. At length, Tecumseh fell, mortally wounded, and the savage warriors dispersed in all directions. Proctor was gone: he had fled at the first onset, leaving his carriage, private papers, and even his sword, behind him.

XII. Besides six hundred prisoners taken by Harrison, several cannon and a large quantity of stores and ammunition fell into his hands. By the victory thus achieved, the territory which Hull had surrendered was entirely recovered, the

IX. QUESTIONS.—36 What were the important consequences of the battle?
X. 37 What accession arrived for Harrison's army? 38. What did Harrison resolve upon? 39. How did the two parts of his army proceed? 40. Why did not Proctor remain at Fort Malden? 41. How is Fort Malden situated? (See map, p. 214.) 42. What is said of the flight of Proctor and the pursuit? 43. When was the battle of the Thames fought?
XI. 44. Give an account of it. 45. Where was the battle fought? (See map, p. 214.)

destruction of Tecumseh's Indian Confederacy was completed, and the war on the western frontier was terminated.

XIII. In the spring of 1813, several months before the successes of Perry and Harrison had been achieved, the Southern Indians were visited by Tecumseh and urged to take up arms against the whites. . The Creeks yielded, and began to commit depredations upon the settlements of the Americans. In the latter part of August, fifteen hundred of their warriors surprised Fort Mims,* on the Alabama River, and massacred nearly three hundred men, women, and children.

XIV. This sanguinary and unprovoked attack aroused the whole South, and a large force, under Generals Jackson and Coffee, marched into the country of the Creeks to avenge the deed of horror. Several battles were fought in quick succession, at Talladega, Autossee, Emucfa, and other places, in every one of which the Indians were defeated.

XV At length a thousand warriors, with their women and children, made a final stand at Tohopeka, or,

---

* The name of this place was also written *Fort Mimms*. The fort was situated on the east side of the Alabama, about ten miles above its junction with the Tombigbee.

XII. QUESTIONS.—46. What were the fruits of Harrison's victory?

XIII. 47. What had Tecumseh been about in the spring of 1813? 48. What followed? 49. What is said of the massacre at Fort Mims? 50. In what direction from Mobile was Fort Mims? (See map, p. 223.)

XIV. 51. What effect did the massacre nave upon the people of the South? 52. What can you say of the battles that were fought? 53. Give the location of the three places named. (See map, p. 223.) 54. What two rivers uniting form the Alabama River? *Ans.*—The Coosa and the Tallapoosa.

1813. as the whites called it, the Horse-Shoe Bend of the Tallapoosa River, where they had established a camp, skillfully fortified. Here, on the 27th of March, 1814, they were attacked by a force of three thousand men, under Jackson. The doomed Creeks, being hemmed in on all sides by their assailants, fought with the energy of despair, and not till almost six hundred of their number were slain did the battle cease : their defeat was complete.

XVI. While these events were transpiring at the South, others of equal moment were taking place at the North. Towards the latter part of April, 1813, General Dearborn, with seventeen hundred men, embarked on board Chauncey's fleet, at Sackett's Harbor, with the design of going against York, the capital of Upper Canada.

XVII. On the 27th, the fleet anchored off that town, and on the same day the troops effected a landing in the face of a severe fire from British and Indians, commanded by General Sheaffe. Still they pressed forward, led by General Pike,*

and were carrying every thing before them, when the enemy's magazine exploded, mortally wounding Pike, and making sad havoc among his men. After a moment's pause, the Americans continued to advance, and were soon in possession of the town.

XVIII. The capture of York having been attained, Dearborn

GENERAL PIKE.

---

* Zebulon Montgomery Pike was born in New Jersey, in 1779. He made two important expeditions; one in 1805 and 6, to explore the sources of the Mississippi, and the other about a year after, to examine the region west of the Red River.

XV. QUESTIONS.—55. Where did the battle of Tohopeka take place? (See map, p. 223.) 56. Give an account of the battle. XVI. 57. What movement was made on Lake Ontario towards the latter part of April? XVII. 58. When did the battle of York take place? 59. Give an account of it. 60. By what name is York now known? *Ans.*—Toronto. 61. How is Toronto situated? (See map, p. 215.)

after several days' delay, during which he received re-enforcements, proceeded to attack Fort George, situated on the Niagara River, near its mouth. The British made but a short defense, and then retreated to Burlington Heights, at the western extremity of Lake Ontario, pursued by a large force, under Generals Chandler and Winder. On the night of the 6th of June, nine days after the capture of the fort, the British suddenly fell upon the camp of the pursuing Americans, and, though they were repulsed, in the darkness and confusion both Chandler and Winder were made prisoners.

XIX. The British in Canada, on being informed that Chauncey's fleet, carrying a large body of troops, had sailed from Sackett's Harbor, sent a thousand men across the lake in Yeo's fleet, to attack the place. Sir George Prevost, the British commander, effected a landing on the 29th of May. The militia fired a couple of volleys upon the invaders, and then, panic-struck, broke and fled. A small body of regulars acted with more firmness. While the advance of the British was held in check by a galling fire from the regulars, General Brown,* the American commander, rallied the militia, and led them by a circuitous route, as if he designed to seize the enemy's boats and cut off their retreat. The stratagem succeeded completely, and the British made a rush for their boats, leaving their dead and wounded behind.

GENERAL BROWN.

XX. Dearborn remained at Ft. George more than a fortnight

---

* Jacob Brown was born in Bucks County, Pennsylvania, in 1775. He died in Washington, in 1828.

XVIII. QUESTIONS.—62. Against what place did Dearborn next proceed? 63. Was Fort George above or below Queenstown? (See map. p. 215.) 64. What success did Dearborn meet with against Fort George? 65. What took place afterward?

XIX. 66. How is Sackett's Harbor situated? (See map, p. 62.) 67. What induced the British to attack the place? 68. When did they attack it? 69. Give an account of the battle.

10*

1813. after the misfortune to Chandler and Winder, without doing any thing. Not so the British. They busied themselves in taking possession of the mountain passes there thus narrowing the limits of Dearborn's position, and cutting off his communications with the country. At length, a detach ment of six hundred men was sent to break up a post which the British had established seventeen miles from the fort. After pro ceeding fifteen miles, the Americans were suddenly surround ed by a body of British and Indians, and compelled to surrender themselves prisoners of war. Dearborn,* not long after, resign ed his command, and was succeeded by General Wilkinson.

XXI. General Armstrong, upon whom President Madison had recently conferred the appointment of Secretary of War devised a plan for the invasion of Canada, by which the two armies—that of the Centre, under Wilkinson, and that of the North, under Hampton—were to form a junction on the St Lawrence, and proceed against Montreal.

XXII. In passing down the St. Lawrence, the fleet of boats employed in conveying Wilkinson's army, was harassed by the British whenever an opportunity occurred. Near Williams burg, a strong detachment was landed to make an advance disperse a body of the enemy, and cover the descent of the fleet. At Chrysler's (*kris'-lers*) Field, a severe battle ensued on the 11th of November, in which the Americans, though losing about one-fifth of their entire force engaged, maintained their position.

---

* Henry Dearborn was born in New Hampshire, in 1751. He was in the battle of Bunker Hill, wa with Arnold in the expedition through the wilderness of Maine, and participated in the battle of Quebec where he was taken prisoner Being exchanged, he served under Gates in the Northern campaign, and did good service at the battle of Monmouth, in Sullivan's expedition against the Indians, and in the suc cessful operations before Yorktown He died in Massachusetts, in 1829.

XX. QUESTIONS.—70 What is said of Dearborn's inactivity at Fort Erie? 71 What, of the activity of the British? 72 Give an account of the mishap to the American detachment 73. Who succeeded Dearborn in the command?
XXI. 74 What office did Armstrong hold? 75. What plan of action did he devise?
XXII. 76. What annoyance did Wilkinson experience while sailing down the St Lawrence? 77 What did he do when near Williamsburg? 78. How is Williams burg situated? (See map, p. 62.) 79. When did a battle take place near Williams. burg? 80. By what name is that battle known? 81. Give an account of it.

XXIII. Hampton,* in the mean time, had entered Canada, encountered the British near St. John's, and been defeated. In consequence of a hostile feeling which existed between him and Wilkinson, he declined to co-operate with that commander, but made his way back to Lake Champlain, and left his army in winter quarters at Plattsburg, under the command of General Izard. Wilkinson went into winter quarters at French Mills, about nine miles east of St. Regis.

XXIV. During 1813, there were many severe battles on the ocean; and though the American seamen were not so uniformly successful as in the preceding year, their gallantry continued to be the theme of admiration. On the 24th of February, the sloop-of-war Hornet, Captain Lawrence, when off the mouth of the Demerara River, fell in with a British brig, which, after an action of only fifteen minutes, struck her colors and raised a signal of distress. She proved to be the brig Peacock, Captain Peake, and was so riddled that she sunk in a few minutes after the surrender, carrying down with her nine of her own crew and three of the Hornet's.

XXV. On his return to the United States, Lawrence was promoted to the command of the frigate Chesapeake, then lying in Boston harbor. In the forenoon of June 1st, the British frigate Shannon, Captain Broke, appeared off the harbor for the express purpose of meeting the Chesapeake. Though the American frigate had imperfect equipments and an ill-assorted crew, while the British ship had a select crew and

---

* Wade Hampton was born in South Carolina, in 1755. He took an active part in the Revolutionary War, serving under Marion and Sumter. After he retired from the army, in 1814, he engaged in agricultural pursuits, and was considered the wealthiest farmer in the United States, owning extensive plantations, and about three thousand slaves. He died in South Carolina, in 1835.

XXIII. QUESTIONS.—82. What misfortune had befallen Hampton in the mean time? 83 How is St. John's situated? (See map, p. 231) 84 What did he neglect to do? 85 Why? 86. Where and in whose charge did he leave his command? 87. How is Plattsburg situated? (See map, p 149) 88. Where did Wilkinson go into winter quarters? 89. Where is St. Regis? *Ans.*—On the south side of the St. Lawrence.

XXIV. 90. What is said of the naval successes of the Americans during the year 1813? 91 Give an account of the action between the Hornet and Pelican.

XXV. 92. How was Lawrence rewarded for his victory over the Peacock? 93. What movement was made by the Shannon? 94. In what condition were the two ships for action?

was in the best possible condition, Lawrence still felt impelled to go out and engage her.

LAWRENCE.

XXVI. At about six o'clock in the afternoon the two vessels met, and a terrific contest of fifteen minutes ensued. Lawrence* was mortally wounded in the early part of the action, and his last injunction as he was borne below was, "Don't give up the ship." The Chesapeake, after having all her superior officers either killed or wounded, was boarded by the enemy and her flag hauled down.

XXVII. The second disaster to the American navy that occurred during the year was the loss of the brig Argus, Captain W. H. Allen,† on the 14th of August. After Allen had conveyed the American minister, Mr. Crawford, to France, he proceeded to cruise in the waters about England, and was successful in taking a large number of prizes and capturing property to the amount of two millions of dollars. While in the English Channel he fell in with the sloop-of-war Pelican, and in the action which ensued, and which resulted in the capture of the Argus, he was mortally wounded. He was taken to Plymouth, England, where he died on the day after the action.

XXVIII. Fortune next favored the Americans. On the 5th of September, Lieutenant Burrows, while in command of

---

* James Lawrence was born in Burlington, N. J., in 1781. He was one of Decatur's party that boarded and destroyed the frigate Philadelphia in the harbor of Tripoli, in 1804.
† William Henry Allen was born in Rhode Island, in 1784. He was the first lieutenant of the frigate United States when that vessel captured the Macedonian.

XXVI. Questions.—95. Give an account of the action.
XXVII. 96. What vessel did Lieutenant Allen command in the summer of 1813? 97. What duty did he perform before making a cruise? 98. What were his successes? 99. When did the Argus and Pelican meet? 100. Give an account of the action between them.
XXVIII. 101. Where did a naval action take place on the 5th of September? 102. Give an account of it. 103. What honors were paid to the dead commanders? 104. Where is Portland? (See map of Maine.)

the brig Enterprise, fell in with the British brig Boxer, Captain Blythe, off the coast of Maine. An action of forty minutes ensued, resulting in the capture of the Boxer. Both commanders were killed in the engagement, and their bodies were buried side by side at Portland, with the honors of war.

XXIX. In 1812, Captain Porter,* commanding the American frigate Essex, in a short cruise captured a number of British merchantmen, and, after an action of only eight minutes, took the sloop-of-war Alert. In 1812 and '13, Porter, in command of the same vessel, made a long and remarkable cruise of more than a year, in the Atlantic and Pacific Oceans. Besides capturing a great many ships, and making prisoners of more than four hundred men, he did immense service to the American shipping by the protection which he afforded.

COMMODORE PORTER.

XXX. At length, on the 28th of March, 1814, he was attacked in the harbor of Valparaiso (val-pa-rī'-so), by two British war vessels that had been expressly dispatched in quest of him, and, after one of the most desperate conflicts of the war, was forced to surrender.

* David Porter was born in Boston, Mass., in 1780. When the frigate Philadelphia was captured by the Tripolitans, in 1803, Porter was made captive and held nineteen months. In 1824 he commanded an expedition against the pirates of the West Indies. He subsequently entered the service of Mexico, as commander-in-chief of her naval forces; but, in 1829, returned to the United States. At the time of his death, which occurred at Constantinople, in 1843, he was consul minister of the United States there.

XXIX. Questions.—105. What were Porter's successes in 1812? 106. What, in 1813?

XXX. 107. Where was he attacked by two British war vessels? 108. Where is Valparaiso? (See map of South America.) 109. Give an account of the action.

REVIEW QUESTIONS.

EVENTS OF 1814, AND CLOSE OF THE WAR.

I. In the early part of 1813, a proposition from the Russian Emperor was received, in which he offered to mediate between the belligerent powers, England and the United States. It was accepted on the part of the American government, and President Madison appointed three commissioners to proceed to St. Petersburg to negotiate a treaty. It was not, however, accepted on the part of the other belligerents; but towards the close of the year the American government was informed that Great Britain was ready to make a treaty of peace. Accordingly, two persons were added to the commission previously appointed, and, in January, 1814, they sailed for Europe, where they joined their three associates. The belligerent governments however continued to prosecute war measures, and even with more vigor than before.

PART OF THE SOREL RIVER.

II. Towards the close of February, 1814, Wilkinson broke up his winter quarters at French Mills and removed to Plattsburg, and Brown marched to Sackett's Harbor, taking two thousand men, mainly for the protection of the fleet there.

III. Late in the following month, Wilkinson* advanced as far as Rouse's Point, where he determined to erect a battery, but the British penetrating his

---

* James Wilkinson was born in Maryland, in 1757. He served in Canada under Arnold, in 1776, and on the staff of Gates, in 1777. During Washington's administration he was engaged on the Northwestern frontier against the Indians, and commanded one of the divisions of Wayne's army in the battle of the Maumee. He subsequently was governor of the Louisiana territory, and an active agent in exposing the plans of Burr, in 1806. He died in Mexico, in 1825.

EVENTS OF 1814, AND CLOSE OF THE WAR.—QUESTIONS.—I. 1. When did a proposition come from the Emperor of Russia? 2. What was it? 3. What action was taken in relation thereto by the American government? 4. What by the British government? 5. Of what was the American government afterward informed? 6. In accordance therewith, what action was taken by the American government?

II. 7. What movement did Wilkinson make toward the close of the winter? 8. To what place did General Brown march?

1814. design, concentrated a force of two thousand men at La Colle Mill, three miles below the point. An attack which he made upon the British, on the last day of the month, was unsuccessful, and he returned to Plattsburg. In consequence of this defeat, he threw up his command and asked to be tried by a court-martial. Gen. Izard was appointed to succeed him.

IV. Brown did not remain long at Sackett's Harbor; but, having been appointed to the command of the army destined to act on the Niagara frontier against Canada, he made haste to carry out the views of the Secretary of War for another invasion of the enemy's territory. Preparations being completed, on the 3d of July a large force, the advance of Brown's command, crossed the Niagara River, and took Fort Erie without a struggle. Pushing forward next day along the bank of the river, the American army reached a plain on the south side of the Chippewa River, in view of the enemy's camp on the other side of that stream.

V. General Brown determined to attack the British in their position; and, apparently, the British commander intended a similar operation against the Americans, for the morning of the 5th beheld both armies deploying into the plain. The battle that ensued was severe, resulting in the defeat of the British, who made good their retreat across the Chippewa. This brilliant victory was owing to the admirable discipline of the American army, no less than to the skill and bravery of General Scott.

VI. The British commander, General Riall, made no at-

---

tempt to dispute the passage of the Chippewa, but, hurriedly burning the bridge after he had effected a crossing, continued his retreat to Burlington Heights, near the head of Lake Ontario. The American army rested but two days after the battle, then advanced across the Chippewa and took post at Queenstown, intending to make a further advance towards Fort George, which the British then held. Not having the necessary cannon with which to attack the fort, they fell back, after a few days, to the Chippewa.

VII. Here, on the 25th of July, Brown was informed that General Drummond, who had reached Fort George with re-enforcements, had crossed the Niagara to attack Fort Schlosser (*shlos'-ser*), where supplies for the American army were deposited. Believing that a demonstration against the forts at the mouth of the river would induce the British to return, Brown ordered Scott to advance with twelve hundred men.

VIII. A march of but two miles had been accomplished when, about sunset, Scott unexpectedly came upon a British force of two thousand men advantageously posted at Lundy's Lane, in the immediate vicinity of Niagara Falls. The most obstinate bat-

---

VI. QUESTIONS.—23. What was Riall's movement after the battle? 24. What Brown's?

VII. 25. Where was Brown on the 25th of July? 26. What information did he get there? 27. Where is Fort Schlosser situated? 28. What order did Brown give to Scott? 29. What was his object?

VIII. 30. Where is Lundy's Lane? (See map, p. 233.) 31. Give an account of the battle fought there while Scott was in command.

1814. tle of the war ensued. Scott took the offensive; and though the enemy outnumbered him, he sustained the unequal contest for an hour, when General Brown, with the main body of the army, arrived upon the field. In the mean time, the British force had been largely augmented by re-enforcements under Drummond, who took the command.

IX. It became evident to Brown that a battery, which the British had placed on a commanding hight, and which swept all parts of the field, must be captured or the Americans be defeated. Upon asking Colonel Miller* if he could take it, the fearless soldier replied, "I'll try, sir." At the head of his regiment, Miller steadily advanced up the hight, while, at every step, his ranks were thinned by the enemy's fire; but his troops pressed forward, and, in one determined charge, gained possession of the battery, and drove the enemy in confusion down the hill.

X. Three times did the British rally and attempt to regain their lost battery, but without success : they were repulsed with fearful loss at every assault. Finally, at midnight, they withdrew, leaving the Americans in quiet possession of the field, each party losing about eight hundred men in killed and wounded. Brown and Scott having both been severely wounded, the command devolved upon General Ripley, who retired with his forces to Fort Erie, where General Gaines arrived soon afterward, and, being a senior officer, assumed the command.

XI. In a few days, General Drummond advanced against Fort Erie, and with a force of five thousand men, commenced a siege. On the 15th of August, eleven days after, the enemy

---

* James Miller was born in New Hampshire, in 1776. He took part in the capture of Fort Erie and in the battle of Chippewa. He died in New Hampshire, in 1851.

IX. QUESTIONS.—32 What, during the battle, became evident to Brown? 33. What question was asked and reply given? 34. Give an account of Miller's heroic achievement.

X. 35. Give a further account of the battle. 36. What officers were wounded in the battle? 37. Who, after the battle, took the command? 38. Whither did Ripley retire? 39. By whom was he succeeded?

undertook to carry the fort by assault, but were repulsed with the loss of more than a thousand men. Though the wounds which Brown had received at Lundy's Lane were yet unhealed, he repaired to the fort and took the command.

XII. Having ascertained that formidable preparations were being made for pressing the siege, he resolved not to await their completion. Accordingly, at noon, on the 17th of September, a sortie was made with nearly the whole of his disposable force. In the space of an hour, the advanced works of the besiegers, which had cost nearly fifty days' labor to erect, were destroyed, and about seven hundred of their number either fell or were taken prisoners. Drummond, upon being informed soon afterward that Izard was approaching with re-enforcements, retired to Fort George. The Americans, in November, abandoned and destroyed Fort Erie, and, crossing the Niagara, went into winter quarters.

XIII. Izard, when he started from Plattsburg on his march for the relief of Brown, left General Macomb* (ma-koom') in command of only fifteen hundred men; but, as the enemy began to threaten Plattsburg, this force was augmented by volunteers from Vermont. Sir George Prevost, at the head of fourteen thousand men, a large number of whom were veterans who had served under Wellington, in Europe, marched against Macomb; and the British fleet on Lake Champlain, commanded by Commodore Downie (down'-e), sailed to attack the American fleet, under Commodore MacDonough (mac-don'-o).

---

* Alexander Macomb was born in Michigan, in 1780. He died at Washington, in 1841.

XI. QUESTIONS.—40. How was Fort Erie threatened by Drummond? 41. What took place on the 15th of August? 42. Who afterward took command at Fort Erie?

XII 43 When did Brown make a sortie from the fort? 44. What induced him to make it? 45. What was his success? 46 Why did Drummond afterward retire to Fort George? 47. What did the Americans do in November?

XIII 48. In what state for defense did Izard leave Plattsburg? 49. How was Macomb's force augmented? 50. What southward movement did Prevost make? 51. What movement was made by Downie?

XIV. Macomb withdrew his forces to the south
1814.　side of the Saranac River, and prepared to dispute any
attempt which the enemy might make to cross, while Prevost
took a position on the north side, where he erected batteries.
For four days the two armies were on the opposite banks of
the Saranac, and all attempts of the British to force a passage
were successfully resisted.

COMMODORE MACDONOUGH.

XV. On the 11th of September, the battle of Plattsburg
and of Lake Champlain took place. The British commenced
the one on the land by opening a heavy cannonade upon the
American works, while at the same time their fleet bore down
and engaged MacDonough's* vessels, which were at anchor
in the bay of Plattsburg. After an action of two hours and
a quarter between the two fleets, flag after flag of the British
struck, and the victory of MacDonough was complete.

XVI. The contest on the land continued throughout the
day. The British undertook to cross the Saranac, making the
attempt in three columns, but without success. After the defeat of Downie, the fire from their batteries slackened, and at
nightfall ceased entirely. They then commenced a hasty retreat,
leaving behind their sick and wounded, and a large quantity of
military stores. Of the army of fourteen thousand men which
Prevost led against Macomb, two hundred and fifty were

---

* Thomas MacDonough was born in New Castle Co., Delaware, in 1783. He was one of Decatur's
party which boarded and destroyed the frigate Philadelphia in the harbor of Tripoli, in 1804. He died at
sea, in 1815.

XIV. QUESTIONS.—52. How did Macomb prepare to meet Prevost? 53. Where
did Prevost take a position? 54. What is said of his attempts to cross the Saranac?
55. Into what body of water does the Saranac flow? (See map, p. 149.)

XV. 56. Give an account of the battle of Lake Champlain.

XVI. 57. Give an account of the battle of Plattsburg. 58. What losses were sustained by each party?

killed or wounded, and more than two thousand deserted. The loss of the Americans was one hundred and twenty.

XVII. During the greater part of 1814 the whole Atlantic seaboard was locked up by British cruisers, from which descents were often made upon small towns. About the middle of August, a squadron of the enemy arrived in Chesapeake Bay, bringing a large body of troops, commanded by General Ross. This force, it was evident, was intended to strike a heavy blow at some of the important cities.

XVIII. Ross, with five thousand men, landed at Benedict, situated on the Patuxent River, twenty-five miles from its mouth. His first object was the destruction of an American flotilla, commanded by Commodore Barney, which had harassed and injured the lighter vessels of the enemy's fleet, but which was then lying in the Patuxent. As the British approached, Barney, rather than have his boats fall into their hands, burnt them.

PART OF VIRGINIA AND MARYLAND.

XIX. Ross's next object was the capture of Washington; but, instead of making a direct march, he proceeded by the way of Bladensburg, where he met with some opposition from the militia under General Winder, but the only

XVII. QUESTIONS.—59. What is said of the operations of British cruisers during the most of 1814? 60. What arrival took place in August? 61. What was the evident intention of the force?

XVIII. 62. Where did Ross land? 63. On which side of the Patuxent is Benedict? (See map, p. 237.) 64. What was Ross's first object? 65. Did he succeed?

1814.   check that he received was from a body of seamen and marines, commanded by Barney.* He reached Washington on the 24th of August, burned the capitol, president's house, and other buildings, and, after effecting this wanton destruction, made a hasty retreat to the shipping, a division of which was still in the Patuxent.

BALTIMORE AND VICINITY

XX. In the mean time, a division of the fleet had ascended the Potomac as far as Alexandria, the people of which, to save their city from bombardment, surrendered their merchandise and shipping to the enemy. The two divisions of the fleet then uniting, it was determined to make an attack on Baltimore.

XXI. On the 12th of September, Ross landed his troops at North Point, fourteen

---

* Joshua Barney was born in Baltimore, in 1759. Though he was but a youth at the beginning of the Revolution, he was appointed master's mate in a sloop-of-war, in which vessel he aided in capturing the town of New Providence, on one of the Bahama Islands. He was engaged in several naval enterprises, and was three times made prisoner. His death occurred at Pittsburg, Pa., in 1818.

XIX. Questions.—66. What was his second object? 67. What route did he take to Washington? 68. On which side of the Potomac is Washington? (See map, p. 237.) 69. In which direction from Bladensburg is Washington? (See same map.) 70. What opposition and check did Ross meet with on his march? 71. When did he reach Washington? 72. What did he effect there? 73. What did he then do?

XX. 74. What had another division of the fleet been doing in the mean time? 75. What did the British then determine upon.

XXI. 76. When did Ross land at North Point. 77. What is the name of the other point at the mouth of the Patapsco? (See map, p. 238.) 78. How far is North Point from Baltimore? 79. What was done by the enemy's vessels on the 12th? 80. How far is Fort McHenry from Baltimore? 81. What befell Ross himself?

miles from Baltimore, while sixteen of the enemy's ships moved up the Patapsco River, to bombard Fort McHenry, commanding the channel, at the distance of about two miles below the city. On his march Ross was met by an advance corps of Americans, and, in a slight skirmish, killed.

XXII. General Brooke, Ross's successor, gave the order to continue the advance, but the progress of the British at one point was disputed, for more than an hour, by a body of militia, commanded by General Stricker. The Americans then fell back in good order, and took a position near the defenses of the city. Brooke resumed the march, but the resolute front which the Americans presented, deterred him from making an attack until he could hear from the fleet.

XXIII. In the mean time, Fort McHenry had been subjected to a heavy bombardment. The firing commenced on the morning of the 13th, and continued till near the following morning, but without making any serious impression. Brooke, therefore, seeing no prospect of success against the city, embarked his troops, and the whole force of the enemy withdrew.

MOBILE AND VICINITY.

XXIV. During the summer, the authorities of Pensacola, then a Spanish port, allowed the British to take possession of their forts, and fit out an expedition against Fort Bowyer (*bo'-yer*), now Fort Morgan, situated at the entrance to Mobile (*mo-beel'*) Bay. On the 15th of September, the fort was assailed by a British

XXII. QUESTIONS.—82. Who succeeded Ross? 93. Give an account of the battle that took place. 84. Why did not Stricker attack the Americans at their position near the defenses of Baltimore?

XXIII. 85. Give an account of the attack upon Fort McHenry. 86. What did Brooke then do?

XXIV. 87. How is Pensacola situated? (See map, p. 223.) 88. Did Pensacola belong to Spain or the United States in 1814? 89. Which of the belligerent powers did the authorities of Pensacola favor during the war? 90. How did that appear? 91. In what direction from Mobile is Fort Morgan? (See map, p. 223.) 92. Give an account of the attack upon Fort Morgan.

1814. fleet, aided by a combined force of Indians and marines; but the enemy were repulsed, losing one of their ships and many men. The other ships effected their escape, returning to Pensacola.

XXV. Florida was then a Spanish province, but it was used by the English, who made Pensacola the rendezvous of their forces, and from that port fitted out expeditions against the United States. The Spaniards made not the least attempt to prevent this abuse of neutral territory; indeed, it is certain they had no disposition to interfere with the operations of the English. Jackson, who, in 1814, was in command at Mobile, placed himself at the head of three thousand men, and marched upon Pensacola. Negotiations failing, he seized the town by force, and compelled the British to leave.

XXVI. Returning to Mobile, he made preparations to meet an anticipated attack upon that place; but learning that the British were about to invade Louisiana for the special purpose of securing possession of New Orleans, he sent the mass of his troops to that city, and reached it himself at the beginning of December. He found the city in no condition for defense, and at once adopted the most energetic measures to oppose the enemy.

XXVII. Towards the middle of December, a British squadron entered Lake Borgne (*born*), the shortest avenue of approach from the Gulf of Mexico to New Orleans, carrying a land force of over twelve thousand men, many of whom were veterans who had served under Wellington. This army was commanded by Sir Edward Pakenham, one of their most distinguished military leaders. On the 14th, Lieutenant Jones, commanding a flotilla of American gunboats, was attacked by

XXV. QUESTIONS.—93 What is said of the use made by the English of Pensacola, and of the disposition of the authorities there towards the United States? 94. State what was done by Jackson

XXVI 95 Where did Jackson go after leaving Pensacola? 96. What did he do there? 97 What information did he receive while there? 98 What course did he then pursue?

XXVII 99 With what force did the British advance against New Orleans? 100· What avenue of approach did they take to that city? 101 Give an account of the action of the 14th of December.

a portion of the British squadron, and, after a sanguinary engagement, was compelled to surrender, thus giving the enemy the control of the route to New Orleans.

XXVIII. The vanguard of the British army landed on the 16th, and marched to a place on the Mississippi, about nine miles from New Orleans, where an encampment was formed on the morning of the 23d. Here the British were attacked by Jackson on the following night. The contest was spirited, and the result advantageous to the Americans, as the enemy's advance was thereby checked, giving Jackson more time to prepare his line of defenses, four miles from the city. On the 28th of December, and again on the first day of the new year, the British attacked the American works, but without success.

XXIX. Pakenham at length determined to make a general assault. Accordingly, on the 8th of January, 1815, the battle of New Orleans, which was the final contest of the war, was fought. The British advanced in the face of a destructive fire from the American batteries : when they were within reach of the muskets and rifles from behind the intrenchments, volley after volley was poured upon them with such terrible effect, that they were thrown into confusion. Pakenham was slain, and his troops fled in dismay, leaving two thousand of their number killed, wounded, and prisoners. The Americans lost only thirteen, seven killed and six wounded.

XXX. A large number of citizens of the United States, belonging to the Federal party,* had been opposed to the war from its very commencement, and they continued to oppose its prosecution till the close. These persons were mostly resi-

---

* The people of the United States were, at that time, divided into two great political parties, calling themselves Democrats and Federalists. The former were in favor of prosecuting the war, while the latter were opposed.

XXVIII. Questions.—102. Of the landing of the British, their march and encampment. 103. Of the battle on the 23d of December. 104. Of the two following attacks.

XXIX. 105. When did the battle of New Orleans take place? 106. Give an account of it. 107. What losses were sustained by both parties? 108. In what direction from Mobile is New Orleans? (See map, p. 223.)

1814.   dents of New England.   They regarded the war as un-
necessary and impolitic; the losses, too, which they
were sustaining in their commerce and fisheries, were not without influence upon them.

XXXI. For the purpose of considering their grievances,
and devising means of redress, a convention was held at Hartford, Connecticut, in December, 1814.   The friends of President Madison and of the war looked upon this assemblage of
delegates, commonly known as the " Hartford Convention," as
a treasonable body; but their doings were, to say the least,
harmless, their principal act being the adoption of a document
which presented a statement of grievances, and recommended
several amendments to the Constitution.   After three weeks
of secret session, the convention adjourned.

XXXII. The joyful tidings of
peace at length reached the
United States.   In February,
1815, an English sloop-of-war
arrived from Europe, bearing a
treaty of peace which had been
agreed upon by British and
American commissioners who
had assembled at Ghent, a city
of Belgium.   The document was
signed on the 24th of December,
fifteen days before the battle of
New Orleans.   The commissioners

HENRY CLAY.*

on the part of the United States, who had negotiated it, were

* Henry Clay was born in Hanover Co., Virginia, in 1777.   He died at Washington, in 1852, and it was
said of him, in a eulogy pronounced by John C. Breckinridge, a political adversary, that. "As a leader in
a deliberative body, Mr. Clay had no equal in America."

XXX.   QUESTIONS.—109. What is said of the course pursued by certain persons
who were opposed to the war?   110. State what is said of their residence, opinions,
&c.
XXXI. 111. Give an account of the "Hartford Convention," and its doings.
XXXII. 112. What news reached the United States in February, 1815?   113.
At what place did the commissioners meet who negotiated the treaty?   114. Who
were the American commissioners?   115. When was the treaty signed at Ghent?

Henry Clay, John Quincy Adams, Jonathan Russell, James A. Bayard, and Albert Gallatin.*

XXXIII. The two great points of dispute—the encroachments upon American commerce, and the impressment of American seamen—which were the main causes of the war, were left untouched by the treaty. The omission, however, was not important, inasmuch as, by the termination of the European war, all encroachments upon American commerce ceased, and, by the great success of the American navy and privateers, the impressment question was effectually disposed of.

* Albert Gallatin was born in Geneva, Switzerland, in 1761. In 1780, he arrived in the United States, and at once aided the Americans, with his hands and money, in their military operations in Maine. He was, at one time, a teacher of French in Harvard College, was several times elected to the House of Representatives from Pennsylvania, and he was Secretary of the Treasury under Jefferson and Madison. His death occurred at Astoria, Long Island, N. Y., in 1849.

XXXIII. QUESTIONS.—116. In what respects was the treaty incomplete and unsatisfactory? 117. By what events were these omissions rendered unimportant?

PRINCIPAL LAND BATTLES OF THE SECOND WAR WITH ENGLAND.

* The asterisk indicates the successful party.

DATES	BATTLES.	COMMANDERS.		MEN ENGAGED.	
		American.	British.	Amer.	British.
1812					
Aug. 5,	Brownstown	Van Horn	Tecumseh* ..	200	600
Aug. 9, {	Maguaga, or 2d of Brownstown	Miller*	Tecumseh ..	600	900
Oct. 13,	Queenstown .	Van Rensselaer	Brock*.	1,200	2,500
1813.					
Jan 22,	Frenchtown	Winchester.	Proctor*	800	1,500
April 27,	York............	Pike*. ...	Sheaffe......	1,700	1,500
May 5,	Fort Meigs	Clay* ...	Proctor ..	1,200	2,000
May 29,	Sackett's Harbor. .	Brown* ...	Prevost ...	1,000	1,000
Aug. 2,	Fort Stephenson...	Croghan* ...	Proctor	100	1,300
Oct. 5,	Thames	Harrison* ...	Proctor	2,500	2,000
Nov. 11,	Chrysler's Field ...	Boyd	Morrison	1,200	2,000
1814.					
March 30,	La Colle Mill	Wilkinson ..	Hancock* . .	4,000	2 000
July 5,	Chippewa .	Brown* ...	Riall ...	1 900	2,100
July 25,	Lundy's Lane . .	Brown* ...	Drummond ..	3,500	5,000
Aug. 15,	Fort Erie (assault)	Gaines* ..	Drummond ..	2,500	5,000
Aug 24,	Bladensburg.. ...	Winder . .	Ross*	3,500	5,000
Sept. 11,	Plattsburg..... ...	Macomb*....	Prevost	3,000	14,000
Sept 12,	North Point... ...	Stricker	Brooke*....	2,000	5,000
Sept. 13,	Fort McHenry. .	Armistead*.	Cochrane. .	1,000	16 ships
Sep. 15,	Fort Bowyer	Lawrence* ...	Nicholls..	120	Mixed
Sept 17,	Fort Erie (sortie) ..	Brown* ...	Drummond ..	2,500	3,500
Dec. 23,	9 miles from N. O.	Jackson	Keane ...	2,000	2,500
1815.					
Jan. 8,	New Orleans	Jackson* .	Pakenham.	6,000	12 000

PRINCIPAL NAVAL BATTLES OF THE SECOND WAR WITH ENGLAND

* The asterisk indicates the successful party.

DATES.	WHERE FOUGHT	VESSELS.	COMMANDERS
1812			
Aug. 13,	Off Newfoundland	Am Frig Essex ..	Porter.*
		Br Sloop Alert	Laugharne.
Aug 19,	Off Massachusetts	Am Frig Constitution .	Hull *
		Br Frig Guerriere	Dacres
Oct. 18,	Off North Carolina	Am. Sloop Wasp	Jones.*
		Br. Brig Frolic	Whinyates
Oct. 25,	Near Canary Islands	Am Frig United States	Decatur.*
		Br. Frig. Macedonian	Carden
Dec 29,	Off San Salvador	Am. Frig Constitution	Bainbridge.*
		Br Frig Java	Lambert.
1813			
Feb 24,	Off Demarara	Am. Sloop Hornet ..	Lawrence.*
		Br. Brig Peacock	Peake
June 1,	Massachusetts Bay	Am. Frig. Chesapeake	Lawrence.
		Br. Frig Shannon	Broke.*
Aug 14,	British Channel ..	Am Brig Argus	Allen
		Br. Sloop Pelican	Maples.*
Sept 5,	Off coast of Maine	Am Brig Enterprise	Burrows *
		Br. Brig Boxer	Blythe.
Sept. 10,	Lake Erie	Am. 9 ves. 54 guns	Perry.*
		Br 6 ves 63 guns	Barclay
1814			
March 28	Harbor of Valparaiso	Am Frig Essex ..	Porter
		Br Brig Phœbe	Hillyar *
		Br. Sloop Cherub ..	Tucker
April 29,	Off coast of Florida	Am Sloop Peacock	Warrington *
		Br Brig Epervier	Wales
June 28,	Near British Channel	Am Sloop Wasp	Blakely.*
		Br Sloop Reindeer	Manners.
Sept. 1,	Near Africa	Am. Sloop Wasp.	Blakely.*
		Br Sloop Avon	Arbuthnot
Sept 11,	Lake Champlain	Am 14 vessels, 86 guns.	McDonough *
		Br. 17 vessels, 95 guns .	Downie.
Dec 14,	Lake Borgne	Am 5 gunboats	Jones
		Br 40 barges	Lockyer *
1815			
Jan 15,	Off New Jersey	Am Frig President	Decatur
		Br. (Squadron)	Hayes.*
Feb. 20,	Off Island of Madeira	Am. Frig. Constitution	Stewart.*
		Br. Ship Cyane	Falcon.
		Br Ship Levant	Douglass.
March 23,	Off Brazil	Am. Sloop Hornet	Biddle *
		Br Brig Penguin	Dickenson.

WAR WITH ALGIERS

XXXIV. During "The War of 1812," the Algerines, believing that the United States were unable to protect their
interests in the Mediterranean, resumed their old practice of

piracy, seized several American vessels, and insulted and plundered the consul of the United States. In May, 1815, a naval force, commanded by Decatur, was sent to the Mediterranean.

XXXV. On the 17th of June, Decatur encountered the largest vessel in the Algerine navy, and captured her, after a running fight of twenty-five minutes. Two days after this success he captured another frigate, with more than five hundred men. He then appeared before Algiers, and compelled the Dey to liberate the American prisoners in his hands, and relinquish all future claims to the annual tribute which the United States had paid to Algiers since 1795, for the purpose of securing the American commerce from molestation in the Mediterranean.

INDIANA.
"This State derived its name from the word *Indian*, the *a* being added, it is supposed, to give it a feminine signification. It was first applied, in 1768, to a grant of land near the Ohio, which a company of traders in that year obtained from the Indians." The State has no motto.

XXXVI. Decatur next proceeded to Tunis (*too'-nis*) and Tripoli, and from both powers exacted payment for American vessels which the English had been allowed to capture in their harbors during the war. They were likewise compelled to make indemnity for other losses which American citizens had sustained at their

---

XXXV. QUESTIONS,—120. Give the account of Decatur's two successes against the Algerine vessels. 121. What did he further accomplish against Algiers?

XXXVI. 122. To what two places did Decatur next proceed? 123. What did he compel the two powers to do?

hands, and to agree to abstain from further depredations upon the commerce of the United States.

XXXVII. During Madison's administration, two States were added to the Union: Louisiana, in 1812, and Indiana, previously a portion of the Northwest Territory, in 1816. Madison, having served two presidential terms, like Jefferson, followed the example of Washington, and declined a second re-election. He was succeeded by James Monroe, also of Virginia.

XXXVII Questions —124. When were Louisiana and Indiana admitted into the Union? 125. Why was not Madison elected President for a third term? 126. By whom was he succeeded?

REVIEW QUESTIONS.

SECTION VII.

FROM THE BEGINNING OF MONROE'S ADMINISTRATION, IN 1817,
TO THE CLOSE OF TYLER'S, IN 1845.

MONROE'S ADMINISTRATION.

JAMES MONROE
Was born in Westmoreland Co., Va.,
April 28, 1758. He served with credit
in the Revolutionary War, participat-
ing in several battles. His death occurred at New York, July 4th, 1831.

I. JAMES MONROE, the fifth President of the United States, was inaugurated at Washington, on the 4th of March, 1817; and his administration commenced under very favorable circumstances.* We were at peace with all foreign powers, our commerce rode every sea unmolested, and the strife at home, between the two great political parties, Democrats and Federalists, had entirely ceased.

II. Towards the close of 1817, the Seminole Indians, joined by some Creeks, commenced depredations on the frontier settlements of Georgia and Ala-

* President Monroe's cabinet consisted of John Quincy Adams, Secretary of State; William H. Crawford, Secretary of the Treasury; John C. Calhoun, Secretary of War; Benjamin W. Crowninshield, Secretary of the Navy; and William Wirt, Attorney-General.

MONROE'S ADMINISTRATION. I. QUESTIONS.—1. When and where was Monroe inaugurated? 2. How did his administration commence? 3. State the three circumstances.

bama. General Gaines was sent against them, but his force being insufficient, General Jackson was ordered into service. Jackson soon overran the Indian country, and being convinced that the Seminoles had been instigated to hostilities by persons in Florida, he seized the Spanish forts, both at St. Mark's and Pensacola.

III. Two British subjects, Arbuthnot and Ambrister, having fallen into his hands, were tried by a court-martial, on a

ILLINOIS.

"Illinois was so called from its principal river. The word, an Indian one, is said to signify the river of men." The first settlements within the present limits of the State were made by the French. The motto of Illinois is given above, on the State seal.

charge of having incited the Indians to hostilities, found guilty, and executed. Jackson's invasion of Florida, a territory belonging to a nation at peace with the United States, and his summary proceedings in the prosecution of the war, were condemned by many persons; but they were approved by the President and Congress.

IV. A treaty was made in 1819, by which Florida was ceded to the United States; but it was not till towards the close of 1820 that the King of Spain ratified the treaty, nor till July, 1821, that the government of Spain surrendered possession of the province. Although the Seminoles, a fierce and

II. QUESTIONS.—4. What troubles commenced towards the close of 1817? 5. Who was first sent against the Seminoles? 6. Who was next sent? 7. Of what was Jackson soon convinced? 8. What did he accordingly do? 9. How are St. Mark's and Pensacola situated? (See map, p. 223, also of Florida.)

III. 10. State the cases of Arbuthnot and Ambrister. 11. What acts of Jackson were much condemned?

11*

MISSISSIPPI.

This State derived its name from the river so called. The word Mississippi is of Indian origin. It was "spelled by some old writers *Miche-Sepe*, and interpreted by them the *Great River*, and the *Great Father of Waters*." A settlement was made by the French, within the present limits of the State, as early as the year 1716. The Seal of the State is represented above. Mississippi has no motto.

warlike Indian race, occupied the best lands in the territory, immigration set in, and a considerable population soon established themselves in the country.

V. The Mississippi Territory, which embraced the present States of Alabama and Mississippi, was divided in 1817, and the western portion admitted into the Union as the State of Mississippi. Illinois (*il-lin-oï*), which up to 1800 had been a part of the Northwest Territory, and from that time to 1809, had formed, with Indiana, the Indiana Territory, and subsequently by itself the Illinois Territory, was admitted into the Union as a State in 1818. Alabama was admitted in 1819. In 1820, Maine, which had, up to that time, been a district of Massachusetts, was organized as a State, and admitted into the Union.

VI. The most important event of Monroe's administration, was the controversy preceding the admission of Missouri (*mis-soo'-rē*) into the Union, by which, for the first time, the

IV. QUESTIONS.—12. State the facts connected with the acquisition of Florida. 13. What is said of the Seminoles and their possessions? 14. Of immigration to Florida?

V. 15. When was Mississippi admitted into the Union? 16. What can you state of the previous history of Mississippi? 17. When was Illinois admitted into the Union? 18. What can you state of the previous history of Illinois? 19. When was Maine admitted? 20. What can you state of the previous history of Maine?

VI. 21. What was the most important event of Monroe's administration? 22. How were the States arrayed on the slavery question?

country was divided upon the slavery question; the States of the North opposing the admission of Missouri as a slave State, while those of the South favored such admission.

VII. In Congress, the debate was long and acrimonious. At length a bill, known as the "Missouri Compromise," was passed, by which it was declared that slavery was prohibited forever in all territory north of thirty-six degrees and thirty minutes north latitude, and west of the Mississippi, Missouri excepted.

ALABAMA.*

Alabama was so called from its principal river. The word is of Indian origin, signifying "here we rest." The territory, comprising the States of Alabama and Mississippi, was originally a part of Georgia; but, in 1802, was ceded to the United States. The seal of Alabama is given above.

Under this compromise, Missouri was admitted into the Union as a slave State, in 1821.

VIII. Another important event of Monroe's administration was the recognition of the Spanish American republics, which had declared and maintained their independence for several years. In 1823, the year following the recognition, President Monroe declared in his annual message, that, "as a principle, the American continents, by the free and independent position

---

* The territory now known as Alabama was originally a part of Georgia. In 1798, all the region comprising the present States of Alabama and Mississippi was organized as the territory of Mississippi. In 1817, its western portion became the State of Mississippi, while the other part continued to be the territory of Alabama until its admission as a State.

VII. QUESTIONS.—23. What is said of the debate in Congress? 24. What bill was passed? 25. What was the important declaration of the bill? 26. What is said of the admission of Missouri?

VIII. 27. What other important event took place during the administration of Monroe? 28. Recite the whole of the "Monroe Doctrine." 29. When and under what circumstances was that "doctrine" put forth?

SEAL OF MAINE.*

which they have assumed and maintained, are henceforth not to be considered as subject for future colonization by any European power ;" a declaration which has since been famous as the " Monroe Doctrine."

IX. During Monroe's administration, two events occurred which are worthy of notice. The first was the President's tour, in 1817, through the eastern and other States, for the purpose of making a personal examination of military posts. The second was the visit of Lafayette to this country. The distinguished visitor arrived in the summer of 1824; and his tour, which was extended through all of the twenty-four States, was everywhere signalized by tokens of respect from a grateful people.

SEAL OF MISSOURI.†

X. Monroe, having served two presidential terms, declined, in imitation of his predecessors, Washington, Jefferson, and Madison, being a candidate for a third term, and was succeeded by John Quincy Adams, of Massachusetts.

---

* Authors are not agreed with regard to the derivation of the name given to this State. The prevailing opinion is that Maine was so called in compliment to Henrietta Maria, wife of Charles I. of England, who, it was supposed, owned the province of Maine, in France. The Coat of Arms of the State of Maine is delineated on the seal (given above), and contains the motto of the State, *Dirigo*, signifying I direct.

† This State takes its name from the great river which passes through it. The word Missouri, signifying Mud River, was applied to the river by the Indians, because of the turbid character of that stream. The motto of Missouri (shown on the seal of the State above) is: *Salus populi suprema lex*—The welfare of the people is the first great law.

IX. QUESTIONS.—30. What account can you give of Monroe's tour in 1817? 31. What of Lafayette's visit to the United States in 1824?

X. 32. Why was not Monroe elected President for a third term? 33. By whom was he succeeded?

JOHN QUINCY ADAMS.

JOHN QUINCY ADAMS
Was born in Braintree, near Boston,
Mass., July 11, 1767. In 1797 he married
a daughter of Joshua Johnson, American
consul at London. His death occurred
at Washington, Feb. 23, 1848.

I. Four candidates were put in nomination to succeed President Monroe, and the consequence was that none of them had a majority of the electoral votes. The election then went to the House of Representatives, for the second time, Jefferson having been thus elected, in 1801 ; and John Quincy Adams was chosen the sixth President of the United States. His inauguration took place at Washington, on the 4th of March, 1825.*

II. On the fiftieth anniversary of American Independence, July the 4th, 1826, occurred the death of the two venerable ex-presidents, John Adams and Thomas Jefferson. As this remarkable coinci-

---

* The cabinet of President John Quincy Adams was constituted as follows: Henry Clay, Secretary of State ; Richard Rush, Secretary of the Treasury ; James Barbour, Secretary of War ; Samuel L. Southard, Secretary of the Navy ; and William Wirt, Attorney-General.

ADAMS'S ADMINISTRATION.—I. QUESTIONS.—1. How many candidates were put in nomination to succeed Monroe? 2. What was the consequence? 3. Where did the election then go? 4. Who was elected? 5. When did his inauguration take place ?

II. 6. What remarkable coincidence occurred during the administration of John Quincy Adams? 7. When did it occur? 8. State the parallels in their lives.

dence took place more than a year after the commencement
of the tenth presidential term, John Adams lived to see his
son President. When it is recollected that Adams and Jefferson were members of the committee that framed the Declaration of Independence; that both signed the important document;
that both had been foreign ministers, vice-presidents, and presidents of the United States; and that each had lived to a venerable age, the coincidence of their deaths is indeed remarkable.

III. The administration of John Quincy Adams was one of
wisdom and peace; and under it the nation made rapid increase in population and wealth. Towards its close the presidential contest for the succession was carried on with great
animation and virulence, and resulted in the election of
Andrew Jackson, of Tennessee.

JACKSON'S ADMINISTRATION.

I. The inauguration of Jackson took place at Washington,
on the 4th of March, 1829,* and the new president at once
commenced a series of vigorous measures which he carried
out for eight years. The practice of removing office-holders,
and appointing the political friends of the President, was
begun by him.

II. In his first annual message to Congress, President Jackson
took strong ground against the renewal of the charter of the
United States Bank, arguing that "such an institution is not authorized by the constitution." Notwithstanding this opposition,

---

* President Jackson's cabinet consisted of Martin Van Buren, Secretary of State, Samuel D Ingham,
Secretary of the Treasury, John H Eaton, Secretary of War, John Branch, Secretary of the Navy, John
McPherson Berrien, Attorney-General, and William T Barry, Postmaster-General The Postmaster-
General was, for the first time, made a member of the cabinet. In 1831, in consequence of a personal
quarrel, changes were made in the cabinet. Edward Livingston was Secretary of State, Louis McLane,
Secretary of the Treasury ; Lewis Cass, Secretary of War, Levi Woodbury, Secretary of the Navy , and
Roger B. Taney, Attorney-General. Other changes afterward took place.

III. Questions —9 What is said of the administration of John Quincy Adams?
10 Of the contest for the presidential succession? 11. What was the result of the
contest?

JACKSON'S ADMINISTRATION.—I. 1 When was Jackson inaugurated? 2 How did
he commence and continue to govern? 3 What practice did he begin?

Congress, in 1832, passed a bill to re-charter the bank, but Jackson vetoed it; and as it subsequently failed to receive sufficient votes to secure its passage over the veto, the original charter expired by limitation in 1836, and the bank then ceased to be a national institution.

III. In 1832, the Northwest frontier suffered from Indian hostilities; but after several skirmishes, most of the savages were driven west of the Mississippi River. Black Hawk, their most

ANDREW JACKSON Was born in Mecklenburg Co., N. C., March 15, 1767. In 1791 he married Mrs. Rachel Robards. His death occurred at the "Hermitage," near Nashville, Tenn., June 8, 1845.

noted leader, and from whom the contest became generally known as *The Black Hawk War*, was taken prisoner. After a detention of some months, during which he was conducted through Washington and other cities, for the purpose of convincing him that resistance against the power of the whites was useless, he was allowed to rejoin his people.

IV. A tariff bill, which had been passed by Congress during the administration of John Quincy Adams, had been

---

II. Questions.—4. What stand did Jackson take with reference to the United States Bank? 5. What was his main objection? 6. What action did Congress take? 7. How came it that the bank ceased to be a national institution?

III. 8. Give an account of *The Black Hawk War*. 9. How was Black Hawk treated after the war?

IV. 10. What is said of a tariff bill, passed before Jackson was President? 11. How was the dissatisfaction increased?

BLACK HAWK.

exceedingly distasteful to the cotton-growing States; and when, in 1832, an act was passed imposing additional duties on foreign goods, the dissatisfaction was greatly increased, especially in South Carolina.

V. A convention, held in that State, declared the tariff acts unconstitutional, and, therefore, null and void. It also declared that duties should not be paid, and proclaimed that any attempts on the part of the general government to enforce the collection of duties would produce the withdrawal of South Carolina from the Union. One of the chief leaders of the nullifiers, as those persons in South Carolina who

JOHN C. CALHOUN.

sustained the declarations of the convention were called, was John C. Calhoun,* who had recently resigned the vice-presidency of the United States. Another leader, of not much less distinction, was Robert Y. Hayne, who, when a United States Senator, in 1830, was the first to declare and defend in Congress the doctrine of nullification, and to whom Daniel Webster, of Massachusetts, then replied in one of the most remarkable

---

* John C. Calhoun was born in the district of Abbeville, S. C., in 1782. He was for six years a representative in Congress; for a number of years was a United States Senator; was Secretary of War in Monroe's cabinet; and was twice elected Vice-President of the United States. In 1845, while Secretary of State in Tyler's cabinet, he was " the author of the annexation of Texas." He died at Washington, in 1850.

V. QUESTIONS.—12. What was declared by a South Carolina Convention? 13. What else did it declare? 14. Who was the great leader of the nullifiers? 15. What high position had Calhoun resigned? 16. Who was another leader of the nullifiers? 17. What did Hayne do in 1830? 18. Who replied to him? 19. What is said of that reply?

speeches ever delivered in Congress. Although Hayne was the first to declare this doctrine in Congress, Calhoun, in a paper known as the "South Carolina Exposition," was its author.

DANIEL WEBSTER.*

VI. In this crisis, President Jackson acted with that promptness and energy which were so characteristic of the man. By his direction an army, under General Scott, was ordered to Charleston; and he issued a proclamation against the nullifiers and their doctrine, which met with a cordial response from every friend of the Union. A "compromise bill," offered by Mr. Clay and passed by Congress, was accepted by Calhoun and his friends, and thus the danger which threatened the Union was averted.

THE SEMINOLE WAR.

VII. Towards the close of 1835, the Seminole Indians, influenced by Micanopy, their head sachem, and by Osceola (os-e-o'-la), the most noted of their chiefs, and a man of great cunning and courage, commenced hostilities against the settlements of the whites in Florida. This outbreak of the Seminoles had its origin

PART OF FLORIDA.

---

* Daniel Webster was born at Salisbury, N. H., in 1782. A large portion of his life was passed at Washington, either as a member of Congress or the cabinet. In 1842, while Secretary of State in Tyler's cabinet, he negotiated with Lord Ashburton a treaty settling the differences between the United States and Great Britain in relation to the northeastern boundary, differences which had disturbed the relations of the two countries for more than sixty years. Webster died at Marshfield, Mass., in 1852.

VI. QUESTIONS.—20. How did Jackson act in this crisis? 21. What was done by his direction? 22. What proclamation did he issue? 23. How was the danger to the Union averted?

in an attempt to remove them from Florida to lands west of the Mississippi, in accordance with the terms of a treaty which had been made with some of the chiefs, but which majority of the tribe did not consider binding.

VIII. In consequence of the offensive conduct of Osceola in opposition to the fulfilment of the treaty, the government agent, General Thompson, put him in irons, and kept him prisoner for six days at Fort King. By feigning penitence and making promises, Osceola obtained his liberty; but, in stead of doing as he had agreed, he placed himself at the head of a war party of Indians and fugitive slaves, and commenced the work of slaughter and devastation.

OSCEOLA.

IX. On the 28th of December, 1835, he approached house in which Thompson and some friends were dining and, making a sudden attack killed five of the number, including Thompson, and carried off their scalps, in revenge for the imprisonment which he had suffered. On the very day of Thompson's death, "Dade's massacre" occurred. Major Dade, with detachment of one hundred and ten soldiers, while marching from Tampa Bay to join General Clinch, at Fort Drane, was suddenly attacked; and that young commander and the whole of his detachment, except four men, were massacred.

VII. QUESTIONS.—24. What troubles broke out in 1835? 25. Why did the Seminoles so act? 26. What was the character of Osceola?

VIII. 27. Why was Osceola put in irons and imprisoned? 28. In what direction was Fort King from Fort Dade? (See map, p. 257.) 29. How long was Osceola kept at Fort King? 30. How did he obtain his liberty? 31. What did he do instead of performing his promises?

IX. 32. How did he have revenge for his treatment at Fort King? 33. Give an account of Dade's massacre. 34. In what direction was Dade marching when he was attacked? (See map, p. 257.)

X. On the 30th of December, two days after, Osceola encountered an American force of six hundred men under General Clinch, at the crossing of the Withlacoochee River, but,
after a hard-fought action of upward of an hour, was compelled to retreat. In February and March, 1836, at the head
of a force of more than a thousand Indians, he fought several
actions against the troops under General Gaines, in the most
important of which, occurring on the 29th of February, near
the scene of Clinch's battle-ground, one American was killed,
and more than thirty, including Gaines, were wounded.

XI. In May, 1836, a
large number of the
Creeks joined the Semi-
noles, and in Georgia and
Alabama, as well as Flor-
ida, committed great de-
vastations, compelling
thousands of whites to
flee for their lives. General Scott, who had been
appointed to the com-
mand in the South, pro-
secuted the war with
vigor, but he was soon superseded by General Jes-
sup. The Creeks were
speedily reduced, and
transported beyond the
Mississippi.

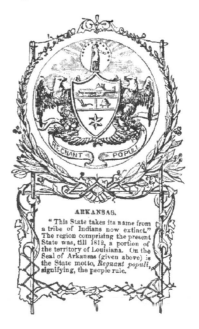

ARKANSAS.

"This State takes its name from
a tribe of Indians now extinct."
The region comprising the present
State was, till 1819, a portion of
the territory of Louisiana. On the
Seal of Arkansas (given above) is
the State motto, *Regnant populi,*
signifying, the people rule.

XII. In October, 1836,
Governor Call, of Georgia, took command of the forces in
Florida. A detachment of more than five hundred of his men

X. QUESTIONS.—35. Give an account of the battle of Withlacoochee. 36. Of the
battles in February and March of 1836.

XI. 37. What took place in May, 1836? 38. Who was then sent against the Indians? 39. Who was next sent? 40. How was the war ended as respects the
Creeks?

encountered the Indians at a place a short distance from the scene of Dade's massacre; and although the enemy dispersed after the action, yet neither in this nor in other battles could the Americans claim a decided victory.

XIII. For upwards of a year did Osceola* conduct the struggle against superior forces, with energy and skill; but, in

MICHIGAN.

Michigan was so called from the lake of the same name. The word Michigan appears to be derived from the Chippewa language, and signifies Great Lake. The motto, *Si quaris peninsulam amænam, circumspice,* If thou seekest a beautiful peninsula, behold it here, is found on the State Seal. The word *Tuebor* means, I will defend it. *E pluribus unum* signifies one composed of many.

October, 1837, he appeared in Jessup's camp, near St. Augustine, with a flag of truce, for the purpose of holding a conference. Suspecting a repetition of treachery, and desiring to prevent further bloodshed, Jessup disregarded the flag and seized the chief, who was taken to Fort Moultrie, and there kept in confinement till his death, which occurred on the last day of January, 1838.

XIV. The capture of Osceola did not end the war with the Seminoles. They amused Jessup for a while with overtures, but he, finding the Indians not sincere, directed Colonel Taylor (afterward General Taylor, and Pres-

---

* Osceola was born in Florida. His father was an Indian trader, an Englishman named Powell, and his mother was the daughter of an Indian chief.

---

ident of the United States) to proceed against them. With about a thousand men Taylor accordingly marched, and on the 25th of December, 1837, encountered the Indians in strong force on the northern side of Lake Okeechobee, and defeated them in one of the most desperate and hotly contested battles in the annals of our warfare with the red men.

XV. Though the Seminoles continued their hostilities through the administration of Jackson, as well as that of his immediate successor, they never again rallied in large force. A treaty was made with them in 1839, but it was not till 1842 that peace was finally secured.

VAN BUREN'S ADMINISTRATION.

I. JACKSON was succeeded in the presidency by Martin Van Buren, of New York. Van Buren's administration was continued during one term, or four years, extending

OCEAN STEAMER.*

from the 4th of March, 1837,† the day of inauguration, to the 4th of March, 1841.

---

* The first regular passages across the Atlantic by steamships were made in 1838, by the Sirius and Great Western.

† President Van Buren's cabinet was constituted as follows: John Forsyth, Secretary of State; Levi Woodbury, Secretary of the Treasury; Joel R. Poinsett, Secretary of War; Mahlon Dickerson, Secretary of the Navy; Benjamin F. Butler, Attorney-General; and Amos Kendall, Postmaster-General. All of these, except Poinsett, had held their respective offices in Jackson's cabinet at the close of his last term. In 1838, Dickerson and Butler resigned, and James K. Paulding was appointed in the place of the former, and Felix Grundy in that of the latter. Grundy was succeeded in 1840, by Henry D. Gilpin, and Kendall by John M. Niles.

XIV. QUESTIONS.—48. Did the capture of Osceola end the war or not? 49. Whom did Jessup order to go against the Seminoles? 50. Give an account of the battle of Okeechobee.

XV. 51. What is said of the subsequent part of the Seminole war?

VAN BUREN'S ADMINISTRATION.—I. 1. Who was Jackson's successor in the presidency? 2. When was Van Buren inaugurated?

II. Soon after his inauguration, a revolution in monetary affairs took place, producing great distress in all branches of business throughout the country. Commerce and manufactures were prostrated, and the crash was finally consummated by the suspension of specie payments by all the banks. In this crisis, the President called an extraordinary session of Congress, but little was accomplished by it for the general relief.

III. In the latter part of 1837 an insurrectionary movement commenced in Canada, having for its object the overthrow of the British rule there, and the establishment of an independent government. The movement enlisted the sympathy of Americans, particularly of those living along the borders in New York, and it engaged their active co-operation. A proclamation, issued by the President, forbidding interference in the affairs of Canada, together with the decided measures taken

MARTIN VAN BUREN
Was born at Kinderhook, Columbia Co., N. Y., December 5, 1782. He was married, in 1804, to Miss Hannah Hoes. His death occurred at Kinderhook, on the 24th of July, 1862.

N. ORR-CO.

II. QUESTIONS.—3. What took place soon after his inauguration? 4. How were commerce, manufactures, and the banks affected? 5. What did the President do in the crisis?

III. 6. What insurrection at the North, beyond the limits of the United States, broke out in 1837? 7. What was its object? 8. What proclamation did the President issue? 9. Why did he find it necessary to issue it?

by the British authorities, had the effect intended, and the attempt at insurrection was suppressed.

HARRISON'S ADMINISTRATION.

WILLIAM HENRY HARRISON
Was born in Berkeley, Charles City Co., Va., Feb. 9, 1773. At the age of nineteen he joined the army. In 1795, he married a daughter of John C. Symmes, who laid out the city of Cincinnati.

I. Van Buren's successor in office was William Henry Harrison, of Ohio, the hero of Tippecanoe and the Thames. The inauguration took place on the 4th of March, 1841. His cabinet was judiciously composed,* and the people anticipated for him a successful administration; but within a month, and after a brief illness of only eight days, he died: the sad event occurring on the 4th of April.

II. By virtue of a provision of the Constitution, John Tyler, of Virginia, then Vice-President, became President; his inauguration taking place on the 6th of April, 1841. Thus, for the first time in the history of the United States, the administration devolved on the Vice-President.

* President Harrison's cabinet was constituted as follows: Daniel Webster, Secretary of State; Thomas Ewing, Secretary of the Treasury; John Bell, Secretary of War; George E. Badger, Secretary of the Navy; Francis Granger, Postmaster-General; and J. J. Crittenden, Attorney-General.

HARRISON'S ADMINISTRATION.—I. QUESTIONS.—1. Who succeeded Van Buren in the presidency? 2. When was Harrison inaugurated? 3. What is said of his cabinet? 4. Of the anticipations of the people? 5. What was the length of his administration? 6. How was it brought to a close?

II. 7. Who was his successor? 8. By what right did Tyler become President? 9. What is noted as peculiar in the accession of Tyler to the presidency?

TYLER'S ADMINISTRATION.*

JOHN TYLER
Was born in Charles City Co., Va.,
March 29, 1790. He was married, in
1813, to Letitia Christian, who died in
1842. In 1844 he married Julia Gardiner.
He died at Richmond, Jan. 17, 1862.

I. In 1842 serious difficulties occurred in Rhode Island, growing out of a movement which was stigmatized by its opponents as the *Dorr Rebellion.* The government of Rhode Island, at that time, was based upon the charter granted by Charles II., in 1663, and consequently no change had taken place in her fundamental law during a period of almost one hundred and eighty years. The movement in 1842 had its origin in a determination among the citizens to substitute a liberal constitution in place of the old charter.

II. The people soon became divided into two parties, those who favored the movement being called the suffrage party, and those who were opposed, the charter party ; and so vio-

* President Tyler retained the cabinet officers of his predecessor until September, 1841, when all but Webster resigned. His cabinet was then constituted as follows : Daniel Webster, Secretary of State ; Walter Forward, Secretary of the Treasury ; John C. Spencer, Secretary of War ; Abel P. Upshur, Secretary of the Navy ; Charles A. Wickliffe, Postmaster-General ; and Hugh S. Legaré, Attorney-General. In May, 1843, Webster resigned, and Legaré was appointed acting secretary in his place. In the following month Legaré died, and thereupon Upshur was transferred to the State Department, and Thomas W. Gilmer was appointed Secretary of the Navy. On the 28th of February, 1844, both Upshur and Gilmer were killed by the bursting of a gun on board the United States war steamer Princeton, while on an excursion on the Potomac. A large party, including the President and many ladies, were on board at the time. John C. Calhoun was then made Secretary of State, and John Y. Mason, Secretary of the Navy.

TYLER'S ADMINISTRATION.—I. QUESTIONS.—1. When did the "*Dorr Rebellion*" occur ? 2. What was the object on the part of those engaged in it ?

lent did the controversy grow that both parties at length appealed to arms. The Governor of the State, at the head of a large military force, marched against a body of the suffrage party, who had appeared in arms at Providence. Upon his approach they dispersed. They again assembled at another place, but, upon being approached, again dispersed without resistance; and this ended the affair. A constitution, the one now in force, was soon afterward adopted.

III. Thomas W. Dorr, the leader of the suffrage party in the insurrection, was afterward arrested, tried, convicted of high treason, and sentenced to imprisonment for life. He was, however, pardoned in 1847; and, at a later period, his civil rights were restored to him, and the record of his sentence was expunged.

FLORIDA.
An unknown land was discovered by De Leon, in 1512. From the abundance of flowers that adorned its forests, and because the discovery happened on Easter Sunday, which the Spaniards call *Pascua Florida*, it was named Florida. Motto of the State: "In God is our trust." The seal is given above.

ANNEXATION OF TEXAS.

IV. A proposition for the admission of Texas into the Union caused excited discussion throughout the whole country during the closing months of Tyler's administration. Texas had been a province of Mexico, but in consequence of the arbitrary policy pur-

---

II. Questions.—3. What division of parties soon took place? 4. What is stated as evidence of the violence of the controversy? 5. Give an account of the "Rebellion."

III. 6. What account can you give of Thomas W. Dorr?

12

IOWA.

Iowa is an Indian name, its signification being, *Here is the place*, or, *This is the spot*. The Indians, having been driven westward across the Mississippi, exclaimed, as they entered the new territory, *E-o-wah!* meaning, Here is the place where we may dwell. The motto of Iowa is, *Our liberties we prize, and our rights we will maintain.*

sued by that government towards her inhabitants, the most of whom were from the United States, they declared their independence, and by force of arms sustained the declaration.

V. A bill for the admission of Texas, under certain conditions, was passed by Congress three days before the expiration of Tyler's term of office, and at once was signed by him. Tyler's last important official act was the signing of the bill admitting Florida and Iowa into the Union. He was succeeded in the presidency by James K. Polk, of Tennessee.

IV. QUESTIONS.—7. What important proposition was made in relation to Texas? 8. What did the proposition cause? 9. What can you state of the previous history of Texas?

V. 10. What progress did the proposition for the admission of Texas make during Tyler's administration? 11. When were Florida and Iowa admitted into the Union? 12. Who succeeded Tyler in the presidency?

REVIEW QUESTIONS.

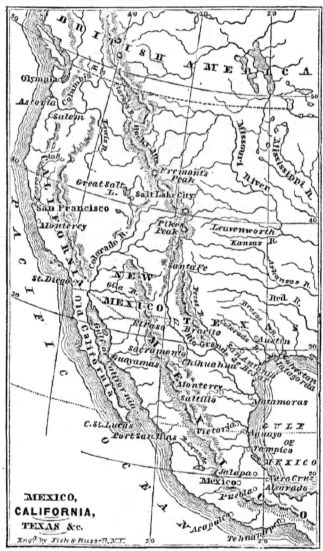

MEXICO,
CALIFORNIA,
TEXAS &c.

Eng.ᵈ by Fisk & Russell, N.Y.

(Questions to be answered from the above map.)

How is San Antonio de Bexar situated? Vera Cruz? Alvarado? Matamoras?
Jalapa? Puebla? Saltillo? Leavenworth? San Francisco? Into what body of
water does the Rio Grande flow? In what direction is Santa Fe from Leavenworth?
Saltillo from Matamoras? Victoria from Saltillo? City of Mexico from Jalapa?

SECTION VIII.

FROM THE BEGINNING OF POLK'S ADMINISTRATION, IN 1845, TO THE CLOSE OF BUCHANAN'S, IN 1861.

POLK'S ADMINISTRATION.

JAMES KNOX POLK Was born in Mecklenburg Co., N. C., Nov. 2, 1795. He was a representative in Congress from Tennessee for fourteen years. His death occurred at Nashville, Tenn., on the 15th June, 1849.

1. POLK'S inauguration took place on the 4th of March, 1845.* His administration continued during only one term, or four years, ending on the 4th of March, 1849; but it was an eventful one. At the beginning of it, he found the country involved in disputes with Mexico, in consequence of the passage of the bill for the admission of Texas. On the 4th of July, 1845, the legislature of Texas approved this bill, and, by the act of approval, Texas was ad-

---

* President Polk's cabinet was constituted as follows: James Buchanan, Secretary of State; Robert J. Walker, Secretary of the Treasury, William L. Marcy, Secretary of War; George Bancroft, Secretary of the Navy; Cave Johnson, Postmaster-General, and John Y. Mason, Attorney-General.

POLK'S ADMINISTRATION.—I. QUESTIONS. 1. When was Polk inaugurated? 2. When did his term of office begin and end? 3. In what disputes were the United States a party at the beginning of his administration? 4. When and by what act was the annexation of Texas consummated?

TEXAS.

"La Harpe, in a letter dated Nasonite (eastern Texas), July 8, 1719, calls the country the province of *Las Tekas*; and this is the first mention of the name in any published works. It may have been the appellation of some petty tribe of Indians living in eastern Texas."†

mitted into the Union, making the whole number of States twenty-eight.

WAR WITH MEXICO.

II. The annexation of Texas led to a war with Mexico ; for, notwithstanding the independence of Texas had been acknowledged by the United States, England, France, and other governments, Mexico still claimed it as a part of her own territory, and considered the act of annexation as sufficient cause of war.

III. The Mexican minister at Washington having protested against the measure of annexation, and returned home, and his government having assumed a belligerent attitude, General Taylor, who was then in command of a camp in the western part of Louisiana, was directed to hold his army in readiness to protect the Texan territory. By the advice of the Texan authorities, he was induced to concentrate his troops at Corpus Christi*

---

* Corpus Christi is a Latin term, signifying *the body of Christ.*   † Texas has no motto.

II. QUESTIONS.—5. What did the annexation of Texas lead to? 6. By what governments had the independence of Texas been acknowledged? 7. What claim did Mexico still maintain? 8. What then was the cause of the war between Mexico and the United States?

III. 9. What course did the Mexican minister pursue? 10. What, his government? 11. Where was Taylor at the time? 12. What direction did he receive? 13. Where did he afterwards concentrate his troops? 14. Into what body of water does the Nueces flow? (See map, p. 271.) 15. Why did Taylor go to Corpus Christi?

(*kor'-pus kris'-te*), situated on the western bank of the Nueces (*noo-ā'-thes*) River, near its mouth, where, in November, his forces amounted to about four thousand men.

EVENTS OF 1846.

IV. The United States, by the annexation of Texas, claimed the Rio Grande (*re'-o grahn'-dā*) as their boundary, while the Mexicans maintained that the western limits of Texas never extended beyond the Nueces. In consequence of these conflicting claims, the country between the two rivers, in time, acquired the appellation of the " disputed territory ;" and when, early in 1846, President Polk ordered Taylor to proceed with his forces to the Rio Grande, across this territory, the advance was treated by the

Mexicans as the actual commencement of hostilities.

V. On his route from Corpus Christi to the Rio Grande, Taylor established a dépôt at Point Isabel (*iz-ā-bel'*), about twenty-one miles northeast of Matamoras (*mat-a-mō'-ras*). On reaching the Rio Grande he took a position opposite Matamoras, and erected a fortress, which was afterward named Fort

---

IV. QUESTIONS.—16. What two boundary claims were maintained? 17. What region was known as the "disputed territory?" 18. What movement did Polk order Taylor to make? 19. How did the Mexicans regard the movement?

V. 20. Where is Point Isabel? (See map, p. 271.) 21. What use did Taylor make of the place? 22. Where was Fort Brown erected? 23. By whom was it erected? 24. Why was it called Fort Brown? 25. Give an account of the disaster to Thornton.

1846.   Brown, in honor of its brave defender. Learning that the Mexicans were assembling troops at a point higher up the river, Taylor sent Captain Thornton, with a party of sixty-three dragoons, to reconnoiter. On the 26th of April, this little band was attacked, and, after a loss of sixteen men, was compelled to surrender.

VI. Thus was shed the first blood in the war. The news of this affair produced the wildest excitement throughout the United States; and a war-spirit, unknown before to exist, was at once aroused. The President sent a message to Congress, announcing that Mexico had "invaded our territory, and shed the blood of our fellow-citizens on our own soil;" and Congress, adopting the spirit of the message, declared that "war existed by the act of Mexico."

VII. The Mexicans, in large force, having crossed the Rio Grande for the purpose, as Taylor thought, of moving against Point Isabel, he marched to the relief of that place, leaving a small garrison for the defense of Fort Brown. Having placed the dépôt in a better condition to resist an attack, he set out on his return to the fort.

VIII. On the 8th of May, the Mexican army, numbering full six thousand men, commanded by General Arista (*ah-rees'-tah*), was discovered upon a beautiful prairie, called Palo Alto* (*pah'-lo ahl'-to*), drawn up in battle array, prepared to dispute his progress. Although the Americans numbered not more than two thousand three hundred men, they pressed forward to the attack; and from noon till twilight, a hot contest was maintained. The enemy then were driven from their position, and the victorious Americans encamped upon the

---

* Palo Alto, a Spanish term, signifying "tall timber."

VI. QUESTIONS.—26. What effect did the news of it have in the United States ? 27. What is said of the President's message? 28. Of the action of Congress?

VII 29 Why did Taylor march to the relief of Point Isabel ? 80. Did he remain at the Point or not? 31. In what direction did he then march ?

VIII. 32 When did the battle of Palo Alto take place? 33 Give an account of it. 34. What loss was sustained by each party ?

battle-field. The loss of the Mexicans was about six hundred ; that of the victors, was only nine killed and forty-four wounded, but among the mortally wounded was the brave Major Ringgold, who died four days after.

IX. On the following day, May the 9th, Taylor resumed his march, and, towards evening, encountered the enemy under Arista, within three miles of Fort Brown, posted in and near a ravine called Resaca de la Palma* (*rä-ºah'-kah dū lah pahl'-mah*). The action was commenced on both sides by the artillery, but the Mexican guns, well aimed and rapidly discharged, were holding the Americans in check, when Captain May was ordered to silence them. At the head of his dragoons, May rushed forward with great fury, killed or dispersed the gunners, and captured General La Vega (*lah vä'-gah*). The charge being supported by the infantry, a general engagement ensued ; and, after a most obstinate resistance, the Mexicans gave way, their retreat becoming a perfect rout. Their loss, in killed, wounded, and prisoners, was at least one thousand, while the killed and wounded of the victors did not much exceed a hundred.

X. During the greater part of Taylor's absence from Fort Brown, a period of nearly eight days, it had been subjected to a bombardment from the Mexican batteries in Matamoras. The garrison made a successful defense, though their heroic commander, Major Brown, was mortally wounded by the bursting of a shell. On the 18th of May, Taylor crossed the Rio Grande and took possession of Matamoras without opposition ; but, owing to the difficulties experienced in getting re-enforcements and supplies, it was not till the end of more than three

---

* Resaca de la Palma, a Spanish term, signifying " a ravine of palm-trees."

IX. QUESTIONS.—35. When did Taylor next meet the enemy? 36. What battle ensued? 37. Give an account of it. 38. What loss was sustained by each party?

X 39. How long had Taylor been absent from Fort Brown? 40 What had occurred there during his absence? 41 What is said of the defense made? 42. What is said of the taking of Matamoras? 43 How is Matamoras situated? (See map, p. 271) 44. How long did Taylor remain at Matamoras? 45. Why did he not advance sooner?

1846.

months that he found himself strong enough to make a further advance.

XI. He then directed his march against Monterey (mon-tā-rā'), an inland city of Mexico, strong in its natural defenses, and, besides, well garrisoned by about ten thousand regular troops, under General Ampudia (am-poo'-de-ah). After garrisoning several towns on his route, he reached Monterey on the 9th of September, with a force of less than seven thousand men. On the 19th he commenced operations; and, after a series of assaults, continued through three days, in which Generals Worth and Quitman rendered brilliant service, Ampudia capitulated on the 24th. An armistice of eight weeks was agreed upon, or the truce was to continue till the expiration of that period, unless instructions to renew hostilities should be received in the mean time from either of the respective governments.

XII. Before the eight weeks had expired, Taylor received orders from Washington, directing him to renew offensive operations. Accordingly, one division of his army, under General Worth, occupied Saltillo (sahl-teel'-yo), while, at a little later period, another division, under General Patterson, took possession of Victoria, with the intention of going against Tampico (tam-pe'-co), but ascertained, before proceeding, that the place had already surrendered to Commodore Conner, commanding the "Home Squadron" in the Gulf of Mexico.

XIII. In the mean time, General Wool, with an army of about three thousand men, had set out from San Antonio de

XI. QUESTIONS.—46. Against what place did he next proceed? 47. In what direction from Matamoras is Monterey? (See map, p. 271.) 48. What is said of its defenses and the garrison then there? 49. When did he capture Monterey? 50. Give an account of the efforts which resulted in the capture. 51. What is said of the armistice?

XII. 52. Why did Taylor renew offensive operations? 53. What was done by General Worth? 54. What, by General Patterson? 55. What, by Commodore Conner? 56. In what direction is Saltillo from Monterey? (See map, p 271) 57. Victoria from Monterey? (See map, p. 268.) 58. Tampico from Monterey? (See same map.)

Bexar (*san an-to'-ne-o dā bā-har'*), a town in Texas, with the design of penetrating the province of Chihuahua (*che-wah'-wah*). After crossing the Rio Grande, and learning that Monterey was in the possession of the Americans, influenced by the advice of Taylor, he abandoned the design against Chihuahua, and joined General Worth at Saltillo.

XIV. In June, 1846, an expedition under General Kearny set out from Leavenworth (*lev'-en-wurth*), on the Missouri River, to conquer New Mexico and California. Kearny accomplished the march of nine hundred miles to Santa Fe (*san'-tah fā*), the capital of New Mexico, and took possession of the country without opposition. After organizing a new government for the place, he proceeded westward, but soon met a messenger who informed him that California was already in possession of the Americans. All the troops with him, except a hundred, then returned to Santa Fe ; and, with the small force remaining, he completed his journey across the continent.

XV. With less than a thousand men, being the main body of Kearny's invading army, Colonel Doniphan, starting from Santa Fe, marched more than a thousand miles through Mexico, and arrived at Saltillo. During this brilliant achievement he fought and was victorious in two battles, one, that of Bracito* (*brah-the'-to*), on the 25th of December, 1846, and the other, of Sacramento (*sah-crah-mane'-to*), on the 28th of Feb-

---

* Bracito, a Spanish word, signifying "Little Arm." It was so called because of the *little arm* or bend in the river where the battle was fought.

XIII. QUESTIONS.—59. How is San Antonio de Bexar situated? (See map, p. 268.) 60. By what name is the place often called? *Ans.*—San Antonio. 61. Where is Chihuahua? (See same map.) 62. What march did General Wool make? 63. Why did he not continue to Chihuahua? 64. What did he do instead?

XIV. 65. What expedition set out in June? 66. In what direction is New Mexico from Leavenworth? (See map, p. 268.) 67. What was Leavenworth then called? *Ans.*—Fort Leavenworth. 68. What did Kearny accomplish? 69. How is Santa Fe situated? (See map, p. 268.) 70. Give an account of Kearny's subsequent movements.

XV. 71. What march did Doniphan make? 72. What two successes did he achieve? 73. How are Bracito and Sacramento situated? (See map, p. 268.)

1846. ruary, 1847. While these events—the successes of Taylor, Doniphan, and others—were transpiring in Texas and the eastern part of Mexico, the Pacific coast had also become the scene of important occurrences.

XVI. Before the breaking out of the war, John C. Fremont,[*] who had been brevetted captain for valuable services rendered the Government in western explorations, was sent to make a survey of the then unknown regions lying between the Rocky Mountains and the Pacific Ocean, as well as to discover, if possible, a new and shorter route than the one already known from the western base of the mountains to the mouth of the Columbia River. After a series of perilous adventures among the mountains, and encounters with hostile Indians, he made his way into California, then a department of Mexico, to recruit his men, secure supplies, and obtain from the Mexican authorities permission to winter in the country.

JOHN C. FREMONT.

XVII. The permission was granted, but in a few days it was revoked, the order of revocation requiring him to leave the country at once, accompanied by a threat of destruction in case of non-compliance. His men being in an exhausted condition and not yet furnished with supplies, and consequently in no condition to repass the mountains at that time, he refused to go. Learning that General Castro, the governor of the province, was mustering a force to come against him, he took

---

[*] Fremont was born in Savannah, Georgia, in 1813. He conducted five exploring expeditions, the first to the Rocky Mountains, and the others as far as California.

XVI. QUESTIONS.—74. On what expedition had Fremont been sent? 75. What trials did he meet with? 76. Why did he enter California?

XVII. 77. Was the permission granted or not? 78. What fickleness did the authorities of California betray? 79. Why did Fremont refuse to go? 80. Of what movement did he soon hear? 81. What defensive course did he then adopt? 82. What did Castro do instead of attacking Fremont?

a position on a mountain peak, thirty miles east of Monterey, where, in March, 1846, he built a rude fort, hoisted the United States flag, and determined to defend himself. Castro gathered a force of not less than five hundred men in the vicinity of the Americans, but spent several days in doing little more than making idle threats.

XVIII. At length Fremont, tired of inaction, and convinced that he could not obtain the needed supplies, withdrew with his party, and, taking a northern route, passed through the valley of the Sacramento, and slowly pursued his journey into Oregon. Here, on the 9th of May, he was overtaken by a messenger with dispatches from Washington, directing him to protect the interests of the United States in California. Retracing his steps, he found Castro already marching against the American settlements on the Sacramento. The settlers flocked to Fremont's standard with such alacrity and in such large numbers that he soon found himself able to confront the Mexican general. Several skirmishes took place, in which the enemy were defeated, and finally compelled to retreat towards the southern part of the province

XIX. On the 5th of July, 1846, California was declared to be independent, and free from all Mexican rule. A few days later, Commodore Sloate, who commanded the United States squadron on the Pacific coast, having previously received information that hostilities had commenced on the Rio Grande, took possession of Monterey. Towards the latter part of the month, Commodore Stockton arrived at Monterey, took command of the squadron, and, with Fremont's co-operation, soon gained possession of the whole of California.

XVIII. QUESTIONS.—83 What did Fremont do in consequence of the inaction of Castro? 84 Why did he retrace his steps from Oregon? 85 What did he find as regards a movement of Castro? 86. How did the settlers act? 87. What successes did Fremont have?

XIX 88 What took place on the 5th of July? 89 What was done by Commodore Sloate? 90 Is the Monterey on the Pacific north or south of San Francisco? (See map, p. 268.) 91. What did Commodore Stockton accomplish?

EVENTS OF 1847.

I. In the mean time, it had been decided by the authorities at Washington that, in order to "conquer a peace," the central part of the Mexican Republic would have to be penetrated, and the capital itself menaced. Accordingly, a plan of invasion was arranged by which Vera Cruz, the most important Mexican city on the Gulf of Mexico, was to be captured; and then an army, under General Scott, was to march through Mexico against the capital. This plan not only deprived Taylor of a large portion of his best troops, but it gave to Scott the chief command of the American forces in Mexico, he being the senior officer.

II. Taylor's last engagement in Mexico was the battle of Buena Vista (*bwā'-nah vees'-tah*), fought on the 23d of February, 1847, nearly five months after his preceding one, that of Monterey. Learning, towards the latter part of February, that Santa Anna (*san-'tah an'-nah*), the ablest of the Mexican generals, with an army of not less than twenty thousand men, was moving to attack his little force of less than five thousand, he took a position at Buena Vista, a mountain pass nine miles in advance of Saltillo, and awaited the approach of the enemy. On the morning of the 23d, the Mexicans appeared, and began the attack. The battle continued until sunset; and, although the Mexicans fought with resolution, and more than once seemed on the eve of victory, their immense superiority in numbers and heroic fighting were of no avail; they were signally defeated, losing, in killed and wounded, about two thousand. The loss of the Americans was between seven and eight hundred. Santa Anna made good his retreat with his

Events of 1847 —I. Questions.—1. What, in the mean time, had been decided at Washington? 2. What plan of invasion was accordingly arranged? 3. How did this operate as regards Taylor's troops and command?

II. 4. Which was Taylor's last battle in Mexico? 5. When did it occur? 6. Give an account of it. 7. What loss did the Mexicans sustain? 8. What, the Americans? 9. What was the effect of the victory along the Rio Grande frontier?

disheartened followers, and, during the rest of the war, the
Americans were left in quiet possession of the frontier of the
Rio Grande and the valley of that river.

SCOTT'S CAMPAIGN IN MEXICO.

III. Scott's campaign
was commenced by an
attack on Vera Cruz,
which was defended by
the strong fortress of
San Juan de Ulloa (*san
whahn dā ool-yo'-ah*),
standing upon the island
of the same name, about
half a mile from the
shore. On the 9th of
March, 1847, he effect-
ed the landing of his
entire army, consisting
of twelve thousand
troops, without the
least casualty; and the city was at once invested from shore
to shore. After a delay of several days, for the purpose of
completing preparations, and also to induce, if possible, the
Mexican commander to surrender, the Americans opened a
tremendous fire from their land batteries, as well as from their
fleet, under Commodore Conner. The bombardment was
continued for five days; and so destructive to life and property was it, that, on the 27th, the city and fortress were com
pelled to surrender.

IV. The march towards the interior was commenced on
the 8th of April, the army taking the national road by the
way of Jalapa (*hal-lah'-pah*). At Cerro Gordo (*thăr'-ro gor'-do*),

III. QUESTIONS.—10. How did Scott begin his campaign? 11. How is Vera Cruz
situated? (See map, p. 279.) 12. How was it defended? 13. When did Scott
effect a landing? 14. Give an account of the operations that followed.

1847. a mountain pass, about fifty miles from Vera Cruz, Santa Anna was strongly fortified, prepared to resist the advance of the Americans. Scott had with him only about eight thousand men—those who were not sick and wounded having been left to garrison Vera Cruz and its fort—while Santa Anna had an army of nearly double the numerical strength of Scott's.

V. On the morning of the 18th, a daring assault was made upon the works of the enemy ; and, before noon, the whole were in the possession of the Americans. Besides losing the most of their artillery and munitions of war, the Mexicans had one thousand of their number killed or wounded, and three thousand made prisoners. On the following day, April 19th, the Americans entered Jalapa: farther on in their march they took without opposition the strong castle of Perote (*pā-ro'-tā*), and, on the 15th of May, they entered the ancient and populous city of Puebla (*poo-ā'-blah*).

VI. The American army had been so reduced by sickness, death, and other causes, that Scott deemed it advisable to rest at Puebla for re-enforcements. After a halt of nearly three months, during which Santa Anna had time to create a new army and to fortify the capital, he resumed his march, passing through a beautiful region without the least resistance, and reaching the town of Ayotla (*ah-yot'-lah*), fifteen miles from the city of Mexico.

VII. Finding that the direct route by the national road was strongly fortified, and being anxious to spare the lives of

---

IV. QUESTIONS.—15. When did Scott march from Vera Cruz? 16. What road did he take? 17. How is Jalapa situated? (See map, p. 279.) 18. Where were the Mexicans posted to dispute Scott's advance ? 19. What is said of the strength of the respective armies?

V. 20 Give an account of the battle of Cerro Gordo. 21 Give an account of the further advance of the Americans, and their three captures 22 In what direction from Vera Cruz is Perote? (See map, p. 279.) 23. In what direction from Vera Cruz is Puebla ? (See same map.)

VI 24 At what place did Scott make a long rest? 25. Why did he remain there so long ? 26. What advantage did this give to the Mexicans? 27 What is said of his further march ?

his men, Scott* turned southward, and, passing around Lake Chalco, encamped at San Augustin (*san aw-gus-teen'*), about ten miles from the capital. Thence the approaches to the city were guarded by batteries at Contreras (*con-trä'-ras*) and San Antonio, and by the strong forts of Churubusco (*choo-roo-boos'-co*) and Chapultepec (*chah-pool-tŭ-p k'*).

VIII. In a night march, the Americans advanced upon Contreras. At sunrise, on the 20th of August, they commenced the attack, and, in less than twenty minutes, the Mexican batteries were carried and the victory was complete. The garrison of San Antonio, being somewhat unsupported by the loss of Contreras, made but a slight resistance, and

GENERAL SCOTT.

then retreated before the pursuing Americans, commanded by General Worth. On the same day, the 20th, a grand movement upon Churubusco was next directed, to which the victory already achieved opened the way. After an obstinate and bloody conflict, the Mexicans, who were commanded by Santa Anna, though numbering at least twenty-five thousand, were driven from the fort and from every part of the battlefield. Some retreated to Chapultepec, the fortress nearest the capital, and others fled to the city itself.

IX. On the day after these two battles, and while Scott was at an advanced position within three miles of the city, Santa Anna asked for an armistice, for the purpose, it was stated, of negotiating a peace. The request was granted, and

---

* Winfield Scott was born in Petersburg, Virginia, in 1786. Died in 1867.

VII. QUESTIONS.—28. Why did Scott turn southward from Ayotla? 29. Where did he encamp? 30. In what direction is San Augustin from the city of Mexico? (See map, p. 279.) 31. How were the approaches from San Augustin to the city of Mexico guarded?

VIII. 32. Give an account of the battle of Contreras. 33. Of Churubusco.

1847. for several days efforts were made to bring the war to a close, but without success. The Mexican commander not only refused to agree to the terms proposed by the Americans; but, while offering others, more becoming a conqueror, he actually violated the armistice by strengthening his defenses.

SANTA ANNA.

X. Scott, losing all confidence in the integrity of his foe, declared the truce at an end, and ordered General Worth to storm the Molino del Rey (*mo-le'-no däle rä*), an outer defense of Chapultepec. Accordingly, on the 8th of September, the attack was made; and, after a hard-fought battle, in which Worth* lost nearly a fourth of his men, the Mexicans were driven from their position. Chapultepec itself, a strongly fortified castle, situated on a lofty hill, was yet to be taken before the capital could be reached.

XI. Several batteries were erected to bear upon the place, and, on the 12th of September, a heavy fire was commenced, which made several breaches through the stone wall defenses. On the next day, the 13th, the battle of Chapultepec was fought. The Americans, in two columns, the one headed by

---

* William Jenkins Worth was born in Hudson, Columbia Co., N. Y., in 1794. In the war of 1812 he performed an honorable part, being twice promoted, once for gallant conduct in the battle of Chippewa, and again for important service in the battle of Lundy's Lane. His distinguished services, in 1842, against the Florida Indians, were also rewarded by promotion. He was with Taylor in Mexico, and for his achievements in the battle of Monterey he was brevetted a major-general. Afterward he joined Scott's army. His death occurred in Texas, in 1849.

IX. QUESTIONS.—34. What request did Santa Anna make? 35. Where was Scott at the time? 36. How did Scott treat the request? 37. What followed for several days? 38. What perfidy was Santa Anna guilty of?

X. 39. What order did Scott give to Worth? 40. When was the battle of Molino del Rey fought? 41. Give an account of it. 42. What yet remained to be done?

XI. 43. How was Chapultepec menaced on the 12th of September? 44. Give an account of the next day's battle.

General Pillow, and the other by General Quitman, advanced to the assault, and in the most gallant style carried the outworks and then the castle, though at the expense of many lives.

XII. Quitman pursued the flying Mexicans; and at night his division rested within the gates of the city, while Worth's division, which had advanced by a circuitous route, halted in the suburbs. During the night, Santa Anna, with most of his army and the principal officers of government, fled from the city. On the following morning, September 14th, the American army passed into the city, and running up the United States flag on the national palace, took for-

WISCONSIN.

"This State takes its name from a large tributary of the Mississippi, having its course entirely within the State. The river was discovered by Marquette, in 1673, who called it, in his Narrative, the *Masconsin*, doubtless from the name of a tribe of Indians then living on its banks. The name was soon afterward changed to Ouisconsin, and finally to Wisconsin." The Seal of the State is given above.

mal possession of the Mexican capital amid the greatest enthusiasm.

XIII. The Mexicans, taking advantage of the weakness of the garrison which Scott had left at Puebla, laid siege to the place; and, after Santa Anna's[*] flight from the capital, he

---

* Antonio Lopez de Santa Anna was born in Jalapa, Mexico, in 1798.

XII. QUESTIONS.—45. What is said of Quitman's and Worth's advance? 46. State what took place on the following morning.

XIII. 47. To what place in the mean time had the Mexicans laid siege? 48. What circumstance had induced them to commence the siege? 49. By whom were they joined during the siege? 50. Why did Santa Anna afterward leave the besiegers? 51. Give an account of the battle that followed.

joined the besiegers with some thousands of his fugitive troops. Learning that General Lane, with a body of recruits, was on his march from Vera Cruz to re-enforce Scott, Santa Anna left Puebla to intercept him. At Huamantla (*whah-mant'-lah*) the encounter took place, and though the Mexicans were vastly superior in numbers to the Americans, the result was, as usual, a total defeat to them.

XIV. On the 2d of February, 1848, a treaty of peace was signed at Guadaloupe Hidalgo (*gwah-dah-loo'-pā he-dahl'-go*), a small town about four miles from the capital, and Mexico was soon after evacuated by the American armies. By the treaty, all the territory north of the Rio Grande, together with the whole of New Mexico and California, was relinquished to the United States. On the part of the United States, it was agreed that $15,000,000 should be paid for the territory, and that debts due from Mexico to American citizens, to the amount of $3,000,000, should be assumed. After the treaty had been ratified by both governments, peace was proclaimed by President Polk, on the 4th of July, 1848.

XIV QUESTIONS.—52. When was a treaty of peace signed? 53 At what place? 54. What territory did the United States acquire by the treaty? 55. What amount of money was paid by the United States? 56. When did President Polk issue a proclamation of peace?

PRINCIPAL BATTLES OF THE WAR WITH MEXICO.

(The Americans were successful in every battle.)

DATES	BATTLES	COMMANDERS		FORCES ENGAGED	
		AMERICAN	MEXICAN	AMER.	MEX.
1846.					
May 8,	Palo Alto	Taylor	Arista	2,300	6,000
May 9,	Resaca de la Palma	Taylor	Arista	2,200	5,000
Sept. 24,	Monterey	Taylor	Ampudia	6,600	10,000
Dec. 25,	Bracito	Doniphan	Ponce de Leon	500	1,200
1847.					
Feb. 23,	Buena Vista	Taylor	Santa Anna	4,700	17,000
Feb. 28,	Sacramento	Doniphan	Trias	900	4,000
March 27	Vera Cruz	Scott	Morales	12,000	6,000
April 18,	Cerro Gordo	Scott	Santa Anna	8,500	12,000
Aug 20, {	Contreras	Scott	Valencia	4,000	7,000
	Churubusco	Scott	Santa Anna	8,000	25,000
Sept. 8,	Molino del Rey	Worth	Alvarez	3,500	14,000
Sept. 13,	Chapultepec	Scott	Bravo	7,200	25,000
Oct. 9,	Huamantla	Lane	Santa Anna.	500	1,000

REVIEW QUESTIONS.

TAYLOR'S ADMINISTRATION.

ZACHARY TAYLOR
Was born in Orange Co., Va., Nov. 24
1784. He was engaged in the War of
1812, the Black Hawk War, the Sem-
nole War, and the Mexican War. Was
never a member of a legislative body.

I. Polk's successor in the presidency was General Zachary Taylor, the hero who had achieved such brilliant victories in the war with Mexico. His inauguration took place at Washington, on the 5th of March, 1849,* the 4th being Sunday. One of the earliest and most difficult of the questions which commanded the attention of his administration, grew out of the acquisition of California and New Mexico.

II. In February, 1848, gold began to be found in California in large quantities. When the news of the discovery reached the Atlantic States, and spread throughout the other States, a wonderful excitement was at once created, and in a very short time thousands of emigrants were

---

* President Taylor's cabinet consisted of John M. Clayton, Secretary of State; William M. Meredith, Secretary of the Treasury; George W. Crawford, Secretary of War; William B. Preston, Secretary of the Navy; Thomas Ewing, Secretary of the Interior; Jacob Collamer, Postmaster-General; and Reverdy Johnson, Attorney-General. The department of the interior had been created by Congress on the 3d of March, two days before Taylor's inauguration.

TAYLOR'S ADMINISTRATION.—I. QUESTIONS.—1. Who succeeded Polk in the Presidency? 2. When was Taylor inaugurated?

II. 3. When was an important discovery made in California? 4. What was it? 5. What was the consequence?

on their way to the land of gold. The rush thither was truly marvelous; not only did people go from the United States, but they likewise flocked from Europe, Asia, South America, and even the isles of the sea.

III. So rapidly did the territory become populated, that in September, 1849, there was a sufficient number of settlers there to constitute a State; and a constitution was then adopted, preparatory to petition-ing Congress for ad-mission into the Union. An article of the Con-stitution, by which sla-very was excluded from California, became a cause for a violent dis-pute, not only in Con-gress, but in the legis-latures of the several States, and among the people throughout the Union. While Con-gress was in session, engaged in angry de-bate, President Taylor, after an administration of only one year, four months, and four days, died on the 9th of July, 1850, at the presidential mansion.

EUREKA.

CALIFORNIA.

"A romance was publis' ed in Spain in 1510, in which the word California, for the first time, occurred. It was ap-plied to an imaginary island located by the romancer, 'in the right hand of the Indies.' Cortez, it is supposed, had read the book, and when he sailed along the west coast of Mexico, in 1535, supposing he was in the region of the island, he called the country Cali-fornia."

FILLMORE'S ADMINISTRATION.

I. By the death of Taylor, the Vice-President of the United States, Millard Fillmore, became President, taking the oath of office on the 10th of July, 1850.*

MILLARD FILLMORE
Was born in Cayuga Co., N. Y., Jan. 7 1800. In 1828, '29, and '20, he was elected to the State legislature of New York In 1832, and subsequently, he was elected representative in Congress.

II. The question in relation to the admission of California had been greatly complicated in Congress, by the application of New Mexico for admission into the Union, and by a claim on the part of Texas to a large portion of New Mexico. For the purpose of making "an amicable arrangement of all questions in controversy between the Free and the Slave States growing out of the subject of slavery," Henry Clay made a proposition, known as the "Omnibus Bill," or the "Compromise Act of 1850."

---

* President Fillmore's cabinet was constituted as follows: Daniel Webster, Secretary of State; Thomas Corwin, Secretary of the Treasury; Charles M. Conrad, Secretary of War; Alexander H. H. Stuart, Secretary of the Interior; William A. Graham, Secretary of the Navy; Nathan K. Hall, Postmaster-General; and John J. Crittenden, Attorney-General.

FILLMORE'S ADMINISTRATION.—I. QUESTIONS.—1. Who succeeded Taylor?
II. 2. How had the question of California's admission been complicated? 3. What was the object of the "Omnibus Bill?" 4. Who offered that bill? 5. By what other name is it also known?

III. Although Mr. Clay's proposition did not pass Congress in the shape offered, the result aimed at was attained, after Taylor's death, by separate bills. These provided for the admission of California as a free State; territorial governments for New Mexico and Utah, leaving the admission or exclusion of slavery to be decided by the people of the respective territories; the settlement of the claim made by Texas; the abolition of the slave-trade in the District of Columbia; and the surrender of fugitives from labor, this last bill being known as the "Fugitive Slave Law."

IV. Fillmore remained President during the unexpired part of the term for which Taylor was elected, a period of nearly two years and eight months, when he was succeeded by Franklin Pierce, of New Hampshire.

PIERCE'S ADMINISTRATION.

I. Pierce was President for only one term, or four years, extending from the 4th of March, 1853,* the day of his inauguration, to the 4th of March, 1857.

II. His administration had scarcely commenced when the controversy was renewed between the slaveholding and non-slaveholding sections of the Union, the one being in favor of, and the other opposed to, the extension of slavery into the Territories of the United States. This fresh outbreak

---

* President Pierce's cabinet was as follows: William L. Marcy, Secretary of State: James Guthrie, Secretary of the Treasury; Jefferson Davis, Secretary of War; James C. Dobbin, Secretary of the Navy; Robert McClelland, Secretary of the Interior; James Campbell, Postmaster-General; and Caleb Cushing, Attorney-General.

III. Questions.—6. In what shape did Mr. Clay's bill afterward appear? 7. What did the separate bills provide for? 8. What was the object of the "Fugitive Slave Law?"

IV. 9. For how long a time was Fillmore President? 10. By whom was he succeeded?

Pierce's Administration.—I. 1. When was Pierce inaugurated? 2. How long was he President?

II. 3. What controversy was renewed at the beginning of his administration? 4. What were the slaveholding States in favor of? 5. What the non-slaveholding? 6. How did this fresh outbreak begin?

13

FRANKLIN PIERCE
Was born in Hillsborough, N. H., Nov.
23, 1804. He was a brigadier-general
in Scott's army in the Mexican War, and
participated in the battles of Contreras
and Churubusco.

had its origin mainly with Congress, in the introduction there of what is known as the "Kansas - Nebraska Bill."

III. By the "Missouri Compromise Bill," passed in 1820, it was provided that, in consideration of the admission of Missouri as a Slave State, slavery should forever be prohibited in all the remaining territories of the United States north of latitude thirty-six degrees and thirty minutes, the southern boundary of that State. By the "Kansas-Nebraska Bill," which Congress passed in 1854, this prohibition was repealed, and the two territories of Kansas and Nebraska were duly organized.

IV. No sooner had the bill passed than emigrants from both sections of the Union began to pour into Kansas, those from the North being determined to make it a free State, while those from the South were equally resolved the other way. And with such undue zeal was the strife carried on, that frequent collisions took place, in which blood was sometimes shed.

III. QUESTIONS.—7. When was the "Missouri Compromise Bill" passed? 8. What was its important provision? 9. When was the "Kansas-Nebraska Bill" passed? 10. What was its important provision?

IV. 11. What began to be done as soon as the "Kansas-Nebraska Bill" was passed? 12. What were the people of the North determined upon? 13. What those of the South?

V. The Kansas controversy, in Congress and everywhere else throughout the Union, as well as the strife in the Territory, contin-

RIVER STEAMER.

ued all through Pierce's administration, and into and nearly to the close of his successor's. In the course of the debate in Congress, Mr. Sumner, of Massachusetts, made a speech, partly directed against South Carolina and some of her representatives. For this he was afterward assaulted by a representative from that State, while writing at his desk in the Senate-chamber, and so seriously injured that he was not able to resume his legislative duties until two years after.

BUCHANAN'S ADMINISTRATION.

I. JAMES BUCHANAN of Pennsylvania, Pierce's successor in the presidency, was inaugurated at Washington on the 4th of March, 1857.* His administration continued one term, ending on the 4th of March, 1861.

II. The slavery question continued to be the prominent topic of discussion in Congress and throughout the country during the four years of his administration, and, even in the last one, the Kansas strife seemed very little nearer a conclusion than it had been at any previous time. As his term of office drew towards its close, no less than four candidates were nominated to succeed him.

---

* President Buchanan's cabinet was constituted as follows: Lewis Cass, Secretary of State; Howell Cobb, Secretary of the Treasury; John B. Floyd, Secretary of War; Isaac Toucev, Secretary of the Navy; Jacob Thompson, Secretary of the Interior; Aaron V. Brown, Postmaster-General; and Jeremiah S. Black, Attorney-General.

V. QUESTIONS.—14. How long did the Kansas controversy continue? 15. What affair took place in the course of the debate in Congress?

BUCHANAN'S ADMINISTRATION.—I. 1. Who succeeded Pierce in the presidency? 2. When was Buchanan inaugurated?

II. 3. What is said of the slavery question? 4. Of the Kansas strife? 5. Of presidential successors?

JAMES BUCHANAN
Was born in Franklin Co., Penn., April
22, 1791. Was a representative in
Congress; envoy to St. Petersburg;
U. S. Senator; Secretary of State; and
minister to England. He died in 1868.

III. The Democratic party was divided between Stephen A. Douglas, of Illinois, and John C. Breckinridge, of Kentucky. The Republican party opposed to the further extension of slavery nominated Abraham Lincoln, of Illinois, while the American party presented for its candidate John Bell, of Tennessee. After an exciting canvass, in which the slavery question was the all-absorbing one, the election resulted in the success of the Republican nominee.

IV. When it became known that Lincoln would be the next President, public meetings were held in Charleston and elsewhere in South Carolina, at which resolutions were adopted in favor of the secession of the State from the Union. In pursuance of a special act of the South Carolina legislature, delegates were elected to assemble in convention at Columbia on the 17th of December, 1860. They accordingly met, but, in consequence of the prevalence of small-pox in that city, an adjournment to Charleston took place, where, on

III. QUESTIONS.—6. How was the Democratic party divided? 7. Who were the other candidates? 8. To what was the Republican party opposed? 9. What was the result of the election?

IV. 10. When Lincoln's success became known, how did the people of South Carolina act? 11. What convention was held in the State? 12. What was done by the convention?

the 20th of December, an ordinance of secession was unanimously passed.

V. In the mean time a great deal of interest was felt respecting the forts in Charleston harbor, only one of which — Fort Moultrie — was garrisoned. Threats had been uttered and demonstrations made which rendered it probable that they would be seized by the South Carolinians. Towards the close of December, as the danger of an attack upon Fort Moultrie became more imminent, the commander, Major Anderson,* convinced that his position there would not be tenable if attacked by well-organized and disciplined troops, on the 26th of December, 1860, withdrew the garrison, which consisted of only about eighty men, and established himself at Fort Sumter.

MINNESOTA.

Minnesota was so called from the river of that name. The word is compounded of two Indian words, *minne*, meaning water, and *sotah*, sky-colored. Minnesota, therefore, is literally, *The State of the sky,*—colored water. The phrase, *L'étoile du Nord,* means, The Star of the North.

VI. The excitement in Charleston, produced by this act of removal, was intense; and it spread with lightning speed over the whole State. The authorities of South Carolina at once

* Major Robert Anderson was born near Louisville, Ky., in 1805. In 1825, he was graduated at West Point. He was in the Seminole War, and with Scott's army in the Mexican War. At the battle of the Molino del Rey he was severely wounded. In May, 1861, he was made brigadier-general in the U. S. army.

V. QUESTIONS.—13. What interest was felt in the mean time? 14. What was the ground of concern respecting the forts? 15. Who commanded Fort Moultrie? 16. How many men did Anderson have with him? 17. What movement did he make? 18. Why did he make the movement?

VI. 19. How did Anderson's removal influence the people of Charleston and the other parts of the State? 20. What buildings did the State authorities seize? 21. What disposition did they make of troops? 22. What was done with a view to a Southern Confederacy?

OREGON.
"As to the name *Oregon*, or the authority for its use, the traveler (Carver) is silent; and nothing has been learned from any other source, though much labor has been expended in attempts to discover the meaning of the word and its derivation. It was most probably invented by Carver."

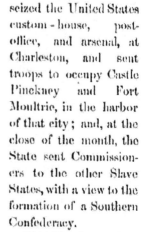

seized the United States custom - house, post-office, and arsenal, at Charleston, and sent troops to occupy Castle Pinckney and Fort Moultrie, in the harbor of that city; and, at the close of the month, the State sent Commissioners to the other Slave States, with a view to the formation of a Southern Confederacy.

VII. On the 10th of January, 1861, the steamer Star of the West, which had been dispatched from New York with supplies and re-enforcements for Fort Sumter, arrived off Charleston, and was fired upon and driven back to sea by batteries erected to command the entrance of the harbor. The Star of the West thereupon returned to New York. During this month, January, five States, viz.: Mississippi, Florida, Alabama, Georgia, and Louisiana, following the lead of South Carolina, passed secession ordinances, and, on the 1st

MAJOR ANDERSON.

VII. QUESTIONS.—23. Give the account connected with the Star of the West. 24. How many States, in January, 1861, followed the lead of South Carolina? 25. When did Texas secede?

of February, Texas did the same.

VIII. Nearly all the forts, arsenals, navy-yards, and custom-houses within these States, and which belonged to the United States, were seized by the secession-ists. Fort Sumter, still held by Major Anderson, and Fort Pickens, near Pensacola, which had been saved by the de-cided action of its com-mander, Lieutenant Slemmer, were the only important forts which remained in the posses-sion of the general gov-ernment on the 1st of

KANSAS.
The name, Kansas, was given to this State from the river of the same name, which received its name from that of a tribe of In-dians. The territory embraced within the limits of the State was a part of the domain bought from France in 1803, under the general designation of Louisiana.

February. The posts at the southern extremity of Florida also remained in the hands of the government.

IX. In the mean time, upon the recommendation of the legislature of Virginia, delegates had been ap-pointed by twenty-one States to a so-called "Peace Conference," to decide upon a plan "for a settle-ment of all difficulties and the preservation of the Union." The convention assembled at Washing-

PENSACOLA AND VICINITY.

VIII. QUESTIONS.—26. What is said of the seizure of forts, arsenals, &c. ? 27. Of Forts Sumter and Pickens? 28. How is Fort Sumter situated? (See map, p. 129.) 29. How is Fort Pickens situated? (See map, p. 295.) 30. What southern posts remained in the hands of the government?

ton, on the 4th of February, and was organized by the unanimous election of ex-President Tyler as chairman. After a session of three weeks it adjourned; and the result of its labors, a series of proposed amendments to the Constitution, was laid before Congress, but .without meeting the approval of that body.

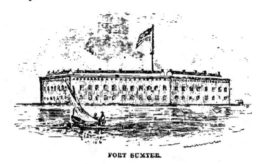

FORT SUMTER.

X. On the very day upon which the "Peace Congress" assembled, February 4th, a congress, composed of delegates from six of the Southern States, met at Montgomery, Ala.; and, four days after, organized a Confederacy, by the adoption of a "Provisional Constitution," calling it the "Confederate States of America." This constitution was superseded, in little more than a month, by one intended to be permanent. On the 9th of February, Jefferson Davis, of Mississippi, was elected President of the Confederacy by the Montgomery Congress, and, on the 18th, he was duly inaugurated.

XI. In this distracted and sad condition were the affairs of the country upon the retirement of Buchanan from the presidency, and the assumption of the office by Lincoln.

IX. QUESTIONS.—31. When and where did the "Peace Convention" meet? 32. How many States were represented there? 33. Upon whose recommendation had the delegates been chosen? 34. Who was chosen president of the convention? 35. Give a further account of the convention and its doings.

X. 36. Where did a second convention meet on the 4th of February? 37. What States were represented in that convention? 38. What was done by the convention? 39. What was done on the 9th and 18th of February?

SECTION IX.

FROM THE BEGINNING OF LINCOLN'S ADMINISTRATION TO THE
CLOSE OF JOHNSON'S.—MARCH 4, 1861, TO MARCH 4, 1869.

LINCOLN'S ADMINISTRATION.

I. On the 11th of February, 1861, Lincoln left his home at Springfield, Illinois, for Washington. On his way he made brief stops at various cities, and was everywhere received with great enthusiasm. It had been arranged that his route from Harrisburgh should be through Baltimore, but, in consequence of the excited state of feeling existing between the political clubs of the last-named city, and desiring to prevent an anticipated outrage, he made a night journey, arriving

ABRAHAM LINCOLN
Was born in Larn Co., Ky., Feb. 12, 1809. He served as captain in the "Black Hawk War;" elected, in 1834, to the Illinois legislature; and in 1846, was chosen representative in Congress.

in Washington at an early hour on the morning of the 22d of February. His inauguration took place on the 4th of March, "amid a greater display of military force than had ever before been witnessed on such an occasion."*

---

* President Lincoln's cabinet was constituted as follows: William H. Seward, Secretary of State; Salmon P. Chase, Secretary of the Treasury; Simon Cameron, Secretary of War; Gideon Welles, Secretary of the Navy; Caleb B. Smith, Secretary of the Interior; Edward Bates, Attorney-General; and Montgomery Blair, Postmaster-General.

13*

II. In his inaugural address, Lincoln announced that he had "no purpose, directly or indirectly, to interfere with the institution of slavery in the States where it exists;" further stating that, in his opinion, he had no right to do so. This assurance, however, did not satisfy the politicians of the South ; the scepter of power had departed from them, and only by setting up a government of their own, with slavery as its corner-stone, could they again expect to rule. Their duty to the General Government they regarded as secondary to their duty to their respective States.

THE GREAT REBELLION.—EVENTS OF 1861.

I. The Confederates soon organized an army, and General Beauregard (bō'-re-gard), who had been a major in the service of the United States, was placed in command of the forces intended to drive Anderson from Fort Sumter. On the morning of the 12th of April, 1861, the first shot was fired upon the fort. After a bombardment of thirty-four hours, the defense being but feeble, in consequence of the smallness of the garrison and a poor supply of ammunition, Anderson was compelled to capitulate. On the 14th he departed with his command, and sailed for New York.

II. The news of this event, as it was flashed along the wires, produced an almost uncontrollable excitement throughout the country ; and the President's proclamation, issued on the following day, April 15th, calling for seventy-five thousand

LINCOLN'S ADMINISTRATION.—I. QUESTIONS.—1. Where did Lincoln live at the time of his election to the Presidency? 2. What can you state of his journey to Washington? 3. When was he inaugurated? 4. What can you state of the occasion?

II. 5. What did Lincoln proclaim in reference to the Slavery question? 6. On what occasion did he proclaim it? 7. How did the politicians of the South receive the assurance? 8. How did they expect to retain power? 9. How did they regard their duty to the Nation?

EVENTS OF 1861.—I. 1. What command was given to Beauregard? 2. When did hostilities actually commence? 3. By whom were they commenced? 4. Why did not Anderson make a better defense? 5. What was the result of the attack?

II. 6. What effect did the news have? 7. News of what? 8. What action did President Lincoln take? 9. What can you state of the response? 10. What took place in Baltimore? 11. Where were the troops going? 12. What meetings of the people were held?

troops, was responded to at once by all the Free States. The national capital being menaced, troops were hurried off for its defense. A Massachusetts regiment, while thus on its way to Washington, was attacked, April 19th, in the streets of Baltimore, by a mob of Southern sympathizers, and two of the soldiers were killed, and a number wounded. This and other acts of the Secessionists aroused the people of the North: a great mass meeting was held in New York city, and similar gatherings took place in other cities, in favor of the Union.

III. Nor were the Confederates inactive. They seized the arsenal at Harper's Ferry. They also made preparations to get possession of the navy-yard near Norfolk: the Union officers there, despairing of a defense, set fire to the government buildings, and scuttled and sunk most of the vessels in the harbor. Immense quantities of ordnance, shot, and shell thus fell into the hands of the insurgents, and they likewise acquired by seizure, arsenals and strongholds in other directions, as well as ships, steamboats, and government property wherever they could find it. In consequence of these acts, President Lincoln issued a proclamation, April 19th, declaring certain Southern ports closed; and, eight days after, he issued an additional proclamation, extending the blockade to all ports in the Slave States south of Maryland.

IV. It can hardly be said that the National Government made any offensive movement before the 24th of May. Then troops were sent into Virginia by order of General Scott, who commanded the army of the United States. Alexandria and

III. QUESTIONS.—13. What activity did the Confederates manifest? 14. How is Harper's Ferry situated? (See map, p 207.) 15. Norfolk? (Same map.) 16. Why did not the Union officers defend Norfolk? 17. What did they do? 18. What then fell into the hands of the Confederates? 19. What else did they acquire? 20. What proclamation did Lincoln issue? 21. Why did he do so? 22. When did he do it? 23. What additional proclamation did he issue?

IV. 24. When did the Government begin in earnest to move against the insurgents? 25. Who, at the time, was in command of the Federal armies? 26. What places did the Government troops occupy? 27. Where are those places? (See map, p 320) 28. What took place at Philippi? 29. At Big Bethel? 30. Where is Philippi? (See map, p. 320) 31. Big Bethel? (Map, p. 312.) 32. Give dates of the battles.

(*Questions to be answered from the above map.*)

Where is Port Hudson? Baton Rouge? Natchez? Vicksburg? Memphis? Fort Pillow? Island No. 10? Paducah? Bowling Green? Fort Donelson? Fort Henry? Arkansas Post? Shreveport? Pea Ridge? Lawrence? Springfield? Corinth? New Orleans? Ship Island? Port Gibson? Huntsville? Little Rock?

Arlington Heights were occupied, and a camp at Philippi was surprised, June 3d, the Confederates being completely routed; but seven days after, a Union force, sent from Fortress Monroe, was severely repulsed at Big Bethel.

V. In the mean time efforts had been made by the Secessionists to take Missouri out of the Union: in this, however, they failed, mainly through the prompt action of General Lyon,* who captured a Confederate camp, defeated the enemy at Booneville, on the 17th of June, and frustrated the designs of the disloyal governor. On the 5th of July, a division of his troops, under Colonel Sigel (seé-gel) defeated a body of the enemy at Carthage; and, on the 2d of August, at Dug Spring, the loyal forces were again victorious; but on the 10th, having been confronted by a vastly superior force, and fearing a retrograde movement would be fatal to the cause, Lyon made an unsuccessful attack upon the enemy at Wilson's Creek, near Springfield, and was killed.

JEFFERSON DAVIS.

VI. The Confederate army, to the number of about one hundred thousand men, occupied a line through Virginia from Harper's Ferry to Norfolk, their strongest position being on the direct road from Washington to Richmond, at a place called

* Nathaniel Lyon was born in Connecticut, July 14th, 1819. He served under Taylor and Scott in the Mexican War, and was promoted for meritorious conduct.

V. QUESTIONS.—33. What efforts had been made meanwhile in Missouri? 34. Why were not the efforts successful? 35. What did General Lyon accomplish? 36. Where is Booneville? (See map, p. 300.) 37. What account can you give of the battle of Carthage? 38. Dug Spring? 39. Wilson's Creek? 40. Where is Carthage? (See map, p. 300.) 41. Dug Spring? 42. Wilson's Creek?

VI. 43. Where is Manassas Junction? (See map, p. 330.) 44. How large an army did the Confederates have in July, 1861? 45. How was the army stationed? 46. What place was then the capital of the Southern Confederacy? 47. What place had been the previous capital? 48. How is Richmond situated? (See map, p. 320.) 49. Montgomery? (See map, p. 223.)

1861.   Manassas Junction.   Richmond was then the capital of the Southern Confederacy, the transfer from Montgomery, their first capital, having been effected in July, and Jefferson Davis had been chosen the President of the so-called "Confederate States of America."

VII. About the middle of July a large army, commanded by General McDowell, marched to attack the Confederates at Manassas Junction.   On the 18th, a division of this army, under General Tyler, encountered the enemy, under General Beauregard, near Bull Run, and after a contest of three hours, fell back to Centreville.   On the 21st occurred the battle of Bull Run.   In this conflict, which was exceedingly desperate, and lasted ten hours, more than forty thousand men were engaged. At length the insurgents, being largely re-enforced, prevailed, and the Union troops, panic-stricken, fled in disorder toward Washington.   The Union loss in killed, wounded, and prisoners numbered nearly three thousand men: the loss of the enemy in killed and wounded did not much exceed half that number.

GENERAL M'CLELLAN.

VIII. On the following day, July 22d, General McClellan succeeded McDowell in the command of the Potomac Army.   McClellan had just closed with credit a brief campaign in West Virginia, where a division of his army, under General Rosecrans (rōz'-krants), had defeated the enemy at Rich Mountain.   This, with other victories, had given him the entire control of that region.   Congress,

VII. QUESTIONS.—50. Who commanded the army opposed to this large one of the Confederates?   51. Give an account of General Tyler's operations.   52. Of the battle of Bull Run.   53. Where is Bull Run? (Map, p. 230.)   54. Centreville? (Same.) VIII. 55. Was McDowell continued in the command of the army?   56. By whom was he superseded?   57. When did the change take place?   58. Where had McClellan previously done good service?   59. What did Rosecrans accomplish?   60. Where is Rich Mountain? (See map, p. 320.)   61. What action did Congress take?   62. The President?

which had met in extra session on the 4th of July, promptly voted to raise 500,000 men, to serve three years or during the war; and in August, the President issued a proclamation forbidding all intercourse with the States in rebellion.

IX. A naval expedition, commanded by Commodore Stringham, was successful in taking, August 29th, Hatteras and Clark, two forts at Hatteras Inlet. A more important expedition, consisting of about fifty vessels, and carrying fifteen thousand men, sailed from Hampton Roads, and on the 7th of November, after a fight of three hours, captured Forts Walker and Beauregard, at the entrance of Port Royal harbor. Commodore Dupont commanded the naval forces on the occasion, and General Sherman * those of the land. This victory secured a fine rendezvous for the blockading squadron, and also a base for subsequent operations during the war. In the mean time, Scott having resigned the command of the Union armies, McClellan was appointed in his place.

X. Affairs in Missouri meanwhile kept growing worse instead of better. Colonel Mulligan, commanding two thousand five hundred men at Lexington, was attacked by a Confederate force of about ten thousand, under General Price, and, after four days' struggle, was compelled to surrender, September 20. General Fremont, who two months before had been placed in command of the Western Department, thereupon marched from St. Louis against Price, who, instead of moving farther northward, retreated in an opposite direction, followed by Fremont. The pursuit was brought to a close at Spring-

---

* Brig.-Gen. T. W. Sherman.

IX. QUESTIONS.—63 What success did Commodore Stringham meet with? 64. How large a fleet sailed from Hampton Roads? 65. Who commanded it? 66. Who commanded the land forces on board? 67. What success did they have? 68. What made the victory particularly important? 69. Where is Hatteras Inlet? (See map, p. 320) 70. Port Royal harbor? (Same map) 71. To what position did McClellan succeed?

X. 72. Give an account of the battle of Lexington, Missouri. 73. Of Fremont's operations. 74. By whom was Fremont succeeded in the command? 75. By whom was Hunter succeeded? 76. Where is Lexington? (See map, p 800) 77. St. Louis? (Same map) 78. Springfield? (Same map.)

1861. field, where Fremont, on the 2d of November, received an order removing him from the command. He was succeeded by General Hunter, who retained the position until the appointment of General Halleck.

XI. In the early part of October, the Confederate army which had threatened Washington began to fall back and the Union army to push forward. A division of General Stone's command, having crossed the Potomac at Edward's Ferry or Ball's Bluff, to make a reconnoissance, was disastrously defeated, October 21, and its commander, Colonel Baker,* killed. In the mean time a number of battles and skirmishes had taken place in Kentucky and in other States. In one at Belmont, Missouri, on the 7th of November, General Grant, who commanded the Union troops, gained credit, though his men finally retired to their boats, the enemy having been largely re-enforced.

XII. On the sea an event had occurred in the mean time which produced great excitement both in the United States and Great Britain, and a war between the two countries seemed for a time imminent. Captain Wilkes, in command of the frigate San Jacinto, intercepted the English steamer Trent in the Bahama Channel, and took from her Messrs. Mason and Slidell, Confederate commissioners to Europe. The two prisoners were then brought to the United States, and placed in Fort Warren, near Boston. As the act committed by Wilkes was contrary to the doctrine of the sanctity of a neutral vessel, a doctrine which had long been avowed by the American Government, and as the British authorities resented the act

---

* Edward D. Baker was born in England. He was a member of Congress from Illinois, and an officer in the Mexican War. At the time of his death he was a United States Senator from Oregon.

XI. QUESTIONS.—79. Give an account of the battle of Ball's Bluff 80. By what other name is it also known? 81. Where is Ball's Bluff? (See map, p. 820.) 82. Give an account of the battle of Belmont. 83. Where is Belmont? (See map, p. 800.)

XII. 84. On what mission were Mason and Slidell sent? 85. Give an account of their captur by Captain Wilkes. 86. What war did the act of Wilkes nearly lead to? 87 What disposition was finally made of the two commissioners? 88. Why were they given up by the United States Government?

as an insult to their flag, the two captured commissioners were put on board an English vessel bound for Europe.

XIII. Since the beginning of the war the United States Government had increased its navy to about two hundred vessels. This had been done by completing those on the stocks, and by purchasing and chartering such steamers and other vessels as were found suitable for the public service. This whole force was required in blockading the ports of the South; and as it was increased in the three succeeding years, the blockade became more effective. Meanwhile the relations of the United States with England and France were by no means amicable. The rebellion had hardly been fully inaugurated before Queen Victoria issued a proclamation, May 13th, acknowledging the South as a belligerent power; and France soon after did the same. The course thus pursued by the two powers was not considered friendly by the Government of the United States.

XIV. During this year the Confederates fitted out a number of privateers to prey upon the commerce of the North. On the 1st of June, the Savannah, a little schooner thus fitted out, captured a vessel; but on the 3d, she fell in with the United States brig Perry, which she mistook for a merchantman, and was easily made captive. Some of the Savannah's crew were afterward tried as pirates, but not convicted. Two months later the Petrel, formerly a revenue-cutter, which had been surrendered to the Confederates at the beginning of the war, ran the blockade of Charleston; but, encountering the United States gunboat St. Lawrence, was sunk with five of her crew.

XIII. QUESTIONS—89. How many vessels were in the United States navy at the close of 1861? 90. How had the increase in the navy been effected? 91. How was the navy employed? 92. What caused unfriendly feelings between the United States on the one side and England and France on the other?

XIV. 93. For what purpose was the schooner Savannah fitted out? 94. What became of her? 95. Of her crew? 96. What became of the Petrel? 97. Give the previous history of the Petrel.

XV. .One of the most successful of the privateers was
1861. the steamer Sumter, Captain Semmes, which ran the
blockade of New Orleans, June 30th, 1861, and having in fifteen
days captured as many vessels, ran into the British port of Nassau, where she was supplied with coal.   The Sumter made other
captures in her subsequent cruise, and then crossed the Atlantic, entering the British harbor of Gibraltar.   Here she
was found by an United States gunboat, and from a Spanish-
port opposite was watched.   Finally she was sold, and her
crew went to England, where a faster steamer, the Alabama,
was being constructed for the Confederate government.
Semmes soon resumed his career of destruction upon the seas,
luring vessels by hoisting the British flag, and then consign-
ing his prizes to the flames.

EVENTS OF 1862.

I. At Cairo the Union troops established a base of operations, General Grant being in command.   From a point on
the Mississippi, a few miles below Cairo, the whole river, to
its mouth, was in possession of the Confederates, and great
preparations were being made on both sides for the mastery
of the river.   The Confederates had also built a line of forts
stretching irregularly from the Mississippi to Cumberland Gap,
the principal ones being at Columbus, Bowling Green, Mill

XV. QUESTIONS.—98. What vessel did Semmes command in 1861? 99. In what
business was the Sumter engaged? 100. From what American port did the Sumter
escape? 101. How many vessels did she capture in fifteen days? 102. Where did
she get a supply of coal? 103. What further account can you give of the Sumter?
104. What vessel did Semmes next command? 105. Where was the Alabama built?
106. By what means did Semmes get possession of his prizes? 107. What disposition did he then make of them ?
EVENTS OF 1862.—I. 1. Where is Cairo situated? (See map, p. 300.) 2. What
was established at Cairo? 3. Who was in command there? 4. How much of the
Mississippi was in possession of the Confederates in the beginning of 1862? 5. What
line of forts had the Confederates built? 6. Give an account of the battle of Mill
Spring. 7. Where is Mill Spring? (See map, p. 320.) 8. Columbus? (Map, p. 300.)
9. Bowling Green? (Same.) 10. Fort Henry? (Same.) 11. Fort Donelson? (Same.)

Spring, and Forts Henry and Donelson. In January, 1862, a division of Union troops under the command of General Thomas, advanced against Mill Spring, and on the 19th a battle took place, resulting in the defeat of the Confederates, and the death of Zollicoffer (*tsol'-le-ko'-fer*), one of their ablest generals.

II. On the 6th of February, Captain, afterward Admiral Foote,* commanding a fleet of gunboats, reduced Fort Henry. Upon the approach of General Mitchell a few days later, Bowling Green was abandoned, the forces retiring to Fort Donelson. Simultaneously with Mitchell's movement, a land and naval expedition proceeded against Fort Donelson, which was

ADMIRAL FOOTE.

assaulted by General Grant on the 15th. The battle lasted the whole of that day with varying fortune, but during the night several thousand men of the Confederate force escaped up the Cumberland, and on the following morning the fort was surrendered, General Buckner and sixteen thousand men becoming prisoners. The evacuation of Nashville and Columbus followed as a necessary consequence.

III. While these events were transpiring, a powerful land

---

* Andrew Hull Foote was born in Connecticut, September 12th, 1806. He spent the most of his life in the naval service of his country. He was an active friend of religious and philanthropic enterprises, being particularly active in discouraging profanity and intemperance. He died in New York, June 26th, 1863, while making preparations to take charge of the squadron off Charleston.

II. QUESTIONS.—12. By whom was Fort Henry captured? 13. When was the capture made? 14. Why did the Confederates abandon Bowling Green? 15. Give an account of the movements against Fort Donelson. 16. What places did the Confederates then abandon? 17. Why did they leave?

III. 18. What expedition sailed from Hampton Roads? 19. When did the vessels reach Hatteras Inlet? 20. When did they commence an attack? 21. What place did they attack? 22. What success did the troops have? 23. Who commanded the troops? 24. What other success did the troops have? 25. What were the successes of the fleet? 26. What expedition was successful? 27. Give an account of the capture of Fort Pulaski. 28. Where is the fort situated?

1862. and naval expedition was fitted out and placed under the command of General Burnside and Commodore Goldsborough. It sailed from Hampton Roads, and, though a destructive storm sprang up soon after, most of the vessels reached Hatteras Inlet by the 17th of January, and entered Pamlico Sound. On the 7th of Feb., the fleet opened a fire upon Roanoke Isl., while the troops landed, and, storming the enemy's intrenchments on the 8th, captured twenty-five hundred prisoners. This success was followed by the destruction of the Confederate flotilla at Elizabeth City, by the seizure of that and other places, and also by a victory gained by Burnside, at Newbern, on the 14th of March. An expedition, fitted out at Port Royal, against certain seaports in Florida, was entirely successful, and, on the 11th of April, Fort Pulaski, at the mouth of the Savannah, was bombarded and captured.

IV. No events of the war produced more interest than those which occurred at Hampton Roads, on the 8th and 9th of March. When Norfolk was abandoned, at the beginning of the war, the steamship Merrimac was sunk. She was, however, soon raised by the Confederates, cut down almost to the water's edge, and covered with a plating of iron. On the 8th of March, she made her appearance in Hampton Roads, sunk the U. S. sloop Cumberland, and compelled the frigate Congress to surrender. Night set in, and it was anticipated, on the next day, all the national vessels in the roads would be destroyed. During the night, however, a newly invented floating battery, the Monitor, commanded by Lieutenant Worden (*wur'den*), arrived from New York, and on the following day encountered the Merrimac. After a contest of several hours, the latter, in a disabled condition, retreated to Norfolk.

IV. QUESTIONS.—29 What havoc was committed on the 8th of March, 1862? 30 Give the previous history of the Merrimac 31. By what name did the Confederates call her? Ans. The Virginia. 32 What was the prospect for the 9th of March? 33. What occurred during the night? 34 What then followed? 35. Where is Hampton Roads? (See map, p. 312.) 36. Norfolk? (Same map.)

V. In Missouri and Arkansas, movements of importance had in the mean while occurred. The Confederates in those States were commanded by General Van Dorn. A division of their army having retreated from Missouri before General Curtis, their forces, to the number of about twenty-five thousand, concentrated at Pea Ridge, where one of the most determined battles of the war was fought. It took place on the 6th, 7th, and 8th of March, and resulted in the signal defeat of the Confederates. Curtis, in his official report, commended General Sigel and others of his officers for their gallant conduct.

VI. Early in March, General McClellan ordered an advance from Washington toward Richmond, the enemy falling back from the position at Centreville and Manassas, which he had occupied nearly a year, and taking up a new line of defense along the Rappahannock. On the 23d, General Shields, commanding a Union detachment, gained a splendid victory at Winchester. McClellan having taken the field, an organization of military departments was effected, Gen. Halleck being assigned to the West, Gen. Hunter to the South, Gen. Butler to the Gulf, Gen. Fremont to West Virginia and Eastern Tennessee, Gen. Banks to the Shenandoah, Gen. McDowell to the Rappahannock, and Gen. McClellan to the Potomac.

VII. After the Confederates had evacuated Columbus, they retreated down the Mississippi to Island No. 10, and to New Madrid, Missouri: they also took a strong position at Corinth.

V. QUESTIONS.—37. Where is Pea Ridge? (See map, p. 300.) 38. Give an account of the battle that took place there. 39. What commendation did General Sigel receive?

VI. 40. What movement was made early in March? 41. What movement did the Confederates make in consequence? 42. What success did General Shields have? 43. What department organizations were effected? 44. Where is Winchester? (See map p. 320.) 45. Into what river does the Rappahannock flow? (Same map.)

VII. 46. To what places did the Confederates retreat from Columbus? 47. What took place at New Madrid? 48. Describe the process by which the Confederates were compelled to evacuate Island No. 10. 49. Where is Columbus? (See map, p. 300.) 50. New Madrid? (Same map.) 51. Island No. 10? (Same map.)

1862. On the 14th of March, General Pope succeeded in taking New Madrid, and on the 16th the bombardment of the island was opened by the gunboat fleet of Commodore Foote. The plan of attack required the co-operation of Pope, but as that officer had no means of crossing the Mississippi, the difficulty was overcome by cutting a canal twelve miles long, through the neck of land formed by a bend in the river opposite the island, by which the needed transports from Foote's fleet were enabled to reach him. As soon as his troops began to cross, April 7th, the enemy proceeded to evacuate the island; and on the following day the place, with about six thousand prisoners, was in the hands of the Unionists.

VIII. In the mean time the main body of the Western army, under Grant, was advancing toward Corinth. On the 6th of April, having reached Shiloh, near Pittsburg Landing, on the Tennessee, here, early in the morning of that day, it was attacked by the enemy, commanded by Johnston and Beauregard. The battle raged till near nightfall, the Union troops being compelled to retreat to the river, where the gunboats aided them to make a stand. The arrival of re-enforcements under Buell enabled Grant to assume the offensive on the following day, and the enemy were finally driven back toward Corinth. The forces engaged in this battle, on both sides, numbered more than a hundred thousand men, and the losses were very severe. Johnston (Albert S.) was killed.

IX. Halleck, having arrived from St. Louis, took command in person of Grant's victorious army. He at once commenced an advance upon Corinth, slowly progressing every day for nearly two months, when, May 30th, the place was found to

VIII. QUESTIONS—52. Where is Corinth? (See map, p. 300.) 53. Shiloh? (Same map.) 54. Into what river does the Tennessee flow? (Same map.) 55. Describe what took place on the 6th of April. 56. Give an account of subsequent operations.

IX. 57. Who then took command of Grant's army? 58. Give an account of his movements. 59. Of Mitchell's movements. 60. Of operations at and near Fort Pillow. 61. Of operations at and before Memphis. 62. Where is Nashville? (See map, p. 300.) 63. Huntsville? (Same map.) 64. Fort Pillow? (Same.) 65. Memphis? (Same.)

be evacuated. A small body of troops under Mitchell meanwhile had marched from Nashville, occupied several towns in Tennessee, and seized Huntsville, in Alabama. The Confederates, after their loss of Island No. 10, made a stand at Fort Wright, or, as it is also called, Fort Pillow. The fleet on the Mississippi, commanded by Commodore Foote, descended the river, and was unsuccessfully attacked by the enemy's fleet near the fort—the fort itself being afterward abandoned. On the 6th, two days later, Commodore Davis, Foote's successor, gained a victory over the fleet defending Memphis, and the town, in consequence, fell into his hands.

X. Lower down the Mississippi, the Union cause had met with a success of still more importance. This was the capture of New Orleans, on the 25th of April. Commodore Farragut's fleet of forty-five vessels, including a number of mortar-boats under the special command of Commodore Porter, ascended the Mississippi, and for six days bombarded Forts Jackson and St. Philip, on opposite sides of the river, about seventy-five miles below the city. Having broken the chain which had been stretched across the stream, Farragut ran past the forts, April 24th, and destroyed a squadron of the enemy's rams and gunboats. As he approached New Orleans, the Confederates set fire to the vast stores of cotton and sugar there. The two forts, Jackson and St. Philip, surrendered to Porter, and then General Butler moved up the river from Ship Island, and, taking formal possession of the city, placed it under martial law.

XI. At Alexandria, McClellan embarked his army, to the

X. QUESTIONS.—66 When was New Orleans captured by the Union forces? 67. When was the capture made? 68. By whom were the victors commanded? 69. Give an account of the achievement. 70. Who then took military possession of the city? 71. Where is New Orleans? (See map, p. 300.)

XI. 72 How large an army did General McClellan have at Alexandria? 73. What movement did he make from Alexandria? 74. Give an account of operations at Yorktown. 75. At Williamsburg. 76. At West Point. 77. Where is Alexandria? (See map, p. 287.) 78. Fortress Monroe? (Map, p. 320.) 79. Yorktown? (Same.) 80. Richmond? (Same.) 81. Williamsburg? (Same.) 82 West Point?

1862. number of eighty-five thousand men, for Fortress Monroe, whence he advanced upon Yorktown. A siege commenced on the 5th of April, and continued, with much fighting, until the 4th of May, when the place was found to be evacuated. The Confederates retreated toward Richmond, pursued by the Union troops; and at Williamsburg, where they were overtaken the following day, a severe action took place. The pursuers at first met with a serious check; but the timely arrival of General Kearny restored the battle, and the enemy fled. A division of the pursuing army proceeded up the York River, and, having landed near West Point, were unsuccessfully attacked on the 7th.

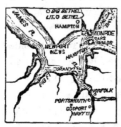

MAP OF NORFOLK AND VICINITY.

XII. President Lincoln at this time visited Fortress Monroe, and having urged a movement upon Norfolk, an expedition was accordingly dispatched under General Wool. Upon approaching the city, the Union commander was met by the civil authorities and informed that the place had been abandoned by the Confederate army. Besides this abandonment, the insurgents had burned the navy-yard near Norfolk; evacuated Craney Island, where they had erected formidable defenses; and they also destroyed their iron-clad vessel, the Merrimac. They needed all their men to oppose the march of McClellan's army against Richmond.

XIII. This army, in the mean time, was steadily advancing. By the 20th of May, most of the troops had reached the

XII. QUESTIONS.—83. What visit did the President make? 84. What did he urge? 85. What success did General Wool have? 86. What previous acts had the insurgents committed? 87. Why did they do so? 88. Where is Norfolk? (See map, p. 312.) 89. Craney Island? (Same map.)

XIII. 90. What advance did McClellan's army make by the 22d of May? 91. When was the battle of Hanover Court House fought? 92. Give an account of the battle of Fair Oaks. 93. What can you state of General McDowell's movements? 94. Into what river does the Chickahominy flow? (See map, p. 29.) 95. Where is Fair Oaks? (See map, p. 313.) 96. Bowling Green? (See map, p. 237.)

Chickahominy, a small river running through a swampy country, and, on the 22d, the stream was crossed. Five days later, a detachment under General Porter defeated the enemy at Hanover Court House. At Fair Oaks, a position within about five miles of Richmond, a bloody battle took place on the last day of May and the first of June, the North losing five thousand men and the South eight thousand, without advantage to either side. McDowell, who had been ordered to co-operate in the movement against Richmond, reached Bowling Green, when he was directed by the President to march for the Shenandoah.

XIV. Banks's division, at the time, was at Strasburg, and this force the enemy formed the plan of capturing; but the Confederates meeting with resistance at Front Royal, Banks became aware of their purpose, and made a masterly retreat to the Potomac. Jackson, the pursuing general, advanced to Harper's Ferry, but, meeting with a repulse, made a retrograde

movement. At Strasburg, he was overtaken, June 1st, by Fremont, who had made a forced march across the mountains, and was driven from the place. Fremont continued the pursuit, fighting an undecisive battle at Cross Keys and another at Port Republic. Although Jackson had failed to capture Banks's army, he had succeeded in preventing re-enforcements being sent to McClellan.

XV. McClellan, believing that the force at his disposal was

XIV. QUESTIONS.—97 Give an account of Banks's retreat from Strasburg 98 Where, on the Potomac, did Jackson meet with defeat? 99 What took place at Strasburg? 100. At Cross Keys? 101. At Port Republic? 102 What was the result of Jackson's expedition? 103 Where is Strasburg? (See map, p. 320) 104. Cross Keys? (Same map) 105 Port Republic? (Same.)

XV. 106 What change of base did McClellan effect? 107 Why did he make the change? 108. What took place while the change was in progress? 109 How was the army protected at Harrison's Landing? 110. Where is the White House? (See map, p. 313) 111. Harrison's Landing? (Same map) 112 What army changes were made?

14

1862.

not sufficient to protect his lines, which extended from the White House, on the Pamunkey, where the army had its supplies, transferred his base of operations to Harrison's Landing, on the James. While this movement was in progress, the Confederates fell upon the Union troops, June 25th, and a series of destructive battles, lasting through seven days, took place. At this new position the Federal army remained until the 14th of August, protected by a fleet of gunboats. Prior to this, the corps of Fremont, Banks, and McDowell had been consolidated with the army of the Potomac, and the command given to General Pope, and, on the 1st of July, the President issued a call for three hundred thousand more volunteers. On the 11th, Halleck was appointed commander-in-chief, Grant succeeding him in the command of the army of the Mississippi.

XVI. Other operations of importance had in the mean time taken place, both in the east and west. General Hunter had made an unsuccessful attempt upon James Island, and great damage had been done to the property of Union people in Missouri, Kentucky, and Tennessee, by guerrilla bands. A severe fight took place on the Yazoo River, July 15th, between the Confederate ram Arkansas and three Federal vessels, after which the ram ran through the fleets of Farragut and Davis to Vicksburg. Some days later she sailed down the Mississippi, to aid in an attack on Baton Rouge. In this movement, which proved unsuccessful, the ram was not able to take part, but on the following day, August 6th, after a brief action with the United States gunboat Essex, she took fire and was blown up. At Iuka (*I-u'-kah*), on the 19th of the following month, Rosecrans fought and dispersed the Confederate force under Price, and on the 4th of October he gained another victory at Corinth.

XVII. Freed from the necessity of defending their own capital, the enemy undertook to menace that of the Union. McClellan was ordered to withdraw from the James and co-operate with Pope against this movement; but before he commenced the transfer of his troops a hotly contested battle was fought, August 9th, at Cedar Mountain, eight miles from Culpepper Court House, between a division of Pope's army, commanded by Banks, and a force under Jackson. The Confederates, though superior in numbers, were unsuccessful. The main army of the enemy, commanded by General Lee, advanced, and, until the close of the month, the struggle between the two great armies was desperate. In a conflict, attended with great slaughter, occurring on the 29th and 30th, and known as the "second battle of Bull Run," Pope was defeated, and at night retreated to Centreville. At Chantilly, two days after, a body of Confederate troops was met and at last driven back, but not till they had killed two valuable Union officers, Generals Stevens* and Kearny.†

XVIII. Pope's army fell back to the intrenchments before Washington, but Lee's, instead of following, turned northward and crossed the Potomac into Maryland. McClellan was then in command of all the troops concentrated near Washington for its defense. He pursued Lee, and, on the 14th of Sep-

---

* Isaac Ingalls Stevens was born in Massachusetts, in 1817. He graduated at West Point, was an officer in the Mexican war, Governor of Washington Territory, and a delegate in Congress.

† Philip Kearny was born in the city of New York, June 2d, 1815. He went to Europe by direction of the United States Government, to report upon the French cavalry tactics, and was promoted for gallant conduct in the Mexican war, losing his left arm. His merits as a disciplinarian were very superior

---

XVII QUESTIONS.—120 What permitted the Confederates to menace the city of Washington? 121 What order was given to McClellan? 122 What took place before McClellan's troops began to move? 123. Give an account of the battle of Cedar Mountain 124. Of the other events of the month 125. Of the battle of Chantilly. 126. Where is Culpepper Court House? (See map, p 320.) 127 Cedar Mountain? 128. Centreville? (See map, p 330.) 129. Chantilly? (Same map.)

XVIII 130 To what position did Pope's army fall back? 131. What did Lee's army do? 132 What duty did McClellan have assigned to him just then? 133. Give an account of the battle of South Mountain 134. Of the surrender of Harper's Ferry. 135. Where is South Mountain? Ans. In Maryland, near Harper's Ferry 136 Harper's Ferry? (See map, p. 320.)

1862. tember, overtook and successfully attacked him at South Mountain. At the same time a strong body of the Confederate army was drawing around Harper's Ferry. These opened fire, and on the 15th the place was surrendered, with eleven thousand men and vast munitions of war.

GENERAL LEE,

XIX. The captors of Harper's Ferry entered Maryland, and, joining Lee at Antietam (*an-te'-tam*), were in time to aid him in the great battle fought there on the 17th. In this contest, which lasted from daylight to nightfall, and which resulted in favor of the Union cause, not less than eleven thousand Federal troops were killed or wounded, while the loss of the enemy was even greater. On the night of the 18th, Lee withdrew his forces across the Potomac, having lost during his campaign in Maryland, in killed, wounded, and prisoners, more than twenty-five thousand men.

XX. In Tennessee and Kentucky, the Confederates were very active during the summer. General Smith moved northward, and defeated a body of Union troops at Richmond, Kentucky, on the 30th of August. His march thence to Frankfort, during which he was joined by a guerrilla force under Morgan, caused great excitement in Cincinnati, and effectual measures were adopted by General Wallace to repel his advance across the Ohio. With the main army, of which

XIX. QUESTIONS.—137. Give an account of the battle of Antietam. 138. What did Lee afterward do? 139. How many men did Lee lose during his campaign? 140. Where is Antietam? (See map, p. 320.)

XX. 141. Give an account of the battle of Richmond. 142. What was done by General Wallace? 143. Through what place did General Bragg march? 144. What place did he intend to attack? 145. Why did he not do so? 146. What took place at Munfordsville? 147. At Perryville? 148. What plunder did Bragg escape with? 149. Who succeeded Buell in the command? 150. How is Richmond, Kentucky, situated? Ans. Near Lexington. 151. Frankfort? (See map, p. 320.) 152. Louisville? (See map, p. 192.) 153. Perryville? (Same.) 154. Munfordsville? (p. 300.)

Smith's was an advanced division, General Bragg marched through Chattanooga, his point of attack being Louisville. Munfordsville, after a day's contest, was surrendered to the Confederates; but Buell, who had followed up Bragg from the South, finally outstripped him, and, arriving at Louisville, put an end to further invasion by the enemy. On his retreat Bragg was successfully attacked at Perryville, October 8th, but he made good his escape, with nearly four thousand wagon loads of plunder. Buell was soon after superseded in the command by Rosecrans.

XXI. Although in the capture of New Orleans, and in other successes, the Federal Government had made progress toward regaining possession of the Mississippi, yet the enemy still held Vicksburg and Port Hudson, and consequently their communication with States on opposite sides of the river continued. An attempt made by Sherman to capture Vicksburg failed, Grant, who had advanced to co-operate, having been compelled to fall back, his line of communication having been cut by the enemy. Sherman's repulse took place on the 29th of December.

XXII. The Army of the Potomac, having made an advance, were in the vicinity of Front Royal on the 7th of November. On that day McClellan was superseded in the command by Burnside, and, later in the month, the troops, led by their new commander, reached the Rappahannock, the design being to march against Richmond by the route from Fredericksburg. Owing to delay in the arrival of pontoons necessary for cross-

XXI QUESTIONS.—154. To what end did the capture of New Orleans tend? 155. What advantage did the holding of Vicksburg and Port Hudson give to the Confederates? 156. When and why did Sherman fail to take Vicksburg? 157. Where is Vicksburg? (See map, p 300.) 158. What was done by the Confederate cavalry? Ans Stuart made a raid into Maryland and Pennsylvania, completely passing around the Union lines.

XXII 159 Who succeeded McClellan in the command of the army, November 7th? 160 Where was the army then? 161 Where is Front Royal situated? (See map, p. 320.) 162 What plan did Burnside undertake to carry out? 163. Why did he not cross the Rappahannock without delay? 164. Give an account of the further operations of Burnside? 165. Where is Fredericksburg? (see map, p 320.)

1862.
ing the river, the enemy had time to throw up strong intrenchments on the hills in the rear of the city. The river was finally crossed on the 12th of December, and Fredericksburg taken possession of; but all attempts to carry the enemy's position failed, and on the 15th the army recrossed the river, having sustained a loss, in killed, wounded, and missing, of over twelve thousand men.

EVENTS OF 1863.

I. On the 1st of January, 1863, President Lincoln issued his memorable emancipation proclamation, declaring forever free all the slaves in the States then in rebellion, excepting in such portions as were occupied by the national troops. This step was taken in accordance with a notice given by the President a hundred days before. By it more than three millions of slaves were declared free. On the same day the city of Galveston was taken by the Confederates, and the naval force before the place captured, destroyed, or dispersed.

II. In the latter part of 1862, Rosecrans moved from the vicinity of Cincinnati, intending to penetrate Alabama, and at Murfreesboro' he encountered the enemy under Bragg. After a severe struggle, which lasted several days, victory, on the 2d of January, 1863, decided in favor of the national forces. Rosecrans remained at Murfreesboro' several months. In June his army was again put in motion, and by a flank movement he compelled Bragg to retreat into Georgia.

EVENTS OF 1863—I. QUESTIONS—1 What Proclamation did President Lincoln issue? 2 When did he issue it? 3 Had he given notice of his intention to issue such a document? 4 When? 5. What was the nature of the proclamation? Ans. "It warned all the insurgents to lay down their arms and return to their allegiance, under the penalty that, in all the districts where the insurrection should be still maintained, with the support of the people, he would, on the first of January then next, proclaim, as a military measure, the freedom of the slaves." 6. What took place at Galveston? 7. Where is Galveston? (See map, p. 268.)

II. 8. What movement did Rosecrans make? 9. Give an account of the battle at Murfreesboro'. 10. Where is Murfreesboro'? (See map, p. 192.)

III. Burnside having, at his own request, been relieved of the command of the Army of the Potomac, was succeeded by Hooker. Toward the latter part of April the army again crossed the Rappahannock, but being met by the enemy under Lee at Chancellorsville, a severe battle was fought on the 2d and 3d of May, to the disadvantage of the national troops. Hooker recrossed

JACKSON (STONEWALL).

the river, and occupied his former camp opposite Fredericksburg. In this attempt the army sustained a loss of about eleven thousand men; that of the Confederates was less, but among their mortally wounded was "Stonewall Jackson,"* one of their ablest generals.

IV. On the 9th of June, Lee's army, numbering nearly a hundred thousand men, began a northward movement, Hooker following. On the 15th President Lincoln issued a call for one hundred thousand men, to repel the invaders, who, crossing the Potomac, on the 27th were near Hagerstown. On the following day the command of the pursuing army was transferred to General Meade. At Gettysburg, in Pennsylvania, Lee concentrated his forces.; and here, on the 1st, 2d, and 3d of July, one of the most important conflicts of the war took

---

* Thomas Jonathan Jackson was born in Virginia, January 21st, 1824. He was a graduate of West Point, served under Taylor and Scott in the Mexican war, and was a professor of the Military Institute of his State. It was remarked by one of his associate officers that in the battle of Bull Run he "stood like a stone wall;" hence he was afterward popularly known as " Stonewall Jackson."

III. QUESTIONS.—11. Who, after Burnside, commanded the Army of the Potomac? 12. Why was Burnside relieved of the command? 13. What movement did the army soon after make? 14. What account can you give of the battle that followed? 15. What did Hooker then do? 16. Where is Chancellorsville? (See map, p. 330.)

IV. 17. How large an army did Lee have on the 9th of June, 1863? 18. What movement did he then make? 19. Who, after Hooker, commanded the Army of the Potomac? 20. Give an account of the battle of Gettysburg. 21. Where is Gettysburg? (See map, p. 320.) 22. Hagerstown? (Same map.)

(*Questions to be answered from the above map.*)

Where is Washington? Richmond? Olustee? Norfolk? Lynchburg? Petersburg? Fredericksburg? Gettysburg? Resaca? Winchester? Harper's Ferry?
Chambersburg? Monocacy? Strasburg? Front Royal? New Market? Martinsburg? Hagerstown? Cross Keys? Chantilly? Philippi? Williamsburg?

place. The invaders were finally defeated, and, with their army reduced one-third, they made a rapid retreat into Virginia.

V. In the beginning of the year a plan of attack against Arkansas Post was concerted by Sherman and Admiral Porter. General McClernand arriving and taking the command of the Army of the Mississippi, the place, with its garrison of five thousand men, was captured on the 11th of January. At this time General Banks was in command of the Department of the Gulf, he having superseded Butler. After making victorious incursions over a large part of Louisiana, he proceeded to invest Port Hudson.

VI. It was the chief object of Grant, then in command of the Army of the Mississippi, to open the great river. His first point of attack was Vicksburg, the strongest post held by the enemy on the Mississippi. Failing to get in the rear of the city, he moved his army down the west side of the river, while Porter's fleet ran by the batteries of Vicksburg. The army then recrossed the Mississippi below Vicksburg, and, near Port Gibson, May 1st, gained a decided victory. General Pemberton, who was the chief in command at Vicksburg, had a force under him of at least thirty thousand men. He sallied forth to attack the rear of the investing army, when a series of battles took place, from the 12th to the 17th of the month, in which he met with defeat. The investment was then made more complete, and the city's defenses were twice assaulted. Pemberton, however, still held out, hoping for relief from General Johnston; but in vain, and, with an

<hr>

V. QUESTIONS.—23. Give an account of the capture of Arkansas Post. 24. Who, after Butler commanded the Department of the Gulf? 25. What did Banks accomplish in Louisiana?

VI. 26. What great object did Grant have in view? 27. How did his army get from the east side of the Mississippi to the vicinity of Port Gibson? 28. What took place near the fort? 29. How did Porter's fleet get below Vicksburg? 30. What battles took place? 31. Give an account of the surrender of Vicksburg. 32. Where is Vicksburg? (See map, p. 300.) 33. Port Gibson? (Same map.) 34. Port Hudson? (Same)

14*

1863.

army on the verge of starvation, he surrendered th city on the 4th of July.

VII. Banks's operations against Port Hudson continue until its commander was informed of the fall of Vicksburg when he too surrendered. Thus was the Mississippi opened In the assaults which had been made upon the enemy's work before Port Hudson, the colored troops, of which there wer several regiments in Banks's army, behaved with so muc bravery as to call forth official commendation. While th Union forces were operating against Vicksburg and Por Hudson, as just related, Colonel Grierson made a cavalry rai of great boldness. Entering the State of Mississippi from th north, he broke the communications of the Confederates destroyed stores, and effected captures, finally reaching Bato Rouge (*bat'-on-roozh*) without serious loss. The news of th victories at Vicksburg, Gettysburg, and Port Hudson, cause great rejoicings among the loyal people of the country.

SEAL OF WEST VIRGINIA.*

VIII. Almost simultaneously wit Lee's invasion of Pennsylvania, bold raid was made into Indian and Ohio by the partisan ranger General Morgan. At first he me with considerable success, plunder ing and destroying as he move eastward; but after having bee pursued day and night for a dis tance of nearly seven hundred miles and baffled by the gunboats in an attempt to recross the Ohio

---

* West Virginia was admitted into the Union in 1863. It includes most of that portion of the old Stat lying west of the Alleghany Mountains—hence its name. The motto of the State, *Montani Semp Liberi*, signifies, *Mountaineers are always free.*

VII. QUESTIONS.—85. What success did General Banks have? 86. What was th consequence? 87. What is said of the conduct of the colored troops? 88. Give a account of Grierson's raid. 89. What effect did the news of victory have?

VIII. 40. Into what States did Morgan make a raid? 41. What success did h have? 42. What pursuit was made? 43. Where was he overtaken? Ans. Nea Kyger's Creek, Ohio. 44. What was the result? 45. What afterward took place?

he was overtaken by General Hobson, July 21st, and a large part of his force captured. He and about five hundred men succeeding in escaping, and were not taken until five days after.

IX. During the year, the principal operations in the Carolinas took place in the vicinity of Charleston. The Confederates undertook to recover their lost possessions in North Carolina, but without success, a demonstration which they made on Newbern failing, as did also their designs against Washington, on the Tar River. On the 7th of April, Admiral Dupont, commanding a fleet of iron-clads, made an attack upon the fortifications of Charleston harbor, but his vessels were driven off. A vigorous attempt to capture Charleston was made on the 10th of July, by the Union land and naval forces, under General Gillmore and Admiral Dahlgren (dal'-gren). Though this also failed, Morris Island, with the exception of its northern portion, containing Fort Wagner, was gained. Twice afterward, on the 11th and 18th, was the fort unsuccessfully assailed. At last the Confederates were forced to abandon the island altogether. During seven days in August, Fort Sumter was subjected to a bombardment so destructive as to reduce it to a mass of ruins, and shells were thrown into the city of Charleston itself.

X. Bragg, who had been compelled by Rosecrans to retreat into Georgia, having been re-enforced by troops from Lee's

IX. QUESTIONS.—46 What can you state of operations in North Carolina? 47. Give an account of the operations of April 7th. 48. July 10th. 49 Of the assaults. 50. What noted officer was killed? Ans. Colonel Shaw, "commanding the first regiment of colored soldiers from a free State ever mustered into the United States service." 51 What took place afterward, during a period of seven days? 52 Where is Charleston? (See maps, pp 79 and 129.) 53. Morris Island? (See map, p 129.) 54. Where was Fort Wagner? 55. What position on the island, beside Fort Wagner, did the Confederates hold? Ans Battery Gregg, situated on the north point of the island 56. Describe the Tar River. (See map, p. 164.)

X. 57. Give an account of the battle of Chickamauga Creek 58. How was Rosecrans's army saved from defeat? 59. What losses were sustained in the battle? 60. What movement did Rosecrans make? 61. Where is Chickamauga Creek? (See map, p 320.) 62. Chattanooga? (Same map.)

1863. army under General Longstreet, turned upon his pursuers near Chickamauga Creek. The battle that followed, September 19th and 20th, was furious; and at the close of the second day General Thomas held a position from which the Confederates vainly by the most desperate efforts endeavored to force him; this alone saved the Union army from utter defeat. On the following day, the entire army of Rosecrans fell back to Chattanooga. In this conflict the loss to the national army exceeded sixteen thousand men: the enemy's was certainly as large.

XI. The army of Rosecrans at Chattanooga was for a time in danger of starvation. Its lines of communication had been cut by the enemy, who also occupied a threatening position on Lookout Mountain and Missionary Ridge. At this time Thomas superseded Rosecrans, and General Hooker opportunely arrived with re-enforcements. Generals Sherman and Grant also arrived, the latter holding the supreme command. Hooker stormed and carried Lookout Mountain, November 24th, and on the following day, Bragg was routed and driven back into Georgia. The losses on both sides were very severe

XII. In the mean time Burnside had been sent from Kentucky to drive the enemy from East Tennessee. Bragg, on being informed of this, detached Longstreet against him; consequently Burnside was besieged in Knoxville for a period of fifteen days. During the siege the enemy made a fierce assault upon Burnside's defenses, November 29th, but were repulsed. The victory at Chattanooga having enabled Grant to send Sherman to the relief of Burnside, Longstreet was compelled to flee. He made good his retreat, succeeding at last in rejoining Lee's army in Virginia.

XI. QUESTIONS —63. What can you state of the condition of the army at Chattanooga? 64 What relief came? 65. What operations took place in November? 66. Where are the two mountains spoken of? Ans. Northern part of Georgia

XII. 67. On what expedition was Burnside sent? 68. What can you state of the siege and assault? 69. What compelled Longstreet to retreat? 70. Where did he go? 71. Where is Knoxville? (See map, p. 192.)

XIII. A great deal of activity was kept up for months by Generals Price, Marmaduke, and others, commanding portions of the Confederate army west of the Mississippi. They, however, met with but little success. Marmaduke was repulsed at Springfield, January 8th, also at Cape Girardeau (*jir'-ar-do*), April 26th, and Price and he at Helena, Arkansas, July 4th. General Steele was afterward sent into Arkansas. He pushed the Confederates with vigor, and by the close of October restored most of the State to the national authority. Bands of guerrillas, however, continued to plunder and destroy; the sacking of Lawrence in Kansas being one of the many outrages thus committed.

XIV. The navy of the United States during the year was very active. It was divided into six squadrons, and employed along the Atlantic seaboard and in the western rivers in blockading duties, and in movements co-operating with the armies of Banks, Grant, and others. A number of vessels were also employed from time to time in cruising after Confederate privateers. The blockade became so effective as to be fully respected by the nations of Europe, Wilmington alone, of all the Confederate ports, on account of its wide and numerous inlets, being at all successful in maintaining an intercourse with Nassau (*nas-saw'*), and other British ports.

XV. Congress, by its several enactments, fully empowered

XIII. QUESTIONS—72. What can you state of the activity of the Confederates west of the Mississippi? 73 What took place at Springfield? 74 At Cape Girardeau? 75. At Helena? 76. At Lawrence? 77 Where is Springfield? (See map, p. 300) 78. Cape Girardeau? (Same map.) 79. Helena? (Same) 80. Lawrence? (Same.)

XIV. 81. Into how many squadrons was the United States Navy divided? 82. How was the navy employed? 83. How were other vessels employed? 84. What is said of the effectiveness of the blockade? 85. Where is Wilmington? (See map, p 320.) 86. What is Nassau? Ans. Nassau is the capital of the Bahama Islands. 87 Where are the Bahama Islands? (See map, p. 10)

XV. 88. What power did Congress confer upon the President? 89 How large was the navy at the close of the year? 90 How many men were in the army? 91. What power did the conscription act confer? 92. How was the great riot in New York brought about? 93. Give an account of the riot. 94. When was West Virginia admitted into the Union? (See note, p. 322.)

1863.

the President to carry on the war, placing at his disposal all the money and men needed. The navy numbered at the close of the year nearly six hundred vessels, carrying twenty-five thousand seamen, and the army consisted of not less than half a million of effective men, of whom above sixty thousand were colored troops. Among the congressional enactments was a conscription act, empowering the President to recruit the army by drafting. By virtue of this authority, he ordered a draft of three hundred thousand men. An opposition to this measure was at once excited, which culminated in a riot in the city of New York, commencing July 13th, while the draft was in progress, and continuing four days. Buildings were sacked and burned, the Colored Orphan Asylum among the number, and the most fiendish acts were committed, particularly against the colored people. At length the police, aided by a military force, quelled the riot, but not before at least a hundred of those engaged in it had been killed.

EVENTS OF 1864.

I. In February, 1864, Sherman,* at the head of twenty-five thousand men, marched eastward from Vicksburg, nearly across the State of Mississippi. An expedition from Memphis, designed to co-operate with him, met with so much opposition from the enemy as to be compelled to put back. Sherman effected the destruction of many miles of railroad, and on his march back to Vicksburg was accompanied by about six thousand of the slaves whom he had liberated. In the same month an expedition from Port Royal, under General Seymour, was made into Florida, which resulted in severe disaster, the Union force being defeated at Olustee, on the 20th inst., with terrible slaughter.

EVENTS OF 1864.—I. QUESTIONS.—1 What march did Sherman make early in 1864? 2 What destruction did he effect? 3. What is stated of the slaves? 4. Give an account of the battle of Olustee. 5. Where is Vicksburg? (See map, p 300.) 6. Memphis? (Same map.) 7. To what place did Sherman's expedition extend? Ans. Meridian (See map, p 300.) 8. Where is Olustee? (See map, p 320.) * Wm T.

II A concentration of forces took place at New Orleans early in 1864 : these, according to the plan of General Banks, were to co-operate with Porter's fleet in an expedition up the Red River as far as Shreveport. General Smith, commanding about ten thousand troops from Vicksburg, preceded Banks, took Fort De Russy, March 14th, and, two days after, entered Alexandria. A column from the main army here joined the expedition. At Cane River the enemy undertook to check the further advance of the Unionists, but they were repulsed. Near Mansfield, on the 8th of April, they were entirely successful, and the Union army during the night retreated to Pleasant Hill : the enemy, following, renewed the attack on the following day, not, however, with a like result. Though the Unionists were successful in this last battle, their losses during the campaign were severe, and Banks ordered the army to fall back to the river.

III. Meanwhile the fleet had made progress up the river, but the retrograde movement of the army decided Porter to return. On his way back he was almost constantly annoyed by the enemy's batteries and sharpshooters on the banks of the stream. The water too had fallen so much that, when his vessels approached the rapids near Alexandria, they could not pass. In this emergency, a plan proposed by Lieutenant-Colonel Bailey was adopted, and under his direction a dam was constructed across the river, by which the boats were enabled to go over the falls. The army returned to New Orleans and the fleet to the Mississippi. General Banks during this expe-

II. Questions.—9. Of what forces was the Red River expedition composed ? 10. How far up the river did General Banks design to go ? 11. What did General Smith accomplish alone ? 12. What took place at Cane River? 13. At Mansfield? 14. At Pleasant Hill ? 15. Describe the Red River. (See map, p. 300.) 16. Where is Shreveport? (Same map.) 17. Fort De Russy ? (Same.) 18. Alexandria ? (Same.) 19. Mansfield ? (Same.) 20. Pleasant Hill ? (Same.) 21. Camden? (Same.) 22. Little Rock ? (Same.)

III. 23. What effect did Banks's retreat have upon Commodore Porter ? 24. What annoyance did Porter experience ? 25. What difficulty did he meet near Alexandria? 26. How was the difficulty overcome ? 27. What movements did the army and fleet then make ? 28. What account can you give of General Steele's movements ?

1864. dition had expected the co-operation of General Steele, from Arkansas. That officer made a successful advance as far as Camden, but the failure experienced by Banks left him no alternative other than a return to Little Rock. On his way he was harassed by the Confederates, and though he defeated them in a battle fought on the 30th of Apr, his losses were severe.

IV. The withdrawal of forces from Vicksburg to engage in the Red River expedition emboldened the Confederates under General Forrest to make a raid into the western part of Tennessee and Kentucky. The garrison at Union City surrendered after a slight resistance. On the following day, March 25th, two unsuccessful attacks were made upon Fort Anderson, near Paducah Early on the morning of the 12th of April an attack was made on Fort Pillow. The garrison, consisting of between five and six hundred men, more than half of whom were colored troops, made a brave resistance, but the place at last was carried by assault, and three hundred of its defenders massacred. In North Carolina the Confederate soldiers were also successful, capturing Plymouth with the aid of the iron-clad ram Albemarle. In October, a little more than six months afterward, the Albemarle was sunk by Lieutenant Cushing, by means of a torpedo. The main defense of Plymouth being thus removed, the town was retaken on the 31st of the same month.

V. The services which General Grant had rendered the country, added to his peculiar fitness as a commander of large armies, induced Congress to revive the grade of Lieutenant-General, with special reference to him. This grade had been

IV. QUESTIONS.—29 Why did Forrest decide upon making a raid? 30 What took place at Union City? 31 At Fort Anderson? 32 At Fort Pillow? 33 Give an account of the loss and recapture of Plymouth 34 Where is Union City? (See map, p 300) 35 Paducah? (Same map) 36 Fort Pillow? (Same) 37 Plymouth? (See map, p. 320.)

V. 38. Why did Congress revive the grade of Lieutenant-General? 39 Give the previous history of the grade. 40 What was done in reference to General Grant? 41 What preparations were begun?

previously conferred on only two persons, Washington and Scott, and on the retirement of the latter, became extinct.   Accordingly the President nominated General Grant for this position, the highest in the military service of the country, and the nomination was confirmed by the Senate on the 3d of March. Vast preparations were at once commenced for two campaigns, one against Richmond by the Army of the Potomac; and the other against Atlanta by an

LIEUT.-GEN. GRANT.

army of a hundred thousand men under Gen. W. T. Sherman. Early in May both armies began to move forward.

VI. To oppose Sherman was an army sixty thousand strong, commanded by Gen. J. E. Johnston. The Union troops advanced from Chattanooga, and, by a flank movement, compelled Johnston to fall back to Resaca. From this position, after a severe contest of two days, May 14th and 15th, he was also obliged to retreat. Other battles were fought, the Union troops carrying line after line of rifle-pits, intrenchments, and fortifications—most of the time through a mountain region— outflanking the enemy and pursuing him to the strong fortifications of Atlanta. Johnston's "retreating policy" was loudly condemned by the Confederates, and he was consequently superseded in the command by General Hood.

VII. From the 20th to the 28th of July, Hood made three

VI. QUESTIONS.—42. What army did Sherman have against him ? 43. From what place did Sherman commence his movement? 44. What took place at Resaca ? 45. What account can you give of the operations before the fortifications of Atlanta were reached ? 46. Who succeeded Johnston in the command of the Confederate army ? 47. Why was Johnston removed ? 48. Where is Chattanooga ? (See map, p. 320.) 49. Resaca? (Same map) 50. Atlanta ? (Same.)

VII. 51. What can you state of the assaults made by Hood ? 52. Of Stoneman's expedition ? 53. How did Sherman manage to divide the Confederate army ? 54. What took place at Jonesboro' ? 55. Why was Hood compelled to evacuate Atlanta? 56. What were the losses of both sides ? 57. Where is Jonesboro' ?

1864.   furious assaults upon the Union troops before Atlanta, but each time he was defeated with heavy loss.   While besieging Atlanta, Sherman sent out cavalry expeditions to destroy the railroads by which it received re-enforcements of troops and supplies.   General Stoneman, commanding one of these, not only failed to perform the task assigned him, but was defeated, and thus the most important road remained in possession of the Confederates.   This road Sherman, however, determined to cut.   Moving with nearly the whole of his army for the purpose, he succeeded in getting between Atlanta and a large portion of Hood's army at Jonesboro, which force he defeated ; and Hood, his army being severed, was compelled, September 2d, to evacuate Atlanta.   Sherman thus gained the object of his campaign, but at a loss in killed, wounded, and missing, of thirty thousand men : the enemy's loss during the same period exceeded forty thousand.

VIII. As has been previously stated, the Army of the Potomac began to move toward Richmond early in May, crossing the Rapidan on the 4th of that month. Though General Meade commanded the army, General Grant was in the field and planned its movements, as well as the movements of the other armies. Lee, who held a position south of the Rapidan, rather than retreat, prepared to resist the progress of the advancing army.   The consequence was a fierce contest, known as the battle of the Wilderness, which, commencing on the morning of the 5th of May, did not end till the close of the 7th, when Lee fell back toward

VIII.   QUESTIONS.—58. When did the army of the Potomac cross the Rapidan? 59. By what other name is the Rapidan also known ? Ans. The Rapid Anna or the Rapid Ann. 60. Into what river does the Rapidan flow ? (See map, p. 330.) 61. Who commanded the Army of the Potomac? 62. What was done by General Grant? 63. Give an account of the battle of the Wilderness. 64. What Union officer of note fell in that battle? Ans. General Wadsworth. 65. How many men were engaged in the conflict ? 66. What recommendation did the President make ? 67. Where is the Wilderness? (See map, p. 330.)

Richmond. Probably not less than two hundred and fifty thousand men on both sides were engaged in it, and the slaughter was terrible. The favorable result of the three days' conflict called forth a proclamation from the President, recommending the following Sunday, May 10th, as an occasion of "thanksgiving and prayer to Almighty God." This recommendation was generally complied with.

IX. Near Spottsylvania Court House, Lee made a stand, and here, during six days, some of the severest fighting of the war took place. The result was again to the advantage of the national arms, and once more the enemy fell back. By a series of successful attacks and flank movements, Lee was driven from one position after another, until, early in June, he was within a short distance of Richmond. In the mean time, important movements in co-operation with Meade were made by the forces in the Shenandoah valley and West Virginia. It had been designed to act against Lynchburg, but reverses prevented the execution of the plan, General Sigel, who was to have cut the western communication of Lee, having met with defeat, on the 15th, near New Market.

X. Another movement, in co-operation with Meade, was made by General Butler, from Fortress Monroe up the James River. Landing at a point on the south side of the river, just above the Appomattox, he made his position secure by strong intrenchments, and thus threatened both Petersburg and Richmond. Expeditions sent by him to cut the enemy's

---

IX. QUESTIONS. 68. Where did Lee make his next stand? 69. Where is Spottsylvania Court House? (See map, p. 330.) 70 What account can you give of the struggle there? 71 What Union officer of note was killed during the contest? Ans. General Sedgwick, on the 9th of May. 72 What movement, in co-operation with Meade, was planned? 73. Where is Lynchburg? (See map, p 320)

X. 74 What movement did Gen. Butler make? 75. What is the name of the place which Butler occupied? Ans. Bermuda Hundred. 76. Give an account of Butler's operations while he was in command there. 77. What change in position was effected by the Army of the Potomac? 78 Where is Fortress Monroe? (See map, p 320) 79 Describe the Appomattox. (Same map) 80. The James. (Same) 81. Where was Fort Darling? (See map, p 318)

1864.

communications were not entirely successful, nor was an attempt made against Fort Darling. He also failed in demonstrations against Petersburg, Beauregard, on his way from the Carolinas to join Lee, having arrived there with a strong force to oppose him. His success, however, in gaining the position he did, was important to a movement made by Grant, by which the Army of the Potomac was transferred across the James to the south side of that river.

XI. The career of three English-built privateers sailing under the Confederate flag was terminated this year. They had for months roamed the seas, and by avoiding armed antagonists had succeeded in pillaging and destroying a large number of American merchantmen. More than sixty vessels, estimated with their cargoes as worth not less than $10,000,000, had been destroyed by the Alabama alone. This privateer was at last discovered by the Kearsarge, Captain Winslow, in the French port of Cherbourg (*sher'-boorg*). Off that harbor an action took place between the two vessels on the 19th of June, resulting in the sinking of the Alabama. Her commander, Captain Semmes, with forty of his crew, was picked up by a British vessel, and, without authority from Winslow, they were all carried to England. The Florida and Georgia were captured, the first by the Wachusett and the second by the Niagara.

XII. A new expedition against Lynchburg was organized, General Hunter taking the place of Sigel. Moving up the Shenandoah valley, Hunter gained a victory over the enemy at Piedmont, June 5th, whence he marched on Lynchburg.

XI. QUESTIONS.—82. What is said of the career of three privateers? 83. What had they done? 84. What destruction had the Alabama alone effected? 85. Give an account of the action between the Kearsarge and the Alabama. 86. What were the names of the other privateers? 87. By what vessels were they captured?

XII. 88. What took place at Piedmont? 89. What can you say of Hunter's further movements? 90. What invasion followed? 91. What took place at Monocacy? 92. What danger was apprehended? 93. Where is the Shenandoah valley? (See map, p. 320.) 94. Piedmont? (Same map.) 95. Martinsburg? (Same.) 96. Hagerstown? (Same.) 97. Monocacy? (Same.)

Finding that re-enforcements from Lee were arriving there, he withdrew, closely followed by a Confederate force, into West Virginia. The valley being thus open, Lee detached twenty thousand men, under General Early, to invade Maryland. Passing through Martinsburg, the invaders crossed the Potomac to Hagerstown, scouring the country in all directions for horses, forage, provisions, and money. With overwhelming numbers, Early defeated General Wallace at Monocacy (*monoc'-ah-se*), July 9th, producing great excitement in Washington and throughout the Northern States, it being feared that the National Capital itself was in danger.

XIII. Grant hurried off troops for the defense of Washington, and these were rapidly joined by others from the loyal States. After threatening both Baltimore and Washington, the Confederates, loaded with plunder, recrossed the Potomac. They were pursued by General Averill, and defeated at Winchester, July 20th, but were in turn victorious on the 24th, their cavalry pursuing the Union troops to Martinsburg. Again did they invade Maryland, penetrating even to Chambersburg, in Pennsylvania. This town they offered to spare upon the payment of $500,000, but, not receiving the money, they burned more than half of the place. On their way back into Virginia they met with opposition from bodies of Union troops, and were badly defeated by Averill, losing their artillery and many prisoners.

XIV. For the defense of the Shenandoah valley, a strong force was at length organized, and put under the command of General

---

XIII. QUESTIONS.—98. What action did Grant take? 99. What large cities did the Confederates threaten? 100. What then did they do? 101. What took place at Winchester? 102. What, four days after? 103. In which direction did the Confederates then go? 104. How was Chambersburg made to suffer? 105. Were the Confederates pursued? 106. With what result? 107. Where is Winchester? (See map, p. 320.) 108. Chambersburg? (Same map.)

XIV. 109. What was at length done for the defense of the Shenandoah valley? 110. Give an account of Sheridan's first battle there. 111. Of his second. 112. His third. 113. Where is Fisher's Hill? (See map, p. 320.) 114. Staunton? (Same map.) 115. Cedar Creek? (Same.)

MAJOR-GENERAL SHERIDAN.

1864. Sheridan. On the morning of the 19th of September, Sheridan marched to attack Early, who, with an army largely re-enforced, was near Winchester. After a stubborn engagement, occurring on the same day, the Union troops gained a complete victory. On the 22d, at Fisher's Hill, they achieved another signal victory, following up their success by a pursuit of the enemy as far as Staunton. After destroying barns and flour-mills, two thousand in all, so as to make the country untenable by a Confederate army, Sheridan returned northward. Before daylight, October 19th, his troops, then at Cedar Creek, were suddenly attacked, he at the time being absent at Winchester, and were driven back four miles. Sheridan, arriving at this critical time, arranged his lines, repulsed an attack of the enemy, and, becoming the assailants in return, completely routed the enemy. The Confederates made no further attempt to invade the North by way of the Shenandoah valley.

XV. Immediately after crossing the Army of the Potomac to the south side of the James, as previously stated, Grant laid siege to Petersburg. On the 30th of July a mine was exploded under one of the enemy's forts, so that a storming party might rush through the gap thus made, and, with the co-operation of other movements, the city be captured. The assault was, however, a disastrous failure. On the 18th of August an important advantage was gained by the seizure of the Weldon Railroad. To regain possession of it, the Confederates made repeated and desperate assaults, but were as often repulsed. A number of conflicts took place by the two great armies of Grant and Lee, on both sides of the James, in September and October, yet Petersburg and Richmond, at the close of the year, were still held by the Confederates, though it was evident their grasp was daily becoming less firm.

XVI. Of all the achievements of the army or navy of the United States during the war, none were perhaps more brilliant than that of Admiral Farragut in Mobile Bay. On the morning of the 5th of August, his fleet of monitors and wooden vessels, two abreast and lashed together, moved up the bay, the admiral being on board his flagship, the Hartford, lashed to the main-top, the better to observe the operations, and give the

REAR-ADMIRAL FARRAGUT.

necessary orders. The vessels succeeded in passing Forts Morgan and Gaines, with no serious disaster beyond the loss of the monitor Tecumseh, which was sunk by a torpedo. An engagement then took place with the enemy's fleet, consisting of the iron-clad ram Tennessee and three gunboats. After a brief encounter, the Tennessee surrendered, Admiral Buchanan, the Confederate commander, being severely wounded; one of the gunboats was captured, but the other two escaped. Meanwhile a co-operative body of troops was landed, and Fort Gaines was taken on the 7th. Fort Morgan held out till the 23d, when it too surrendered.

XVI. QUESTIONS.—121. How is Farragut's achievement in Mobile Bay spoken of in comparison with other achievements? 122. What was the name of Farragut's flag-ship? 123. Where did Farragut take a position during the battle? 124. What disaster befell one of the fleet? 125. State what afterward took place. 126. What at Fort Gaines. 127. At Fort Morgan. 128. Did the two vessels that escaped reach Mobile? Ans. One was so badly injured that she had to be destroyed. 129. Where is Mobile? (See map, p. 300.) 130. Fort Morgan? (Same.) 131. Fort Gaines? (Same.)

1864.

XVII. After the fall of Atlanta, Hood, with increased forces, assumed the offensive by attempting to destroy Sherman's communication; but being followed by the latter he withdrew into northern Alabama. Leaving General Thomas to watch Hood, Sherman returned to Atlanta, which city he destroyed, and on the 15th of November commenced his memorable march to the sea-coast. His army advanced through Georgia, living upon the country. The State capita and other large towns were occupied by him, and on the 10th of December the vicinity of Savannah was reached. Three days after, Fort McAllister was carried by assault, and by this achievement a communication was opened with the fleet

General Hardee, in command a Savannah, perceiving the prepara tions which Sherman was making for a grand assault, effected his escape on the night of the 20th, and on the following morn ing the Union army entered th city.

XVIII. In the mean time Hood advanced into Tennessee, whil Thomas fell back toward Nashville. At Franklin, November 30th, a fierce battle was fought, at the close of which th

NEVADA.—This State derived its name from the Sierra Nevada, the mountain range bounding it o the west. The two words, *sierra* and *nevada*, are Spanish, the former signifying mountain range, ar the latter snow-clad or snow-covered. The State was admitted into the Union in 1864.

Union army fell back to the outer line of the Nashville intrenchments, three miles from the city. With a view to compel Thomas to abandon the defense of Nashville, Hood made preparations to blockade the Cumberland, and cut the railroads leading to the city; but, before he could put his plan into execution, Thomas attacked him, December 15th, renewing the battle on the following day, and finally routing him with very great loss. Hood, with the remnant of his army, retired to Alabama.

EVENTS OF 1865.

I. The active operations of 1865 began with the reduction of Fort Fisher, situated at the mouth of Cape Fear River. This was the main defense of Wilmington. In December, 1864, General Butler, with about six thousand troops, had effected a landing near the fort, for the purpose of operating in conjunction with Admiral Porter's fleet; but, deeming the works too strong to be carried by his force, returned to Fortress Monroe. In January, 1865, the enterprise was renewed by General Terry, with eight thousand men, including Butler's force. Under cover of a fire from the fleet, the troops were landed on the morning of the 13th, and on the 15th the works were carried, after desperate hand-to-hand fighting. The fall of Fort Fisher carried with it the other defenses on the river, the Confederates were driven from Wilmington, and the city was occupied by the Federal troops on the 22d of February.

II. General Sherman, having halted at Savannah only long

EVENTS OF 1865.—I. QUESTIONS—1. How is Fort Fisher situated? 2. Describe the Cape Fear River. (See map, p. 164.) 3. What can you state of Butler's preparations to attack Fort Fisher? 4. Why did he not make the attack? 5. What force afterward made a successful attack? 6. Give an account of the capture. 7. What were the consequences of the capture?

II. 8. When did Sherman move from Savannah? 9. When did he take Columbia? 10. How was the capture of Charleston effected? 11. What is said of Fort Sumter? 12. Give a further account of Sherman's march northward. 13. At what place did the battle on the 16th of March occur? Ans. Averysboro'. 14. The battle on the 19th and 20th? Ans. Bentonville. 15. What place did Sherman reach on the 13th of April? 16. What retreat did Johnson make? 17. Where is Raleigh? (See map, p. 320) 18. Goldsborough? (Same map) 19. Hillsboro'?

15

MAJOR-GENERAL SHERMAN.

1865.

enough to refit his army, entered upon a campaign through the Carolinas, and by the 1st of February his whole force was again in motion. On the 17th he captured Columbia, thus rendering it necessary for the Confederates to evacuate Charleston. General Gillmore, commanding the land forces operating against Charleston, from the coast, took possession of the city on the 18th, and the national flag floated once more from Fort Sumter. Sherman continued his march northward, entering North Carolina, while General Schofield from Newbern, and General Terry from Wilmington, co-operated with him. On the 16th of March, and on the 19th and 20th, he encountered the enemy, repulsing them in both engagements. On the 21st he occupied Goldsborough, and on the 13th of April reached Raleigh, Johnston retreating beyond Hillsboro'.

III. Sheridan, in the mean time, was making a raid up the Shenandoah valley. At Waynesborough, March 2d, he attacked and routed Early. Marching onward, through Charlottesville, he destroyed the railroads and the canal by which Richmond and Lee's army received supplies, and finally formed a junction with the Army of the Potomac south of Petersburg. As the issue of the great struggle became more dubious to the Confederates, their Congress, after considerable opposition, passed a bill to increase their military forces by arming the slaves. Lee, seeing that he was hemmed in, determined, if possible, to divide Grant's army, and, by getting into its rear, force it to abandon its lines. With this intention he made a sudden dash at Fort Steadman, and captured it; but there his success ended, for on the same day, March 25th, the fort was retaken, and, still later in the day, a forward movement, ordered by General Grant, was completely successful.

IV. On the 29th of March the final movement of the national forces around Richmond began, and, after ten days' marching and fighting, the campaign was finished. On the 3d of April both Petersburg and Richmond were occupied by Grant's victorious troops, Lee and his army having fled the day before toward Lynchburg, and Jefferson Davis toward the sea-coast. The retreating troops were hotly pursued by Sheridan, and, on the 9th of April, Lee surrendered what remained of his army to General Grant. From this period the history of the war is but a record of national successes, in the surrender of the several remaining Confederate commanders.

V. The hearts of the loyal people were throbbing with ecstasy at a triumph so long struggled for, and the dawn of peace appeared; but this feeling of joy was suddenly turned into mourning. In less than one week after Lee's surrender, April 14th, President Lincoln was assassinated by a desperado acting in sympathy with the Confederate cause, and an attempt was also made upon the life of Mr. Seward, the Secretary of State.

VI. The intelligence of this sad event filled every loyal

IV. QUESTIONS.—28. When did the great final military movement commence? 29. How long did it continue? 30. In what direction did General Lee retreat? 31. When were Petersburg and Richmond captured? 32. What direction did Jefferson Davis take? 33. What further account can you give of Davis? Ans. He was captured at a place in Georgia, and then, at Fortress Monroe, put in close confinement. 34. After Lee's surrender, what did the other Confederate commanders do?

V. 35. What sad event took place? 36. When was President Lincoln assassinated? 37. When did he die? Ans. He lingered a few hours in an insensible condition, expiring on the morning of the 15th. 38. What attempt at assassination was made, but without success?

VI. 89. How did the news of the President's death affect the people? 40. How did the people manifest their grief? 41. What may be truly said of Mr. Lincoln?

1865. heart throughout the land with overwhelming sorrow; and even those against whom the murdered President had so long contended, expressed the strongest feeling of regret that so wicked and, to them, useless, if not baneful, an act should have been committed. The demonstrations of grief throughout the North were unprecedented, and for several weeks all the great cities were draped in badges and emblems of mourning. The funeral cortege of the deceased President was followed by hundreds of thousands of the citizens of the republic, as it wended its way from the capital to his former home at Springfield, where the remains were deposited ; and it may be truly said that upon no President since Washington, and no personage in the history of the country, were the affections of the people more warmly bestowed, and that none was ever more generally or more sincerely lamented.

JOHNSON'S ADMINISTRATION.

I. Upon the death of Mr. Lincoln, which occurred on the morning of the 15th of April, the Vice-President, Andrew Johnson, of Tennessee, was sworn into office, and thereupon assumed the duties of President of the United States.* The assassin of the lamented President eluded pursuit until the 26th, when, on being tracked to his hiding-place and refusing to surrender, he was shot. It appearing that the assassination was part of a conspiracy to disorganize the Government, by the simultaneous destruction of its principal executive officers, a trial was had ; and, of the seven persons tried and found guilty, four were hanged and the others imprisoned.

* President Johnson retained the Cabinet of his predecessor, which then consisted of William H. Seward, Secretary of State ; Hugh McCulloch, Secretary of the Treasury ; Edwin M Stanton, Secretary of War ; Gideon Welles, Secretary of the Navy , James Harlan, Secretary of the Interior , James Speed, Attorney-General , and William Dennison, Postmaster-General.

JOHNSON'S ADMINISTRATION.—I. QUESTIONS.—1. When did Mr. Lincoln's death occur ? 2 Who then became President ? 3. What was the fate of the person who shot Mr. Lincoln ? 4. What can you state of the conspiracy ?

II. Hostilities having ceased, the work of "Reconstructing the Union" began. On the 29th of April, the President issued a proclamation removing restrictions on commerce in the South; and, a month after, a proclamation of amnesty was addressed to a large class of those who had been concerned in the rebellion. Three-fourths of the States having ratified the resolution of Congress proposing an amendment to the Constitution, by which slavery should be abolished, the formal

ANDREW JOHNSON
Was born in Raleigh, N. C., Dec. 29, 1808. Served nine years at the business of a tailor. Was five times a Representative in Congress, and twice Governor of Tennessee.

announcement that slavery was constitutionally abolished was made on the 18th of December.

III. Upon the assembling of Congress, in December, 1865, it appeared that the entire debt of the Government amounted to about two billions seven hundred millions of dollars, the great bulk of which had been contracted in the prosecution of the war. To raise the enormous sums required during the contest, loans were offered, and were freely taken by the

II. QUESTIONS.—5. As soon as hostilities were ended, what began? 6 What proclamation was issued April 29th? 7. May 29th? 8. What can you state in relation to the abolition of slavery?

III. 9. The debt of the Government? 10. Of loans? 11. Duty on importations? 12. Taxes on incomes? 13. Revenue-stamps? 14. Gold, as an article of merchandise?

loyal people. Still further to increase the ability of the treasury to meet the heavy drain upon it, the duty on importations had been increased, taxes had been imposed on incomes and manufactures, and revenue-stamps required to be placed on bonds, mortgages, and other documents. A general suspension of specie payments by the banks of the North having taken place at the close of 1861, specie circulation soon gave way to that of paper, and gold became an article of merchandise, commanding a high premium.

IV. In March, 1865, Congress passed an act known as the Freedmen's Bureau Bill. By the term Freedmen were meant all the colored people of the South, who, at the breaking out of the Rebellion, were slaves; but who had afterward been declared free by proclamation of the President. The bill had for its object the supervision and relief of freedmen and loyal refugees. A second bill, amending and continuing in force the first, although vetoed by the President, was passed in July, 1866.

V. It soon became evident that Congress and President Johnson were at variance on the subject of "Reconstructing the Union," the former being opposed to the restoration of the late insurgent States to their former political standing, until certain guarantees of protection should be extended to the colored population, and other conditions complied with by the States. A Reconstruction Act was, however, passed by Congress, notwithstanding the veto of the President, March 2d, 1867, and two Supplementary Reconstruction Acts were also passed, in like manner.

VI. In March, of the same year, a bill to regulate the tenure of certain civil offices was passed over the President's

---

IV When was the Freedmen's Bureau Bill passed? Who were meant by the term Freedmen? What was the object of the Bill? What is said of the second Freedmen's Bureau Bill?

V. What soon became evident as between Congress and the President? What position did Congress take? What is said of the Reconstruction Bill? Of the two Supplementary Acts?

veto. By this bill it is declared that persons holding, or appointed to, any civil office, by and with the advice and consent of the Senate shall be entitled to hold such office until a successor shall have been, in like manner appointed and duly qualified. This is known as the *Tenure-of-Office Bill.*

VII. During the year 1867, Nebraska was admitted into the Union, and the territorial possessions of the United States were very much enlarged by the addition of A l a s k a, formerly known as Russian America. This vast tract of land was purchased of Russia, the price agreed to be paid being $7,200,-000 in gold.

VIII. In August, 1867, the President suspended Mr. Stanton, the Secretary of War from office, because, "upon important questions, the views of

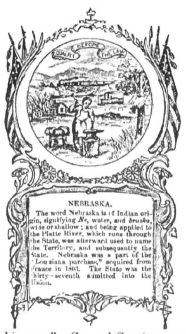

NEBRASKA.

The word Nebraska is of Indian origin, signifying *Ne*, water, and *braska*, wide or shallow; and being applied to the Platte River, which runs through the State, was afterward used to name the Territory, and subsequently the State. Nebraska was a part of the 'Louisiana purchase," acquired from France in 1803. The State was the thirty-seventh admitted into the Union.

the secretary differed from his own." General Grant was appointed to discharge the duties of the office. In December, the President notified the Senate of the change he had made, and of his reasons for so doing. The Senate having duly considered the reasons, passed a resolution of non-concurrence

---

VI. State what you can in relation to the Tenure-of-office Bill.

VII. What is said of the admission of Nebraska? What is said of Alaska?

VIII. From what office was Mr. Stanton suspended? By whom was the suspension made? Why was it made? What course in relation to the matter did the President afterward take? What course and action did the Senate take? What course did Mr. Stanton take?

in the suspension; and, thereupon, January 13th, 1868,
1868.   Mr. Stanton resumed the exercise of the duties of
Secretary of War.

IX. On the 21st of February, the President sent a message
to the Senate, declaring that he had removed Mr. Stanton from
office, and had placed General Lorenzo Thomas in his stead
until a successor should be appointed.   This produced great
excitement in both houses of Congress.   The Senate passed a
resolution notifying the President " that under the Constitution and laws of the United States, he had no power to remove the Secretary of War and designate any other officer to
perform the duties of that office."

X. On the 24th, a resolution, impeaching President Johnson of high crimes and misdemeanors, was adopted by the
House of Representatives.   In accordance therewith, nine
articles of impeachment, prepared by a committee of the
House, were, on the 2d of March, adopted; and seven mana-
gers were thereupon selected from among the members of the
House, to conduct the impeachment before the Senate.

XI. Two more articles of impeachment having been added,
in which the President was charged with declaring that Congress, as then constituted, was an illegal body, the trial was
begun on the 30th of March.   On the 16th of May a verdict of
acquittal was declared on the eleventh article; and, ten days
after, a like verdict was rendered on two other articles, when
the Senate, as a court, adjourned and the trial ended.   On the
same day, May 26th, Mr. Stanton resigned his position as
Secretary of War.   In the fall of the same year (1868), General Grant was elected President to succeed Johnson.

IX What course did the President take in the following February? What was the
effect in Congress?   What resolution did the Senate pass?

X. What resolution was afterward adopted by the House of Representatives?
What subsequent action was taken by the House?

XI. How many articles of impeachment, in all, were brought against the President? What charge was made in the last two? What is said of the trial and the
result? What course did Mr. Stanton then take? Who was elected President of the
United States to succeed Johnson?

CHRONOLOGICAL TABLE

OF IMPORTANT EVENTS RELATING TO THE HISTORY OF THE UNITED STATES.

1492. America discovered by Christopher Columbus,....... Oct. 12
1497. Labrador discovered by John and Sebastian Cabot, . . July 3.
1498. Coast of North America explored by Sebastian Cabot.
Continent of South America discovered by Columbus, Aug. 10.
1499 South America visited by Amerigo Vespucci.
1512. Florida discovered by Juan Ponce de Leon,......... April 6.
1513. The Pacific Ocean discovered by Vasco Nuñez de Balboa, Sept. 29.
1520. Carolina visited by Lucas Vasquez de Ayllon.
1521. Mexico conquered by Fernando Cortez.
1524. Coast of North America explored by John Verrazani.
1528. The conquest of Florida undertaken by Pamphilo de Narvaez.
1534 The St. Lawrence River discovered by James Cartier,. June
1539. Ferdinand de Soto undertook to conquer Florida.
1541 The Mississippi River discovered by De Soto.
1562. Colony of Huguenots settled at Port Royal entrance
1564 Colony of Huguenots settled in Florida
1565 St. Augustine, Florida, founded by the Spaniards,.. .. Sept 18.
Huguenot colony in Florida destroyed by the Spaniards, Oct 1
1583. Newfoundland taken possession of by Sir H. Gilbert .
1584. Amidas and Barlow explored the coast of North Carolina.
1585. First attempt to form a settlement at Roanoke.
1587. Second attempt to form a settlement at Roanoke.
1602 Cape Cod discovered by Bartholomew Gosnold, ... May 24.
1605 Port Royal, in Nova Scotia, settled by the French.
1606. London and Plymouth Companies received charters,.. April 20.
1607. Jamestown settled by the London Company, ... May 23.
The Plymouth Company began a settlement on the Kennebec River,......... .... Aug 21.
1608. Quebec settled by the French, under Champlain, ... July 3.
1609 Virginia received its second charter,............ . June 2.
The Hudson River discovered by Henry Hudson, ... Sept 21.
1610 "The Starving Time" in Virginia
1612 Virginia received its third charter,..... ... . March 22.
1613. Pocahontas married to Rolfe, ... April.

1613. French settlements in Maine and Nova Scotia destroyed
       by Samuel Argall.
1614. The coast of New England explored by John Smith.
       New York settled by the Dutch.
1616. The culture of tobacco commenced in Virginia.
1620. Commencement of Negro slavery in the English colonies, Aug.
       Charter granted to "The Council of Plymouth," ..... Nov. 3.
       Massachusetts settled at Plymouth, ... Dec. 21.
1621. Treaty with Massasoit made, ... April 1.
1622. First Indian massacre in Virginia, ... April 1.
1623. New Hampshire settled at Little Harbor and Dover ..
1633. Connecticut settled at Windsor, ... Oct.
1634. Maryland settled at St. Mary's, ... April 6.
1636 Rhode Island settled at Providence.
       Harvard College founded.
1637. The Pequod War.
1638. Delaware settled near Wilmington, ... April.
1641 New Hampshire settlements united to Massachusetts.
1643. Union of New England colonies formed, ... May 29.
1644. Second Indian massacre in Virginia, ... April.
1645. Clayborne's Rebellion in Maryland.
1650. North Carolina settled on the Chowan River.
1651. The "Navigation Act" passed by Parliament.
1652. The Maine settlements united to Massachusetts.
1655. Civil War in Maryland.
       New Sweden conquered by the Dutch, ... Oct.
1663. Carolina granted to Clarendon and others.
1664. New York became an English Province, ... Sept. 8.
       New Jersey settled at Elizabethtown.
1670. South Carolina settled on the Ashley River.
1673. Virginia granted to Culpepper and Arlington.
1675. King Philip's war commenced, by an attack upon Swan-
       zey, ... July 4.
1676. Bacon's Rebellion.
1680. Charleston founded.   ·
       New Hampshire made a Royal Province, ... Sept. 28.
1682. Pennsylvania settled.
       Delaware granted by the Duke of York to William Penn, Aug. 31.
1686. Andros arrived at Boston as governor of New England, Dec 30
1689. King William's War commenced. Attack upon Dover, July 7.
1690. Schenectady, burned by the French and Indians, ... Feb. 8.
       Port Royal taken by the English under Phipps, ... May.

1692. " Salem Witchcraft" delusion prevailed.
1697. King William's War terminated by the "Treaty of
  Ryswick," .... Sept. 20.
1702. Queen Anne's War commenced.
1710. Port Royal, Nova Scotia, captured by the English,... Oct. 13.
1713. Queen Anne's War terminated by the "Treaty of
  Utrecht," .... April 11.
1729. North and South Carolina became separate provinces, July.
1732. Washington born in Westmoreland county, Virginia,. Feb 22.
1733. Georgia settled at Savannah,..................... Feb. 12.
1741. "The Negro Plot" in New York.
1744. King George's War commenced in America.
1745. Louisburg captured by the English, ... June 28.
1748. King George's War terminated by the "Treaty of Aix
  la Chapelle," .... Oct. 18.
1753. Washington sent with a letter from Dinwiddie,. ... Oct. 31.
1754. Washington delivered St. Pierre's reply to Dinwiddie,. Dec. 11.
  The battle of the Great Meadows, ... May 28.
  Congress of Commissioners met at Albany ... . June
  The battle of Fort Necessity, ... July 4.
1755. French expelled from Nova Scotia by Monckton, ... June.
  Braddock's defeat at the battle of Monongahela,. .... July 9.
  The British defeat by Dieskau near Lake George, ... Sept. 8.
  Dieskau defeated by the British at Lake George,..... Sept. 8.
1756. Great Britain declared war against France,. .... May 17.
  France declared war against Great Britain, ... June 9.
  The French, under Montcalm, captured Oswego, ... Aug. 14.
  Indians defeated at Kittaning,................... Sept 8.
1757. Fort William Henry surrendered to Montcalm, ... Aug 9.
  The massacre at Fort William Henry, ... Aug. 10.
1758. Lord Howe killed in a skirmish near Ticonderoga,.... July 6.
  Abercrombie repulsed by Montcalm at Ticonderoga,... July 8.
  Louisburg taken by Amherst and Wolfe,. .... July 26.
  Fort Frontenac surrendered to the English,...... ... Aug. 27.
  Grant defeated by Aubury near Fort Duquesne....... Sept. 21.
1759. Ticonderoga and Crown Point abandoned by the French.
  Niagara surrendered to the English, under Johnson,... July 25.
  Battle of Montmorenci, ... July 31.
  Battle of the Plains of Abraham,.................. Sept. 13.
  Quebec surrendered to the English, ... Sept. 18.
1760. The French, under De Levi, attempted the recovery of
  Quebec (battle three miles above the city),....... April 28.

1760. Montreal and the rest of Canada surrendered to the
       English, ... Sept 8
1763 The peace of Paris between Great Britain and France, Feb. 10.
       Florida ceded to Great Britain by Spain,............. Feb 10.
1765. The Stamp Act passed by Parliament,................. March 8
       A colonial Congress met at New York,............... Oct 7.
1766. The Stamp Act repealed by Parliament,............... March 1:
1767. A bill imposing duties on glass, paper, etc., passed,.... June 29.
1768. A body of British troops arrived at Boston, ... Sept. 27
1770. "The Boston Massacre,"............................. March 5.
       All duties, except on tea, repealed by Parliament,..... April 12
1773. The cargoes of tea at Boston thrown overboard,...... Dec. 16
1774 "Boston Port Bill" passed by Parliament,. .... March.
       "The First Continental Congress" met at Philadelphia,. Sept. 5
1775. The battle of Lexington,.............................. April 19
       Ticonderoga, New York, captured by Allen and Arnold, May 10
       Crown Point, New York, captured by the Americans,.. May 12.
       Washington elected commander-in-chief,............. June 15.
       The battle of Bunker Hill, ... June 17.
       Washington took command of the army,............. July 12.
       Montreal surrendered to Montgomery, ... Nov. 13
       Battle of Quebec,.................................... Dec 31.
1776. Norfolk, Virginia, destroyed by Lord Dunmore,.. ... Jan 1.
       Boston evacuated by the British troops, ... March 1.
       The battle of Fort Moultrie, South Carolina, ... June 28
       The Declaration of Independence,.................. July 4.
       The battle of Long Island, New York, ... Aug. 27
       The city of New York abandoned by the Americans,... Sept 15
       The battle of White Plains, New York,............. Oct. 28.
       The battle of Fort Washington, New York,.... .... Nov. 16
       Fort Lee, New Jersey, taken by the British,.... ... Nov. 18.
       Gen Lee surprised and taken prisoner, ... Dec 13
       The battle of Trenton, New Jersey,................ Dec 26
1777. The battle of Princeton, New Jersey,................ Jan 3
       Tryon's first expedition against Connecticut,........ April
       Meigs's expedition against the British at Sagg Harbor,. May 23.
       Invasion of New York by Burgoyne,................ June
       Ticonderoga abandoned by the Americans,... . ... July 5
       The battle of Hubbardton, Vermont,............. July 7
       Gen. Prescott captured by Colonel Barton, ... July 10.
       Murder of Miss Jane McCrea, near Fort Edward, . .. July 27.
       Fort Schuyler, New York, besieged by St Leger,.... Aug

1777. The battle of Oriskany, near Fort Schuyler,......... Aug 6.
    The battle of Fort Schuyler,..................... Aug. 6.
    The battle of Bennington, Vermont,.............. Aug 16.
    The battle of Brandywine, Pennsylvania,.......... Sept. 11.
    The battle of Bemis Heights, or first of Stillwater,... Sept. 19.
    The battle of Paoli, Pennsylvania, ... Sept. 20.
    Philadelphia entered by the British,.............. Sept 26.
    The battle of Germantown, Pennsylvania,.......... Oct. 4.
    Forts Clinton and Montgomery taken by the British,.. Oct. 6.
    The battle of Saratoga, second of Stillwater,.. ...... Oct. 7.
    The surrender of Burgoyne,...................... Oct. 17.
    The British repulsed at Fort Mercer, New Jersey,.... Oct. 22.
    The British repulsed at Fort Mifflin, Pennsylvania,.... Oct. 22.
    Articles of Confederation adopted by Congress,...... Nov. 15.
    Fort Mifflin abandoned by the Americans, ... Nov. 16.
    Washington encamped at Valley Forge, Pennsylvania, Dec. 11.
1778. American Independence acknowledged by France,.... Feb. 6
    Treaty of Alliance with France,.................... Feb. 6
    British commissioners sent to America.
    Philadelphia evacuated by the British,.............. June 18.
    The battle of Monmouth, New Jersey,....... ...... June 28.
    The battle of Wyoming, Pennsylvania, and massacre, July 3.
    The French fleet under D'Estaing arrived,........... July 11.
    The battle of Rhode Island,.................. ...... Aug 29.
    Grey's ravaging expedition to the eastward, ... Sept.
    Ferguson's expedition against Egg Harbor,.......... Oct.
    The massacre at Cherry Valley, New York,...... .. Nov 11,12
    The battle of Savannah, Georgia,.................. Dec. 29.
1779. Sunbury, Georgia, captured by the British, ... Jan 9.
    The battle of Kettle Creek, Georgia,.. .... Feb. 14.
    The battle of Brier Creek, Georgia,.......... ...... March 3.
    Tyron's second expedition against Connecticut, ... March.
    Stony Point, New York, captured by the British,..... May 31.
    Verplanck's Point, New York, captured by the British, June 1.
    War declared against Great Britain by Spain,........ June 26.
    The battle of Stono Ferry, South Carolina.......... June 20.
    Tyron's third expedition against Connecticut .... July.
    The battle of Stony Point, New York, ... July 15.
    British garrison at Paulus Hook surprised by Lee,... July 19
    The battle of the Penobscot, Maine,................ Aug. 13.
    Sullivan's expedition against the Indians
    "The battle of the Chemung," New York,.......... Aug. 29.

1779. Savannah besieged by the French and Americans,. ... Sept. Oct
       Jones's naval battle off the coast of England, ... Sept 23.
       D'Estaing and Lincoln repulsed at Savannah,..... .. Oct 9.
1780. Charleston besieged by the British, ... Ap. May.
       The battle of Monk's Corner, South Carolina, ... April 14.
       Charleston surrendered to the British, ... May 12.
       The battle of Waxhaw, South Carolina,............. May 29
       The battle of Springfield, New Jersey,............. June 23.
       French fleet arrived at Newport, Rhode Island,. ... July 10.
       The battle of Rocky Mount, South Carolina,........ July 30.
       The battle of Hanging Rock, South Carolina,....... Aug. 6.
       The battle of Sanders Creek, South Carolina,........ Aug. 16.
       The battle of Fishing Creek, South Carolina,........ Aug. 18
       Arnold's treason.
       André executed as a spy at Tappan, New York,..... Oct. 2.
       The battle of King's Mountain, South Carolina,.... Oct. 7.
       The battle of Fishdam Ford, South Carolina,........ Nov. 12.
       The battle of Blackstocks, South Carolina,......... Nov. 20.
1781. Revolt of the Pennsylvania troops, ... Jan 1.
       The battle of the Cowpens, South Carolina,. .... Jan 17.
       The revolt of New Jersey troops,................ ... Jan. 18.
       Arnold's depredation in Virginia,..... .... Jan.
       Cornwallis's pursuit of Morgan and Greene, ... Jan. Feb.
       Articles of Confederation ratified by the States.
       The battle of Guilford Court-House, North Carolina,.. March 15.
       The battle of Hobkirk's Hill, South Carolina, ... April 25.
       Siege of Ninety-Six by General Greene............. May, Jun
       The battle of Ninety-Six, South Carolina,......... June 18.
       Colonel Hayne executed by the British at Charleston, July 31.
       Arnold's expedition against Connecticut, ... Sept.
       The battle of Fort Griswold, Connecticut,.......... Sept. 6.
       The battle of Eutaw Springs, South Carolina,....... Sept 8.
       The siege of Yorktown, Virginia, ... Oct.
       The surrender of Cornwallis at Yorktown,......... Oct. 19.
1782. Preliminary articles of peace signed at Paris,........ Nov. 30.
1783. Cessation of hostilities proclaimed in the American
       army,....................................... . April 19.
       Savannah, Georgia, evacuated by the British,....... July 11.
       Definitive treaty of peace signed at Paris,......... Sept. 3.
       American army disbanded by orders of Congress,.... Nov. 3.
       New York evacuated by the British, ... Nov. 25.
       Charleston, South Carolina, evacuated by the British, Dec. 14.

1783. Washington resigns his commission,................. Dec 23.
1787. Shays's Rebellion in Massachusetts.
     Constitution of the United States agreed on by the
       convention of delegates at Philadelphia,.......... Sept 17.
1789. The first Congress under the Constitution met at New
       York, ... March 4.
     Washington inaugurated President of the United States, April 30.
1790. Harmar defeated by the Indians in Indiana,......... Oct.17,22
1791. United States Bank established at Philadelphia.
     Vermont admitted into the Union,................ Mar. 4.
     St Clair defeated by the Indians in Ohio,........... Nov. 4.
1792. Kentucky admitted into the Union .... June 1.
1793. The difficulties with France.
1794. Wayne defeated the Indians on the Maumee,......... Aug. 20.
     "Whisky Insurrection" in Pennsylvania.
1795. "Jay's Treaty" with Great Britain ratified,........... June 24.
     Treaties with the Western Indians, Spain, and Algiers,
1796. Tennessee admitted into the Union, ... June. 1.
1797. John Adams inaugurated President of the United
      States,.. March 4.
1799. The death of Washington, ... Dec. 14.
1800. The seat of government removed to Washington.
     Treaty of peace conducted with France,............. Sept. 30.
1801. Thomas Jefferson inaugurated President,.... .... March 4.
     War declared against the United States by Tripoli..... June 10.
1802. Ohio admitted into the Union .... Nov. 29.
1803. Louisiana purchased of France,..................... April 30.
     Commodore Preble sent against Tripoli.
1804 The frigate Philadelphia destroyed by Decatur,.... ... Feb 15.
     The duel between Hamilton and Burr,............... July 11.
1805. Derne, a Tripolitan city, captured by Eaton,......... April 27.
     Treaty of peace concluded with Tripoli,............. June 3.
1806 British blockade from the Elbe to Brest declared,...... May 16.
     Bonaparte issued his "Berlin Decree,".............. Nov. 21.
1807 British "Orders in Council" prohibited coast trade
     with France,.................................... Jan. 7.
     American frigate Chesapeake attacked by the Leopard. June 22.
     British armed vessels ordered to leave the United States, July.
     British "Orders in Council" prohibited all trade with
      France and her allies,........................... Nov. 11.
     Aaron Burr tried for treason, and acquitted,......... Sept.
     Bonaparte issued his "Milan Decree,".............. Dec. 17.

1807. Embargo on American ships laid by Congress, ...   Dec 22
1809. Commerce with Great Britain and France interdicted
        by Congress,................... .... March 1
        James Madison inaugurated President,........ .. . March 4
1811. Action between the President and Little Belt.. ..... May 16
        Battle of Tippecanoe, Indiana, ... Nov 7.
1812. Louisiana admitted into the Union .... April 8
        War against Great Britain proclaimed by the United
        States, ... ˙ . June 18
        Invasion of Canada by Gen. Hull, ... July 12
        Surrender of Fort Mackinaw, Michigan,.......... July 17
        The first battle of Brownstown, Michigan,. ... . Aug. 5.
        The second battle of Brownstown,. .... Aug 9.
        Surrender of Detroit, Michigan, by Gen. Hull,.... . Aug 16
        British sloop Alert taken by the Essex,...... ..... Aug. 13
        British frigate Guerriere taken by the Constitution,.. Aug. 19
        The battle of Queenstown, Canada,.. . ... Oct 13
        British brig Frolic taken by the Wasp, ... Oct. 18
        British frigate Macedonian taken by the United States, Oct. 25
        British frigate Java taken by the Constitution,........ Dec. 29
1813. The battle of Frenchtown, Michigan,............ Jan. 22
        British brig Peacock taken by the Hornet,.......... Feb. 24
        Madison commenced a second presidential term, . . March
        The battle of York, Canada, ... April 2
        Fort Meigs, on the Maumee, besieged by Proctor, ... May 1.
        The battle of Fort Meigs, Ohio, ... May 5.
        Fort George, Canada, taken by the Americans, ... May 27
        The battle of Sackett's Harbor, New York,.. ...... May 29
        American frigate Chesapeake taken by the Shannon,.. June 1
        The battle of Fort Stephenson, Ohio,.............. Aug 2
        American brig Argus taken by the Pelican,.......... Aug 1
        Creek War commenced by the massacre at Fort Mims, Aug. 30
        British brig Boxer taken by the Enterprise, ... Sept 5.
        Perry's victory on Lake Erie, ... Sept 10
        The battle of the Thames, Canada,......... ...... Oct 5
        The battle of Chrysler's Field, Canada, ... Nov. 11
1814. The battle of Tohopeka, the last of the Creek War, .. March
        American frigate Essex taken by the British war ves-
        sels Phœbe and Cherub,. .... March
        The battle of La Colle Mill, Canada,.............. March
        British brig Epervier taken by the Peacock,......... April 2
        British sloop Reindeer taken by the Am. sloop Wasp . June 28

1814. Fort Erie captured by the Americans,............... July 3.
    The battle of Chippewa, Canada,. .... July 5.
    The battle of Lundy's Lane, or Bridgewater, Canada, July 25.
    The first battle of Fort Erie, Canada,.............. Aug. 15.
    The battle of Bladensburg, Maryland,.............. Aug. 24.
    The city of Washington taken by the British,....... Aug. 24.
    British sloop Avon taken by the Am. sloop Wasp,... Sept. 1.
    McDonough's victory on Lake Champlain,.......... Sept. 11.
    The battle of Plattsburg, New York, ... Sept 11.
    The battle of North Point, Maryland,.............. Sept. 12.
    The battle of Fort McHenry, Maryland,.......... ... Sept. 13
    The battle of Fort Bowyer, Alabama, ... Sept. 15.
    The second battle of Fort Erie, Canada,........... Sept. 17.
    The British driven from Pensacola by Gen Jackson,. Nov. 7.
    The battle on Lake Borgne, Louisiana,..... .. .. Dec. 14.
    Hartford Convention,............ .. .. Dec
    The battle nine miles from New Orleans,........... Dec. 23.
    Treaty of peace between the United States and Great
       Britain,....................................... Dec. 24.
1815. The battle of New Orleans,...................... Jan. 8.
    The U. S. frigate President captured by a British
       squadron, ... Jan. 15.
    The Cyane and Levant taken by the Constitution,.... Feb. 20.
    The British brig Penguin taken by the Hornet,...... March 23.
    War with Algiers declared by Congress,............ March.
    Commodore Decatur sent against Algiers,.......... May.
1816. Bank of United States rechartered for twenty years,... April 10.
    Indiana admitted into the Union,..... .... Dec. 11.
1817. James Monroe inaugurated President,.............. March 4.
    Mississippi admitted into the Union,.............. Dec. 10.
    The Seminoles and Creeks commenced depredations.
1818. General Jackson went against the hostile Indians, . March.
    Arbuthnot and Ambrister executed, ... April 30.
    Pensacola seized by General Jackson, ... May 24
    Illinois admitted into the Union, ... Dec. 3.
1819. Alabama admitted into the Union.................. Dec. 14.
1820. Maine admitted into the Union,................... March. 15.
    Florida ceded to the United States by Spain, ... Oct.
1821. Missouri admitted into the Union,................. Aug. 10..
1824. Lafayette visited the United States, ... Aug.
1825. John Quincy Adams inaugurated President,........ March 4.
1826. Death of the two ex-presidents, Adams and Jefferson, July 4.

1829. Andrew Jackson inaugurated President,........ .... March 4.
1831. Death of Ex-president Monroe,................... July 4.
1832. "The Black Hawk War."
      "Nullification" in South Carolina.
1833. Removal of the Government funds from the U. S. Bank, Oct.
1835. War with the Seminoles commenced.
      Gen. Thompson and friends massacred by the Seminoles, Dec. 28.
      Major Dade and party massacred by the Seminoles,.. Dec. 28
1836. Arkansas admitted into the Union,.......... ..... June 15.
1837. Michigan admitted into the Union,.. ... . Jan. 26.
      Martin Van Buren inaugurated President,. .... March 4.
      The battle of Okechobee, Florida, ... Dec. 25.
1838. "The Canadian Rebellion."
1841. William Henry Harrison inaugurated President,...... March 4.
      Death of William Henry Harrison, ... April 4.
      John Tyler inaugurated President, ... April 6.
1842. The war with the Seminoles terminated.
      The ' Dorr Rebellion" in Rhode Island.
1845. Joint resolutions for the annexation of Texas signed by
          President Tyler,.............................. March 1.
      James K. Polk inaugurated President,............. March 4.
      Florida admitted into the Union, ... March 3.
      Texas admitted into the Union, ... Dec. 29.
1846. Thornton's party captured by the Mexicans, Texas,... April 26.
      Fort Brown bombarded by the Mexicans, ... May.
      The battle of Palo Alto, Texas, ... May 8.
      The battle of Resaca de la Palma, Texas, ... May 9.
      Congress declared "war existed by the act of Mexico," May 11.
      Taylor crossed the Rio Grande and took Matamoras,.. May 18.
      Monterey, Mexico, surrendered to Gen. Taylor, ... Sept. 24.
      The battle of Bracito, Mexico, ... Dec. 25.
      Iowa admitted into the Union,.................... Dec. 28.
'847. The battle of Buena Vista, Mexico,................ Feb. 23.
      The battle of Sacramento, Mexico,.......... .. .... Feb. 28.
      The surrender of Vera Cruz to General Scott, ... March 27
      The battle of Cerro Gordo, Mexico, ... April 18.
      The battle of Contreras and Churubusco, Mexico, ... Aug. 20.
      The battle of Molino del Rey, Mexico,............. Sept. 8.
      The battle of Chapultepec, Mexico,............. ... ... Sept. 13.
      City of Mexico entered by the Americans under Scott, Sept. 14.
      The battle of Huamantla, Mexico,...... .... Oct. 9.
1848. Treaty of peace signed at Guadalupe, Hidalgo,....... Feb. 2.

1848. Wisconsin admitted into the Union,............... May 29.
1849. Zachary Taylor inaugurated President,............ March 5.
1850. The death of President Taylor, ... July 9.
     Millard Fillmore inaugurated President,.......... July 10.
     California admitted into the Union, ... Sept. 9.
1853. Franklin Pierce inaugurated President,............ March 4.
1854. "Kansas-Nebraska Bill" passed,................. June.
1857. James Buchanan inaugurated President,.......... March 4.
1858. Minnesota admitted into the Union, ... May 11
1859 Oregon admitted into the Union,............ ..... Feb 14.
     John Brown's raid into Virginia, ... Oct 16.
1860. Secession Ordinance passed by South Carolina,..... Dec. 20.
1861. Secession of Mississippi, Florida, Alabama, Georgia,
        Louisiana, Texas, Virginia, Arkansas, and North
        Carolina declared.
     Steamer Star of the West, off Charleston, fired into,. Jan. 9.
     Kansas admitted into the Union,................. Jan. 29.
     "Southern Confederacy" formed at Montgomery,
        Ala.,..................... .... Feb. 4.
     Jeff. Davis inaugurated President of the "Confed-
        eracy,"................................... Feb 18.
     Abraham Lincoln inaugurated President of the
        United States,............ .... March 4.
     Fort Sumter attacked by the Confederates,........ Ap 12, 13.
     President Lincoln calls for 75,000 troops,.......... April 15.
     Volunteer troops attacked in Baltimore,.......... April 19.
     The President issues a second call for troops,...... May 4.
     Union victory at Philippi, Virginia,............... June 3.
     Confederate victory at Big Bethel, Virginia,........ June 10.
     Union victory at Romney, Virginia,............... June 11.
     Union victory at Booneville, Missouri,............ June 17.
     Meeting of Congress in Extra Session, ... July 4
     Battle of Carthage, Missouri,.................... July 5
     Battle of Rich Mountain, Virginia,. .... July 11.
     Battle near Centreville, Virginia,................ July 18.
     Confederate Congress meets at Richmond,....... .. July 20.
     Battle of Bull Run, Virginia, ... July 21.
     Battle of Dug Spring, Missouri,.................. Aug. 2.
     Battle of Wilson's Creek, Missouri,............... Aug. 10.
     Forts Hatteras and Clark, N C, captured,........ Aug 29
     Confederates take Lexington, Missouri,.......... Sept. 20.

1861. Battle of Edward's Ferry, or Ball's Bluff, Virginia,.. Oct. 21.
      Capture of Port Royal entrance by Union fleet, ... Nov. 7.
      Battle of Belmont, Missouri,..................... Nov. 7.
      Mason and Slidell taken from English steamer,..... Nov. 8.
1862. Battle of Mill Spring, Kentucky,................. Jan. 19.
      Fort Henry captured by Union fleet,.............. Feb. 6.
      Roanoke Island captured by Union forces,......... Feb 8.
      Fort Donelson captured by Union forces, ... Feb. 16.
      Battle of Pea Ridge, Ark,..................... Mar. 6, 8
      U. S. ves. Congress and Cumberland sunk by the
          Merrimac,........ .... March 8.
      Engagement between the Monitor and Merrimac,... March 9.
      Newbern, N. C., captured by Union troops,....... March 14
      Battle at Winchester, Virginia,.................. March 23.
      Battle of Pittsburg Landing, or Shiloh, Tenn.,...... Ap. 6, 7.
      Capture of Island No. 10, Mississippi River,....... April 7.
      Fort Pulaski, Ga., captured by Union fleet,........ April 11.
      New Orleans captured by Union forces,........... April 25.
      Battle of Williamsburg, Virginia,................. May 5.
      Norfolk, Va , surrendered to the Unionists,........ May 10.
      Confederates retreat from Corinth, Miss ,.......... May 28, 29
      Battle of Seven Pines, or Fair Oaks, ...May 31, June 1
      Memphis, Tenn., surrendered to the Unionists,..... June 6.
      Seven days' contest on the Virginia peninsula, June 25 to July 1
      The President calls for 300,000 more troops,....... July 1.
      Battle of Cedar Mountain, Virginia,.............. Aug. 9.
      Pope's battles between Manassas and Washington,..Aug 23, 30
      Battle near Richmond, Kentucky,................ Aug 30.
      Invasion of Maryland by Lee's army,............. Sept 5.
      Battle of South Mountain, Maryland,........ ...... Sept. 14.
      Harper's Ferry surrendered to the Confederates,.... Sept. 15.
      Battle of Antietam, Maryland,.................. Sept. 17.
      Battle of Munfordsville, Kentucky,........ ...... Sept. 17.
      Battle of Iuka, Mississippi,..................... Sept. 19.
      Battle of Corinth, Mississippi,.................... Oct. 4.
      Battle of Perryville, Kentucky,... .... Oct. 8.
      Battle of Fredericksburg, Virginia,. .... Dec. 13.
      Union Repulse at Vicksburg, Mississippi,......... Dec. 29.
      Battle of Stone River, or Murfreesboro', Tennessee,. Dec 31.
1863. The President's Emancipation Proclamation issued,. Jan 1.
      Battle of Murfreesboro' resumed and ended,....... Jan. 2.

1863. Arkansas Post captured by Union forces, ... Jan. 11.
Bombardment of Fort Sumter, South Carolina, ... April 7.
Union cavalry raid, under Grierson, in Mississippi,.. April.
Battle at Port Gibson, Mississippi,............ . May 1.
Battle of Chancellorsville, Virginia,.............. May 2, 3.
Battle of Raymond, Mississippi,.................. May 12.
Union victory near Jackson, Mississippi,. .... May 14.
Battle of Champion Hill, Mississippi,.... . ... May 16.
Battle at Big Black River, Mississippi, ., ... May 17
Second invasion of Maryland by Lee's army, . . . June.
West Virginia admitted into the Union,...... ... June 20.
Battle of Gettysburg, Pennsylvania, ... July 1–3
Vicksburg surrendered by the Confederates, . . . July 4.
Port Hudson surrendered by the Confederates, ... July 8.
Great riot in New York city,...... ....July 13–16.
Morgan defeated near Kyger's Creek, Ohio,. ..... July 21.
Morgan captured near New Lisbon, Ohio,... .... July 26.
Fort Wagner, S. C., captured by Union troops, ... Sept 6.
Battle of Chickamauga, Georgia, ...Sept. 19, 20.
Knoxville, Tenn., invested by the Confederates,.... Nov. 18.
Union victory at Lookout Mountain, Georgia,...... Nov. 24.
Union victory at Missionary Ridge, Georgia,.. ... Nov 25
Union victory at Knoxville, Kentucky,. .... Nov. 29.
1864. President orders a draft for more men,...... ..... Feb 1
Battle of Olustee, Florida, ... Feb. 20.
Grant created Lieutenant-General.. .... March 3
Fort De Russy, La., captured by Union troops,.... March 14
Battle of Cane River, Louisiana,........ ... . March 26.
Battle of Mansfield, or Sabine Cross Roads, La,... April 8
Battle of Pleasant Hill, Louisiana, ... April 9
Fort Pillow, Tenn., captured by the Confederates,... April 12
Plymouth, N. C., surrendered to the Confederates,.. April 20.
Army of the Potomac commenced a forward move-
    ment,..... .... May 3
Battle of the Wilderness, Virginia, ... May 5–7.
March from Chattanooga against Atlanta commenced, May 7.
Battles near Spottsylvania Court House, Virginia, . May 7, 12.
Battle of Resaca, Georgia, ... May 15.
Battle of New Market, Virginia, ... May 15.
Army of the Potomac crossed to south side of the
    James, ... June 14.

1864. Battle between the Kearsarge and Alabama,....... June 19.
      Invasion of Maryland by Early's army,.... ...... July 5.
      Battle of Monocacy, Maryland,.............. .... July 9.
      President calls for 500,000 volunteers,............ July 18.
      Battles before Atlanta, Georgia, ...July 21, 22, 28
      Chambersburg, Pa, sacked and burned, ... July 30.·
      Explosion of mine and Union repulse at Petersburg, July 30.
      Confederates defeated in Mobile Bay, Ala ,........ Aug. 5.
      Weldon railroad seized by Union troops,.. .... Aug. 18.
      Atlanta, Ga, captured by Union army,......ь..... Sept. 2.
      Battle of Winchester, Virginia,................. Sept. 19.
      Battle of Fisher's Hill, Virginia, ... Sept. 22.
      Battle of Cedar Creek, Virginia,. ... . Oct. 19.
      Confederate ram Albemarle destroyed by torpedo, . Oct. 28.
      Plymouth, N C., recaptured by Union troops,...... Oct 31.
      Nevada admitted into the Union, ... Oct 31.
      Battle of Franklin, Tennessee,.................. Nov. 30.
      Battle near Nashville, Tennessee,... .... Dec. 16.
      Savannah, Ga, captured by Union army, ... Dec. 21.
1865 Fort Fisher, N C, captured by Union troops,.. ... Jan 15.
      Constitutional Amendment abolishing slavery passed
          by Congress,.... ... . Jan. 31.
      Columbia, S. C., captured by Union troops,. ... ... Feb. 17.
      Charleston, S. C, captured by Union troops, ... Feb. 18.
      Wilmington, N. C, captured by Union troops,...... Feb. 22.
      Battle of Bentonville, North Carolina,....... ... .Mar. 19, 20
      Battle near Goldsboro', North Carolina,....   .. March 21
      Battle of Fort Steadman, Virginia, ... March 25.
      Petersburg and Richmond captured,............. April 3.
      Surrender of Lee's army, ... April 9.
      Mobile, Ala, captured by Union forces,. .... April 13.
      President Lincoln assassinated,.. .... April 14.
      Andrew Johnson inaugurated President,. .... April 15.
      Surrender of Johnston's army,..... . ... April 26.
      Jefferson Davis captured in Georgia,. .... May 10.
      Close of the Great Rebellion.
      Slavery declared abolished,.................... Dec. 18.
1867. Nebraska was admitted into the Union.......... ...March 1.
      Alaska was purchased for $7,200,000..... ....June 20.
1868. The House of Rep. impeached President Johnson.....Feb 24.
      The President was declared acquitted. ....April 26.

PRESIDENTS AND VICE-PRESIDENTS OF THE UNITED STATES

NO.	PRESIDENTS.	RESIDENCE.	INAUGURATED.	VICE-PRESIDENTS.
1	George Washington	Virginia	April 30, 1789	John Adams
2	John Adams	Massachusetts	March 4, 1797	Thomas Jefferson
3	Thomas Jefferson	Virginia	March 4, 1801	Aaron Burr. George Clinton.
4	James Madison	Virginia	March 4, 1809	George Clinton. Elbridge Gerry.
5	James Monroe	Virginia	March 4, 1817	Daniel D. Tompkins
6	John Q. Adams	Massachusetts	March 4, 1825	John C. Calhoun.
7	Andrew Jackson	Tennessee.	March 4, 1829	John C. Calhoun Martin Van Buren
8	Martin Van Buren	New York	March 4, 1837	Richard M. Johnson
9	William H. Harrison	Ohio	March 4, 1841	John Tyler.
10	John Tyler	Virginia	April 6, 1841	
11	James K. Polk	Tennessee	March 4, 1845	George M. Dallas
12	Zachary Taylor	Louisiana	March 5, 1849	Millard Fillmore
13	Millard Fillmore	New York	July 10, 1850	
14	Franklin Pierce	New Hampshire	March 4, 1853	William R. King
15	James Buchanan	Pennsylvania	March 4, 1857	John C. Breckinridge
16	Abraham Lincoln	Illinois.	March 4, 1861	Hannibal Hamlin Andrew Johnson.
17	Andrew Johnson	Tennessee	April 15. 1865	
18	Ulysses S. Grant	Illinois.	March 4, 1869	Schuyler Colfax.

(Questions to be answered from the above Table, and in connection with the preceding one.)

1 When was Washington inaugurated President of the United States? 2 How many years did he serve? 3 Who, during the same period, was Vice-President? 4. What States were admitted into the Union while Washington was President? 5. Who succeeded Washington in the presidency? 6. When was John Adams inaugurated? 7. How many years did he serve? 8. Who, during the same period, was Vice-President? 9 Were any States admitted into the Union while John Adams was President? 10. Who succeeded John Adams in the presidency? 11. When was Jefferson inaugurated? 12. How many years did Jefferson serve? 13. Who was the Vice-President during his first term of office? 14 Who, during the second? 15. What State was admitted into the Union while he was President? 16. By whom was he succeeded? 17. When was James Madison inaugurated? 18. For how many years was he President? 19. Who were the Vice-Presidents during that period? 20. Name the two States that were admitted into the Union during his presidency? 21. Who was his successor in office? 22. When was Monroe inaugurated? 23. How many years was Monroe President? 24. Who, during the same period, was Vice-President? 25. Name the five States that were admitted into the Union during Monroe's presidency? 26. Who succeeded Monroe in the presidency? 27. When was John Quincy Adams inaugurated? 28. Did he serve four or eight years? 29. Who was Vice-President during that time? 30. Were any States admitted into the Union while John Quincy Adams was President? 31. Who succeeded him in the presidency? 32. When was Jackson inaugurated? 33. Was he President four or eight years? 34. What two States were admitted during Jackson's administration? 35. What two during Tyler's? 36. What two during Polk's? 37 Which one during Fillmore's? 38. Were any admitted during Pierce's? 39. What three were admitted during Buchanan's? 40 What was the length of Jackson's administration? 41. Of Van Buren's? 42 Harrison's? 43. Tyler's? 44. Polk's? 45. Taylor's? 46. Fillmore's? 47 Pierce's? 48. Buchanan's? 49. Who were Vice-Presidents during Jackson's administration? 50 Who was during Harrison's? 51. Tyler's? 52 Polk's? 53. Taylor's? 54. Fillmore's? 55. Pierce's?

SETTLEMENT AND ADMISSION OF THE STATES.

STATES.	SETTLED.			ADMITTED.
	When.	Where.	By Whom	
Virginia	1607	Jamestown	English ..	*
New York.......	1614	New York......	Dutch	*
Massachusetts ...	1620	Plymouth	English ...	*
New Hampshire .	1623	Little Harbor ..	English .	*
Connecticut.....	1633	Windsor	English ...	*
Maryland	1634	St Mary's	English ...	*
Rhode Island	1636	Providence	English ..	*
Delaware........	1638	Wilmington	Swedes ...	*
North Carolina...	1650	Chowan River ..	English ...	*
New Jersey	1664	Elizabeth.......	Dutch	*
South Carolina ...	1670	Ashley River...	English ...	*
Pennsylvania	1682	Philadelphia ...	English ...	*
Georgia	1733	Savannah	English ..	*
Vermont	1724	Fort Dummer...	English ...	1791
Kentucky........	1775	Boonesboro.....	English ...	1792
Tennessee.......	1757	Fort Loudon....	English ...	1796
Ohio............	1788	Marietta	English ...	1802
Louisiana	1699	Iberville	French....	1812
Indiana	1730	Vincennes.....	French...	1816
Mississippi	1716	Natchez	French....	1817
Illinois.........	1720	Kaskaskia......	French....	1818
Alabama	1711	Mobile	French....	1819
Maine	1625	Bristol	French....	1820
Missouri	1764	St. Louis	French....	1821
Arkansas	1685	Arkansas Post.	French...	1836
Michigan........	1670	Detroit......	French ..	1837
Florida.........	1565	St. Augustine...	Spaniards .	1845
Texas..........	1692	S. A. De Bexar..	Spaniards .	1845
Iowa	1833	Burlington......	English ...	1846
Wisconsin.......	1669	Green Bay.....	French....	1848
California	1769	San Diego......	Spaniards .	1850
Minnesota......	1846	St. Paul	Americans	1858
Oregon	1811	Astoria	Americans	1859
Kansas	....	....	Americans.	1861
West Virginia...	....	....	....	1863
Nevada.........	....	Carson City.....	Americans.	1864
Nebraska.......	....	....	....	1867

Bracket note at right of Admitted column: The Thirteen Original States.

(Questions to be answered from the above Table.)

When and where was Virgina settled? New York? Massachusetts? New Hampshire? Connecticut? Maryland? Rhode Island? Delaware? North Carolina? New Jersey? South Carolina? Pennsylvania? Georgia? When was Vermont admitted into the Union? Kentucky? Tennessee? Ohio? Louisiana? Indiana? Which five States were admitted during the five succeeding years? When were Arkansas and Michigan admitted? Florida and Texas? Iowa? Wisconsin? California? Minnesota? Oregon? Kansas? West Virginia?

GENERAL REVIEW QUESTIONS.

(One of these questions, in most cases, is sufficient for a lesson; and then the pupil had better answer it in writing in the form of a composition.)

* See the Chronological and other tables at the end of the History.

THE DECLARATION OF INDEPENDENCE.

A DECLARATION BY THE REPRESENTATIVES OF THE UNITED STATES OF AMERICA, IN CONGRESS ASSEMBLED, JULY 4TH, 1776.

WHEN, in the course of human events, it becomes necessary for one people to dissolve the political bands which have' connected them with another, and to assume, among the powers of the earth, the separate and equal station to which the laws of nature and of nature's God entitle them, a decent respect to the opinions of mankind requires that they should declare the causes which impel them to the separation.

We hold these truths to be self-evident :—that all men are created equal ; that they are endowed by their Creator with certain unalienable rights ; that among these are life, liberty, and the pursuit of happiness. That, to secure these rights, governments are instituted among men, deriving their just powers from the consent of the governed ; that, whenever any form of government becomes destructive of these ends, it is the right of the people to alter or to abolish it, and to institute a new government, laying its foundation on such principles, and organizing its powers in such form, as to them shall seem most likely to effect their safety and happiness. Prudence, indeed, will dictate that governments long established, should not be changed for light and transient causes ; and, accordingly, all experience hath shown, that mankind are more disposed to suffer while evils are sufferable, than to right themselves by abolishing the forms to which they are accustomed. But, when a long train of abuses and usurpations, pursuing invariably the same object, evinces a design to reduce them under absolute despotism, it is their right, it is their duty, to throw off such government, and to provide new guards for their future security. Such has been the patient sufferance of these colonies, and such is now the necessity which constrains them to alter their former systems of government. The history of the present king of Great Britain is a history of repeated injuries and usurpations, all having in direct object the establishment of an absolute tyranny over these States. To prove this, let facts be submitted to a candid world :—

He has refused his assent to laws the most wholesome and necessary for the public good.

He has forbidden his governors to pass laws of immediate and pressing importance, unless suspended in their operation till his assent should be obtained; and, when so suspended, he has utterly neglected to attend to them.

He has refused to pass other laws for the accommodation of large districts of people, unless those people would relinquish the right of representation in the legislature; a right inestimable to them, and formidable to tyrants only.

He has called together legislative bodies at places unusual, uncomfortable, and distant from the depository of their public records, for the sole purpose of fatiguing them into compliance with his measures.

He has dissolved representative houses repeatedly, for opposing, with manly firmness, his invasions on the rights of the people.

He has refused, for a long time after such dissolutions, to cause others to be elected; whereby the legislative powers, incapable of annihilation, have returned to the people at large for their exercise; the State remaining, in the mean time, exposed to all the danger of invasion from without, and convulsions within.

He has endeavored to prevent the population of these States; for that purpose, obstructing the laws for naturalization of foreigners; refusing to pass others to encourage their migration hither, and raising the conditions of new appropriations of lands.

He has obstructed the administration of justice, by refusing his assent to laws for establishing judiciary powers.

He has made judges dependent on his will alone for the tenure of their offices, and the amount and payment of their salaries.

He has erected a multitude of new offices, and sent hither swarms of officers, to harass our people, and eat out their substance.

He has kept among us, in times of peace, standing armies, without the consent of our legislature.

He has affected to render the military independent of, and superior to, the civil power.

He has combined with others to subject us to a jurisdiction foreign to our constitution, and unacknowledged by our laws; giving his assent to their acts of pretended legislation:

For quartering large bodies of armed troops among us:

For protecting them, by a mock trial, from punishment for any murders which they should commit on the inhabitants of these States:

For cutting off our trade with all parts of the world:

For imposing taxes on us without our consent:

For depriving us, in many cases, of the benefits of trial by jury:

For transporting us beyond seas to be tried for pretended offenses:

For abolishing the free system of English laws in a neighboring province, establishing therein an arbitrary government, and enlarging its boundaries, so as to render it at once an example and fit instrument for introducing the same absolute rule into these colonies:

For taking away our charters, abolishing our most valuable laws, and altering, fundamentally, the powers of our governments:

For suspending our own legislatures, and declaring themselves invested with power to legislate for us in all cases whatsoever.

He has abdicated government here, by declaring us out of his protection, and waging war against us.

He has plundered our seas, ravaged our coasts, burnt our towns, and destroyed the lives of our people.

He is, at this time, transporting large armies of foreign mercenaries to complete the works of death, desolation, and tyranny, already begun, with circumstances of cruelty and perfidy scarcely paralleled in the most barbarous ages, and totally unworthy the head of a civilized nation.

He has constrained our fellow-citizens, taken captive on the high seas, to bear arms against their country, to become the executioners of their friends and brethren, or to fall themselves by their hands.

He has excited domestic insurrections amongst us, and has endeavored to bring on the inhabitants of our frontiers the merciless Indian savages, whose known rule of warfare is an undistinguished destruction of all ages, sexes, and conditions.

In every stage of these oppressions we have petitioned for redress, in the most humble terms; our repeated petitions have been answered only by repeated injury. A prince whose character is thus marked by every act which may define a tyrant, is unfit to be the ruler of a free people.

Nor have we been wanting in attention to our British brethren. We have warned them, from time to time, of attempts made by their legislature to extend an unwarrantable jurisdiction over us. We have reminded them of the circumstances of our emigration and settlement here. We have appealed to their native justice and magnanimity, and we have conjured them, by the ties of our common kindred, to disavow these usurpations, which would inevitably interrupt our connections and correspondence. They, too, have been deaf to the voice of justice and consanguinity. We must therefore acquiesce in the necessity which denounces our separation, and hold them, as we hold the rest of mankind—enemies in war—in peace, friends.

We, therefore, the representatives of the United States of America, in general Congress assembled, appealing to the Supreme Judge of the world for the rectitude of our intentions, do, in the name and by the authority of the good people of these colonies, solemnly publish and declare, that these United Colonies are, and of right ought to be, free and independent States; that they are absolved from all allegiance to the British crown, and that all political connection between them and the State of Great Britain is, and ought to be, totally dissolved; and that, as free and independent States, they have full power to levy war, conclude peace, contract alliances, establish commerce, and to do all other acts and things which independent States may of right do. And, for the support of this declaration, with a firm reliance on the protection of Divine Providence, we mutually pledge to each other our lives, our fortunes, and our sacred honor.

The foregoing declaration was, by order of Congress, engrossed, and signed by the following members:

JOHN HANCOCK.

New Hampshire.
Josiah Bartlett,
William Whipple,
Matthew Thornton.

Massachusetts Bay.
Samuel Adams,
John Adams,
Robert Treat Paine,
Elbridge Gerry.

Rhode Island.
Stephen Hopkins,
William Ellery.

Connecticut.
Roger Sherman,
Samuel Huntington,
William Williams,
Oliver Wolcott.

New York.
William Floyd,
Philip Livingston,
Francis Lewis,
Lewis Morris.

New Jersey.
Richard Stockton,
John Witherspoon,
Francis Hopkinson,
John Hart,
Abraham Clark.

Pennsylvania.
Robert Morris,
Benjamin Rush,
Benjamin Franklin,
John Morton,
George Clymer,
James Smith,
George Taylor,
James Wilson,
George Ross.

Delaware.
Cæsar Rodney,
George Read,
Thomas M'Kean.

Maryland.
Samuel Chase,
William Paca,
Thomas Stone.

Charles Carroll, of Carrollton.

Virginia.
George Wythe,
Richard Henry Lee,
Thomas Jefferson,
Benjamin Harrison,
Thomas Nelson, jun.,
Francis Lightfoot Lee,
Carter Braxton.

North Carolina.
William Hooper,
Joseph Hewes,
John Penn.

South Carolina.
Edward Rutledge,
Thomas Heyward, jun.,
Thomas Lynch, jun.,
Arthur Middleton.

Georgia.
Button Gwinnett,
Lyman Hall,
George Walton.

UNITED STATES.

The device of the Seal of the United States was adopted June 20, 1782, as follows: "Arms—Pale-ways of thirteen pieces, argent and gules; a chief azure; the escutcheon on the breast of the American eagle displayed proper, holding in his dexter talon an olive-branch, and in his sinister a bundle of thirteen arrows, all proper, and in his beak a scroll, inscribed with this motto, "*E pluribus Unum.*" For the *Crest*—over the head of the eagle, ... a glory, on breaking through a cloud, proper, and surrounding thirteen stars, forming a constellation, argent, on an azure field."

ORIGIN OF THE

CONSTITUTION OF THE UNITED STATES.

I. WHEN the Revolutionary struggle commenced, there were three forms of Colonial government in force among the colonies, namely: the Provincial or Royal, the Proprietary, and the Charter.

II. The Provincial or Royal government was that which was under the control of a governor, who, appointed by the king, administered affairs according to instructions from his royal master. The colonies of this class were New Hampshire, New York, New Jersey, Virginia, North Carolina, South Carolina, and Georgia.

ORIGIN OF THE CONSTITUTION.—I. QUESTIONS.—1. What forms of government existed among the colonies previous to the Revolution?

II. 2. What was the Provincial or Royal government? 3. Which of the colonies were Provincial or Royal?

III. The Proprietary government was that which was under the control of one or more proprietors, who derived their authority by grant and privileges conferred by the king. Pennsylvania, Delaware, and Maryland, were subject to the proprietary rule.

IV. The Charter government was that wherein certain political rights were secured to the people by royal charter. Massachusetts, Rhode Island, and Connecticut, were charter governments.

V. In July, 1775—a year before the Declaration of Independence—Dr. Franklin submitted to Congress a sketch of Articles of Confederation between the colonies. By this plan it was proposed to establish a Confederation, and continue it until a reconciliation with Great Britain should take place; or, in the failure of that event, to make it perpetual. It appears, however, that Franklin's plan was never discussed.

VI. On the 11th of June, 1776,—the very day on which the Committee to prepare the Declaration of Independence was chosen—Congress resolved that a committee should be appointed to prepare and digest a form of Confederation, to be entered into by the colonies.

VII. On the 12th of July following, this committee, consisting of one from each State, reported a draft of Articles of Confederation, which was considered and debated from time to time, until the 15th of November, 1777, when, with some amendments, it was adopted.

VIII. These Articles of Confederation were ratified in 1778 by all the States except Delaware and Maryland, and by

---

III QUESTIONS.—4. What was the Proprietary government? 5. Which of the colonies were subject to the Proprietary rule?

IV. 6. What was the Charter Government? 7. Which of the colonies were provided with charters?

V. 8. When was a sketch of Articles of Confederation first submitted to Congress? 9. By whom was it submitted? 10. What was proposed by Dr. Franklin's plan?

VI. 11. When was the Committee to prepare the Declaration of Independence appointed? 12. What resolution was passed by Congress on that day?

VII. 13. Of how many persons did the committee consist? 14. When did they submit their report? 15. What was done with the report?

*1

Delaware, in 1779; but, in consequence of the delay on the part of Maryland, they did not go into effect until the 1st of March, 1781, the day on which they were signed by the delegates from that State.

IX. It was soon found that the Articles of Confederation were not adequate to the wants of the Government. They were deficient as regards the regulation of commerce, the settling of controversies between the States, and the making of treaties with foreign nations; and especially deficient in not conferring the necessary power upon Congress to liquidate the debts incurred during the war.

X. Consequently, a convention of delegates from all the States, except Rhode Island, met at Philadelphia, in May, 1787, for the purpose of revising the Articles of Confederation; but it was thought best by a majority of the delegates to adopt an entirely new form of government, instead of making any attempts to amend the defective one then in existence. Accordingly, after four months' deliberation, the present Constitution, —except some changes which were made in after years,—was adopted by the Convention on the 17th of September, 1787.

XI. The new Constitution was submitted to the people, who, in the newspapers, legislative halls, and elsewhere, discussed it with earnestness and thoroughness. It met with considerable opposition, but, by the 4th of March, 1789, when it went into operation, it had been adopted by all the States, with the exception of North Carolina and Rhode Island.*

---

* Delaware adopted it on the 7th of December, 1787; Pennsylvania, on the 12th of December, New Jersey, on the 18th of December, Georgia, on the 2d of January, 1788; Connecticut, on the 9th of January, Massachusetts, on the 6th of February; Maryland, on the 28th of April; South Carolina, on the 23d of May; New Hampshire, on the 21st of June; Virginia, on the 26th of June, New York, on the 26th of July; North Carolina, on the 21st of November, 1789; and Rhode Island, on the 29th of May, 1790.

VIII. Questions.—16. When did the States ratify the Articles of Confederation? 17 When did the Articles of Confederation go into effect?

IX. 18. What was soon ascertained with reference to the Articles of Confederation? 19. In what respects were they deficient?

X. 20. What convention was held in May, 1787? 21. What was done by the convention?

XI. 22. To whom was the Constitution submitted? 23. Where was it discussed? 24. When did it go into operation? 25. Which of the States had adopted it at that time?

THE CONSTITUTION

OF

THE UNITED STATES OF AMERICA.

PREAMBLE.

WE, the people of the United States, in order to form a more perfect union, establish justice, insure domestic tranquillity, provide for the common defense, promote the general welfare, and secure the blessings of liberty to ourselves and our posterity, do ordain and establish this CONSTITUTION for the United States of America.

ARTICLE I.

THE LEGISLATIVE DEPARTMENT.

SECTION I.

All legislative powers herein granted shall be vested in a Congress of the United States, which shall consist of a Senate and House of Representatives.

PREAMBLE —26. What is the introductory part of the Constitution called? 27. What is the object of the preamble? *Ans.*—To state the purposes of the Constitution. 28. How many and what purposes are stated in the preamble? 29. By whom was the Constitution ordained and established? 30. Recite the preamble. 31. How many and what departments of government are established under the Constitution? *Ans*—Three : the legislative, the judicial, and the executive. 32. What is the legislative department? *Ans.*—The power that enacts the laws. 33. What is the executive department? *Ans*—The power that enforces the laws. 34. What is the judicial department? *Ans*—The power that interprets the laws.

ARTICLE I.

THE LEGISLATIVE DEPARTMENT.

SEC I —35. Of what does Article first of the Constitution treat? 36. In whom is the legislative power vested? 37. Of how many and what branches does Congress consist?

SECTION II.

1st. Clause. The House of Representatives shall be composed of members chosen every second year by the people of the several States, and the electors in each State shall have the qualifications requisite for electors of the most numerous branch of the State legislature.

2d Clause. No person shall be a representative who shall not have attained to the age of twenty-five years, and been seven years a citizen of the United States, and who shall not, when elected, be an inhabitant of that State in which he shall be chosen.

3d Clause. Representatives and direct taxes shall be apportioned among the several States which may be included within this Union, according to their respective numbers, which shall be determined by adding to the whole number of free persons, including those bound to service for a term of years, and excluding Indians not taxed, three-fifths of all other persons.* The actual enumeration shall be made within three years after the first meeting of the Congress of the United States, and within every subsequent term of ten years, in such manner as they shall by law direct. The number of representatives shall not

---

Sec. II —*1st Clause.*—38. By whom are the representatives chosen ? 39. How often are they chosen ? 40. What qualifications are requisite for electors or representatives? 41. What is an elector? *Ans* —One who has the right to vote in choosing an officer. *2d Clause.*—42. How old must a person be before he can be a representative? 43. How long must he have been a citizen of the United States ? 44. What is the requisite in regard to his habitation ? 45. Now name the three qualifications requisite for a representative. *3d Clause.*—46. How are representatives and direct taxes apportioned among the States ? 47. How are the respective numbers of the representative population of the several States to be determined? 48. What provision is made in regard to Indians? 49. What is meant by "all other persons?" *Ans.*—Slaves. 50. When was the first census or enumeration to be made? 51. How often thereafter is the census to be made? 52 How many inhabitants at least are required for one representative? 53. If a State should not have that number, what is the law ? 54. Was the first representation in Congress based upon the actual population of the several States ? 55. Which State at first sent the greatest number of representatives? 56. Which two States sent the smallest number? 57. Of how many members did the first House of Representatives consist? 58. Of how many does the present House consist? *Ans.*—

* See Article XIV p 39.

exceed one for every thirty thousand, but each State shall have at least one representative; and until such enumeration shall be made, the State of New Hampshire shall be entitled to choose three, Massachusetts eight, Rhode Island and Providence Plantations one, Connecticut five, New York six, New Jersey four, Pennsylvania eight, Delaware one, Maryland six, Virginia ten, North Carolina five, South Carolina five, and Georgia three.

4th Clause. When vacancies happen in the representation from any State, the executive authority thereof shall issue writs of election to fill such vacancies.

5th Clause. The House of Representatives shall choose their speaker and other officers; and shall have the sole power of impeachment.

SECTION III.

1st Clause. The Senate of the United States shall be composed of two senators from each State, chosen by the legislature thereof, for six years; and each senator shall have one vote.

2d Clause. Immediately after they shall be assembled in consequence of the first election, they shall be divided as

---

4th Clause—59. How are vacancies in the representation of a State to be filled? 5th Clause—60. By whom is the speaker of the House of Representatives chosen? 61. By whom are the other officers of the House chosen? 62. What sole power has the House? 63. What is meant by impeachment? *Ans.*—An impeachment is an accusation against a public officer, charging him with misconduct in the discharge of his official duties.

Sec. III—1st Clause.—64. Of whom is the Senate composed? 65. By whom are the senators chosen? 66. For how long a period are they chosen? 67. How does the mode of electing a senator differ from that of a representative? *Ans.*—A senator of the United States is chosen by the legislature of his State; a representative is chosen by the people. 68. How do their terms of office differ? *Ans.*—A senator is chosen for six years, a representative for only two. 69. How many votes is each senator entitled to? 70. Have the large States any more senators than the small ones? 2d Clause.—71. Into how many classes were the senators at first divided? 72. In what order were their seats of office vacated? 73. What proportion of the Senate is elected every second year? 74. How often is one-third elected? 75. When may the executive of a State fill a vacancy in the Senate? 76. For how long a time does a senator so appointed hold his office? 77. How is the vacancy then filled? 78. Now state how vacancies in the Senate are filled.

equally as may be into three classes. The seats of the senators of the first class shall be vacated at the expiration of the second year, of the second class at the expiration of the fourth year, and of the third class at the expiration of the sixth year, so that one-third may be chosen every second year ; and if vacancies happen by resignation, or otherwise, during the recess of the legislature of any State, the executive thereof may make temporary appointments until the next meeting of the legislature, which shall then fill such vacancies.

3d Clause. No person shall be a senator who shall not have attained to the age of thirty years, and been nine years a citizen of the United States, and who shall not, when elected, be an inhabitant of that State for which he shall be chosen.

4th Clause. The vice-president of the United States shall be president of the Senate, but shall have no vote, unless they be equally divided.

5th Clause. The Senate shall choose their other officers, and also a president *pro tempore*, in the absence of the vice-president, or when he shall exercise the office of president of the United States.

6th Clause. The Senate shall have the sole power to try all impeachments. When sitting for that purpose, they shall all be on oath or affirmation. When the president of the United States is tried, the chief-justice shall preside : and no person shall be convicted without the concurrence of two-thirds of the members present.

3d Clause.—79. How old must a person be before he can be a senator ? 80 How long must he have been a citizen of the United States? 81 What is required of him in regard to residence? 82. Now name the three requisites for a senator 83. How do they differ from those of a representative ? (See page 12.) *4th Clause —* 84. Who is president of the Senate ? 85 When only is he entitled to vote? *5th Clause.*—86. What officers are chosen by the Senate ? 87 What is meant by a ' president *pro tempore ?* ' *Ans* —A " president *pro tempore*" is one chosen only for the time being 88. When does the Senate choose a " president *pro tempore ?*" *6th Clause —*89 What sole power has the Senate ? 90 What sole power has the House ? (See page 13.) 91. Under what solemnity does the Senate sit for the trial of impeachment? 92 When does the chief-justice preside in the Senate ? 93. Who presides when the president of the United States is tried ? 94. What proportion of the Senate is necessary to a conviction?

7th Clause. Judgment in cases of impeachment shall not extend further than to removal from office, and disqualification to hold and enjoy any office of honor, trust, or profit under the United States; but the party convicted shall nevertheless be liable and subject to indictment, trial, judgment, and punishment, according to law.

SECTION IV.

1st Clause. The times, places, and manner of holding elections for senators and representatives, shall be prescribed in each State by the legislature thereof; but the Congress may at any time by law make or alter such regulations, except as to the places of choosing senators.

2d Clause. The Congress shall assemble at least once in every year, and such meeting shall be on the first Monday in December, unless they shall by law appoint a different day.

SECTION V.

1st Clause. Each house shall be the judge of the elections, returns, and qualifications of its own members, and a majority of each shall constitute a quorum to do business; but a smaller number may adjourn from day to day, and may be authorized to compel the attendance of absent members, in such manner, and under such penalties, as each house may provide.

2d Clause. Each house may determine the rules of its pro-

7th Clause.—95. How far may judgment extend in cases of impeachment? 96. To what is the convicted party further liable?

SEC. IV.—*1st Clause.*—97 What is prescribed by each State legislature in regard to elections for senators and representatives? 98 What power has Congress over such regulations? *2d Clause.*—99. How often does Congress assemble? 100. On what day is it prescribed that the meeting shall take place? 101 May a different day be appointed? 102 How?

SEC V —*1st Clause.* 103. Of what is each house constituted the judge? 104. What proportion constitutes a quorum? 105. What is meant by a quorum? *Ans*—By a quorum is meant a sufficient number to do business. 106. What power do a smaller number possess, as regards adjourning? 107. What else may they do, as regards absentees? *2d Clause.*—108. What power has each house, over the rules of its proceedings? 109. What power does each house possess for enforcing its rules?

ceedings, punish its members for disorderly behavior, and, with the concurrence of two-thirds, expel a member.

3d Clause. Each house shall keep a journal of its proceed ings, and from time to time publish the same, excepting such parts as may in their judgment require secrecy ; and the yeas and nays of the members of either house on any question, shall, at the desire of one-fifth of those present, be entered on the journal.

4th Clause. Neither house, during the session of Congress, shall, without the consent of the other, adjourn for more than three days, nor to any other place than that in which the two houses shall be sitting.

SECTION VI.

1st Clause. The senators and representatives shall receive a compensation for their services, to be ascertained by law, and paid out of the treasury of the United States. They shall, in all cases, except treason, felony, and breach of the peace, be privileged from arrest during their attendance at the session of their respective houses, and in going to and returning from the same ; and for any speech or debate in either house, they shall not be questioned in any other place.

3d Clause.—110. What is required of each house, in respect to keeping a journal ? 111. How is publicity given to the proceedings of Congress ? 112. What part of its journal may either house withhold from publication ? 113. When shall the yeas and nays be entered on the journal ? *4th Clause.*—114. For what length of time may either house adjourn without the consent of the other ? 115. How is each house restricted, as regards the place to which it may adjourn ?

SEC. VI.—*1st Clause.*—116 Are members of Congress compensated for their services ? 117. How is the compensation determined ? 118. Are members of Congress paid by their States, respectively, or by the general government ? *Ans*—The sena-tors and representatives in Congress are not compensated for their services by the in-dividual States, but by the general government, out of the treasury of the United States. 119 What personal privileges are members of Congress entitled to ? 120. What are the three exceptions to the general privilege that the Constitution allows to Congressmen ? 121. In what does treason consist ? (See page 32.) 122. What is felony ? *Ans*—A felony is understood to mean a crime punishable with death. 123. What is meant by a breach of the peace ? *Ans.*—"A breach of the peace is a viola-tion of the public order." 124. For what are members of Congress not to be ques-tioned ?

2d Clause. No senator or representative shall, during the time for which he was elected, be appointed to any civil office under the authority of the United States, which shall have been created, or the emoluments whereof shall have been increased, during such time ; and no person holding any office under the United States, shall be a member of either house during his continuance in office.

SECTION VII.

1st Clause. All bills for raising revenue shall originate in the House of Representatives; but the Senate may propose or concur with amendments as on other bills.

2d Clause. Every bill which shall have passed the House of Representatives and the Senate, shall, before it become a law, be presented to the president of the United States ; if he approve, he shall sign it ; but if not, he shall return it, with his objections, to that house in which it shall have originated, who shall enter the objections at large on their journal, and proceed to reconsider it. If, after such reconsideration, two thirds of that house shall agree to pass the bill, it shall be sent, together with the objections, to the other house, by which it shall like-

---

2d Clause —125. To what offices cannot members of Congress be elected? 126, Suppose that a person holds an office under the United States, what then ?

Sec VII.—1st Clause —127. In which branch of Congress must all bills for raising revenue originate ? 128 What power has the Senate over such bills? *2d Clause.* —129 After a bill has passed both houses of Congress, what must be done with it? 130 What must the president do with the bill? 131. What is the president's act of objecting to a bill called? *Ans.*—The president's act of returning a bill with his objections, is called a veto 132. Why was the veto power given to the president? *Ans.*—The veto power was given to the president to enable him to protect the executive department of the government against the encroachments of the legislature; also with a view to greater security against the enactment of improper laws. 133. When the president vetoes a bill, what is the duty of the house to which it is sent? 134. When is the bill sent to the other house? 135. What accompanies the bill to the other house? 136. Then what does that other house do with the bill? 137 If two-thirds approve of the bill, what then? 138. Now state how a bill may become a law, notwithstanding the veto of the president. 139. When the two houses reconsider a vetoed bill, how do they determine the votes? 140. What record of names is imperative? 141 State how a bill may become a law, even though the president has neither signed nor vetoed it 142 In what case does a bill fail to become a law, though it has passed both houses of Congress, and is not vetoed?

wise be reconsidered, and if approved by two-thirds of that house, it shall become a law. But in all such cases the votes of both houses shall be determined by yeas and nays, and the names of the persons voting for and against the bill shall be entered on the journal of each house respectively. If any bill shall not be returned by the president within ten days (Sundays excepted) after it shall have been presented to him, the same shall be a law, in like manner as if he had signed it, unless the Congress by their adjournment prevent its return, in which case it shall not be a law.

3d Clause. Every order, resolution, or vote, to which the concurrence of the Senate and House of Representatives may be necessary (except on a question of adjournment), shall be presented to the president of the United States ; and before the same shall take effect, shall be approved by him, or, being disapproved by him, shall be repassed by two-thirds of the Senate and House of Representatives, according to the rules and limitations prescribed in the case of a bill.

SECTION VIII.

The Congress shall have power

1st Clause. To lay and collect taxes, duties, imposts, and excises ; to pay the debts and provide for the common defense and general welfare of the United States ; but all duties, im-

---

3d Clause.—143 What is necessary to be done with orders, resolutions, and votes, requiring the concurrence of both houses before they can take effect ? 144 What is the object of the provision? *Ans.*—If it were not for the provision, Congress might pass laws, calling them orders or resolutions, and thus evade the president's veto. 145. When the president vetoes an order, resolution, or vote, what course does it take ? 146. In what case, requiring the concurrent action of both houses, has the president no veto power?

SEC VIII.—*1st Clause.*—147 What power has Congress in regard to taxes, duties, imposts, and excises? 148. What are taxes? *Ans.*—Contributions of money exacted by government from individuals, for public purposes. 149 How many kinds of taxes are there ? *Ans.*—Two kinds; direct and indirect. 150 What are direct taxes? *Ans.*—Those laid directly on the person or property of individuals. 151 What are indirect taxes? *Ans.*—Those laid on the importation, exportation and consumption of goods. 152. What are duties? *Ans.*—Taxes on the importation and exportation of goods. 153. What are imposts? *Ans.*—Taxes on goods imported. 154 What are excises? *Ans.*—Taxes on goods produced or manufactured in the country

posts, and excises shall be uniform throughout the United States;

2d Clause. To borrow money on the credit of the United States;

3d Clause. To regulate commerce with foreign nations, and among the several States, and with the Indian tribes;

4th Clause. To establish a uniform rule of naturalization, and uniform laws on the subject of bankruptcies, throughout United States;

5th Clause. To coin money, regulate the value thereof, and of foreign coin, and to fix the standard of weights and measures;

6th Clause. To provide for the punishment of counterfeiting the securities and current coin of the United States;

7th Clause. To establish post-offices and post-roads;

8th Clause. To promote the progress of science and useful arts, by securing for limited times to authors and inventors the exclusive right to their respective writings and discoveries;

9th Clause. To constitute tribunals inferior to the Supreme Court;

2d Clause.—155 What power has Congress in regard to borrowing money? *3d Clause*—156. What, in regard to regulating commerce? *4th Clause.*—157 What, in regard to a rule of naturalization? 158. What is meant by naturalization? *Ans*— The act by which a foreigner becomes a citizen of the United States. 159. How long must a person reside in the United States before he can be naturalized? *Ans*— Five years at least 160 What power has Congress in regard to bankruptcies? 161. What is meant by bankruptcies? *Ans*—A person is a bankrupt when he is unable to pay his just debts. *5th Clause*—162. What power has Congress in regard to coining money? 163. What, in regard to the value of money? 164 What, in regard to foreign coins? 165. What, in regard to weights and measures? *6th Clause*—166. What power has Congress in regard to counterfeiting? *7th Clause.*—167 What, in regard to post-offices and post-roads? *8th Clause*—168 In what way may Congress promote the progress of science and arts? 169 For how long a time is the author of a book entitled to the exclusive right of publishing it? *Ans*—Twenty-eight years. 170 What is the right called? *Ans*—A copyright. 171. May a copyright be renewed? *Ans*—At the expiration of the twenty-eight years, the copyright may be renewed for the further period of fourteen years 172. For how long a time is the inventor of a machine entitled to the exclusive right of manufacturing it? *Ans*—Fourteen years. 173 What is the right called? *Ans*—A patent right 174 Can a patent right be extended? *Ans*—The commissioner of patents is authorized, at the end of the fourteen years, to extend the patent right for the further period of seven years.

10*th Clause.* To define and punish piracies and felonies committed on the high seas, and offenses against the law of nations;

11*th Clause.* To declare war, grant letters of marque and reprisal, and make rules concerning captures on land and water;

12*th Clause.* To raise and support armies; but no appropriation of money to that use shall be for a longer term than two years;

13*th Clause.* ·To provide and maintain a navy;

14*th Clause.* To make rules for the government and regulation of the land and naval forces;

15*th Clause.* To provide for calling forth the militia to execute the laws of the Union, suppress insurrections, and repel invasions;

16*th Clause.* To provide for organizing, arming, and disciplining the militia, and for governing such part of them as may be employed in the service of the United States, reserving to the States respectively, the appointment of the officers, and the authority of training the militia according to the discipline prescribed by Congress;

17*th Clause.* To exercise exclusive legislation in all cases

---

9*th Clause.*—175. What power has Congress in regard to judicial tribunals? 10*th Clause.*—176. What, in regard to piracies, felonies, etc.? 177 What is piracy? *Ans*—Robbery on the high seas. 178 What is meant by the term "high seas?" *An.*—The "high seas" are all the waters oft he ocean beyond the boundaries of low-water-mark. 11*th Clause.*—179. What power has Congress in regard to declaring war? 180. What, in regard to "letters of marque and reprisal?" 181 What are "letters of marque and reprisal?" *Ans*—Commissions granted by the government to individuals, authorizing them to seize the persons and property of the citizens or subjects of a nation that refuses to make satisfaction for some injury which it has committed. 182. What power has Congress in regard to rules concerning captures? 12*th Clause*—183 What power has Congress in regard to armies? 184 In what way is such power restricted? 13*th Clause.*—185. What power has Congress in regard to a navy? 14*th Clause.*—186. What power, in regard to the government of the land and naval forces? 15*th Clause*—187 What power, in regard to calling forth the militia, etc.? 16*th Clause.*—188 What power, in regard to organizing armies, and disciplining the militia? 189. What, in regard to governing the militia? 190. What reservations are secured to the respective States? 17*th Clause.*—191. What power has Congress in regard to the seat of government, and to places purchased for certain purposes set forth? 192. What is the district occupied by the seat of government called? *Ans — The District of Columbia.*

whatsoever, over such district (not exceeding ten miles square) as may, by cession of particular States, and the acceptance of Congress, become the seat of the government of the United States, and to exercise like authority over all places purchased by the consent of the legislature of the State in which the same shall be, for the erection of forts, magazines, arsenals, dock yards, and other needful buildings;—and

18*th Clause.* To make all laws which shall be necessary and proper for carrying into execution the foregoing powers, and all other powers vested by this Constitution in the Government of the United States, or in any department or officer thereof.

SECTION IX.

1*st Clause.* The migration or importation of such persons as any of the States now existing shall think proper to admit, shall not be prohibited by the Congress prior to the year one thousand eight hundred and eight; but a tax or duty may be imposed on such importation, not exceeding ten dollars for each person.

2*d Clause.* The privilege of the writ of habeas corpus shall not be suspended, unless when, in cases of rebellion or invasion, the public safety may require it.

---

193. How large was the District of Columbia originally? *Ans*—A tract ten miles square. 194. From what States had it been derived? *Ans.*—Maryland and Virginia. 195. Is the District of Columbia at present ten miles square? *Ans*—The portion which had been derived from Virginia having been ceded back to that State in 1846, the District of Columbia is now confined to the Maryland side of the Potomac. 196. What consent is requisite before the United States can acquire property in a State, for the erection of forts, magazines, etc.? 18*th Clause.*—197. What general powers are conferred upon Congress in regard to making laws?

SEC. IX.—1*st Clause*—198. What restriction was imposed upon Congress, in regard to the migration or importation of certain persons? 199. Who were meant by "such persons?" *Ans*—Slaves. 200. What was the great object of the clause? *Ans.*—To enable Congress to put an end to the importation of slaves into the United States, after the year 1808. 201. In what way was Congress left to restrain the importation, without actually forbidding it? 202. When was the importation actually prohibited? *Ans.*—On the first of January, 1808. 2*d Clause*—203. What is said of the writ of habeas corpus?

3d Clause. No bill of attainder or *ex post facto* law shall be passed.

4th Clause. No capitation or other direct tax shall be laid, unless in proportion to the census or enumeration herein before directed to be taken.

5th Clause. No tax or duty shall be laid on articles exported from any State.

6th Clause. No preference shall be given, by any regulation of commerce or revenue, to the ports of one State over those of another: nor shall vessels bound to, or from, one State, be obliged to enter, clear, or pay duties in another.

7th Clause. No money shall be drawn from the treasury, but in consequence of appropriations made by law; and a regular statement and account of the receipts and expenditures of all public money shall be published from time to time.

8th Clause. No title of nobility shall be granted by the United States: and no person holding any office of profit or trust under them, shall, without the consent of the Congress, accept of any present, emolument, office, or title, of any kind whatever, from any king, prince, or foreign state.

---

204. What is a writ of habeas corpus? *Ans.*—A written command from a judge or other magistrate, directing that the body of a certain person shall be brought before him   205. What is the object of the writ? *Ans.*—The object of a writ of habeas corpus is to provide a means of redress for all manner of illegal imprisonment. 206. Repeat the clause in relation to the writ of habeas corpus. 207. In what cases may the privilege of the writ of habeas corpus be suspended? *3d Clause.*—208. What is said of bills of attainder or *ex post facto* laws?" 209 What is a bill of attainder? *Ans.*—An act of the legislature, inflicting the punishment of death, without trial, upon persons supposed to be guilty of high crimes   210 What is an *ex post facto* law? *Ans.*—A law which renders an act punishable in a manner in which it was not punishable at the time of its commission   *4th Clause.*—211 In what way may Congress lay a capitation or other direct tax?   212. What is meant by a capitation?   *Ans.*—A direct tax upon individuals. 213. How is the census to be taken? (See page 12.) *5th Clause.*—214. What prohibition is imposed upon Congress in relation to articles exported from any State?   *6th Clause.*—215. What preference is forbidden in relation to a regulation of commerce or revenue?   216. What freedom have vessels that are bound from one State to another?   *7th Clause.*—217. Under what circumstances only can money be drawn from the national treasury?   218. What publication must be made in regard to receipts and expenditures of all public money?   *8th Clause.*—219. What is said in the Constitution about titles of nobility?   220. What is said of office-holders accepting presents, etc.?   221. Under what circumstances may an office-holder accept a present?

SECTION X.

1st Clause. No State shall enter into any treaty, alliance, or confederation; grant letters of marque and reprisal; coin money; emit bills of credit; make any thing but gold and silver coin a tender in payment of debts; pass any bill of attainder, *ex post facto* law, or law impairing the obligation of contracts, or grant any title of nobility.

2d Clause. No State shall, without the consent of the Congress, lay any imposts or duties on imports or exports, except what may be absolutely necessary for executing its inspection laws: and the net produce of all duties and imposts, laid by any State on imports or exports, shall be for the use of the treasury of the United States; and all such laws shall be subject to the revision and control of the Congress.

3d Clause. No State shall, without the consent of Congress, lay any duty of tonnage, keep troops, or ships of war in time of peace, enter into any agreement or compact with another State, or with a foreign power, or engage in war, unless actually invaded, or in such imminent danger as will not admit of delay.

---

222 Repeat the clause relating to titles and presents.

Sec. X.—*1st Clause.*—223. What prohibition is placed upon the several States as regards treaties, alliances, or confederations? 224. What, as regards letters of marque and reprisal? 225. What, as regards the coining of money? 226 What, as regards bills of credit? 227. What is meant by bills of credit? *Ans*—Bills of credit, within the meaning of the Constitution, are bills intended to circulate as money among the people. 228. What is constituted a legal tender in payment of debt? 229. What prohibition is placed upon individual States, in regard to a bill of attainder? 230. What, in regard to an *ex post facto* law? 231. What, in regard to a law impairing an obligation? 232 What, in regard to a title of nobility? 233 Recite the clause just considered. *2d Clause.*—234. What prohibition are individual States under, as regards imposts or duties? 235. In what case only, may a State lay any imposts or duties? 236. What are inspection laws? *Ans.*—Laws requiring certain articles of commerce to be examined by officers called inspectors. 237. What is the object of inspection laws? *Ans.*—To protect the public against fraud or imposition on the part of the producer, and to cause improvement after improvement in the quality of articles produced. 238. What disposition must be made of the net produce of all duties and imposts laid by individuals? 289. What are the inspection laws of individual States, as regards imports or exports, subject to? *3d Clause,*—240. What prohibition are individual States under, as to the laying of a duty of tonnage?

ARTICLE II.

THE EXECUTIVE DEPARTMENT.

SECTION I.

1st Clause. The executive power shall be vested in a president of the United States of America. He shall hold his office during the term of four years, and, together with the vice-president, chosen for the same term, be elected as follows :

2d Clause. Each State shall appoint, in such manner as the legislature thereof may direct, a number of electors, equal to the whole number of senators and representatives to which the State may be entitled in the Congress : but no senator or representative, or person holding an office of trust or profit under the United States, shall be appointed an elector.

---

241. What is a duty of tonnage? *Ans.*—A duty of tonnage, or a tonnage duty, is a tax laid on vessels at a certain rate per ton 242. What prohibition are individual States under as to the keeping of troops? 243. What, as to the keeping of ships of war? 244. What, as to an agreement or compact with another State, or with a foreign power? 245. What, as to engaging in war? 246. Under what circumstances, then, may a State engage in war?

ARTICLE II

THE EXECUTIVE DEPARTMENT.

SEC. I.—*1st Clause.*—247. Of what does Article II of the Constitution treat? 248. In whom is the executive power of the United States vested? 249. What is the president's term of office? 250. How often may a president be re-elected? *Ans.*—The Constitution does not limit the number of terms for which a president may be re-elected. 251. Who was the first president of the United States? *Ans.*—Washington. 252. For how many terms did Washington serve? *Ans.*—Two. 253. Why was not Washington elected for a third term? *Ans.*—At the close of his second term of office, Washington declined to be a candidate for a third term. 254.—What has been the effect of his declination? *Ans.*—Washington's example, in declining to be elected for a third term, has become a precedent by which subsequent presidents have been guided. 255. How many and what presidents have served two terms each? (See History, p 309.) 256. Which has the longest term of office; the president, a senator, or a representative? 257. What term has each? 258. What is the vice-president's term of office? 259. Who was the first vice-president of the United States? *Ans.*—John Adams. 260. By whom are the president and vice-president chosen? *Ans.*—The president and vice-president are not chosen by the people directly, but by electors. 2*d Clause.*—261 In what manner does each State appoint electors? 262. What number of electors is each State entitled to? 263. Who are prohibited from being electors?

[The electors shall meet in their respective States, and vote by ballot for two persons, of whom one at least shall not be an inhabitant of the same State with themselves. And they shall make a list of all the persons voted for, and of the number of votes for each ; which list they shall sign and certify, and transmit sealed to the seat of government of the United States, directed to the president of the Senate. The president of the Senate shall, in the presence of the Senate and House of Representatives, open all the certificates, and the votes shall then be counted. The person having the greatest number of votes shall be the president, if such number be a majority of the whole number of electors appointed; and if there be more than one who have such majority, and have an equal number of votes, then the House of Representatives shall immediately choose by ballot one of them for president; and if no person have a majority then from the five highest on the list, the said House shall in like manner choose the president. But in choosing the president, the votes shall be taken by States, the representation from each State having one vote ; a quorum for this purpose shall consist of a member or members from two-thirds of the States, and a majority of all the States shall be necessary to a choice. In every case, after the choice of the president, the person having the greatest number of votes of the electors shall be the vice-president. But if there should remain two or more who have equal votes, the Senate shall choose from them by ballot the vice-president.]

THE TWELFTH AMENDMENT TO THE CONSTITUTION.

1st Clause. The electors shall meet in their respective States, and vote by ballot for president and vice-president, one of whom, at least, shall not be an inhabitant of the same State with themselves ; they shall name in their ballots the person voted for as president, and in distinct ballots the person voted for as vice-president, and they shall make distinct lists of all persons voted for as president, and of all persons voted for as vice-president, and of the number of votes for each, which lists they shall sign and certify, and transmit sealed to the seat of the government of the United States, directed to the president of the Senate ;—the president of the Senate shall, in the presence of the Senate and House of Representatives, open all the certificates, and the votes shall then be counted ;—the person having the greatest number of votes for president, shall be the president, if such number be a majority of the whole num-

---

264. What has been done with the original clause of the Constitution prescribing the proceedings to be taken to elect a president and vice-president? *Ans.*—It has been repealed, and its place supplied by the twelfth amendment to the Constitution. 265. Where do the electors for president and vice-president meet? 266. In what way do they vote? 267. What is prescribed respecting one of the persons for whom they shall not vote ? 268. How is it required that their ballots shall be made out?

ber of electors appointed : and if no person have such majority, then from the persons having the highest numbers, not exceeding three, on the list of those voted for as president, the House of Representatives shall choose immediately, by ballot, the president.   But in choosing the president, the votes shall be taken by States, the representation from each State having one vote : a quorum for this purpose shall consist of a member or members from two-thirds of the States, and a majority of all the States shall be necessary to a choice.   And if the House of Representatives shall not choose a president, whenever the right of choice shall devolve upon them, before the fourth day of March next following, then the vice-president shall act as president, as in the case of the death or other constitutional disability of the president.

2d Clause. The person having the greatest number of votes as vice-president, shall be the vice-president, if such number be a majority of the whole number of electors appointed; and if no person have a majority, then, from the two highest numbers on the list, the Senate shall choose the vice-president : a quorum for the purpose shall consist of two-thirds of the whole number

269. After voting, what lists are they required to prepare ? 270. What provision must be complied with, before the lists can pass out of their hands ? 271. After the lists are signed, certified and sealed, to whom are they directed ? 272. To what place are they then transmitted ? 273. What does the president of the Senate do with the certificates ? 274. How is it determined who is elected president ? 275. Now describe the manner in which the electors choose a president. 276. In the event of no choice being made by the electors, by whom is the president chosen? 277. From how many and what candidates must the House of Representatives choose the president ? 278. In what way must the choice be made ? 279. How are the votes taken in choosing the president ? 280. How many votes is each State entitled to ? 281. How many is each entitled to, when voting by electors ? 282. In choosing the president by the House of Representatives, how many constitute a quorum ? 283. In such case, how many States are necessary to a choice? 284. Whenever the right of choosing a president devolves upon the House of Representatives, till what time may the right be exercised ? 285. Now describe the manner in which the House of Representatives choose a president 286. In the event of both the electors and House of Representatives failing to choose a president, what takes place? 287. How is it determined whom the electors have chosen for vice-president? 288. In the event of no person having a majority of electoral votes, by whom is the vice-president chosen? 289. When choosing a vice-president, how many senators are requisite to a quorum? 290. How many are necessary to a choice ? 291. What is said of the eligibility to the office of president, as compared with that of vice-president ?

of senators, and a majority of the whole number shall be necessary to a choice.

3d Clause. But no person constitutionally ineligible to the office of president, shall be eligible to that of vice-president of the United States.

4th Clause. The Congress may determine the time of choosing the electors, and the day on which they shall give their votes; which day shall be the same throughout the United States.

5th Clause. No person except a natural born citizen, or a citizen of the United States at the time of the adoption of this Constitution, shall be eligible to the office of president; neither shall any person be eligible to that office who shall not have attained to the age of thirty-five years, and been fourteen years a resident within the United States.

6th Clause. In case of the removal of the president from office, or of his death, resignation, or inability to discharge the powers and duties of the said office, the same shall devolve on the vice-president, and the Congress may by law provide for the case of removal, death, resignation, or inability, both of the

---

4th Clause —292. What power has Congress over the time of choosing the electors? 293 What, as to the day on which the electors shall vote? 294 In the event of Congress determining the day on which the electors shall give their votes, what sameness is prescribed? 295. When are the electors chosen? *Ans.*—On the Tuesday next after the first Monday, in the last November of each presidential term. 296. Where do the electors meet to give their votes? *Ans.*—In their respective States, at a place appointed by the legislature thereof. 297. What place is usually appointed for their meeting? *Ans.*—The capital of their State. 298 When do the electors meet to give their votes? *Ans*—On the first Wednesday in the last December of each presidential term *5th Clause.*—299 What person, as regards his place of birth, cannot be eligible to the office of president? 300 How old must a person be to be eligible to that office? 301. How many years must a person, to be eligible to that office, have resided within the United States? 302. Now state the legal qualifications of a president. 303 Recite the clause relating to the qualifications. *6th Clause* —304. In what contingencies does the office of president devolve on the vice-president? 305. What provision is made by the Constitution for the case of removal or death, etc., of the president?

president and vice-president, declaring what officer shall then act as president, and such officer shall act accordingly, until the disability be removed, or a president shall be elected.

7th Clause. The president shall, at stated times, receive for his services a compensation, which shall neither be increased nor diminished during the period for which he shall have been elected, and he shall not receive within that period any other emolument from the United States, or any of them.

8th Clause. Before he enter on the execution of his office, he shall take the following oath or affirmation :—

" I do solemnly swear (or affirm) that I will faithfully execute the office of president of the United States, and will, to the best of my ability, preserve, protect, and defend the Constitution of the United States."

SECTION II.

1st Clause. The president shall be commander-in-chief of the army and navy of the United States, and of the militia of the several States, when called into the actual service of the United States; he may require the opinion, in writing, of the principal officer in each of the executive departments, upon any subject relating to the duties of their respective offices; and he shall have power to grant reprieves and pardons for offences against the United States, except in cases of impeachment.

---

806. What, for the case of removal, etc, of both president and vice-president? 307 In the case of removal, etc., of both president and vice-president, what officer shall, by law of Congress, act as president? *Ans*—The president of the Senate, *pro tempore*, shall act as president. 308. What is to be done, in case there is no president of the Senate? *Ans*—Then the speaker of the House of Representatives shall act as president. 309 How long shall such officers, acting as president, continue to act? *7th Clause*—310. What does the Constitution provide as regards the compensation to be allowed to the president? 311. What restriction is imposed, in regard to any other emolument? 312. Recite the clause relating to the president's compensation. 318. What is the salary of the president? *Ans*—$25,000 a year, together with the use of the presidential mansion and its furniture. 314. What is the salary of the vice-president? *Ans.*—$8,000 a year. *8th Clause.*—315. What does the president do, just before entering on the execution of his office? 316. Repeat the oath or affirmation taken by the President.

2d Clause. He shall have power, by and with the advice and consent of the Senate, to make treaties, provided two-thirds of the senators present concur; and he shall nominate, and, by and with the advice and consent of the Senate, shall appoint ambassadors, other public ministers and consuls, judges of the supreme court, and all other officers of the United States whose appointments are not herein otherwise provided for, and which shall be established by law; but the Congress may by law vest the appointment of such inferior officers as they think proper, in the president alone, in the courts of law, or in the heads of departments.

3d Clause. The president shall have power to fill up all vacancies that may happen during the recess of the Senate, by granting commissions, which shall expire at the end of their next session

SECTION III.

He shall, from time to time, give to the Congress information of the state of the Union, and recommend to their consideration

---

SEC. II.—*1st Clause.*—317 In what relation does the president stand toward the army and navy? 318. When only can he command the militia? 319. Whose opinions may he require in writing? 320. Upon what subjects may he require the opinions? 321. Is he bound to be guided by such opinions? *Ans.*—He is not. 322. What executive departments have been established by Congress? *Ans.*—Six, namely: (1) Department of State, (2) Department of the Navy, (3) Department of War, (4) Department of the Treasury, (5) Post-office Department, and (6) Department of the Interior. 323. For what purpose were they established? *Ans.*—For the purpose of aiding the president in the executive and administrative business of the government. 324. How are the heads of the departments appointed? *Ans.*—By the president, with the advice and consent of the Senate 325. How is the attorney-general appointed? *Ans.*—In like manner with the heads of the departments 326. Of whom does the president's cabinet consist? *Ans.*—Of the heads of the Departments and the attorney-general of the United States. 327. What power has the president in relation to reprieves and pardons? 328 What is a reprieve? *Ans.*—A limited suspension or delay of the execution of a sentence in a criminal case. 329. With what exception is the president vested with the power to grant reprieves and pardons? *2d Clause.*—330. What power has the president relative to treaties? 331. In whom is the appointing power vested? 332. What is the first step in making an appointment? 333. What offices are enumerated, for which the president and Senate make appointments? 334. What may Congress do in relation to the appointment of inferior officers? *3d Clause.*—335. What vacancies can the president fill? 336. When does such appointment expire?

such measures as he shall judge necessary and expedient; he may, on extraordinary occasions, convene both houses, or either of them; and in case of disagreement between them, with respect to the time of adjournment, he may adjourn them to such time as he shall think proper; he shall receive ambassadors and other public ministers; he shall take care that the laws be faithfully executed, and shall commission all the officers of the United States.

SECTION IV.

The president, vice-president, and all civil officers of the United States, shall be removed from office on impeachment for, and conviction of, treason, bribery, or other high crimes and misdemeanors.

ARTICLE III.

THE JUDICIAL DEPARTMENT.

SECTION I.

The judicial power of the United States shall be vested in

Sec. III —337. What information is the president required to give to Congress? 338. What recommendations is he required to make? 339. In what way are the recommendations made? *Ans.*—By means of written messages. 340 Was the reading of written messages always the practice? *Ans*—The first two presidents, Washington and Adams, used to meet both houses of Congress, and make their recommendations by verbal addresses. 341. Is Congress obliged to adopt the president's recommendations? *Ans* —Congress is under no obligation to adopt the recommendations of the president. 342 When may the president convene both houses? 343. May he convene only one house? 344. When? 345. When may the president adjourn Congress? 346. What is the duty of the president respecting ambassadors, etc.? 347 What is his duty respecting the execution of the laws? 348. What is his duty respecting the granting of commissions?

Sec. IV—349. For what crimes may government officers be removed from office? 350 How may the removal be effected?

ARTICLE III.

THE JUDICIAL DEPARTMENT

Sec. I.—351. Of what does Article III. of the Constitution treat? 352. In what is the judicial power of the United States vested? 353. How long do the judges hold their offices? 354. What is established as to the compensation of the judges? 355. How can the judges be removed from office? (See page 14.) 356. How is the supreme court of the United States organized? *Ans.*—The supreme court of the United States is composed of one chief-justice and eight associate justices, any five of whom constitute a quorum. 357 What is the salary of the chief-justice? *Ans.*—$6,500 a year 358. What is the salary of each associate justice? *Ans*—$6,000 a year.

one supreme court, and in such inferior courts as the Congress may from time to time ordain and establish. The judges, both of the supreme and inferior courts, shall hold their offices during good behavior, and shall, at stated times, receive for their services a compensation, which shall not be diminished during their continuance in office.

SECTION II.

1st Clause. The judicial power shall extend to all cases, in law and equity, arising under this Constitution, the laws of the United States, and treaties made, or which shall be made under their authority ; to all cases affecting ambassadors, other public ministers, and consuls; to all cases of admiralty and maritime jurisdiction ; to controversies to which the United States shall be a party ; to controversies between two or more States ; between a State and citizens of another State ; between citizens of different States; between citizens of the same State claiming lands under grants of different States ; and between a State, or the citizens thereof, and foreign States, citizens, or subjects.

2d Clause. In all cases affecting ambassadors, other public ministers and consuls, and those in which a State shall be a party, the supreme court shall have original jurisdiction. In all the other cases before mentioned, the supreme court shall have

SEC. II—*1st Clause*—359 Name the first of the nine subjects in which the United States courts have jurisdiction. 360 Name the second, concerning ambassadors, etc. 361 Name the third, concerning certain jurisdiction. 362 The fourth, concerning controversies with the United States. 363 The fifth, concerning controversies between States. 364 The sixth, concerning controversies between a State and citizens. 365 The seventh, concerning controversies between citizens. 366. The eighth, concerning controversies between citizens claiming lands. 367 What is the last of the nine subjects? *2d Clause*—368. In what cases has the supreme court original jurisdiction? 369 What is meant by original jurisdiction? *Ans*—The original jurisdiction of a court is that in which a suit originates or commences. 370 What is meant by appellate jurisdiction? *Ans*—The appellate jurisdiction of a court is that in which the decision of an inferior court is taken on appeal. *3d Clause.*—371 Before whom must the 'trial of all crimes" be held? 372. What cases are exceptions to the law? 373 By whom are impeachments tried? (See page 14) 374. Where must the trial of a crime committed within a State be held? 375. Where, when not committed within a State? 376 Repeat the entire clause just considered.

appellate jurisdiction, both as to law and fact, with such exceptions, and under such regulations, as the Congress shall make.

3d Clause. The trial of all crimes, except in cases of impeachment, shall be by jury; and such trial shall be held in the State where the said crimes shall have been committed; but when not committed within any State, the trial shall be at such place or places as the Congress may by law have directed.

SECTION III.

1st Clause. Treason against the United States shall consist only in levying war against them, or in adhering to their enemies, giving them aid and comfort. No person shall be convicted of treason unless on the testimony of two witnesses to the same overt act, or on confession in open court.

2d Clause. The Congress shall have power to declare the punishment of treason; but no attainder of treason shall work corruption of blood, or forfeiture, except during the life of the person attainted.

ARTICLE IV.

MISCELLANEOUS PROVISIONS.

SECTION I.

Full faith and credit shall be given in each State to the public acts, records, and judicial proceedings of every other State. And the Congress may by general laws prescribe the manner

---

SEC III —*1st Clause.*—377. Of how many things does treason against the United States consist? 378. What are the two things? 379. What is necessary to a conviction of treason? 2d *Clause*—380. What power has Congress relative to the punishment of treason? 381 What punishment has Congress accordingly declared? *Ans*—Congress has declared that the punishment of treason shall be death by hanging. 382. How does the Constitution limit the consequences of attainder? 383. What is meant by attainder? *Ans*—Attainder means a staining, corruption, or rendering impure 384. What is meant by corruption of blood? *Ans*—By "corruption of blood" a person is disabled to inherit lands from an ancestor; nor can he either retain those in his possession, or transmit them by descent to his heirs

ARTICLE IV.

MISCELLANEOUS PROVISIONS.

SEC. I.—385. Of what does Article IV. treat? 386. How are the public acts, etc, of the several States, to be treated in each State? 387. How are they to be proved?

in which such acts, records, and proceedings shall be proved, and the effect thereof.

SECTION II.

1st Clause. The citizens of each State shall be entitled to all the privileges and immunities of citizens in the several States.

2d Clause. A person charged in any State with treason, felony, or other crime, who shall flee from justice, and be found in another State, shall, on demand of the executive authority of the State from which he fled, be delivered up, to be removed to the State having jurisdiction of the crime.

3d Clause. No person held to service or labor in one State, under the laws thereof, escaping into another, shall, in consequence of any law or regulation therein, be discharged from such service or labor, but shall be delivered up on claim of the party to whom such service or labor may be due.

SECTION III.

1st Clause. New States may be admitted by the Congress into this Union; but no new State shall be formed or erected within the jurisdiction of any other State, nor any State be formed by the junction of two or more States, or parts of States, without the consent of the legislatures of the States concerned, as well as of the. Congress.

2d Clause. The Congress shall have power to dispose of and make all needful rules and regulations respecting the territory or other property belonging to the United States; and

---

Sec. II.—*1st Clause.*—388. What privileges and immunities are the citizens of each State entitled to? *2d Clause.*—389. What is said of persons charged with crime, fleeing into another State? *3d Clause.*—390. What is said of persons escaping from service or labor? 391. What persons are referred to in the third clause? *Ans —* Fugitive slaves, and persons bound by indentures of apprenticeship.

Sec. III.—*1st Clause.*—392. By whom may new States be admitted into the Union? 393. What is said of the formation of new States? 394. How many States belonged to the Union at the adoption of the Constitution? (See page 10.) 395. How many belong to the Union now? *2d Clause —*396 What power has Congress respecting the territory or other property belonging to the United States? 397 What construction as to claims is not to be put upon any part of the Constitution?

3*

nothing in this Constitution shall be so construed as to preju-
dice any claims of the United States, or of any particular
State.

SECTION IV.

The United States shall guarantee to every State in this
Union a republican form of government, and shall protect
each of them against invasion; and, on application of the
legislature, or of the executive (when the legislature cannot
be convened), against domestic violence.

ARTICLE V.

The Congress, whenever two-thirds of both houses shall
deem it necessary, shall propose amendments to this Constitution; or, on the application of the legislatures of two-thirds of
the several States, shall call a convention for proposing amendments, which, in either case, shall be valid to all intents and
purposes, as a part of this Constitution, when ratified by the
legislatures of three-fourths of the several States, or by conventions in three-fourths thereof, as the one or the other mode of
ratification may be proposed by the Congress; provided, that
no amendment which may be made prior to the year one
thousand eight hundred and eight shall in any manner affect
the first and fourth clauses in the ninth section of the first
article; and that no State, without its consent, shall be
deprived of its equal suffrage in the Senate.

Sec. IV.—398. What guarantee does the Constitution make to the several States
in respect to their form of government? 399. In what two events are the United
States bound to protect individual States?

ARTICLE V.

MODE OF AMENDING THE CONSTITUTION.

400. Of what does Article V treat? 401. In what two ways may amendments to
the Constitution be proposed? 402. What two ways are provided for ratifying
amendments? 403. What three restrictions upon the power of making amendments
were originally imposed by the Constitution? 404. Why have two of the restrictions lost their force? 405. What do " the first and fourth clauses" referred to, declare? 406. What permanent restriction upon the power of making amendments
still exists in full force?

ARTICLE VI.

1st Clause. All debts contracted, and engagements entered into, before the adoption of this Constitution, shall be as valid against the United States under this Constitution as under the Confederation.

2d Clause. This Constitution, and the laws of the United States which shall be made in pursuance thereof, and all treaties made, or which shall be made, under the authority of the United States, shall be the supreme law of the land; and the judges in every State shall be bound thereby, any thing in the constitution or laws of any State to the contrary notwithstanding.

3d Clause. The senators and representatives before mentioned, and the members of the several State legislatures, and all executive and judicial officers, both of the United States and of the several States, shall be bound by oath or affirmation to support this Constitution; but no religious test shall ever be required as a qualification to any office or public trust under the United States.

ARTICLE VII.

The ratification of the conventions of nine States shall be sufficient for the establishment of this Constitution between the States so ratifying the same.

ARTICLE VI.
ADDITIONAL MISCELLANEOUS PROVISIONS.

1st Clause.—407 What debts and engagements does the Constitution, recognize? *2d Clause*—408. What is declared to be the supreme law of the land? 409 By what are the judges in every State bound? *3d Clause.*—410 Who, besides the judges, are bound to support the Constitution? 411. In what way shall they be bound? 412. What prohibition is made in regard to religious tests?

ARTICLE VII

413. How many States were necessary to ratify the Constitution, in order to its establishment? 414 Where did the Convention meet which framed the Constitution?—*Ans.* Philadelphia 415. In what year was it framed? (See p 10) 416. Who was the president of the convention? *Ans.*—George Washington. 417. How many delegates signed the Constitution? 418. Which of the thirteen States was not represented in the convention? *Ans.*—Rhode Island 419 How many States ratified the Constitution before it went into effect? *Ans.*—Eleven 420. Which of the thirteen States did not ratify the Constitution until afterward? *Ans.*—North Carolina and Rhode Island failed to ratify the Constitution until after it had been ratified by the other eleven States and had gone into operation.

AMENDMENTS,

PROPOSED BY CONGRESS, AND RATIFIED BY THE LEGISLATURES OF THE SEVERAL STATES, PURSUANT TO THE FIFTH ARTICLE OF THE ORIGINAL CONSTITUTION.

ARTICLE I.

Congress shall make no law respecting an establishment of religion, or prohibiting the free exercise thereof; or abridging the freedom of speech, or of the press; or the right of the people peaceably to assemble, and to petition the government for a redress of grievances.

ARTICLE II.

A well-regulated militia being necessary to the security of a free State, the right of the people to keep and bear arms shall not be infringed.

ARTICLE III.

No soldier shall, in time of peace, be quartered in any house without the consent of the owner; nor in time of war, but in a manner to be prescribed by law.

ARTICLE IV.

The right of the people to be secure in their persons, houses, papers, and effects, against unreasonable searches and seizures, shall not be violated; and no warrants shall issue but upon probable cause, supported by oath or affirmation, and particularly describing the place to be searched, and the person or things to be seized.

AMENDMENTS

421. How may the amendments to the Constitution be regarded? *Ans.*—All the amendments to the Constitution, with the exception of the 12th, may be regarded as a declaration, securing to the people and States certain rights, beyond the possibility of being encroached upon by Congress. *1st Article.*—422. What declaration does the first amendment make, respecting religion? 423. What, respecting the freedom of speech? 424. What, respecting the freedom of the press? 425. What, respecting the right of petition? *2d Article.*—426. What is the declaration respecting the right of the people to keep and bear arms? *3d Article*—427. What is said of quartering soldiers? *4th Article.*—428. What is said of searches and seizures?

ARTICLE V.

No person shall be held to answer for a capital or otherwise infamous crime, unless on a presentment or indictment of a grand jury, except in cases arising in the land or naval forces, or in the militia, when in actual service in time of war or public danger; nor shall any person be subject for the same offense to be twice put in jeopardy of life or limb; nor shall be compelled in any criminal case to be a witness against himself, nor be deprived of life, liberty, or property, without due process of law; nor shall private property be taken for public use, without just compensation.

ARTICLE VI.

In all criminal prosecutions, the accused shall enjoy the right to a speedy and public trial, by an impartial jury of the State and district wherein the crime shall have been committed, which district shall have been previously ascertained by law, and to be informed of the nature and cause of the accusation; to be confronted with the witnesses against him; to have compulsory process for obtaining witnesses in his favor; and to have the assistance of counsel for his defense.

ARTICLE VII.

In suits at common law, where the value in controversy shall exceed twenty dollars, the right of trial by jury shall be preserved; and no fact tried by a jury shall be otherwise re-examined, in any court of the United States, than according to the rules of the common law.

---

429 What is said of the issuing of warrants? *5th Article.*—430 What is said of holding persons to answer for crimes? 431. What is said of a second trial for the same offense? 432 What is the meaning of the clause, that no person shall "be twice put in jeopardy," etc.? *Ans.*—It means that no person shall be a second time tried for the same offense, of which he has been legally acquitted or convicted. 433. When shall not a person be compelled to witness against himself? 434. What guarantee of protection to life, liberty, and property is given? 435. When only can private property be taken for public use? *6th Article.*—436 What right shall a person accused of crime enjoy? 437. What right, as to the witnesses against him? 438. What right, as to the witnesses in his favor? 439 What right, as to the assistance of counsel? *7th Article.*—440. In what suits shall the right of trial by jury be preserved?

ARTICLE VIII.

Excessive bail shall not be required, nor excessive fines imposed, nor cruel and unusual punishments inflicted.

ARTICLE IX.

The enumeration in the Constitution of certain rights, shall not be construed to deny or disparage others retained by the people.

ARTICLE X.

The powers not delegated to the United States by the Constitution, nor prohibited by it to the States, are reserved to the States respectively, or to the people.

ARTICLE XI.

The judicial power of the United States shall not be construed to extend to any suit in law or equity, commenced or prosecuted against one of the United States by citizens of another State, or by citizens or subjects of any foreign State.

ARTICLE XIII.*

SECTION I.—Neither slavery nor involuntary servitude, except as a punishment for crime, whereof the party shall have been duly convicted, shall exist within the United States, or any place subject to their jurisdiction.

SEC. II.—Congress shall have power to enforce this article by appropriate legislation.

---

* For the twelfth amendment, see page 25.

---

441. In what way only shall the re-examination of facts tried by a jury be made? *8th Article.*—442. What is said of bail, fines, and punishments? *9th Article.*—443. What is said of rights retained by the people? *10th Article.*—444. What is said of the powers reserved to the States? *11th Article.*—445. What i said of the restriction upon the judicial power? *13th Article.*—Section I.—446 What is said of slavery and involuntary servitude? Sec. II.—What power has Congress with reference to this subject? Give the history of Article XIII. of the Constitution. (See history, p. 341.) *14th Article.*—When was the 14th Article adopted? *Ans.* Having been ratified by three-fourths of the States it was declared adopted on the 28th of July, 1868. Sec I.—Who are declared to be citizens of the United States? What restriction is imposed upon the States with regard to the privileges or immunities of citi-

ARTICLE XIV.

SECTION I.—All persons born or naturalized in the United States, and subject to the jurisdiction thereof, are citizens of the United States and of the State wherein they reside. No State shall make or enforce any law which shall abridge the privileges or immunities of citizens of the United States; nor shall any State deprive any person of life, liberty, or property, without due process of law, nor deny to any person within its jurisdiction the equal protection of the laws.

SEC. II.—Representatives shall be apportioned among the several States according to their respective numbers, counting the whole number of persons in each State, excluding Indians not taxed. But when the right to vote at any election for the choice of electors for President and Vice-President of the United States, Representatives in Congress, the executive and judicial officers of a State, or the members of the legislature thereof, is denied to any of the male inhabitants of such State, being twenty-one years of age, and citizens of the United States, or in any way abridged, except for participation in rebellion or other crime, the basis of representation therein shall be reduced in the proportion which the number of such male citizens shall bear to the whole number of male citizens twenty-one years of age in such State.

SEC. III.—No person shall be a Senator or Representative in Congress, or elector of President and Vice-President, or hold any office, civil or military, under the United States, or under any State, who, having previously taken an oath, as a member of Congress, or as an officer of the United States, or

zens? What, with regard to the lives, liberty, or property of persons? What, with regard to the protection of the law given to persons? Sec. II.—How are representatives and direct taxes apportioned among the States? How does this provision of the Constitution differ from the one formerly in force? (See Article I, Sec. II., 3d clause, p. 12) When shall a reduction be made in the basis of representation to which a State may be entitled? Sec. III—What class of persons, in consequence of their rebellious acts, are deprived of certain exalted privileges? Name the privileges which are withheld from them. Is it possible for any person belonging to that

as a member of any State Legislature, or as an executive or judicial officer of any State, to support the Constitution of the United States, shall have engaged in insurrection or rebellion against the same, or given aid or comfort to the enemies thereof. But Congress may, by a vote of two-thirds of each House, remove such disability.

Sec. IV.—The validity of the public debt of the United States, authorized by law, including debts incurred for payment of pensions and bounties for services in suppressing insurrection or rebellion, shall not be questioned. But neither the United States nor any State shall assume or pay any debt or obligation incurred in aid of insurrection or rebellion against the United States, or any claim for the loss or emancipation of any slave; but all such debts, obligations, and claims shall be held illegal and void.

Sec. V.—The Congress shall have power to enforce, by appropriate legislation, the provisions of this article.

ARTICLE XV.

Section I.— The right of citizens of the United States to vote shall not be denied or abridged by the United States, or by any State, on account of race, color, or previous condition of servitude.

Sec. II.— The Congress shall have power to enforce this article by appropriate legislation.

---

class to have the privileges accorded him? How? Sec. IV.—What shall not be questioned as regards the debts of the United States? What debts, obligations, and claims are declared illegal and void? What restriction is imposed upon the General Government and individual States, with respect to such debts, obligations and claims? Sec. V —What legislation may Congress enact, in regard to the provisions of Article XIV.?

CPSIA information can be obtained
at www.ICGtesting.com
Printed in the USA
LVHW031246291120
672944LV00009BA/366